To Heather
all good wishes.
Yours sincerely
Fred. (Cysmith)

GRANDAD'S WARS

CYSMITH

MINERVA PRESS
MONTREUX   LONDON   WASHINGTON

GRANDAD'S WARS
Copyright © Cysmith 1995

All Rights Reserved

ISBN 1 85863 534 9

First published 1995 by
MINERVA PRESS
1 Cromwell Place
London SW7 2JE

Printed in Great Britain by
B.W.D. Printers Ltd., Northolt, Middlesex

GRANDAD'S WARS

TABLE OF CONTENTS

LIST OF ILLUSTRATIONS

INTRODUCTION

These memoirs are in no way intended as a diary, although some effort has been made to introduce some sort of chronological sequence. Most of the incidents recorded, happened to the author himself, or to the ship in which he was serving at the time. There are a few incidents in which we were not the prime actors; chiefly the incidents of the "Talamba" and the dropping of the atom bombs on Hiroshima and Nagasaki. I was involved in all the events recorded, either through my presence or my near proximity. Many of the events were undisclosed to the public until many years after the war had ended. Perhaps the reader may have heard of some of the events previously, and for those few exceptions, I seek your sympathetic indulgence, for many things happened to many people during those SIX momentous years of World War II, when TRUTH was ever stranger than FICTION. In NO case is there a question of spinning a TALL yarn, as many folk assume most sailors' stories to be.

In writing, I dedicate these memoirs to my dear wife, who was never informed of my whereabouts, other than by announcements on the radio or in the press some time later. It was always just plain, C/O C.P.O. London.

Throughout the war, my wife bore the strain and suspense with cheerful forbearance and fortitude and with complete faith that all would be well. IN REALITY a TRUE WOMAN. September 1947

In passing, I would like to thank those wonderful folk that had more faith in my writing than I did, namely my whole family; my niece Wendy and her husband Derek; and the two friends from the United States Navy, Walt and Jane le Compte, whose yacht CALLISTO was berthed near "Owl-n-Pussy Cat" in Saint Katharine's Dock, London, during 1993. A special thanks too, to Kelvin, who helped with the production of this book, not forgetting the invaluable assistance of my wife, both physically and materially, in making this project possible.

December 1993.

MY FIRST IMPRESSIONS

The year was 1913 and the date was July 29th. It was to be my most memorable day, the time was unknown for the reason that no clock was visible. In any case, even had there been a clock in the room, I was unable to record the time. For this seeming lack of intelligence on my part, the explanation was that I had just been born and that I would henceforth, at least for some time, be a screaming infant. The screaming was because some unknown assailant had very recently delivered, on my buttocks, a resounding smack. In that year, and under the existing circumstances, the finances of the family to which I had been born would simply not justify the use of a midwife or any other person that may have required payment for their services. The birth, so I have been told, was in the front bedroom of number 39 Long Street, Ipswich, in the county of Suffolk.

The house itself was typical of the working class houses of the times, all being rented, and comprised of two up and two down with another small room attached downstairs, very like an after thought. This small extra room measured some six by eight feet in length, served as a kitchen-cum-bathroom-cum-laundry room as it contained a gas cooker of indifferent performance, a brick work copper with fire grate beneath, and the proverbial large china sink. Also, there was an exit door leading to a small backyard that boasted a coal shed and a water closet. The latter was reached by descending a couple of steps. As in most houses of this type and class this was commonly referred to as the "privy" and only called a closet if some visitor of local renown was talking of the subject in question. This privy had the nasty habit of becoming water logged in very wet weather, being some fifteen inches or so below the surface of the yard. In fact, it often became waterlogged for the sole reason of revenge, joke, or just sheer cussedness by some prankster. Many a quiet "smoke or rest period" was spoiled in this fashion by someone else. To return to the problem of the birth of yours truly. I was taken into the kitchen-cum-bathroom for my initial cleansing by one of two people, who had acted as my unofficial nursemaid. These good folk were either Mrs Ellis, from across the road, and whose husband was in the Royal Navy serving as a medical petty officer, or, Mrs Osborne from next door who had herself given birth to numerous offspring; I recollect about ten or eleven. The reason for the choice of Mrs Ellis was, I understand, because much of the husband's medical knowledge had rubbed off onto his wife. This neighbourly assistance was general practice on these occasions, for nobody could afford the employment of a midwife, much less a doctor, both of whom would have required payment of a few pence which was just unaffordable. In any case, a birth was treated as one of the common ailments of the time, and was in the same category as a cough or cold. One either survived the complaint or just succumbed to it. As simple as that. Thus it is sufficient for me to relate, that Mother and myself survived my arrival into the waiting world.

At 39 Long Street, sharing the home with me were six brothers and two sisters, besides, of course, Mother and Father, as it was customary, even in those days, to have parents. So, eleven of us completed the SMITH family and I was to be the last in the line of succession. Not that there was much of anything to succeed to apart from the name. The task of nursing me, apart from Mother, fell chiefly to my two sisters, Win and Kate. There are, of course, some recollections of others being involved, but by that time, it was hardly a question of nursing but one of minding and watching to make sure that I did not promote trouble.

Heading the pecking order in the family was father, who more often than not enjoyed his pints of beer in preference to anything else. Next should have been Mother, but more often than not she was compelled to forgo that doubtful privilege. This was through force of circumstances, for Mother usually had several small meagrely paid jobs which necessitated her absence. These jobs, such as house cleaning or laundry for some neighbour, were undertaken in order that the school attenders of the family might feed when possible. However, Mother always ensured that there was always something to appease the young hungry stomachs, be it only with bread and dripping, or a smear of margarine. In short, life always became very interesting to a very high degree, and this not only applied to eating, but to the whole way of life at number 39 Long Street. Never a dull moment, at least in the sense of it being dull.

The area in which we lived was only a few minutes walk from the quite busy docks which were situated at the bottom of the street, with a cut between the Bakers; Mr Aldertons; and a public house, called, I believe the "Steam Packet", in Duke Street. Before entering this area one had to cross the main road, Fore Street, and the junction with Back Hamlet. The important landmark here was the public house called the "Earl Grey" that looked towards Fore Street. At the bottom of Back Hamlet, on the other side from Earl Grey, stood the Ship Inn, well noted for its stabling yards with the carters' horses and, of course, the almost constant supply and smell of manure. This then, was the start of Long Street which was clearly marked by a round brick building in the centre of the road. This small building had no roof and only one small entrance-cum-exit. From here, the constant smell of stale urine was very evident, as it was much used by the males of the area, it being the "urinal" or toilet. No modern day cleansing here, as all that it boasted was an automatic flushing device that suffered inconsistent action, leaving the smells to enter the surrounding street. Moving up Long Street from here, on the left one encountered Southgate's scrap yard, which was piled some ten to fifteen feet high with old bedsteads, pots and pans, bicycle frames, corrugated iron and in fact anything of a metal base that could be converted to hard cash. In addition to this were piles of old rags and newspapers, all left in the open to get wet or dry as the weather dictated. Moving further up the street, one came to a small shop whose chief display was an almost permanent window occupation by a ginger cat and a tabby cat, both of dubious sex and parentage. Amongst the other displays were sweets and toffee apples when in season, together with a small assortment of various vegetables. All seemed to live happily side by side. Immediately opposite was the works yard of Ransome Sims and Jefferies, whose foundries were some goodly distance down Duke Street and backed on to the Docks. Opposite this factory yard was Baker Street, which held the entrance to the maltings of the local brewery. All the various smells combined to make an indefinable, overpowering, throat-catching scent that could almost be tasted. In spite of this drawback, the occupants of the area seemed to thrive, bodily and physically. Crossing Baker Street, one came across the local cobbler, Mr Wheeler, who always seemed to have a smile and cheery word for all comers. More of this gentleman later. Passing up the street, in Long Street, one encountered the normal type of houses for the area. Next to Mr Wheeler was a smartish looking terraced house occupied by an elderly lady whose name has slipped my memory, almost a recluse, so that nothing much was known of this person. Sounds almost like a police report on somebody's character. Next door to this was a rather buxom lady, Mrs Bloomfield, whose husband made infrequent appearances, and was presumably employed in the seafaring business, although this was uncertain. Moving another door up, were the Osbornes, the lady who may have been my temporary midwife. Then we come to the Smiths; yours truly, who were separated from the Carneys by a covered passage that supported part of the bedrooms of both houses. The Carneys were not as prolific as the rest of the residents as they had only two sons and one daughter, leaving only five to share the accommodation. The younger son, Teddy, and his sister, Ivy, were always later to become mixed up with the rest of us in our escapades. Then we come to another lady who shall remain unknown, as memory has again failed me. Finally, on our stretch of the road, we come to the Everetts who were associated with the Barge traffic. Moving on, we come to the so-called posh part of the street, as these houses sported a small front garden between the front door and the pathway. This did not indicate that the residents were in any way superior to the remainder of the street, just that it may have helped to give one that impression. Here, there were four such houses occupied by Messers Rix, Brunning, Kett, and again, an unknown. That just about completed the length of the street. Of course, we knew many of the folk on the other side of the road, The Plumes, Bartram, Ellis, Grey, Webbs, Dolby and Jay and Patricks to mention a few, the latter being the Cycle shop. Needless to say, none of the folk live there any more, for some years later, the area was demolished and modernised. In fact, when I last visited the area some five years ago, I was completely lost, or at least disoriented. Before moving on to more mundane things, I must add a little more to the local geographic features. Almost opposite the first house of the posh folk, just recently mentioned, was a cul-de-sac disguised by the name of Stanhope Street. This ran for some couple of hundred yards wherein several houses were situated. In these, lived a few more of what would now be called the gang, although we just called ourselves pals, which included the sisters of any of the chums. This was a completely sexless gathering, at least among the school fraternity, for it became a case of sharing all things. As I have already said, our family of eleven resided in the two up and two down terraced house.

Fortunately, at least as far as room was concerned, my two eldest brothers were in the Navy and the Army, for the year was already 1914 before I knew much about it. These were Jim and Bert, the former being in the Navy, and Bert (Gordon), the Army, where already at the age of eighteen he was a Company Sergeant Major. There is little that I can remember of those days until about the end of 1917. I can clearly remember that there was some white covering on the ground, be it frost or snow, I could not tell. The back door from our kitchen opened on to the yard, and gave way to a gate that admitted one to the passage between our house and that of the Carneys. This, in turn, led to the street, and this was used by the army as a kind of sentry box. Here the soldier on guard would stand through the night.

Being a good citizen, and probably hoping that some kind person would treat her own soldier son in a kindly manner, Mother would send out a jug of hot tea during the evening and late at night. The task of taking the tea out to the guard, fell to sister Win, who was about seventeen or eighteen. As was natural, then as now, Win had a soft spot for one of the sergeants, or he may have been a corporal, for he had some stripes on his uniform. As Win was also my unofficial nurse maid, it became the known thing that I should accompany her on these tea parties, so that I soon became known to the members of the guard. Romance for sister Win was not allowed to develop, for the army thought that all those soldiers should be moved elsewhere, probably to France where the war was still being fought over patches of mud. New faces arrived for the tea parties, but no more romances for Win. It was also somewhere about this time that enemy Zeppelins, airships. were making their nightly raids on various towns, to the annoyance of the general public. During one of these raids, a pilot from Martlesham managed to intercept one of the machines, and managed to inflict severe damage to the airship, which eventually caught fire as it made for the coast to the east of Ipswich. That blazing machine I saw as we watched from the passageway between our house and the Carneys. This machine was, I believe, that which was destroyed by Flight Lieutenant Warnford V.C RFC. During this episode, Father, who was a big man, standing some six foot plus and built like the proverbial traction engine, had decided that the best place for him was under the stairs in case the enemy could see him. The incident was the talk of the town for weeks, especially amongst those who had seen the ball of flame moving slowly across the eastern sky, gradually loosing height until it crashed somewhere miles away.

It would be convenient here to give the reader some idea of the SMITH Family. As I have just mentioned, Father was a big man in size, whose trade was that of journeyman builder, and his work reputation was a by-word in the town and surrounding areas. That reputation was off-set by his big failing, that of his liking and desire for his pints of beer. It was common knowledge to know that Mother often had to meet him from work and more or less beg for some weekly housekeeping money. This, when received, would be in the region of a one pound note and if mother was lucky, a few more coins might be added. This as far as I can recall was to sustain the rest of the family and to pay the rent, plus any other commodity that had to be paid for. Even on the occasions such as Christmas, the amount might possibly be raised to One pound Ten Shillings; equal to 150 pence of today's money. As for Mother, one cannot attempt to offer sufficient compliments, for although she was only small, about five feet nothing, quite good looking in a homely fashion, and in all respects a LADY, for in every respect, she was the soul of gentility, always willing to help or assist any person in any way possible. Of my sisters Win and Kate, I have already spoken, and of my two eldest brothers in the Navy and Army. Brother William came next, a rather dapper fellow of smart appearance and carriage. Then came Len, rather well built and employed by the local baker, Mr Tricker. Next came Glen, who actually worked for no pay at a garage until he joined the Navy, this was to allay Father's fears that he was one of the unemployed. Next was Ralph, who suffered an accident when young and had his right knee-cap removed, leaving him a permanent cripple in that he was unable to bend the leg. Last of all, came me, just plain Fred, with no embellishments and no second name.

My next recollection of the war days was that of what I now know to be the "Armistice Day", November 11th at 11 a.m. My brothers and some pals had taken me to Alexandra Park at the top of the hill that formed Back Hamlet. This was a favourite place for play, especially in the forbidden part of the park that consisted of bushes and shrubs surrounded by wire fencing. These compounds made ideal areas for hide and seek and such games. On this particular day, we had been playing until the stomach dictated that it was time for something to eat. We were just making our way through the park gates and were turning into Back Hamlet just when the air raid sirens started to sound. All of us had heard them before, but never during the day. Fear and probably some panic set in, and we all ran hell for leather down the hill and turned into Long Street before the sirens stopped. It was then that we noticed that other people were not moving or trying to make for cover as we had been told to do when we heard the sirens. It was not until we all arrived home quite breathless that Mother explained to us about the sirens sounding to mark the end of the war. That afternoon, all the neighbours started to make merry and there was much happiness everywhere, as it meant that soon the sons and fathers who had gone to war would be coming home again. It also meant that as I was still a youngster of some five years old, I benefited much from any sweets or goodies that might have been going.

Instead of meaning better things for everybody, the war having ended, it meant that there were more men to do the few jobs that were available, as even the women and girls had been working in the factories, making munitions, driving trams and horse buses and many other of the jobs that had been done by the men. However, the war was over, and the nation as a whole celebrated. Some more than others, and one fellow in particular, as he had a leg missing from just above the knee, and he hobbled round with a single crutch. Whether the wound was caused by the enemy or not, we never did know, except that under certain inebriated conditions he would become the terror of the area, as he would somehow balance on one knee and swing the crutch about his head and yell like the proverbial dervish, defying all and sundry to get near him. My best description of him is that he would best suit Long John Silver in any pantomime play, except that he had no parrot. That was Mr Warren or "Stumpy", as all people called him, and he lived in a little courtyard just below the sweet shop and almost next door to Southgate's scrap yard.

It would be about this time that I was taken to my first school, a place that was run by the Church of England. In fact I am sure that it was called St Clements C. of E. Infants School. Here then, I was deposited in the early morning to be called for later on. Not being sure of the routine of schools, and although I could see myself to the toilets, I was somewhat bashful in asking if I might go to the toilets. The result was, in spite of imposing severe restrictions on myself by crossing my legs and holding myself, a somewhat large puddle appeared on the floor, much to my dismay, disgust and annoyance, for I had to suffer the indignity of remaining in wet trousers until I was collected. Not a very impressive start to a nondescript school term. At this school, we were taught to form our letters and numbers which we wrote on slates. It was not until we progressed to the more senior of the infant classes that we were allowed to use paper of any sort, and then only for special work. School hours were from 9 a.m. to 4 p.m. with a break of about an hour or so at mid day. During this break, one would run like the wind to get home and have some sort of meal. This would be anything that Mother could conjure up. Probably some soup made from a supply of bones and vegetables with a thick slice of bread to fill in the corner of one's stomach. If finances were favourable, one would have perhaps a bloater with bread, or if extra cash had been made available one could have a piece of streaky pork. Then it would be a race back to school so as not to get a black mark for being late. This proved all good training for the later years, as by the age of seven, just after the three week August break, I was sent to Cavendish Street School. This was an elementary school about a mile from our home. Here I was placed in the first class of all, Standard One, under the eagle eye of Mrs Martin, a sharp featured, rather elderly woman, who at least managed to instil a moderate amount of knowledge to my not readily receptive brain. School hours here were 9 a.m. to 4.30 p.m. with a break for the midday meal of about one-and-a-half hours. As before, it was a question of getting home for a mid-day meal and back again. By the end of the year, I was able to complete the home journey in about 15 minutes running time, with a gradual improvement as time passed by. Also by the end of the year, my progress was such that I was able to move to standard 2, where a Miss Roper became our teacher. Miss Roper was, if anything, the complete opposite to Mrs Martin, being young and as us young fellows thought, quite good looking, so that the majority of the lads put themselves out to please her. This was particularly the case when answering her questions. Looking back, I feel sure that this was part of her teaching technique. All hopes of any young romance by the lads was immediately crushed by the appearance of the senior class teacher, a Mr Overfield, who taught the standard 7 and X7 pupils. By the end of the second year, my knowledge had expanded to the point where I was able to do addition and subtraction, simple stuff only, and I had started to spell easy words. I must have been an average pupil for at the end of the year I was able to progress to standard 3. Here we were met and taught by Mr Staines who tolerated no nonsense from any boy, for in his class there were no girls.

From my experience of Mr Staines, who, although very strict, was a wonderful teacher, the imparting of knowledge was his main object in life. If one did not pay attention to instructions, one was punished by having so many cuts of the cane. The amount was usually three or more, all on the one hand; the non-writing hand. Should the offence be really serious, then punishment was six cuts, three on either hand. It was a point of honour that one did not resist punishment but that one held out the hand at full arm's length with the palm of the hand facing upwards. Judging the moment, Mr Staines, "Harry", would deliver stroke number one like the striking of a snake. The second stroke would follow in due course, and after careful deliberation, followed by the remainder of the punishment which had previously been announced to the class. All punishments were carried out in full view of one's classmates, who were never backward at informing the offender that he was a coward of the first order. Such remarks would in no way be tolerated, not at least if the offender was one of the Long Street boys, with the consequential challenge to a bout of fisticuffs. These challenges usually took place in the playground during the dinner break when the news of the fight had been passed through the various classes of the school. Pupils who witnessed the bouts would form a ring and the contestants would enter, without any preliminaries or seconds. The fight would continue, without rounds, until one or the other of the contestants either withdrew or the fight was broken up by the appearance of one of the teachers. This would then mean that the offenders would each be punished in front of the class for fighting in the school grounds. The teacher, having administered the punishment, would then demand that the contestants shake hands and, as further proof of the end of hostilities, would sit the offenders together in the same desk. More often than not, this resulted in long lasting friendships between the opponents, but not always. I will state here, in case folk may think me a stranger to the truth, I very often was awarded cuts, as we called the cane, and quite often became involved in the fisticuffs. The occasions, I hasten to add, were always in defence of my honour, especially after some rather extensive punishment, or having been falsely accused of cheating. Having been punished by the teacher, it became the end of the matter, and it did one no good to go home and tell one's parents, as then one got punished by a "clip" from the head of the house. Although this type of punishment may seem harsh, in my opinion, it never did any of us any real harm, except to our dignity. In fact, I feel that it really toughened us up a bit more, for these were tough times, but it did not affect our sense of discipline in any way. Those in authority, we felt, had the right to order the comings and goings of us lads, and authority was respected in all ways at all times. Obviously, one did try to kick over the traces at times, for after all, we were fast growing up, and one would not have been recognised if one had not tried to take over the reins, even at an early age.

Again, at the end of the year, classes were changed and this time, Mr Staines came with us to standard 4, where we really had to buckle down to the bookwork, for this was the year in which one would sit what would now be called the eleven plus exam. On the result of this examination, one would either go on to the middle school, "Central" or the Municipal school from where one might be able to attain a Grammar School entry.

Such dizzy heights were definitely beyond me, for in no way could I envisage passing such an examination. Even if I had been able, I am sure that my parents would have been unable to afford my going to such a school. However, there was no need to worry, for I suspect that I was a write-off for the Municipal School right from the first question on the first paper. The question was that I translated the following; "à vous marches comme ça." This I assumed to be French, so being quite honest, I wrote on my paper that I did not understand French. Needless to say, I did not pass for the Municipal School, but I got a recommendation to apply for the Central School. When I told Mother she was more than pleased for me to go BUT, family finances forbade such a step. This did not bother me, for it meant that I would have deserted my pals in Long Street, and to me I felt that loyalty was more important. With the results of the examination made known, it seemed that the school attitude changed completely. Mr Staines became quite friendly towards me, and it seemed that with my promotion to standard 5, I was to be the star pupil of the class. This was possibly because of the recommendation to go to the Central School, and my not having taken it up. Much of this latter assumption was most probably my own imagination.

Just prior to this episode, which I will refer to as the eleven plus examination, it was the practice of the male members of the family to go to the place where Mother was working in the early morning. The purpose of this visit was to collect what food may have been left from the employers' tables. This would be placed in a bag, usually a fish creel, for collection by the Smith boys. The best contributor to this menu was a lady that lived at the top end of Berners Street, almost opposite the Ipswich and East Suffolk General Hospital, before it was moved to Foxhall Heath. The bag was highly prized by the recipients, for it could contain anything edible, from a stale ham sandwich, a piece of stale fruit cake or – treasure amongst treasures – a piece of fresh unrequired buttered toast from the morning's breakfast table. These selections of goodies were sorted over in the gardens of Christchurch Park, just below the Arboretum. Those that had collected the goodies had what they wanted, and the remainder would be taken home for the rest of the family. Naturally, when I went on these expeditions I, being the youngest, took last pick, and not always with good grace. That was life, and one had to take it as it came. Of course, many of the tit bits did come my way through a certain amount of blackmailing the elder brothers, as sometimes they indulged in a quiet smoke or some other small misdemeanour. On the whole, the young boys of the family lived and shared as one, whenever that was possible.

One of the main pastimes during the winter evenings, was to watch for the Gaslamp Lighter coming round to light the street lamps. The lamp was positioned at the top of a post, some twelve or fourteen feet high, and was actuated by means of a chain attached to the on or off switches of the lamp. The usual man was an expert at this operation, for he would come round on his cycle with a long hooked pole, and almost without stopping, would skilfully engage the hooked pole with the appropriate chain. A quick jerk, and the light would come on or off according to requirement. Just below the lamp was positioned a stout metal bar for resting a ladder against when servicing the lamp. One of the tests for becoming a member of the Long Street fraternity, was to shin up the lamp post, transfer one's body to the ladder bar, hang on for five seconds and then drop to the ground. Easily done when one can shin up a fourteen foot lamp post, transfer one's weight to the ladder bar, hang on for five seconds, then drop to the ground. This was part of the test of entry to the Long Street Fraternity.

In the Spring, there was always the road tarring operations to distract one's attentions. The evening before the actual operation, large carts would deposit loads of sand at places about fifteen yards apart on each side of the street. With the disappearance of the workmen, an impromptu seaside developed in the street, for this was too much for the smaller children to let pass by. After all, they had heard from elder brothers or sisters just what the seaside was like, with loads of sand to play with. Amazingly, not much of the sand ever seemed to be missing by the next morning. Honesty appeared to reign when the simple pleasures were meted out. The next morning the Tar Engine would arrive, already belching columns of black smoke where the tar was being heated. About three men would be positioned at each sand heap ready to throw the shovelled sand on the hot tar when it was sprayed on the roadway. This was done as the metal tar tank was horse drawn along the roadway while two men would pump the hot tar over the road. The operation would usually last the best part of the day, and any sand that may have been left over was rapidly and magically disappearing to various back gardens or yards. This latter event was the bane of the parents, for it meant that all the youngsters would be almost covered in as much tar as had been sprayed on the road.

At about the same time that these events occurred, Mr Wheeler, the cobbler, asked if I would like to do some errands for him and for which I would be paid. No second offer was needed for this chance to earn a few coppers, during my out of school hours. It was on that first evening that I earned my first few coins. The errand was to fetch some bruised oranges from the wholesaler in Brook Street. When I collected this fruit, there must have been some fifty or sixty bruised oranges in a sack, and these I delivered to Mr Wheeler, after I had inspected and taken for myself the best of the oranges. Curious to know why he wanted the fruit, I was told that it was for making home-made orange wine. I was then given a demonstration of what to do with the oranges, which were then put into a large earthenware bowl and left to ferment. Much later on, when he judged the drink to be ready, the concoction was siphoned into bottles and placed under the floor boards of the shop. I do not know just how many bottles of wine there were under the boards, but there seemed to be an enormous number. Some of the other jobs that I was paid for, were the delivery of some of the repaired boots and shoes, and also taking some boots and shoes to the boot factory on the Woodbridge Road for them to be machine sewn by the factory machines, which took about ten minutes for each boot or shoe. Then, it would be a fast run home for dinner or tea and more jobs or school, whichever the occasion demanded.

Amongst our friends in Long Street were several large families connected with the river barges and the docks. This was always of great interest to us, for whenever we knew that the barges were due to arrive at Ipswich, the families would inform each other, and the children of the barge crews would be invited to meet the barges. If one was friendly with these children, one also had an invite to meet the barge on its way in to the docks. Sometimes, it could even mean meeting the barge some way down the river, perhaps opposite Pondhall Farm or, if one was extra lucky, at Nacton Shore, depending on the state of the tides. If luck was in, one would walk to the shore at the arranged pick up point, and the barge skipper would arrange for a skiff to be sent to pick up the guests. A quick trip out to the barge and then a scramble on board, where one's place was in a position at the stern near the huge steering wheel. All this adventure, if such it could be called, certainly helped to allay any sense of boredom that might have been prevalent. In fact, the days seemed so full of things to do that there never seemed to be enough days in any week.

In the winter months, there would be the gathering of the broken branches for the fires, and there was usually the snow clearing to be done. For this one usually got one penny for each house front cleared. In the spring, there were the gardens to be cleared and dug which meant more pennies. There was always the horse manure to be collected from the streets, which would be sold for one penny a bucketful. This was never very difficult to do, as almost every trader had a horse and cart. One has heard of the "Cries of London" and the various wares that were so sold, but no mention was ever made of the Ipswich Cries of "Horse Muck a penny a pail". A half a dozen pails full would ensure that one had a good meal next day, for the fertiliser was always in great demand for the allotments that many people rented for a few pence per week. Much of this interest in gardening was the requirement for a supply of cheap vegetables for many hungry mouths.

Helping to pick the early fruits would also provide some extra cash. If other excitement was needed, there were always the parks, where, more often than not, the park keepers were hostile to young lads who trespassed on their domains. It could be quite a common sight to see a keeper chasing some seven or eight young lads who had perhaps done nothing more than throw sticks at the conkers on the trees. Should one be unlucky enough to be caught, a smart "clip" on the ear would prove a good deterrent against early repetition.

During the summer, one would have a prolonged holiday of three weeks from school. This was originally instituted so that the school children could help with the harvest, or, if no harvesting was available, so there would be early apples and plums to pick which all helped to swell the meagre purses of the locals. Whatever task was undertaken it was done with as much speed as possible so that more time was available for other money making projects. The money so earned would be offered to Mother to help towards the household budget, and she would usually give one a copper or so back for one's own use. This would normally be spent on a penny saveloy or some pork scratchings from the local butcher. There was never any food wasted, for any scraps from one meal, if not sufficient to meet the next meal, would go into the pot for making some soup. So, it was with a sense of pride and achievement that one contributed as much as one could.

It was also about this time that father rented an allotment on the Nacton Road, some distance past the present Race Course Hotel, and about four miles from Long Street. This allotment was cultivated at weekends and in the evenings during the summer, if Father felt that way inclined. The only snag to this arrangement was that I, being the only junior male available, would be required to help with the cultivation of the plot. This meant walking to the allotment, where one would work either raking the soil or stone picking, and helping in general. If Father felt in a benevolent mood, I would be given a penny to catch the tram from The Earl Grey pub to the Royal Oak pub on the Felixstowe Road, and then have to walk about one and a half miles to the allotment. Much the same procedure would be taken for the return journey after work stopped. This may seem like rather tough treatment when compared with the amount of walking done by the youngsters of today. The only way to get to any destination was to walk it, unless some benevolent person provided the coin with which to travel. If one did not comply with the wishes of one's elders, the result was usually some physical discomfort administered very promptly. For these trips to the allotment, one would be dressed in the oldest and oddest assortment of clothing that was readily available. My usual rig for these expeditions was, an old shirt, trousers and jacket, all several sizes too big or too small, with an old chamber pot hat tied to the jacket button-hole with string. Somewhere in the family possessions there is a snapshot picture of me so-dressed ready for the hike to the allotment. Should one have objected to the current fashion parade, then parental chastisement would be the order of the day. In all this, I had to bear the remarks and jeers of my chums, for they were never very backward at making fun of anything or anyone at anytime. However, the allotment trips had some advantage, for I had asked if I might have a small patch of ground in which to grow some flowers. This I was allowed to do, and several of the other allotment holders would buy the young plants or flowers from me for a few pence. Admittedly, the cash was always welcomed, but the real thrill was being able to take Mother some flowers when I went home each time.

Mother really adored flowers and shrubs, in fact, she was really a walking encyclopaedia as regards nature. Very often on Sunday afternoons, Mother would take us for a walk, most probably by the river from Cliff Quay as far as Pondhall Farm and back home across the fields and Nacton Road. During these walks, it would be a continuous nature study lesson, or Mother would reminisce about her young days. These chats were very interesting, as Mother was at one time head cook to various wealthy families in many localities. At one time, Mother lived at Spencers Wood, Reading. Whether it was that she had worked there or not, I do not know. Whatever it was, there must have been some strong reason attached, for she often spoke of Spencer's Wood. On one occasion that I recall, Mother went to Reading for a few days to attend somebody's funeral, leaving us young ones in the care of our elder sister. It must have been something of importance as a telegram boy had called, and Mother received a letter from Reading containing some money for her fare. It was only a flying visit, for Mother was back within a couple of days. Some few days after that, we were visited by an uncle from Dereham in Norfolk. He had been a Captain in the Grenadier Guards during the war. All this was very exciting, and would have been intriguing had I been a few years older, but I had to wait several years to hear the story of these visits by Mother. It was shortly after these events that brother Gordon, Bert as we called him, came home from the army, and arranged a trip for us that were at home, to visit the Aunt Mary that lived at Tunstall near Wickham Market. That aunt had a pub, The Green Man, also a large garden and orchard with a pond and ducks. The orchard part was most interesting, for I was able to help myself to apples and fruit, much to my later discomfort. This trip was undertaken in a motor car, hired for the day apparently, so that when we came home the car was loaded with fruit and was piled about us on the back seat. Not only me, and I think the whole family had loaded as many apples as possible into the car, for we had never seen so many apples before, and we also brought home a duck that had been killed while we were there. When we arrived home at Long Street, almost the whole street population turned out to meet us, for it was an unheard of thing for any resident of the street to use a car. Had the football pools been in existence at the time, then I am sure they would have been convinced that we had a good win. The social standing of the SMITHS went up dramatically. What happened next, was that father, being the head of the family, went to get out of the car, a real vintage model, with high sides and a running board, with spare tyre attached. Not readily realising that the car was full with apples, he opened the door with a flourish, so the apples rolled onto the roadway. This was much to the delight, joy and benefit of the neighbours who did not wait to be invited to help themselves. Father was furious, and immediately expressed his feelings in no uncertain terms, again, much to the delight and entertainment of the onlookers. That, as I remember, was my first ride in a car, and was to be the last for many years.

One of the usual pastimes of the youngsters of Long Street, was to go to the docks and the barges for some fishing for eels. Should the skipper of the barge happen to be a parent of one of our fraternity, then we would use the barge for our fishing in preference to the quayside. One always managed a better catch from the outside of the barge, probably because of the edible refuse that was thrown overboard. The small eels would be thrown back while the larger ones would be offered for sale to any likely purchaser. Yes, one never lost an opportunity to make a few pence, for money meant food, and there was never too much of that.

Another of our profitable schemes was to watch for the arrival of boats carrying Locust Beans, which would be unloaded at R.W. PAUL'S or Cranfield's Flour mills. These beans would be unloaded by the grain elevators ready for making into cattle food cakes. Any of the beans that missed the loading trays would fall to the dockside, to be pounced on by hungry youngsters. After all, we too were animals of some degree, and our need was as dire as the farm animals. We would only leave the dockside when our pockets were crammed full, or the unloading was completed. The beans were about four inches long, black or dark brown (the fruit of the Carob Tree), and quite hard to bite, but being delightfully sweet when eaten. Having a pocket full of these beans was as good as having a pocketful of coins, for the beans could be sold to school mates. The rate of exchange was about five sticks for one penny. This would depend on the size of the beans that had been salvaged for sale. Of course, if two or three boats were unloading at the same time, the prices of the beans would fall. We needed no stock exchange to fix the price of beans, just common sense, a sense of fairness and a flair for bargaining. Just what the nutritional value of the beans happened to be, was anybody's guess, though they certainly did us no harm. How could they when they put meat on the bones of cattle? At least, that was our reasoning although I suspect that our parents or any medical staff would have thrown up their hands in despair. Such reasoning I think went for all foods, be it fruit or vegetable; if an animal could eat it and suffer no harm, then so could we.

Another of our favourite foods was crab. These were obtainable from Southgates, a brother of the rag and bone merchant and the scrap yard. Crabs that were sold were about two pence each, depending on size and whether the claws were missing or not. If both claws were missing in the cooking process, then the crab would cost about half the normal price. The claws could be brought separately, about three a penny and usually sold by the handful. Having purchased a crab, one had to clean and dress it for eating with bread. Crab became a SMITH delicacy, for the dressing of crab needed dexterity and patience and we all became expert in this field. The body of the crab would be eaten by the elder members of the family and the juniors would be given the legs, not the claws, to crack and clean of meat. As one became older or went to work and could afford two pence for a crab, then Sunday tea was assured. No doubt the members of the youth of Long Street heard of our liking for crabs. This one day, led to the youths going to the docks, catching several crabs, which incidentally were not edible, and deciding to deposit them live in the front bedroom of the Smith residence. To do this was no mean feat, for one would have to climb a drain pipe while carrying the live crabs and nothing was heard or seen of the intruders, so that when Father retired that night he encountered several live crabs on the floor and on the bed. Everybody that was already in bed was wakened by the yells and the language that resulted. It was hard to tell whether he was calling for the police or the fire brigade. From the sounds, it seemed as though the murder squad was required. All I know is that we all had to scramble round and find the crabs, which again caused more commotion when one of us got a nip from a belligerent crab. Although Father threatened every person with the weight of the law, obviously no culprit was found.

I also remember that brother Len, the one that worked at Trickers the Bakers, kept pigeons in the yard. A kind of shed was built right at the bottom of the yard and in this shed the pigeons were kept. The eggs were a constant source of food for they laid almost daily and would be eaten raw. It was not until Len found out that the eggs were being eaten that he made us stop the pilfering by threats of violence. Whenever the birds were released for a flight, probably in the evening more often than not, a bird would be missing on their return home. Whether the birds that went missing really got lost, or whether somebody had a cheap meal, is completely unknown, for the mystery was never solved. Also at the bottom of the yard and on the ground in the pigeon pen, was an air vent to the brewers malting. Through this vent we would often talk to the workman, who was always the same man, and sometimes he would give us some of the unripened malt for the birds. This arrangement was fine, until it was discovered that when the pigeons were cleaned out, much of the sweepings were pushed through the vent, to the man's annoyance. This caused the supply of malt to cease with the ultimate disposal of the pigeons.

Also in the yard we had another lean-to, which housed the mangle. A big iron instrument standing about five feet high with massive wooden rollers. Since I was the only one not at work, it was my lot to turn the mangle for Mother on washdays. This involved feeding the wet washing between the rollers and turning the large handle while Mother caught the semi-wet washing on the other side. If one was not completely alert or was day-dreaming, the result was some severely squashed fingers, for the rollers were kept closed by a large leaf spring similar to the leaf on a lorry, but not quite as large. The mangle was carefully looked after, for this was a source of income to Mother. Very often a neighbour would bring the washing round to be mangled for a small fee. This task was considered by me to be a contribution to the household budget although I never actually contributed any cash. Mother however, always made it up in lots of little ways, such as being allowed to sit up late when there was a fireworks display. This would be in Alexandra Park which we could see from our front bedroom window, and would finish sometime just after 11 p.m. usually on a Saturday.

Shortly after the episode of the crabs, brother Jim came home from China, where he had been in service with the Navy. This was the first time that I had seen him, at least to my knowledge, for when he had been home previously, I had been too young to understand. Hearing him talk of the Navy, must have inspired me some way, as from then on, it was to be my ambition to join the Royal Navy. This would have been about 1923, and early the following year, Jim was posted to the Navy Training Establishment at Shotley. Here, he would sometimes pay for Mother and myself to visit him if he was on duty at the weekend. This we did by catching the bus from the Old Cattle Market and it took about three quarters of an hour for the trip. Naturally, Jim would show us round the Establishment and then take us into his mess for tea. He was a Petty Officer at the time and seeing and tasting what I thought was a banquet, it really inspired me to join the Navy. Indeed, where else could one possibly eat like that?

Also about this time, Jim took Mother and myself to see a house in Gladstone Road that he thought of buying. This would have been for Mother more than anything else and although I was not consulted, the house was finally purchased through a building society. This meant a move of house to 23 Gladstone Road, and the leaving of my chums in Long Street although I met them daily at school. Mother did try to get me transferred to Clifford Road School but this was not allowed, so I had to remain at Cavendish Street School which suited me. The move to Gladstone Road meant that now I had to walk all the way to the allotment, which was possibly some half to a mile nearer but there were no trams or buses available for making the trip. It did not really matter, for some time after this, Father gave up the allotment, either voluntarily, or because the ground was needed for building purposes. This did not unduly bother me, for it meant that I no longer had to go to the allotment. However the house at Gladstone Road had a small garden and it then became my task to keep it tidy. This carried on until 1925 when there was a General Strike by all workers. This included Father who was what was known as a Journeyman Builder. Daily he would return home, not having any work. Sometimes he would return somewhat inebriated much to the disgust and annoyance of the rest of the family. Where he got the money from is a mystery, but we suspected that he either did some small private jobs or else his pals treated him. The drinking became a trial for the family, for he would verbally abuse one after the other for some length of time. This would greatly upset Mother, who would retire to the kitchen and shed many tears. On one occasion, brother Bert, who was home at the time, remonstrated with father and things improved for some time. By that Christmas, Father had returned to the drink habit, causing much unhappiness in the family. By next summer, all domestic bliss had disappeared so that father was warned by the elder sons to mend his ways. This apparently did not suit for without more ado Father left home without a farewell or apology. Mother, my sisters and next elder brother Ralph all expected a daily return. We did occasionally hear of him from some source or other and he did put in an appearance at some odd times.

By now, it was time for me to leave school and go to work for I had reached my fourteenth birthday and it was imperative that I should help out with the family budget, if only to help support myself. Jobs were not easy to come by, so that when I had the chance to become an errand boy at the Grocers, 'Miller & Steel' in the Butter Market, I did not hesitate to accept. This meant that I would work five and a half days a week from 8.30 a.m. to 5.30 p.m. Monday to Friday and half a day on Saturday to finish at 1 p.m. This was to be for the princely sum of five shillings per week, (in today's money, 25 pence). From that I gave Mother two shillings, (ten pence) and with the other three shillings I was expected to more or less clothe myself. The work was not easy, for it meant being at the beck and call of all the staff and delivering groceries to customers at various addresses round the town. This sometimes meant several miles of cycling on an old heavy trade cycle with a carrier in the front that held a goods basket. At times, it was a case of cycling quite a few miles with perhaps one or two small items.   Customer Service was the motto of the firm and the requirements of the customer were paramount, whatever the errand boy's ability to comply.   Sometimes in bad weather, in pouring rain or sleet and snow the trips were never pleasant, the front loaded cycle would get out of control with the result that the groceries finished in the roadway.   One would try one's best to avoid such spills but this was not always possible, so that the scattered goods would be scooped up and dusted down and hopefully delivered to the customer without question.   More often than not the goods would be taken by a servant who was usually quite pleasant so perhaps a cup of cocoa would be offered.   I was not yet at the stage where I could be offered a glass of cooking sherry, or such like.   With perhaps three or four trips like this on a bad day, one would be absolutely shattered by the time one packed up work for the day.   This was especially so if one was wet through.   At such times I regret to admit, one's temper was not always at its best.   It was on one such day that I had just returned from a long wet run, and it was just about finishing time that I was told to deliver a large jar of marmalade to one of the customers.   This I did with as much good grace as I could muster.   On return to the shop, at well past closing time I was met by the assistant manager to be informed that I had broken the jar of marmalade.   This I knew to be untrue, so I expressed myself most forcefully.   In the morning, I was called to the manager's office to explain the broken jar of marmalade.

This I could not do, as I did not know of any breakage, other than as explained to me the previous evening.   The result was, that I was accused of telling lies, which really got me wound up.   Without more ado, I mounted the cycle and went to the customer's house and saw the servant that had taken the pot.   On confronting her, she admitted to me that she had dropped it later and thought that it was better that I took the blame, for she would have been required to pay for it.   I guess that the same could have been said for me, and told her so.   The result of this was that she told her mistress and that the lady of the house telephoned the shop manager to that effect.   After that a great improvement in the shop staff attitude towards me resulted, for it seemed that I would not be set upon even to the extent of going to the source of any bother.   Also, remembering the attitude of the assistant manager and the manager when interviewed, I decided that I would ask for a rise in pay.   The manager whose name was also Smith, asked me several questions about what I intended, and finally asked if I would like to train as a shop assistant in the shop. First, I wanted more money for my wages and having got that, (a rise of two shillings), I told him that I would think about the offer. I told Mother that evening about the pay rise and the offer of being a shop assistant. First Mother agreed that I should keep half the pay rise, and secondly, that I should have to make up my own mind. I explained to Mother about my wanting to join the Navy when I was old enough, and of this she had already guessed my desires.

For some time now, I had been running round the park in the early mornings and doing various exercises that I thought would help me develop physically, ready for the navy. I was already fairly fit at having been organ blower at the local church for some considerable time. The church was St Clements in the church lane of that name and I was paid threepence per service, (just over 1p), in today's coinage. This job consisted of three services on Sunday and one midweek service in the evening, thus giving me another shilling a week. Sunday services were the worst ones, for here the organist, Mrs Carter, would play through what I deemed to be her whole repertoire after each service. I think that this must have been her only chance each week to play the organ without restrictions, for she would play the organ at full volume and with all the stops out, making me pump like one possessed. There was no such thing as electric organs. It was the usual thing for me to pump in my vest during these performances. Most times one had some sort of audience and it delighted me to think that no matter how Mrs Carter played, I could always keep the bellows full. When there were no onlookers, I would get my revenge on Mrs C. by letting the wind gradually reduce in the bellows so that she would play at volume to suddenly find there was no sound issuing. This would mean that Mrs Carter would pump the foot pedals of the organ in a most demanding and annoyed manner, as a signal that air was out of the bellows. This to me meant that I should pump with renewed vigour resulting in a sudden and unexpected blast of noise, depending on which pedal had been pressed. This unexpected sound, probably out of tune or key, would for the moment hold Mrs Carter quite bewildered and the wrong notes would echo and re-echo through the church with deafening noise. An immediate lessening of the demand for air was the immediate result until the organist, carried away with the delights of music would get a repeat performance of the empty bellows. Revenge was mine, and we learned to respect each other's ability for we were both masters of our respective jobs. My pay for these services was accumulated until the end of the quarter when I would receive untold wealth of thirteen shillings, (65p today). With this money I would normally buy clothing or boots and treat mother and myself to a piece of fried fish and chips, (two pence today) and then look forward eagerly to the next quarter's payment.

Time rolled by, and I began to fill out bodily and grow in size, so that using a little of my extra money each week, I joined some keep fit and weight lifting classes at the Social Settlement in Fore Street, just round the corner from Long Street. Also I managed a few lessons in Boxing as one always needed to be alert and ready for when the big day came that I would join the Navy. At the age of fifteen and without hesitating I reported to the recruiting office for the Navy. Here the Chief Petty Officer recruiter gave me several tests, mostly general maths and figures, and some dictation and told me to write why I wanted to join up. In all the tests as well as the physical, I passed O.K. and then came the blow that stunned me, as I was told that I was too young, and to come back when I was another three months older. Sadly I went back to work and in no sweet temper, for I had taken the time to go to the recruiter in my dinner hour. It is quite possible that I sulked somewhat for everybody seemed to annoy me for the rest of the day. However, time passed, so that I eventually reported again to the recruiter, who recognised me, at least by name. Again the tests and again the results as before. This time I was told that although I was now old enough, the Navy had stopped recruiting for the time being. By Christmas, I began to despair and weekly I pestered the Recruiting Officer until I think he got fed up with me and passed my name to those that said YES. Some time later during the February, I received a letter telling me that I was again to report to the Recruiting Office early in March. Time could not pass quickly enough and eventually I was informed that I was accepted for the Navy and that my joining instructions would be sent to me after I had completed a form which my Father would have to sign. Naturally I consulted Mother, for she was my confessor. The paper also needed the signature of some person in authority to act as witness. This was no bother for I knew that the vicar of the church would witness for me. The bother would be to get Father home in time to sign and at the same time be sober enough to do it. Acting on Mother's advice I arranged with the vicar, the Rev. Knapp, to meet us at our home about 6.30 p.m. on a Monday. On that particular evening I managed to coax Father away from his work before he went to the pubs. To do this, I had to bribe him with six bottles of beer that would be available on completion of the signing. Fortunately everything went according to plan and without waiting I got the papers in a sealed envelope and delivered them at once to the Recruiting Officer. It now only needed patient waiting for the commencement of my dreams and the informing of the world in general. Soon a letter arrived telling me that I was to join the Navy in the April following. The time dragged until just before the big day when I gave in my notice at work ready to finish at the weekend. No longer would I be an errand boy, and life seemed very rosy. Here, I will admit, that there were several shocks to be overcome. First, the real big difference in visiting the training establishment as a guest of a Petty Officer brother, and joining the Navy as a recruit. Jim was by now serving in H.M.S. Nelson, while Glen had left the training establishment some few years earlier, and was serving in the Mediterranean in H.M.S CERES. My orders clearly stated that I was to report to the Recruiting Officer at 8.15 a.m. on 23rd April 1929 for the Royal Navy, so I said my farewells to friends and chums that weekend.

I JOIN THE ROYAL NAVY

On this day, 23rd April some countless years ago, St George battled with the Dragon, at least that is according to legend. This was 1929 and the only Dragon to be battled with as far as I was concerned, was that of getting into the Navy. Although that day is now some sixty plus years ago, I can still remember it quite clearly. For me it was to be the most important day of my life. That is why, after having said adieu to Mother and the family, I found myself on the doorstep of the Recruiting Office, trembling slightly, either from excitement or fear of the unknown. Having rung the bell (it was a private house in Oxford Street) I was told to enter by the Recruiting Officer. Already inside the room, was another young fellow, whom I had seen on a couple of occasions before. Without further delay, we were given instructions to get ourselves to the Railway Station ready to catch a train for Manningtree and thence on to Harwich. The train was scheduled to leave Ipswich at about 9.50 a.m. and we were expected to be on it. Navy Authorities would be meeting the train at Harwich and as he told us, we were now in the navy so there was to be no delaying our getting there. Obviously we were in civilian clothes, so had anybody suggested that we were playing truant from school, we would have been indignant to say the least. Were we not the upholders of all the Naval traditions known and unknown? Apart from that, we both anticipated that within a few days at least we should be on our way to the lands of sunshine and fortune.

I found that my companion's name was Charles and that his surname was Stimpson and that although unknown to us, we were destined to spend the next year or so in each other's close company. Having caught the train as detailed by the Recruiter, we both started on the sandwiches that our parents had given us for we had been obliged to have an early breakfast about 6.30 a.m. Trains were changed at Manningtree, as we had been told and we were soon off to Harwich ready for the welcome that we were sure awaited us. Arriving at Harwich, we certainly had a welcome, but not quite what we expected. Standing on the platform, just idly minding our own business, we were most rudely awakened by a shout from a huge blue uniformed brass buttoned person with each arm covered in gold braid. The shout was, "who are you two then?" It was on the tip of my tongue to remark that I was one of the "Pirates of Penzance," but having been told that we were already in the Navy I thought better of it and just muttered that we were new Naval Recruits from Ipswich. Having established that we were indeed two of the expected recruits, this person told us to wait by the exit as he was expecting to gather some more recruits from another train that was shortly due to arrive. Very soon, a train arrived apparently from London, and the same brass buttoned gold lace adorned figure returned with three more lads about our own age. Surely there could not be any more recruits expected, as we had been told that recruiting had been stopped or delayed. How wrong we both were. It was here that another person dressed as a sailor, said to the tall big person with the armful of gold lace, something about a boat being ready to shove off, and that he would be back in an hour. It was fortunate that I had some idea of the navy, due mainly to my brothers, that I recognised the big fellow as a Naval petty officer and the younger sailor as a leading seaman. I was just about to impart my knowledge to Charles when an abrupt order called for silence. We were then informed that in future one would only talk if one was spoken to. What a welcome! No wonder there was a mutiny on the Bounty, I thought. At this point the Chief Petty Officer told us to fall in, and then started putting us in some order, at the same time ordering us to remain silent. With that accomplished, we partly marched and partly walked to the Jetty where a picket boat was puffing clouds of black smoke. Yes, we were off to sea be it only across the river to Shotley Pier, which I instantly recognised from my previous visits with Mother. Again we were told in no uncertain terms, to get into the picket boat but not down in the cabin. For the short trip across the River Stour, we seated ourselves round the foot of the funnel, for the wind was quite keen, still not daring to talk. On arrival at Shotley Pier, there was a shout of "make it lively then", and the leading seaman told us to fall in on the pier. He need not have bothered, for waiting for us at the top of the steps was a petty officer who ordered us to "fall in" and told us that an able seaman, or it may have been ordinary seaman would take us onwards. Having just fallen in by order of the petty officer, we decided that to take up our previous positions was the best plan. This we did, so that the seaman was somewhat surprised by our sense of discipline.

To those that can remember, and to those that only have history books to inform them of events, the year 1929 was the time of depression following the First World War. Also, this time was shortly after the General Strike of 1926, when every working man that had been to war, was wanting his correct rewards for winning that war. This strike also included a lot of folk that had never donned uniform or even done any war work. A golden opportunity to climb on the band wagon if one may steal a phrase. Hence, joining one of the armed forces was a definite chance for a wage and a regular mealtime, as all jobs were at a premium. If one had a job, especially if it was a reasonable wage payer, one just carried on working at it. There was very little chance of betterment in any job. Not only that, but this was also the time long before decimal currency was thought of, just plain pounds shillings and pence, twelve pence to the shilling and twenty shillings to the pound. I leave the mathematicians to work out the answers, although I have endeavoured to convert some already.

Having got ourselves into some semblance of order, the seaman asked us all for our papers that had been given to us by the recruiter. Having checked the papers against the numbers of recruits, he stuffed them inside his uniform, rubbed his hands on his trousers and said, "Let's be having you then." This was all Dutch to us, and we understood much more clearly when he called, "Right turn - double march." I feel sure that all five of us readily grasped his meaning for at a steady pace we rapidly cleared the pier. Immediately in front of us were three long flights of stone steps, now known to be called "Faith, Hope and Charity", that consisted of almost one hundred steps from top to bottom. Naturally, the lads in the lead started to walk up the steps in perhaps a dignified manner.

"HALT," shouted like a thunder clap, brought us to an instant stop. Unseen by us, another Petty Officer had seen us and intervened in our walk up the steps. Without more to do, he took the seaman aside and apparently gave him a telling off. Next, it was our turn to get the lash of his tongue, for he told us in no uncertain words that now that we were joining the Navy it was customary for recruits to double (run) at all times even though there were numerous steps in front of us. Somewhat crestfallen at our errors, we were already moving when again he called, "HALT." Again we stopped, and again we were lectured on not doing as we thought, but to await orders to move. Then, it was "carry on" and again the shouted "Halt", as we started off up the steps. Again the tongue lashing about orders being given to the senior hand of the party which in no way could have been us seeing that we were not even "Nozzers" (New Entries) yet. With that, and an acknowledgement by the seaman, we started off up the steps again, this time at the double. By the time we were at the top of the first flight, our breath was coming in sharp gulps for this was something that we were not prepared for. I suppose the Navy did have a little compassion, for the seaman told us to "halt" and to get our breath back. How grand it was just to stand and try to breathe normally. One of the fellows who had joined us from the London Train sat down on the steps in almost a state of collapse. Our rest period was short lived, for coming down the steps was another tall brass buttoned gold lace covered figure.

"Double march," shouted the seaman in almost the same tones as the Petty Officer, so that we again started off at the run. As we passed the figure coming down, our seaman friend shouted, "Eyes right," and saluted the officer who incidentally was wearing black gaiters. This denoted that he was a Gunnery Officer. Trying to show off my knowledge of the navy, I also saluted the Officer, and, to the amazement of us all, we got a smile in return. The smile was not meant for me however, for I received a telling off by the seaman, who informed us that only the person in charge should salute. At the top of the steps, we were ordered to halt and stand easy, so that we could fully recover from our mountain climbing efforts. Relief did not last long for we were soon doubling at a brisk pace across what our leader termed the quarter-deck. By this time, I was beginning to wonder if everybody in the navy was being trained to be a super athlete for we never seemed to stop running. I was really glad that I had been doing some training, for even though I was out of breath, I could still keep going which was more than could be said for some of the group. Stopping at a gateway that led to the road, we were inspected by another officer who had several seamen and petty officers with him. Here our seaman friend left us and we were taken over by a petty officer, with red badges on his arms. He was instructed to take us to the New Entry Block down in "Nozzers Lane." To get there we passed by the edge of the large parade ground and then down a slight incline where there were three or four buildings which looked like elongated bungalows. As we marched down the roadway, one could see clearly across the River Orwell towards Felixstowe. We were stopped outside the first of the buildings and were told that here would be our home for the next few days.

Coming from one of the other buildings was an elderly looking Chief Petty Officer who took over from the petty officer. The Chief Petty Officer welcomed us with, "Good morning Gentlemen." What a difference from some of the other forms of greeting that we had experienced that morning. Telling us to go inside the building he followed us in and told us about what the various rooms were as we passed them. One was the night heads, another the wash place while another was the store. All these would be explained later when the remainder of the recruits arrived. In the meantime we were detailed to take our bedding which he would supply us with and put it on the first of the beds as we entered the dormitory. I was detailed to take the second bed in the row, the first being already occupied and Charles was told to take the third bed. The other lads were detailed to take the first three beds on the opposite side. At least we were beginning to know one another for as we collected our bedding we exchanged names and a few personal details such as where we were from and what we had been doing before coming to the navy. This little interlude was short lived for the Chief Petty Officer told us to leave everything and fall in outside. With that, two of us were told to follow him while the others would wait outside the Mess, which was I believe No 29. Following in the C.P.O.s footsteps we went past several other messes, all of which were empty. Just then, a bugle blared out from the tannoys and the call I recognised was "Cooks to the galley." So, the navy would hopefully give us something to eat. Before many minutes had passed, we were outside the galley in the Long Covered Way. Here we followed the C.P.O. into the galley which was a hive of activity while the chief spoke to another person in white apron and trousers. After some talk and some laughter we two were each given a large dish containing some mashed potatoes, several large sausages and some carrots. Then, in another dish, we were given a large portion of jam tart. Never had I seen such a large jam tart and as we were told, this was between us five recruits. Although I had never starved before, I had at times been very hungry so this time my mouth started to water. If the Navy could feed me like this, then what did it matter if they told me off for some silly thing. After all, words didn't fill the stomach and one could always let the words pass over one. Yes, I was learning fast. Again we followed the Chief back to our Mess where the others had laid a large table for six of us. Yes, this was for the fellow that had the bed next to me but he was not a new entry like us. He had several badges on his arm and the chief introduced us to him. He was an Instructor Boy and apparently we would have to treat and respect him as though he were our instructor, which in reality, he was. Apparently he would be attached to our intake of recruits until we joined the barracks properly. As we later learned from him, it would be in about five weeks' time, provided we passed our tests. Having eaten our dinner, I felt like a bloated little pig, we were shown how and where to wash up and put the gear away. There was then about ten or fifteen minutes to wait before we would be required to go to the sick bay for a medical inspection. During this short break, one of the lads from London decided to have a smoke while resting on his bed. Suddenly it seemed that an earthquake had occurred, for from seemingly nowhere the Instructor Boy was pushing the lad off the bed, and had snatched the cigarette from his mouth. At the same time he was really going to town by telling the lad that he had committed a most horrible crime, for which he must be reported to the chief. This took place almost immediately, as the C.P.O. had apparently heard the noise from his mess next door and had appeared to see just what was wrong. All of us were then told to fall in and pay attention while we were told that trainees especially Boys, were NOT allowed to smoke. It was then that we were told to empty our pockets for an inspection to see if there were any more cigarettes on anybody. Any cigarettes were confiscated by the chief but this did not affect me for I did not smoke. A short lecture by the chief regarding the ways and rules of the Navy followed, before we were marched to the sick bay for medical inspection by the Navy Doctor. The Instructor Boy, Storrey I believe, marched us by various ways to the sick bay close by the Hospital, describing the various places en route. Once inside the sick bay, we were left to our own devices for some while, until an attendant came out and told us to strip to the waist. One by one we entered the examination room. Here a youthful looking doctor examined us and asked us several questions regarding present and past health.

With a friendly pat on the rump he remarked that I would do for the present and told me to join the others who were rapidly getting dressed.

I was now at a slight disadvantage for I was the last to be examined. However the others told me that as soon as I was ready we had to fall in outside. Here the Instructor Boy marched us at the double to a building about five minutes away. This he told us, was so that we could get ourselves a "Shotley Trim" as he called it. Five of us went into the barber's shop, accompanied by the Instructor Boy who spoke to one of the two barbers. In a moment the first lad was being trimmed. It would have been more appropriate to say "Shorn", for the barber ran the shears over the lad's head, from back to front. It certainly became a uniform haircut for we all got the same treatment, leaving us with less than a quarter of an inch of hair. One of the London lads complained about the shortness and was promptly told that if he wanted his hair back on, he was at liberty to sort out what he wanted from the pile of hair on the floor. Also I was not too pleased with the treatment but thought that I had better not say anything. When we again fell in outside, I looked at my watch and noticed that it was only seven minutes from my previous look, and five of us had been trimmed, to match the current fashion.

Again, it was double march but this time only for a short spell as the next stop was just round the corner to a place called "Clothing Store." Here we each were given a towel, a block of yellow soap, a tooth brush and a tin of tooth powder. For this, we had to sign a form before being permitted to leave the store. Next, it was to the Bathhouse, and here, we were allowed to sport ourselves under the hot shower; no bath and no privacy. Here too, we found that our elderly C.P.O. was in attendance. After we had soaped and cleaned ourselves, the water was turned off and we each had to parade in front of the Chief in the nude. Arms were raised above the head while each boy was inspected both from the back and front. All this was apparently to make sure that no boy was bringing "illegal lodgers" or strange diseases into the establishment.

It was when this small episode was finished that we were marched back to our temporary home in Nozzers Lane. Here we were surprised to find that we had some more company in the form of several young fellows already in uniform. Some even had badges on their arms. As a result of enquiries, we found that these fellows were recruits the same as us, except that they came from the Royal Hospital School at Greenwich and there, they had to wear the uniform of the school. In actual fact they were already part of the way trained, as their schooling was on nautical lines. To us, they were a source of information and it was good to hear them explain different things that had so far been absolute riddles. It seemed that their fathers had previously been in the navy and had consequently elected that their sons should go to Greenwich. By this time also, the new arrivals had been collecting their bedding so that we now had some two dozen in our hut. We were also told that tomorrow there would be some more recruits arriving through the day and that it would be our duty to help them when they arrived. After tea, the Chief and the Instructor Boy marched us all down to the lower playing fields where there was a large cinder race track and a spare field which we used to kick a football about. During this impromptu football match, some other fellows came down to the track, and they were all dressed in sports wear. Not taking any notice of us, they all did various running exercises on the track. This as we were told was in preparation for the sports day when all boys would compete against others at track and field events. So it seemed that we should have time for some sport. Little did we dream that nearly half of our time at Shotley would be spent in sporting events of some kind or other. All too quickly the time passed until we were ordered to fall in and were marched back to our quarters or hut. I had not yet got used to the naval terms of calling the living quarters a Mess, that would soon happen, though. Again we heard the bugle's call of "Cooks to the galley," so it seemed that we were to be fed again. Of course, after the strenuous day that we had gone through, running everywhere and then football in the evening, I must admit that I was ready for something to eat. Falling in, the chief read us out some orders, which seemingly were our duties while at Nozzers Lane.

About half way through the orders, I heard my name mentioned for I was to be the "Night Heads Boy." What a wonderful title, but was to be quickly disillusioned when one of the Greenwich school boys told me what it involved. The night heads was the other name for the lavatories to be used only at night. At all times when the rest were cleaning up the messroom etc., I would clean and tidy the night heads. As these already appeared spotless or so I thought, I did not have much to do so just whiled away my time reading the notices that were displayed about the room. A voice soon woke me from my dreaming for it informed me in the most severe terms that I was supposed to be cleaning my station. Again I was dumb struck, so that I asked another Greenwich lad just what was my station to be cleaned. In reply to his question, "What job have you got?" he laughed when I replied, "Night Heads." "That," he said, "is your station." Without waiting for more telling off, I grabbed some cleaning material and made to look as though I was busy cleaning up the place. As I was doing this, I heard that clanging of metal dishes signifying that the supper had arrived and was being dished out. This was great, especially if our training were to be all sport and feeding. Supper that night consisted of cheese and pickles with thick slices of bread and margarine, to be backed up with some very thick cocoa served up in a big tin mug. After that one had another session of clearing and tidying up one's station. This was fine until about twenty minutes to nine that evening, when it seemed that all the boys wanted to go to the toilet. Many of them had never had to clean a toilet or had only known of the public toilets. Consequently they were not too particular in their use of the "Night Head", or else they would have hopefully displayed some thought for the cleaner; ME. This meant that by the time the Chief came in to order us to bed just before 9 p.m. I was very busy cleaning up and was last in bed after being told off for being so slow with the cleaning station. That was one of the reasons that I had been given the bed near the entrance door of the mess. Somebody's brain must have been ticking over much faster than mine had done.

Having got safely into bed, we were beset by the single blast of the bugle followed by the shouted order, "Stand by for rounds." These naval terms were intriguing to say the least. This then, to be followed by some officer following a man with a candle lamp, which seemed most comical considering that the electric lights were burning. I asked the Instructor Boy about this after all had passed by and he informed me that it was a tradition from Nelson's days. This little conversation started off a general talk which was quickly stopped by the Instructor who had come back at the noise. This again was tradition as no unnecessary noises were allowed after the night rounds as they were called. The following morning, it was just becoming daylight when the bugle started again. This was reveille and we were ordered to get up and get washed and clean our teeth. This was while being watched by the Instructor, just to make sure that no one dodged it. The dodging part could be understood as there was no hot water in which to luxuriate. While this was happening some of the boys who had been detailed as cooks had gone to the galley to fetch cocoa and biscuits. As this arrived, it was measured out into enamel mugfuls for each of us, with plenty left over, and the biscuits were square and about three eighths of an inch thick. Not like the biscuits we had at the grocer's shop, but rather harder and quite pleasant to taste. These I would imagine would go well with some cheese, so, as soon as the instructor said that there were some spare biscuits, I took a couple, for as I thought any emergency. Never before had I had biscuits for early morning tea. Soon, this repast was forgotten in the round of cleaning as I had to clean the Night Heads. Plenty of soap and water for scrubbing everywhere and then dry up all the floor while all the windows in the messroom were flung wide open. These would remain open until the evening. At about half past seven, the bugles again sounded for cooks to the galley and we all eagerly awaited breakfast. We were not disappointed, when we found that it was egg and bacon with tomatoes. This the Greenwich lads term "Train smash." Train smash or not, I enjoyed it. The dishing up was done by the other fellows who were designated cooks. Again the cleaning up period until about 8.45 a.m. when we fell in for morning assembly. Here the Chief placed us in the care of the Instructor Boy and gave him instructions as to where we were to report. Such places as "Ships Office", "Duck Suit test," "Gymnasium" and some others that I cannot remember. The chief would in the meantime, collect some more recruits from Harwich and bring them over to the mess. So, we were to get some more mess mates to swell our ranks.

Away we marched, the Greenwich lads leading by order of the Instructor Boy, as they at least understood some of the orders, so that we others just followed. At a place marked "Ships Office" we were halted and taken inside. There, one at a time, we were given a number to remember. This was called a "Ship's Book Number." I must apologise here, for I am fast getting like the old chief told me, "Brains like a rocking horse." Then moving to another desk, we were given another number which we were told, there was no need to remember. That I can still remember. It was our Official Number and mine was C/JX 133067, while Charles who had joined with me was C/JX 133066. Those numbers were most important for the number was YOU, no matter where in the world you went, or what you did, that number was your body and nobody else's. Almost the same as having a convict's number. Here also, we had to sign several forms ready for our pay and other matters. We were also asked if we wished to make an allotment. Not for me, I had already had enough of the allotment on Nacton Road. However when one of the Greenwich boys told me just what an allotment was, I decided on the spot to allot Mother some of my money. Not that it was a lot, being just five shillings a week, (25 pence), so that I allotted Mother about half a crown, (12.5 pence), each week. Later on, Mother told me that she was putting it in the bank for me as I would need it. With the business there finished, we were marched to the swimming baths for a swim, so we were told. Arriving there, we were told to remove boots, shoes and socks, as these were not allowed inside the baths. Also, we were told that we were not permitted to run while in the baths. The swimming instructor promptly added that the baths were not a refuge for boys that objected to running, or who wished to dodge "doubling." On finding out that we could all swim, we were told to get undressed and don a pair of swim trunks. No fancy fashions these, just plain triangles of white drill that tied at each side with tapes. When all were thus equipped, we were lined up at the deep end and told to jump in. As quickly as possible, we swam as ordered, towards the shallow end where a couple of the lads gave up.

The rest of us were told to swim back to the deep end where we were permitted if we wished, to get out or to go back to the shallow end where we were to get out. Those of us that returned to the shallow end had to report to the swimming instructor who took our names and ship's book numbers telling us that next time we came to the Baths, we were to report to him for the "Duck Suit Test." This was a test that all boys at Shotley had to pass before they were allowed to leave the establishment to go to sea. He also told us just what the test entailed, saying that we had done the preliminary test today. There was really no need to worry about this as the Instructor, our own Chief, had taken our names and he would ensure that we did the test properly the next time.

Again it was "fall in and double march," this time to the clothing store where we were to be measured for our kit. In reality, it was not so much to measure us as to get an idea of the numbers of the various sizes that would be required, for this was to be NO Bond Street

Tailors and Fittings. About four or five different sizes of everything and we would all be fitted out. None of this gear would be issued at the moment. This was just a bit of preparation. We were then marched back to the mess again, as I and several of the others were hoping that it would be for dinner as our stomachs were beginning to rumble with hunger. We had now been steadily on the go since 8 a.m. Just as we reached the mess, the bugle sounded for cooks to the galley. As I was now a cook, it was time to grab your apron and get to the cookhouse as quickly as possible. Not only that but we now had some more boys to join us, for Chief had collected these from Harwich Station and these were apparently the rest of our classmates. Whether it was stew or not, I do not remember, except that whatever it was, we were all ready and waiting for it. By the time we had finished and us cooks had cleaned up the dishes and pans it was almost time to get moving again. This time, as we now had a complete class, we were given some drilling and marching by the Instructor Boy for about half an hour, before marching out of the gate towards the main establishment.

Passing through the gate, we passed on our left, the tall mast surrounded by a huge netting and rigging. At the foot of the mast was a colossal figurehead, presumably that of the ship from which the mast came. This mast towered upwards one hundred and eighty feet before tapering to a lightening conductor. Just as we got passed the mast we were ordered to wheel right and at the same time smarten up and double march. This as we were told was the quarter-deck and one always doubled across this deck besides which, one always saluted when coming on to the quarter-deck. This is apparently an age old custom and tradition that started long ago when a crucifix was mounted on this deck, and the sailors of old times would cross themselves before the crucifix and before moving on. Whether this was true or not, that is what we were told. Somehow, I do not disbelieve it for the Navy is full of old customs and traditions. Reaching the end of the quarter-deck, we turned to the left and marched on for some distance before being called to a halt. Here we were told to go through a small gateway on a pathway through some gardens which led us to the Sick Bay. At this point, the new lads were marched into the sick bay for their medical inspections while we others were marched back to the Clothing Store. On being dismissed, we entered the store in sequence of our ship's book numbers and started to collect various items of our kit. I had never had so many clothes in my life. Some of the clothing we had to try on in case it did not fit, but for many of the articles, it was a case of sizes one to five, being gauged from the measurements given the previous day. All this kit was eventually piled into a huge canvas kitbag that would soon bear our names and official numbers. It was just like Christmas and waiting for Santa Claus, the only snag was, there was no Santa to carry the now overflowing kit bags away on his sledge. These we had to shoulder and carry as we marched back to our mess some hundreds of miles away. At least, that is what it seemed by the time we arrived back at the mess.

As there was quite some time before our next meal, the Chief started to help us sort out our kit. Pots of black and white paint were already laid out on some tables, and these were accompanied by several large squares of flannel on tin trays. Onto these trays was poured some of the paint and the wood strip with our names carved on, were dipped carefully in the paint. Black clothes were marked with white paint and white clothes marked with black. There was a standard method of marking all clothes in identical places so that all names were in line.

It was not long after the quick demonstration of how to mark one's kit that there was a commotion outside the mess and a strange Petty Officer arrived with about twenty young fellows dressed in civilian clothing. These, we learned after the chief had had a talk with the P.O., were the rest of our intake to make up our class. Also, just then the welcomed call of "Cooks to the galley" was made. Our Chief detailed a couple of the newcomers to go with the usual cooks so as to start learning, as he called it "THE ROPES." This was all to the good, for it gave some of us a chance to exchange names and other details about one another. Apparently they all came from long distances away, Scotland, Ireland, and there was one fellow from the Falkland Islands. Like us, they did not take long to settle in, for there is nothing like a meal to get strangers talking, and getting on a friendly basis.

That afternoon, all of us, about thirty-eight, were taken to the sick bay for medical inspection. Those that had been inspected the previous day, were sent in first. Here, we endured a series of nude gymnastics such as jumping over a chair and doing press ups and running on the spot at speed. Then, it was chest test and inspections to see if one could still breathe O.K. and then weighing in and eyesight and hearing tests. All through this period of individual gymnastics, the Medical Officer kept calling a series of numbers that a companion wrote down on each person's papers. Our old family doctor, Frankie Adams, had never given us such a testing as this. Eventually the M.O. asked me a few questions about my health in general, which I answered satisfactorily, or so I thought, so with a friendly smile he declared me fit for the R.N. On returning to the mess, tea was ready and welcomed and the Chief informed us that the next day we should be going to the New Entry mess at the Annexe on the far side of the Ipswich Road.

The next day after loading our belongings on to a lorry, we were marched to the Annexe where our Instructor boy was already waiting for us. Having unloaded the lorry with our belongings the Chief gave us a short lecture on No Smoking and other prohibited things, and also told us that from then on, it was to be all things at the "Double." Also my new duties were COOK so that a new apron which had to be kept clean was given me. This suited me fine as I had noticed that by careful watching and wangling of the dishes, the cooks at least, could always manage a little extra with their helpings. This was what was called "perks", which is a Naval shortened version of perquisites. There were many such peculiar words and sayings that only the Navy uses and understands. In fact, many of the sayings and words used in everyday life today are derived from old Naval sayings and they are too numerous to mention here. Our chief was full of such sayings and went to great lengths to explain many of them to us and to ensure that we understood them. Chief was also our Father Confessor and as he said, "Your nursemaid and mentor," he also added that we were not to expect him to clean our boots and such like, although he did instruct us just how to get a polish on the boots when we got them, which if all went well would be the next day.

After almost a repetition of the previous evening when the officer came round with a lantern, we were that tired that I don't think any of us wanted to talk. Reveille sounded just after I got to bed, or so it seemed, for I hardly touched the pillow before I was out for the count and the bugle was sounding. Wash under the cold shower, clean one's teeth, under the eagle eye of Chief and many of the lads were sent back for trying to dodge the cold water. Then, came the clean ship routine, for the establishment was after all, H.M.S. GANGES hence the use of the term, SHIP. Breakfast of bacon and train smash, as the Greenwich lads called it, (bacon and tomatoes), with thick slices of bread and mugs of tea. Then again, a quick clean up everywhere and also getting oneself ready for the day. All that this entailed was getting smartened up and looking clean and tidy.

With these small details attended to, we were marched to the Clothing Store for the remainder of our kit which was parcelled up in a blanket after we had tried on such things as jumpers, trousers, caps and such like that needed fitting. All this would have to be marked and the names sewn in, in coloured cotton, white or black, and in the case of the blanket sewn in black wool. It was also explained to us that, from then on any gear that was lost would have to be replaced at our own expense and we should have to give detailed accounts of how it was lost. By the time all the kit was packed in the kitbag, I imagine that it must have weighed some seventy or eighty pounds and all names to be sewn in. How thankful I was that my name only had five letters and one initial. Anybody with a long name was at an immediate disadvantage, for while I would be sewing only six letters somebody else with a name like "Somerfield" and perhaps two initials would take twice as long as me. This could mean a certain curtailment of one's own free time, if there were to be any. Every evening after instructions, there was a wild scramble to get one's kitbag out and start sewing in the names on various articles. Not even Rumpelstiltskin had any comparison to us in those far off early days, especially when one got a hole in one's sock, as one had to darn it straight away. Many of the lads tried to disguise such matters much to their dismay and disgust, for either the chief or the instructor boy would soon spot such errors and award such punishment as they thought fit. To complain would mean extra punishment such as sweeping up after the others had turned in for the night. All this sewing had to be completed as soon as possible and in any case before the end of the four weeks or it would mean being "Back Classed" and doing a further four weeks at the Annexe.

It was one morning after breakfast about ten days into the Annexe time that we were doing drill, (Square Bashing), that I suddenly collapsed and fell out of line. The guardsman that dropped his rifle was as nothing compared to the bawling out that I started to get. It was only when the Instructor realised that I had passed out that I received attention. By that time, there were three of us on the ground as casualties from inoculations. One of the others included my friend Stimpson who had joined with me. All three of us woke up in the Hospital ward having been brought down in an ambulance. Apparently it was a case of mild Vaccinia for none of us had been vaccinated before. However we all three stayed in the Royal Naval Hospital at Shotley for about six days. During these few days we were first "starved" and then well fed for a couple of days before being discharged to duty again. Returning to the New Entry Mess at Annexe and reporting to the Chief we were lectured on the need to look after our health, and then informed that we were still expected to pass the final inspection in two weeks time with the rest of the class. This meant, that the speed of plying the needles had to be redoubled. Later by hard work, I made it and then, with a final sigh of relief, I declared to the Chief that I had finished my sewing of names. This resulted in an inspection of the neatness and style of the sewing which he passed as O.K. and then told me to help my chums that had longer names. This was, I suppose, a lesson in team work which the Chief readily emphasised. Nobody was allowed to relax and do nothing. As the chief said, "No free rides for anybody." Needless to say, I suddenly discovered that I had many chums who all presented me with some sewing so that I took a piece of kit from several of the fellows with the longest names and this seemed to satisfy quite a few, but not all. In addition to all this sewing etc., one had to keep one's boots highly polished if that were possible. This necessitated the deft use of the toothbrush handle an old rag with plenty of spit and lots of polish. Also, we had been issued with a pair of gaiters that needed cleaning, especially the brasswork which had to be cleaned daily. No rest for the wicked, and I never realised that I had at some time been so wicked, and as Chief would say, "the Devil finds work for idle hands", adding that there was room for only one devil, and that was himself. By the end of the third week, we were all considering ourselves fully blown sailors when to our disgust we were all given a kit inspection to prepare us for the big day the next week when the Commander of the establishment would inspect us, before we should be transferred to the main barracks. All the personal kit of each boy had to be rolled to a certain length, the length of the Seamanship Manual. Each piece would then be stopped, tied with clothes stops at a regulation distance from each end. All names had to be shown between the stops so that apart from the names, all kits would look the same and each piece of clothing would be laid out in regulation order. Pictures of this lay out were hung about the large room where we were to lay out the kits so there was no excuse for not knowing. When Chief had finished his inspection, nobody had got off Scot free from a telling off about something being wrong with the kit, be it in the lay out or in the neatness or otherwise of the sewing of the names. Eventually kits were passed as being O.K. and then stowed away, after all faulty pieces had been recorded and they were required for fresh laundering. This laundering would be done by ourselves in our spare time, such as it was.

This laundering and the kit laying out was a favourite form of punishment, inflicted by both the Chief and the Instructor Boy, both of whom always seemed to have an excuse for the award. Much of this, as discovered later was awarded with the idea of smartening everybody up so that when the kit muster inspection came, everything would be on top line. The daily lot of Physical Training and drilling was also increased and we seldom went anywhere but at the double march. Eventually the great day came for the big inspection by the Commander of the establishment. This person was a most imposing figure, as he had three wide gold braided bands of lace on each sleeve and his most distinctive mark was that in place of one hand, he had a silver coloured hook. In fact, he was referred to as "Hooky Walker", the Walker part being his surname. This alone, instilled a sense of fear into any new entry like ourselves. As a point of interest, I met him in London a good many years later when he was working at Admiralty and I was a civilian working in Berkeley Square. Yes, we did exchange pleasantries although I hardly think that he remembered me. Just a chance, and a pleasant two minute interlude. I will add here, that he was then a Vice Admiral at that time, and that there was no feeling of fear on my part. However the inspection was completed without incident, except that the great man did find fault with a few of the kits that were displayed. After seeing us march and drill, he told us all that we had done well and that the following day, a Friday, we should move as a class to the main barracks, and that we should all be closely watched to ensure that we made favourable progress in our chosen careers. The rest of the day was given to packing our kits and making ready for the move to the main establishment. Friday dawned much as any other day at the end of May, and after breakfast and a good clean up of the mess room we were "fallen in" ready for marching to our new home. We were leaving the Annexe for the last time, at least for many of us, and proudly we marched to the calling of the Instructor Boy's, "Left, Right," as he called the step from time to time. A smart "eyes left" as we passed some officer going in the opposite direction. No, I did not salute this time for I was in the ranks and I feel that I would have been truly in the muck had I done so.

Through the gates of "Ganges", past the figure-head on the left under the mast, another quick eyes right and "Double March" as we cleared the "Quarter-deck" on the right. Then on down the "Short Covered Way" to where our new mess was situated at the bottom on the left. Here we "Halted" and were met by another Chief P.O. who introduced himself as C.P.O. Hayes and told us he was then our new Instructor, together with another C.P.O. whose name eludes me. Almost in a flash, we were dismissed and told to get our kits inside the mess and to sort ourselves out. This was in distinct contrast to the shepherding that we had received at Annexe, the reason being that we were now in the Navy properly and from there on all things would be done in strictly Naval fashion. We now realised just how much we had been molly-coddled before. However there was no time to think of past pleasures, for we were told that during the afternoon we should be going to the gymnasium for our first real shake down.

After everybody had put their kit on a bed in the long dormitory, we were mustered and informed that as of now there would be no walking on the highly polished wood blocked deck that did really look a picture. It would have graced many a stately home and was justly the pride of C.P.O. Hayes. If one wished to walk on the deck, then it would be with boots or shoes of all kinds taken off. Only stockinged or bare feet would be allowed on the deck. This became a real exercise in speed, removing and putting on boots which had to be laced and tied in the correct manner. Also, we were detailed for our various mess duties and mine became one of the polished deck sweepers and cleaners. To do this, first one had to sweep up properly and then with an old blanket secured to a large square metal weight, we, the sweepers would put down bees wax polish and on hands and knees would shine it to mirror brightness. Then would come the polishing part with the heavy metal weighted blanket. This would be pulled up and down the sleeping area so that not a blemish remained on the blocks. Such a polish has to be seen to be believed and many are the hours of petty punishment that were awarded to maintain that polish, while many young lads sweated over that task. This task had to be performed during the intervals that the cooks were getting the meals served out. The only saving grace of this job, was that as a polished deck cleaner, one was excused falling in while waiting for the meals. This was fine if the weather was inclement, as although the outside entrance of the mess was under the covered way, the wind always had a nasty habit of blowing straight into the covered way to the discomfort of anyone that was there. That night, before "pipe down," (Naval for silence), and rounds, (everywhere to be spick and span), when the inspecting officer came round to see that all was correct. This dignitary was accompanied by the usual retinue of Naval Police, a Royal Marine, a bugler and the bearer of the candle lamp. To this Officer the Chief would report that his charges were turned in, (asleep in bed or presumably so), and that the mess was correct. All this is purely Naval Routine, at least it was. Whether the same ancient drills are still carried out is not known but I would assume that they are. Why I suggest this is because at some much later date, when as a civilian instructor to the Sea Cadets as late as 1991, many of these drills and customs were still carried out. My apologies for the slight digression.

Saturday as is usual in the Navy, is general clean up day, weather and the exigencies of the service permitting. It is very seldom that much is allowed to interfere with the normal Saturday routine. This is the day when all spaces and compartments are cleared and cleaned out for inspection by the Commander or Executive Officer. In reality, much of the equipment that is removed from these spaces usually joins up behind the inspecting officer and his retinue, to be replaced as before in the same spot once the inspection is over. Of course, there are occasions when one gets caught out and the Inspecting Officer doubles back on his tracks, with the intention of catching out the offenders. However, the normal Saturday routine usually proceeds without much bother. Some Captains and Commanders have been known to wear white cotton gloves when doing this Saturday inspection. The idea being, that if there is any dust or dirt where the gloves have been, it will be revealed with startling clarity. At Ganges, such things were generally unnecessary as the Instructor would normally spot such offences before the Officer came round. While on the subject of "Cleaning Ship," (Saturday Routine) it was the normal practice for the Divisional Officer to award a large fruit cake to the mess of his division that had the cleanest mess. This could have been high domestic diplomacy, for the cake to the boys was far more important than anything, as the boys were a hungry lot. All this cleaning was preceded by a general assembly of the whole establishment to exercise fire stations and drill. This was always done to perfection and the equipment of hoses and pumps mounted on carriages were thoroughly exercised. On being informed the whereabouts of the fire, some several hundred lads carrying hoses and pulling the pumps, would dash to the scene. Heaven help any passer-by that managed to get in the way, as it would be a sure hospital case. Very often, the whole pump and carriage would be overturned at the sheer speed of taking corners, resulting in grazed hands or legs to say the least. As soon as the hoses were rigged, the order would be passed for the sea water to be switched on. Again, it was a question of keeping well clear, for the squirting of water by fire hose is most probably every young boy's dream of pure delight. We were no exceptions, and very often the hoses were misdirected against some unfortunate in another division, or it could even have been, intentional. It is probably appropriate here, to explain the Division formation of the establishment. The entire personnel of the "Ganges" was divided into "Divisions" named after old Admirals such as Drake Raleigh Benbow Hawke, all depending on the number of lads in the establishment. At the time, there were six divisions of about three hundred plus boys. Some divisions contained a few more than others and these were the senior boys who would be awaiting draft, or a new intake from Annexe such as ourselves. Each division was a close knit unit, comprising of perhaps four or five messes of anything up to forty boys who in turn were again a close knit unit. This always showed in the competitive spirit as one mess competed against another and the best competitors would represent the division and finally the Establishment.

Saturday and Sunday afternoons were devoted to sports on a mess or divisional basis. All other days were set aside for instructions in Squad Drills, Seamanship, Boatwork, Gunnery and Schoolwork, these being the chief items that the Instructors endeavoured to conjure into our befuddled brains. Oh yes, those very early days in the Navy were a whirlpool of dormant knowledge that was eager to make itself manifest at some later date. Just how the instructors ever managed to impart any knowledge into our seemingly dim-witted heads is nothing short of a miracle. Lest the reader should imagine that the evenings were our own time, I would hasten to disillusion them, for each evening would be taken up with some sport or other. One was not allowed to rusticate at all. The sports included any that developed the team spirit and also lots that were individual events and these included all the well known sports, from rugby and soccer to sailing and boxing. If one was no good at a particular sport, one still had to partake as detailed, if only to make up numbers.

Sunday morning was Parade and Church morning. The day would start as a normal morning with cleaning and polishing until breakfast time. After that, it would be a mad rush to complete all one's tasks in time for the muster for the big Parade at 9 a.m. on the extensive parade ground. This being our first Sunday Parade, (called Divisions), it was to be the wearing of our then best suits and collars and caps with the "Ganges" cap ribbon. This would be the first time ever that we had worn them. At about 8.40 we were ordered to fall in for inspection by the instructor, which was most critical, then followed a full scale lecture by the Chief on how to march and drill smartly. At the conclusion of the lecture, we were marched under the care of the Chief to the parade ground at the extreme back, almost off the parade. There then followed much juggling of bodies until our Instructor was satisfied with our position and formation. We being New Entries, would be the last to march off the parade and march past the reviewing officer who would be the Captain of the Establishment. Soon bugles blared for the general assembly. Every boy stood perfectly still while the bugles sounded, no matter where they happened to be or what they were doing. This, we learned was to be the general practice, so as to ensure that the bugle call was properly heard. No sooner had the bugles ceased their blaring, than some two thousand boys ran onto the parade ground to take up their predetermined positions according to their Division and Mess. Each lad knew exactly where to go as it was part of the daily performance of parading. All this, and much more was explained to us as we watched, as after that parade we should be taking full part in the parade. For some time, about seven minutes, each lad was inspected, first by the Instructor then the Divisional Officer. Eventually the Officer would report his Division correct to the Executive Officer who would report to the Captain who had just arrived. All this would take some considerable time, so, to prevent the paraded lads from becoming restless, the Royal Marines Band would play a selection of tunes while we stood at ease, still and waiting for the resulting orders. This particular Sunday, the whole assembly was ordered to close on the rostrum where the Captain stood, just to the west of the Mast. Before the assembly marched to the rostrum, we New Entries were told to stand easy and to listen very carefully to what we were about to be told. All it really amounted to was, that we should turn to the right in our ranks, close on the new end lads, then a left turn, and an order to advance in column. This we had practiced somewhat at the Annexe so that we knew what to do. All it really meant, was that instead of being four deep to march, there were about ten or eleven lads abreast one another and only four lines of lads. This meant that the whole mess was condensed into a block sixty foot across the front and about eight foot deep. This exercise was called advancing in column of messes. This incidentally needs quite a lot of practice to get the exercise correctly performed, as if not the result is a chronic concertina motion, which is greatly frowned upon by the drill instructors. In fact some drill instructors have been known to go berserk over some exhibitions of the bad carrying out of this exercise. Being the last mess of all, it was fairly well carried out and we closed on the rest of the establishment without sending our new Chief into tantrums of rage. With the closing of all messes and divisions, the Captain awarded some trophies to some boys who had been sent up to the rostrum, I think it was caps of some sort for representing the establishment at some sport. With the little ceremony over, the whole parade was turned about and we marched back to our original positions, at the back of the parade ground. Again we were told to pay attention to instructions for we should shortly be marching past the Captain. This would be in a similar fashion to that which we had just done, except that having marched past the Captain and various other officers, we should have to turn right in columns of four and march off the parade. As the Chief told us, he wanted "lots of swank and tons of bull," as we marched past the Captain, or he would want to know why. The swank part was easily understandable but just what had a lot of bull to do with it? Surely we were not going to be taken to some animal farm especially in our best uniforms. Ignorance is bliss, or was.

Whether it was pride or concentration on our marching, I do not know, but whatever it was, we survived the ordeal, as I am sure that each one of us new entries was somewhat scared by the array of gold lace as we marched past. No sooner were we off the parade ground, than we were given the order to double march. We were off again, and the little respite offered by the parade ceremony was soon over. Straight to the huge gymnasium where we were greeted by several white shirted instructors wearing badges of crossed clubs on their chests. These were the P.T.I.s so I was told. All of them were very muscular and they all looked remarkably fit and smart. We were not allowed to linger on the physical attributes of the instructors, as we were quickly told to march inside where other instructors would direct us to our seats. I for one was about to wonder what this was all in aid of, when a church bell began to toll. A lad next to me who had been at Greenwich School whispered to me that we were going to church and that we were the first ones here. I then guessed that we should be in the front seats probably under the glaring eyes of the instructors. I was correct in my guess of being in the front row, but hopelessly wrong in the rest of my guess. Before we were really seated, the remainder of the lads started to file in and here they were shepherded in by the P.T.I.s. A Royal Marines Band sat in the far front corner of the hall and when the lads were seated, the band started to play soft classical music. The reason was that officers entered and sat down on the rows of chairs that were facing us. After some several minutes, the whole assembly stood up and we noted that the Captain and his wife came in and took seats on the very front of the assembled officers. Then followed the Chaplain and what I presumed to be the choir, although none of them wore cassocks or surplices. Without more delay the church service started with the singing of the usual hymns and psalms. This was the first time for quite a few years that I had been to church and not had to pump the organ. At the end of the service the chaplain made one or two announcements which were of little concern or interest to us. With the singing of the final hymn, "Eternal Father strong to save". which was sung with much gusto by all, the service closed with the singing of the National Anthem. The Captain and Officers with their wives and ladies were then allowed to leave the church (gymnasium) while we remained seated until the officers were well clear. Then, the P.T.I.s. came into their own by starting from the back of the gym, they allowed the boys to leave one row at a time after they had told the "stool boys" to remain at the back end of the hall. I had heard of people being termed "stool pigeons" and wondered if there was any relationship. I was to find out the next Sunday as I was detailed to be one. This meant taking the mess stools to church before one went to divisions and collecting the same when church was finished and they were to be returned to the mess. No such trick as forgetting the job, as this was marked off on the duties board, or one was given the job as a form of punishment. It seemed that all the awkward and detestable jobs were incorporated in the Naval register of punishments, as being a "stool boy" involved doing the job in one's best rig which invariably got dirtied in some small way, so that an extra period of time was required to clean the suits. Failure to do this could result in further awards of punishment, a truly wicked and vicious circle if ever there was one. After the church parade which usually finished just before dinner, one would find a few moments, if possible, in which to remove one's suit and fold it carefully inside out. No knife edged creases were allowed, as it was all clothes were folded inside out, so that all creases went inwards. I never did find out the object of this, unless it was to present a clean outside image to the inspecting officer. The uniform trousers had to be folded to the width of the Seamanship Manual, seven folds being the usual regulation number of folds. The only exception to this was if one was small in height or extra tall. This task being completed and gear stowed away carefully, no throwing it on the bed and leaving it for mum or the maid to put away. Chief was both Mum and maid to us, and if he found anything not put away, he would place it in his office to be recovered by forfeiting an inch of soap for each article. This was termed the scran bag, with the key being held only by the instructors. The soap forfeiture would be used in cleaning the mess during the clean ship periods. .

My next interesting event came very quickly; the following Wednesday morning, when the whole mess was ordered to lay out their kits. This was a repetition of the final kit muster at Annexe, except that it was completed by the Chief who was just as thorough in all details. When all was ready for inspection, the chief reported to the Divisional Officer who inspected each kit in minute detail. We were allowed only an hour in which to lay the kit out before the inspection. Fortunately some of us had been schooled by the Greenwich boys who taught us how to be ready for quick inspections.

Chief made copious notes on each boy's kit as he passed with the Div. Officer and as each was passed, the boy was permitted to pack his kit away. Again the mad scramble to get everything cleared away and stowed so that no penalties were incurred. After that came the stand easy and general tidy up. Then a double march to the Parade Ground or the Drill Shed for pay parade, depending on the state of the weather. Within a few moments of our arrival the bugles sounded for the assembly. This time there was a slight difference, which had already been explained to us, so that we arranged ourselves in our Ship's Book numbers. Being new entries, we were all at the rear of the columns that were lined up, so that we would be some of the last to be paid. In all, there were about four columns of about five hundred boys to be paid. Slowly each column moved forward as each boy was paid. The drill was identical for all. As the lad in front moved up to the table that was supervised by a Pay Officer and others, one would stand to attention, remove one's cap as we had been drilled to do, crown up and call out one's ship's book number. Nothing much to that one might think, no, not so easy when having to do it while being visually inspected at the same time. Eventually my turn came to get my pay. Smartly, at least I thought so, I stepped up to the table and very promptly forgot my number so that without any more waiting the next lad was called and I was stood aside. It was only when the lad that followed me called his number that mine came back to me. No such luck as being allowed to enter the queue. There I had to stand, stiffly to attention until the very end, which fortunately was not very far off. First the Pay Officer called my number, promptly I stepped smartly forward in the proper manner, removed my cap, called my number correctly and was again refused. Four times in all did I repeat the performance before the Pay Officer placed one shilling, (five pence today), on the crown of my cap. All boys received the same amount, unless Boys First Class, or Badge Boys, who all received extra. Then came the telling off first by the Pay Officer, then another Officer of Lieutenants rank, and finally the prize telling off by the chief.

If one was not detailed for early sport that afternoon, one made a beeline for the canteen after assembly. This was a mad scramble, for if one was a new entry and was at the rear of the parade ground one was at the tail end of roughly two thousand boys. Having successfully reached the canteen counter, one would order what one desired, usually a bag of dates, a bar of Sharpes Toffee, and a cream bun and bar of chocolate, normally referred to as a quim and a bar. Hundreds of these parcels had already been prepared in advance and anticipation of the hundreds of orders for a quim and a bar and a bagger, with the possible addition of a stamp for writing home. Oh yes, one had to write home, otherwise if one's parents enquired whether Tommy or Johnny was well, the Chief would cause one's life to be a misery by inflicting punishment. Not so much that Chief wished to find favour with the parents should they arrive at the Gates, but that it was a reflection on his ability to take care of the offender. After all, he was both mother and father to us, at least according to him.

Wednesday evening's tea was usually a simple affair, very plain, probably bread and jam or suchlike, as the catering officer was aware that many buns and dates etc had been consumed during the afternoon. With tea over, it would be a rush to get the mess stools to the gymnasium ready for the movies that would be shown. These films were normally cowboy or comedy but with an occasional good film to be put on. This was a grand time for the boys to exhibit their wit, especially when there was a breakdown in the film or the villain of the film made indiscreet remarks. In fact, any incident that was not quite in order gave ample scope for the wits of the establishment to display their mettle. I must add that the duty instructors who were always present, ensured that no boy got out of hand, and all remarks were obviously made in good fun, or the use of the proverbial stonicky would have been prominent. Stonicky, is the Shotley term for a short piece of rope that the instructor usually carried in his pocket, and in the old days of sail, it would have been termed a "starter." These were used to prompt the slow fellows to get a move on, and were part of the petty officers accoutrements. Before leaving the weekly Wednesday routines, I feel that I must state that the rest of our pay, about four shillings each week, (twenty pence today), would be placed to our credit for our own usage at a later date. Also, it was possible if one required, to allot a small amount home each week, in order to help out the finances of the family.

With the training starting in earnest, seamanship, boatwork, squad drill, gunnery and school, all compulsory, all in addition to keeping ourselves and our kit clean, time soon passed. Soon it was just over a month that we had been in the main establishment and we found that at school one day we were given an examination in the work that we had covered at school. From the results of this examination, it would be decided whether one would progress to other fields or remain in the seaman's class, or perhaps qualify for accelerated advancement at a later date. The results did not take overlong to be published and to my amazement, I with quite a few others, qualified for the accelerated advancement at the age of 17-and-a-half, instead of having to wait until the age of 18, for promotion to Ordinary Seaman or the equivalent. The Chief announced the results one evening at tea, and there were many congratulations between the boys who had passed. This meant that those that passed the exam, would be moving to another mess very soon. My pal Stimpson, who had joined with me, qualified for the Telegraphist branch as he was more brainy than me having gone to the Municipal School. However, we were both destined to remain together for many more months, for that weekend, we were sent to our new mess, No 8 in the Long Covered Way near the top, and in the Rodney Division.

Here our Instructors met us, and as usual detailed us for our various duties in the mess. Again, I was detailed as a Cook. Here our instructors were, Yeoman of Signals Bryant and Petty Officer Telegraphist Pitts. Both of these were grand instructors right from the start, instilling in all of us some special pride at being selected for the Communication Department. The whole of us would work as one class for the present and we would be having instructions that were common to both Tels and Signals.

Here again, we were given some new books to study as they contained instructions of special interest to us. In addition to new studies, there were signal flags, about eighty different ones, the Morse code, the semaphore alphabet and the international code. Quite a lot to digest for the moment, as well as having to remember the seamanship and knots and splices that we had already been taught. Soon, the idea that although we were a new mess, there were already lads in the establishment that were junior to us in the length of time in the service and we did not hesitate to let them know it. Our mess, No. 8, was the only Signal mess in the Rodney Division so that as our Instructors informed us, we were to prove to the rest, that we were not only better than they were, but we were superior to them. The instructions went on at a rapid pace and soon we were anticipating our first signals exam. Whether we should be selected for Visual Signals or Telegraphists depended on this examination. With the results came the knowledge that Stimpson and myself would be parting company as regards instruction, for it seemed that my knowledge of Maths was not enough to carry me through to Telegraphist, for Tels required detailed and extensive knowledge of mathematics and mine was lacking. As events proved I was not to regret the non selection. Thus, yours truly became a budding signal boy, and I did not regret it.

From now on, as Yeo Bryant informed us, we would eat, live and sleep signals, so that every action would be interpreted into signal form or language. One of the first things that we had learned, was the phonetic alphabet as well as the naval signal flags. It would now be a crime to refer to any flag or single letter by its designated title, but rather by its phonetic equivalent. The Morse code was speeded up, as was the semaphore exercises that we practiced sometimes twice each day. As our Yeoman said, we should eat, live and sleep signals. It certainly became very true, for if one so much as looked at a comic or boys paper, it was some form of punishment that resulted. These punishments were seldom anything physical, but rather a deprivation of privileges, such as stoppage of pictures on Wednesdays, or doing a clean up duty. Whatever they were, they always seemed endless in their variety and application. The physical punishments were reserved for the inclination of the Divisional Officer or The Commander and Captain.

Signals and schoolwork took precedence over all else, and were about equally divided.

Here I must comment on the Schoolmaster that we were delivered to. Not very tall, rather tubby, a wonderful disposition, and a Navy rugby player, who lived by the name of Mr Middleton, (Tich), as known in the rugby world. He would literally talk the knowledge into to our heads, and his only method of inflicting himself on any boy not paying attention, was to break off small pieces of chalk, then with deadly aim, the small piece of chalk would hit the offender in the side of the neck. More of the teacher later, except to say that he was highly qualified in the educational world.

Meanwhile, the signals' menu was proving satisfying in every sense, and our knowledge developed surprisingly. With our class of about twenty-four, we would move to any place in the establishment, purely by using signals. For example, if one wanted to move from the halt, the signal for speed of the fleet will be 10 knots, equalling quick march, or a right turn would be Blue Nine, (fleet will alter course together 90 degrees to starboard). The main point to remember was, that whatever order was given to a marching body of men, the same thing could be done by signal. The difference being, that only signal personnel would know the orders. This knowledge would cause much consternation when in company with or near Gunnery Classes, as they would have no idea what the signal classes would be doing. Should a signal class and a gunnery class meet in a narrow road, more often than not, the gunnery class would be halted while the signal class would be manoeuvred round them, thus giving the signals class the advantage and many smiles of superiority. Even when we spoke to each other, it was either by using the Morse code or the semaphore, as we were now reaching almost talking speeds. In addition to this, it had the added advantage of not being read, only by signal and telegraphists boys or ratings. All these points made for added interest by the communications lads. Sometimes, I felt sure, that if the average civilian could have heard us talking in our signals language, they would have condemned us all as being lunatics from outer space. In any case it pleased us youngsters to be able to go round the establishment, calling out genuine signals such as, G 20. (double march) or Four Numeral Blue (left incline) or Uncle Issac, (stop or halt). The amazing thing about this manoeuvring was that it would be done for exhibition on special occasions, where each lad would represent a ship in formation at sea. No opportunity was ever lost by the signal classes at exercising what we called "marching manoeuvres" and especially at the double. The only real problem became that of remembering all the coded signals that were employed. If one were a little slow in recalling the meaning of certain signals, it could result in chaos on the parade, or as would be the case, at sea. This would of course, reflect on the Instructor's teaching ability and of course, his mess mates would not be slow in deriding him at his failings. As ever, the class would reflect the ability of the instructor, no matter what category, so that it became a matter of pride that the class did not let the instructor down, only at their own peril.

Somewhere in all this swotting and burning of the midnight oil, we had to fit in our seamanship training, for although signal boys under training, one was not allowed to forget that one was basically a seaman. Woe betide any signal boy that had forgotten how to splice, or their bends and hitches (knots), as these were constantly in use. Also, in the early August we were given three weeks leave. During this leave, I must confess that I boasted of my achievements in the navy, while talking to my old pals, most of whom had taken unto themselves girl friends, so that really I was not one of their clan, so to speak, and I did not see very much of them. Time passed very quickly and before I was really aware of it leave was over, so that in a sense I was glad to go back to "Ganges" and get back to signals.

On return from leave we were mustered on the "quarter-deck" as we returned, where we were searched for cigarettes or matches, these being valuable and prohibited commodities for the boys, as smoking was not permitted while under training, no matter what one's age may have been. This was punishable by the Captain's punishment award of six cuts of the cane on one's buttocks while wearing only a thin pair of duck trousers. The person who administered the cuts was the Master at Arms who after due ceremony would produce the cane for inspection, and the offender would be instructed to lie across a box horse after he had been examined by the doctor. At the order from the commanding officer, "Commence the punishment," the Master at Arms would deliver the first stroke of the number that had been awarded. It would have to be a very serious case to warrant more than six cuts which was the usual for smoking, and getting caught. Each stroke would be delivered precisely and counted by several officers, even though only six cuts were ordered. It was then, on the final stroke that the M.A.A. would report "Punishment completed" at which the offender would again be examined by the M.O. If passed as fit, the offender then went straight to the Sick Bay for treatment of the cuts. I should here remark that it was a point of extreme dishonour if the culprit screamed or even whimpered during the punishment, even though the pain was sufficient to cause a breach of honour. No matter what happened, the report would somehow reach the culprit's chums who would suitably comment round the mess, to the satisfaction or otherwise of the offender. Should one offender have taken his punishment with dignity and honour, he would proudly display his wounds to the rest of the mess the same evening. Not a pleasant sight, but having received at one time six of the best for bad language to another boy, I think that the bruising resulting from the cuts was worse than it looked as the pain of the cuts was over within minutes, although I must admit, that sitting down was rather uncomfortable for some time after. So much for the searching on return from leave, as this usually resulted in some mess being placed in quarantine because one of the members had been in contact with some infectious complaint or some other minor complaint that necessitated segregation. Normally all boys returned in a very healthy state, and a deluge of hot showering with plenty of disinfectant and carbolic soap would normally clear matters. It would then be a matter of having all one's clothes taken from one and the lot would be fumigated as we called the process that followed. No slur attached to this process.

Quickly one buckled down to work, and swotting with a vengeance became the order of the day, for in October we were due for another examination, which would be roughly half way through our signals course. On this examination depended whether or not we should receive our crossed flags badges denoting that we were now Signal Boys and receive extra pay for being graded as first class boys. The increase of pay would be about two shillings weekly and of that we should receive sixpence for our pocket money, (two-and-a-half pence today), but then it was riches untold. If one did not pass this coming exam, one would be reverted to Seaman Boy and have to start again. The ambition of every boy at Shotley, was, I think, to get to sea as soon as possible. With each examination, the signal knowledge became more involved with subjects not related to signals. A certain amount of Gunnery and Torpedo knowledge, also a small amount of aircraft operating. These subjects would eventually be taken in depth as one progressed in signals as would the subject of seamanship.

Eventually October arrived and the day of the examination drew near so that there was much consultation with the Yeoman and our chums by asking and answering questions that would be directed at almost anybody and at any time. In fact it was Yeoman Bryant's favourite to call us at Reveille with a simple signal question because as he informed us, it would usually be just as you woke up that some ship would start making signals to you. How true it all became later on. However, the day of the exam came and partnering off with our particular chums we made to read the flashing light signals that would take some half an hour. With that finished it was the turn of the semaphore to be taken down. With each of these subjects one would endeavour to read the signals at eighteen words a minute with only making a few mistakes as the passing marks were in the 90 per cent area. As speedily as possible one read through one's signals exercise and made any corrections that one wished. Much depended on the intelligent reading of the signal and the interpretation of any obvious errors. I would add here, that half way through the semaphore exercise, the yeoman would turn round so that one would be reading the signals backwards. Another trick of his would be to make us read signals through the wrong end of the telescope to give us the idea of distance and simulated awkward conditions. All clever stuff, that made for really good signalmen in the future. For the rest of the examination it was a written and oral test conducted by qualified Signals Officers of various grades. Needless to say, the whole class suffered badly from jitters in case they may have failed and would be reverted. However, it was a happy class when the results became known, for we had all passed and with fairly good marks. That night, there was no swotting or studying, as all the mess became apprentice tailors for there were the coveted signal badges to be sewn on all uniform jumpers, and to be ready for the next day's parade. Yes, I am sure that there was no smarter mess on the parade ground the next morning than No. 8 mess. To improve on this matter, the mess had done extremely well in the sports world as we had won the mess trophy for cross country. This was followed some weeks later by the Division winning the Divisional trophy. This meant that the Divisional Officer, Lieut. Grant, would supply us with a slap-up supper. This meant that some fifty of us that had taken part in the cross country race would be able to eat bangers and chips and cream cakes to our stomachs' content to be followed by bars of Sharpes Creamy Toffee. Here we probably did a bit of cheating on our Divisional Officer, for many of us hid some of the goodies for our pals that had done duty for us during the training periods. It would also be about this time that I was selected for the pulling boats crew which would race against other Divisions. To my surprise, the Instructor selected me as the stroke oar for the Division. In this race, we were towed out past the Spit Buoy off Harwich until we were a mile from Shotley Pier, where the finishing line was established. Twelve well trained boys pulled like Trojans in quite a choppy sea. Not an easy job pulling a SIXTEEN FOOT ash oar for a mile with a cross wind, and a two ton cutter (pulling boat) to move along. However the result was a good win for Rodney by some ten lengths. This gave us another Divisional Supper, which was worth every bit of effort that we could have put into winning, at least that was our opinion, for what was a little effort compared with a slap-up supper.

Apparently these kinds of suppers were the rewards for winning any big event in the sporting world at Shotley, so that each lad did his utmost to achieve and partake in the mess supper supplied by the Divisional Officers.

I have previously mentioned the mast just inside the main gate. This mast was originally the mizzen mast of one of the old sailing ships of the line. For those that are unacquainted with sailing ships, the mizzen mast is the rear one on a three masted ship, or the rear one on a two masted ship. I believe that the mast was from the old Ganges, but in this, I may be wrong. Not that it matters unduly, for the mizzen masts in all ships of the line were almost the same height, and some thirty foot shorter than the main mast. This particular mast was some one hundred and eighty feet high, with the rigging reaching up to about one hundred and seventy feet. The last ten feet or so, was bare of rigging in any sense, so that if one wished to reach the button on top, one had to shin up the bare pole. On the very top of the pole, was a round platform, some foot across, and this was termed the button. Projecting from this button was a rather robust lightning conductor of about four feet in height. Any boy reaching the top would use this as a hand hold while he stood on top, his only support. Also, any boy having reached the top and having stood on the button was eligible to be the Button Boy in the event of Manning the Mast and Yards, of which there were three, the topsail yard, the mainsail yard and the lower yard. The lower yard was by far the biggest and was some foot or so in diameter with the other yards being appropriate size and length. On each yard there were two methods of reaching the ends. One was by walking on the yard and holding the manrope which was about waist high, and the other method was to lower oneself on to the footropes slung under the yard and work a way out to the end. The quicker method was the first one, as here one could almost run to the end, if one was sure footed enough. Of course, it was much easier to do either on this mast at Shotley than it would have been at sea, especially if the ship were rolling or pitching. In any case the Shotley mast was a good test of nerves for any boy, and we were all encouraged to climb it for our own satisfaction. This was because that at some time during one's stay at Shotley the mast had to be climbed as a test and one could be failed if the test was not satisfactorily carried out.

The test itself was usually done towards the end of the period at Shotley, and consisted of climbing the rigging one side and coming down the other. Sounds simple enough, but to complete it properly, one had to surmount the obstacle of the futtock rigging. This was situated about half way up by the first platform, called the half moon and although there was a way through to the upper rigging, one had to use the futtock which actually carried one backwards while climbing it. Having negotiated the obstacle so far, one grabbed the hand rail over one's head, drew oneself up level with the platform, kicked one's feet away from the rigging, and hey presto, one was over the futtock. The easy way through was originally intended for those persons, like Marines who carried their arms for fighting, and who fought from the tops, as there very often were small cannon mounted in the tops. As was remarked, the mast had to be climbed up one side and down the other, negotiating the futtocks en route, while the exercise had to be completed in three minutes or under. Its a wonderful exercise if one is fit. Unfortunately, the establishment is no longer there, just derelict buildings, though the mast is still standing, saved I believe by ex-boys as a memento of their past experiences. For our test, we were marched to the foot of the mast and lined up six deep. This is the number of climbers that the mast will take each time. The first six were lined up, told to man the rigging, each boy standing on the bottom rung, and the order is then given "Way aloft." A mad scramble to be in front, as the rigging tapers towards the top from the bottom. Those that are in the front at the halfway or futtock, are usually the first ones all the way as by the time the top is reached, there is only room for one person at a time. On reaching the ground, one is timed by stop watch, each lad will report to the Instructor, "Mast drill completed." If one watches the climbers all the way, one will note that some of the lads employ various tactics in an effort to reduce their time. Although the time allowed is three minutes for the whole drill, I would imagine that a certain leeway is allowed as in practice, only the lads that are in the lead can hope to complete in the time allowed. Occasionally one encounters the odd boy that cannot face the climb, or perhaps cannot negotiate the futtock on the way down, or perhaps the lad's nerve gave way at the last moment. This would mean that the Instructor would have to go up and coax the lad down, as under the circumstances, it would have been no good trying to shout instructions to the lad. Should the lad have lost his nerve and fallen, there was an enormous safety net some eight feet from the ground, and surrounding the whole mast area. Even so, it is far better to come down than to fall down. One thing I should have mentioned about this drill, like all other achievements by any mess, it was a matter of pride and honour that the mess did not possess any "chickens" as the non-mast drill boys would be called. If a mess had one of these non competitors, lads from the other messes would on passing the mess concerned, commence crowing or clucking like a chicken. This would obviously lead to trouble, if only as a question of fisticuffs. Our mess was extremely lucky in this, as we had all our mess pass with little or no bother. Another step on the road to getting our sea-legs.

During the time at Shotley, one was taught to wash and mend one's clothes, and to do them properly, for the Instructors had eyes like the proverbial hawks. The laundry of the establishment was situated not far from the hospital and sick bay in a road called Laundry Hill. This also was a place of punishment when required. To return to the laundering of clothes. The laundry itself was allocated to a Division and the messes would use the laundry as detailed by the Divisional Officer. Junior messes would be allocated first sessions from 0530 until about 0700 on a particular day. This meant that the lads would be up very smartly, then under the eye of the instructor the washing would be carried out in huge bowls that lined the room. As the pieces were washed and inspected by the instructor, they would be placed in a huge spin drier (Hydro) which was operated by the instructor when he judged the machine to be full. Probably some dozen lads' washing would be done at any one time, and then placed on huge clothes horses that were slid into the walls where heat would be turned on. The washing would then be dry and ready for collecting at dinner time or at the end of the morning instruction periods. Normally it was the responsibility of the owners to collect their washing from the laundry. In practice some half dozen lads were detailed, and under the orders of a petty officer boy, they would collect for the mess, remembering that all clothes were marked by names. Occasionally a piece of laundry would be misplaced which would be returned to the mess concerned as most of us knew everybody in our own messes. I did not hear of any of the lads losing any such clothing for we knew that it would be somewhere in our own division. Mind you, the penalties for stealing clothing were quite severe, even by navy standards. This would be in addition to what one's mess mates might take it into their heads to award as their ideas of punishment.

During all these routine comings and goings, one had to take part in the various sports that were currently in season. There was inter mess boxing, or as they called it mess milling. The mess would be lined up in two ranks, tallest lads on the right and shortest on the left. The fellow in front or behind you, was the lad that you had to box in the ring. Needless to say, it was sometimes a one-sided affair but that made little difference to the three minute scramble. From this, the best would be selected for the Divisional Boxing and then if any good, one could represent the establishment against other services. In the mess competition, I managed to get a win and so passed to the Divisional competition. There however, I was easily defeated, having spilled quite a fair amount of blood before the fight was stopped. The main thing in this competition, was to put up a show as this was entertainment for the establishment. No such thing as a fight to the finish and nobody got really hurt, as the referee would stop the fight if it was in the slightest way an unequal fight. The other sports were usually football, cricket, rugby, swimming, running, and many other events that I had not taken part in. Whatever it was, one had to compete before one was informed that a better fellow had been found. Most diplomatic were some of the instructors, while others would just simply inform one that they were not much good at the particular event.

The highlight of the sports calendar was as ever, the Establishment Sports Day in the latter part of June. Here, the complete establishment took part in all track and field events on a divisional basis. Points were awarded as usual to the winners and on to the last competitor. The scores were kept by the Schoolmasters and pay departments on very large blackboards at each end of the sports track on the lower fields. The entire boys establishment would take part over the two days, each division competing against the others, with the lads cheering their respective divisions. Almost a gala occasion, except that there were no ice cream vans or such like for every boy would be taking part, and such luxuries were banned for the period of the sports by the Divisional Officers. In fact, the establishment took on an air of the Olympics training centre before any particular event. There was a keenness by everybody to beat the other persons or divisions and there would be no let up until the end of the last event. Sometimes one could almost feel the tense atmosphere that existed, especially if one division seemed to be favoured. All parents and friends would be invited to attend if they wished. Many would not be able to attend because of distances or financial difficulties, as it must be remembered that at that time, the country was just beginning to recover from post-war depression and the General Strike of 1926. There were some civilian visitors present but these could easily have been the wives or friends of the Officers. I cannot recall seeing any of the boys with their families. However the sports went with a real swing, with first one division leading, then another, but always with Rodney Division near or in the lead. The last race of the second day for the boys, was the long relay race, where each division had entered some eighty boys. Each boy would run a quarter of a mile, making it twenty miles of relay for each team. First one division, then another, would be in the lead, depending on how they had placed their best runners. At the halfway stage, Rodney were in second place and we still had our best runners to come. Slowly we forged up to first place and then, with our good runners, we forged ahead until at the finish, we were nearly a whole lap, a quarter of a mile, in the lead. Needless to say, the lads of our division went wild with delight. Not only that, but we had won the most trophies and were the champions. This acme of delight was only surpassed when the Divisional Officer told us that evening, that there would be a divisional supper for all the division. Perhaps he had plenty of money, but that did not worry us. The supper was our main concern. One must not think that we suffered starvation rations, far from it. It was just a case of healthy young lads always being ready for something extra, as we were always engaged in some strenuous sport.

Our next big event was the Ipswich British Legion Fête on Christchurch Park. The best teams at Gunnery, Field Gun; Seamanship, and Signals were selected to attend and give a display to the public. This was a much prized event as there was always plenty of food for the competitors, besides being able to mix with the civilian population, which I think the majority of the lads missed, during their spell at Shotley. Our Signal Class was selected for this event and display. Early on the morning in question, all lads taking part in the Fête caught the special buses to Ipswich or went by lorry to accompany the equipment for the displays. On arrival at the display ground, we all had to help unload and place out the equipment, ready for the coming displays. I must add here, that we were accompanied by the Royal Marine Band, which would play appropriate tunes as we gave our display. Previously we had been told about our attending the Fête, and as I lived in Ipswich, Mother made a point of being there for the show. Yes, I felt quite proud of myself as we all marched on with the band, knowing Mother was watching from somewhere in the crowds. The display from the "Ganges" lasted some sixty to seventy minutes, our particular part of the display being about the middle. This consisted of marching and counter marching, all to signals that were hoisted on a mast that we had brought with us. Each lad represented a ship and the signals were again the genuine signals that would have been made to ships at sea. When the whole display was over, the public gave us many rousing cheers and hand clapping. In fact, I must admit that this cheering and clapping affected all lads, and for myself, there has only been one occasion since when I have been so affected to the state of embarrassment. That however, will come much later in the story and many years later in time. As we marched off the show ground, I noticed that Mother was standing not far from the exit, so that instinctively I straightened up a little more, if that were possible. Then, the usual service routine of halting and dressing ranks, plus the usual "bull" of numbering and reporting to various officers until we were finally dismissed after various warnings about not being late for the final assembly and bussing back to Shotley. Meeting Mother was quite a thrill, I being in my best uniform with gold crossed flags badge. Mother had brought me the usual parcel of goodies which included a large bread pudding, and which I would share later with my particular pals. For a couple of hours, one was free of the Navy routines and many a stealthy smoke was enjoyed by some of the lads, for the public made no effort to hide their pleasure at offering any lad a cigarette. Mother and I watched the rest of the various performances before we were all called by the bugler sounding the call for general assembly. Our brief sojourn in the realms of civilian company was at an end, so with regret we said our adieus to the various friendships that had been made and renewed that afternoon. By the time we had been paraded and mustered, no lads missing for this was a point of honour; we embussed and returned to Shotley.

The very next week, we embarked on the nerve racking business of our final exams at Shotley. These lasted all week without a break, except for sleeping and the necessary cleaning routines. These examinations in various subjects, all relating to signals were again visual, written and oral, where the marks required for passing were all above the eighty per cent and the marking was not generous on the part of the examiners. From the completion of the exams, one was allowed to wear blue uniform with collar and cap with "Ganges" Cap Ribbon, as one became part of the ship for work. As far as we were concerned, it meant being a messenger during the day and evening as most Officers had personal messengers allocated to them. Then again, as we should be working odd hours we were permitted to use our mess during the off-duty times. Much of the off-duty times being spent in preparing our hammocks and bedding for going to sea. For this we waited very patiently, as during the waiting period, we had our Mid-summer leave of three weeks. On return, after the usual medical inspections and searches, we resumed our messenger duties while we waited for the orders detailing us for our ships in the middle of September. My details were finalised and I was to be drafted to *H.M.S. Marlborough* of the third Battle Squadron, a battleship based at Portland, Dorset. Many were the questions that we bombarded our Instructor with regarding our drafting. As ever, Yeo Bryant was a mine of information, telling us everything we required to know about our new ships, and lots that we did not need to know. No longer were we the stupid new entries that he had first known us to be. Against all orders, we lads made a collection between us and bought him a silver ball point pen which were then the latest things out for such folk as Yeomen of Signals. He had really put us on the road in the best possible way, and although Ben Bryant is no longer with us in body, I still wish to thank him for his kindnesses and his ever ready ear for a lad's troubles and for setting us right for the signal ratings of the future.

It was just as I was about to leave Shotley, that Mother wrote to me, telling me that brother Glen, who was in the Navy, serving on *H.M.S. Ceres* in the Mediterranean, had been involved in an accident on board the ship and was at that moment transferred to the Naval Hospital at Bighi in Malta. I think it must have been fairly serious and when I spoke to Yeo Bryant about it, he enlightened me quite a lot when I told him a little about the accident. Not that I knew a lot except that Glen would be sent home on the next possible ship and would be going to the Naval Hospital at Haslar. One just had to be content with what little knowledge one had.

H.M.S. MARLBOROUGH

The day of drafting to *Marlborough* came and I, with several other lads were called early, given an early breakfast collected our kitbags and hammocks and mustered outside the mess ready to go. Kit bags and hammocks were loaded on to lorries and then we were taken to Ipswich by special bus. As far as I can remember, the train left Ipswich about 0930 or thereabouts and we were taken round London by train. It was destined that we were not to see anything much of London. This was probably just as well, for we had amongst us, several lads from London and the powers that be had the thought that perhaps some of the lads might 'unconsciously' go home. However, the train rattled on through London and we eventually arrived at Weymouth Station. Here, there was much commotion as some two hundred lads sorted out their baggage and hammocks, ready for their allocated ships. Some were going to ships other than the *Marlborough*. Again the loading of lorries and transportation to the docks, and again the sorting out of baggage. Again, we loaded our gear, but this time onto a drifter, (a kind of fishing boat), used for fleet stores ships. This drifter took us to the middle of the harbour where our future home was at anchor or moored. I was still not sufficiently a sailor to know the difference, but was very soon to find out. Then again, it was time to unload and collect gear and take it to the mess that you had been assigned to. Thank goodness it was supper time for we were all very hungry, only having had packaged meals on the train. Then came the problem of finding somewhere to sling one's hammock which Stimpson and myself did in a lobby leading to the sick bay. Oh yes, my pal Stimpson was with me and we should be together for a while yet.

The next morning was quite bright but with a wind blowing so that one needed to watch where one stood or stopped if one wished to retain one's cap. After breakfast, and assembly where all boys mustered together, we were told that the ship would take on some hundreds of tons of coal and that we should be required to assist. This meant that we were to change into overalls and other odd gear. My job was to be with one of the coal barrows. When we again mustered, the coaling lighter was already alongside and various winches were already working. Having been allocated the job of barrow boy, like many of the other boys who came with me, we collected our barrows, or perhaps truck would be a more suitable word and mustered in line by the coal hoists. Once the job was started, it went with great speed and without a break, and by 1045 we had taken on board, according to some of the engine room folk, some two hundred tons. To me this was a colossal amount of coal as I had never seen so much except in the coal yards of Melonie and Golder on the docks at Ipswich. This coal I learned later, was not for the engine rooms but for domestic use in the many galleys. *The Marlborough* was oil driven, and probably if I had been observant, I would have noticed the oiler alongside while we were dashing to and fro with the coal barrows. By the afternoon, after we had cleaned away all traces of the coaling dust, the wind started to blow quite hard and the pipes were made stating that the ship would proceed to sea at 1600, (4 p.m.). During the afternoon the ship's company were very busy securing the ship for sea and at 1540, the pipe called Special Sea Dutymen to their stations. This did not mean much to me because as far as I knew I was not one of those folk. At least, I was not until an Instructor took a close look at me, and seeing that I was a signal boy, told me to report to the signal bridge. Climbing several ladders and decks, I eventually found what was later found to be the flag deck, as here were familiar surroundings with flag lockers and halyards. Seeing a yeoman of signals standing near by, I reported to him that I had been told to report to the flag deck.

"Good," said the yeoman, "we can do with some extra bodies." With that, he told me to get my oilskin and report to the signalman on the fxle, by the anchors. Having got the oilskin coat, I duly reported to the signalman by the anchors who was already busy tying a canvas wallet of flags to the guard-rail. Here he gave me instructions of what he had to do, and that as he gave me the flags, I was to put them away and also to give him what flags that he would call for. All these flags in the wallet were on staves about three feet long, with each one rolled up and placed in a separate pocket of the wallet. That part was easy. It was when they came to weigh anchor that the tricky part came. The huge iron shackles possibly weighing one hundred and twenty pounds or more, would clank their way over the hawse-pipe, to slither along the deck to the capstan where they would disappear down through the deck to the cable locker. Our job on the fxle, was to signal to the captain on the bridge, the amount of cable that was on deck at the hawse-pipe. This was done by counting the number of shackles either side of the joining shackle; which was a different design from the ordinary shackles. The amount of cable would be marked by wire bindings on the studded links, thus if there were four shackles of cable on deck, the fourth studded link from the joining shackle would be marked with the wire bindings. This I found was fairly easy to understand provided one did not let one's attention wander from the job. As the signalman told me, there was not a lot in this until one was letting the anchor go, when one had to be really on one's toes as three or four shackles could go out before a stop was made. Incidentally, a shackle of cable is a definite measurement, as there are a certain number of shackles that make up a cable. Then a cable's distance is one tenth of a mile, being two hundred yards. More of the mathematics and measurements at a later stage. As the signal number was reduced, so the amount of cable would be signified by that numbered flag. Naturally, I thought it would go to the figure one. This was not so, as just after signalling two shackles on deck, the officer called out, "Up and Down." Immediately the signalman told me to show flag U for uncle, which meant that the cable was up and down, or that the ship's stem was immediately over the anchor. The next moment it was "Anchor away" at which flag "A" was displayed, and the ship started to move out of harbour, in company with the *Iron Duke* which was the next ship of the squadron. Although flag signals were made by the flagship, I was too busy with my job on the fxle to attend to other signals. This was one thing that Yeoman Bryant had installed into our minds, that when reading or doing a signal job, one should never allow one's mind to be distracted by other things, and it proved over the course of time, to be very sound advice. Our job had finished, and we were then getting our equipment packed up and getting back to the bridge, before the ship got out to sea. It was while I was reporting to the yeoman that I noticed a youngish officer with heavy gold lace on his left shoulder so that I asked the signalman just what that denoted. The heavy gold lace he told me, were called aguillettes and the person in question was the Flag Lieutenant to the Squadron Rear Admiral. I was quite surprised when he came over and spoke to me about where I had come from. When I told him that I had arrived yesterday from "Ganges", he seemed quite surprised that I had been given some real signal work so soon, and suggested that I had done quite well in helping out with the cable flags. I did not like to mention that I had been detailed to report by another unknown instructor who had seen me idling on deck. Silence, so they say, is golden, and I thought it best not to dispute the wisdom of that saying.

Everything on board seemed vastly different from Shotley as here, all orders to the ship's company were transmitted by loud speakers and preceded by a pipe. Many were hard to interpret but, by asking questions, one soon started to get the idea of things in general. It was also learned that the *Marlborough* was a kind of training ship for it seemed that most lads from "Ganges" were sent here to finish their training and get some sea experience. By now, the ship was some way outside the harbour and with the wind and sea being a little boisterous, the movement became a little uncomfortable and my stomach started to raise objections. It was not long before I started to feel a little sea sickness coming on, so that I looked for somewhere quiet, as I hoped, to hide myself. Before very long, just when I thought that I had found the ideal spot, one of the instructors came along and told me to muster on the upper deck behind "Q" turret which was midships. Here I found many of the lads that had journeyed down to Portland with us yesterday. Most of them had noticed that I had been on the fxle when the ship was weighing anchor, and I was asked many questions about what I had to do, as they all expected to have to do similar jobs in the future. It was a question of exchanging knowledge of jobs, as one never knew when it might be their turn to do the same job. Such chatter helped to take our minds off the state of the weather and the movement of the ship, which was now becoming quite violent. Not many of the lads went to tea or supper that evening although I did manage to digest a piece of bread and butter. Quite readily we all slung our hammocks and turned in with very little fuss or bother for the movement had now reached a point where one did not want to move very much. The next morning when we were called, some of us went to have a look at the weather before doing anything else. Strangely enough, the ship was on her own somewhere in the middle of the ocean, and it was while idly looking round that I became violently sick and dashed to the side to ease my stomach.

Yes, I really did feed the fishes, so that going back below again, I was tempted to turn in again in my hammock. It was just as well that I did not, or shall I say that perhaps I was rather slow in making up my mind. The instructor came along and more or less shook all boys from their hammocks. Not a very nice thing to do, or so I thought. However this was no more than it should be for we were in the navy to take ships to sea, "And by golly," said the instructor, "that is just what you will do." Some of us only pecked at our breakfast, and again I only ate bread and margarine with just a small drop of tea. As the instructor told us, it is better to have something inside one, than to try to be sick on an empty stomach, which was good advice, for as the day progressed, I was not sick again. There had not been any let up in the weather all day and that night was a repetition of the last. By the next morning, the weather had abated somewhat, and we woke to find the ship at anchor in Torbay. Not that it mattered to me, for one place was as good as another and I was fast learning the ropes of being in the navy.

That morning when we mustered after breakfast, I was told that I would be the flag lieutenant's messenger. Making enquiries as to my duties, I was told that I should report to the Officer's Marine servant who would be about from 0830. Promptly on time, I reported as instructed to the marine servant, who told me of my duties such as doing messenger for the Officer, and he also instructed me that I should clean the aguillettes on the jacket of the Officer. Fortunately, for me, it was only an old suit that had been used at sea in bad weather, and just as I was about to start the process with a special tin of Bluebell metal polish, there was an almighty roar and some strange expletives, that I immediately stopped. I was asked who had told me to do such a stupid thing, so that I remarked that I thought that the aguillettes looked rather green and dirty so that I would clean them up a bit. For this, I obviously earned the servant's gratitude, for when I told him about it, he looked really worried until I told him what I had said to the Flag Lieutenant. That Marine was quite a good pal after that for he always managed to secure some extra little tit bits of food which I could always collect from the Pantry. From there on, I was the Flag Lieutenant's messenger, not that I profited from such a job, except perhaps that I had much more running about than I might otherwise have done. The only consolation for me, was that I had the same boss all the time, and when the other officers got to know me, I was not bothered with them for running their messages. Of course, I was not excused the usual signal boy's signal exercises where usually the Flag Lieutenant watched from the back of the Bridge. He would also watch while the signal boys did their semaphore and flashing exercises each morning and quite often in the evening. To be non-navy fashion, being Flag's messenger had quite a few advantages, for being available on the bridge, one saw many of the signals that were made and received, so that I soon became quite good at reading the various signals. This was the case when in company with other ships, although I suspect that many of the signals were totally unnecessary but were made for the benefit of passing time and to keep the signal staff on their toes. Time passed very quickly as although we did quite an amount of sea time, we never went anywhere in particular except to sea and back again. Christmas came, with leave to all the ship's company. Being boys, we were given fourteen days' leave to take us over the Christmas and the New Year. I think that everybody made the best of the time, for it was on the cards that the next Christmas, most of us would not be in the U.K., but most probably spread over the world as this was the time that the navy had many ships. In fact it was a common thing to do more foreign service than home time. One would be exceptionally lucky to be posted to a ship in the Home Fleet for a couple of years. Normally one expected to do two lots of foreign service to one home posting, and one would count oneself lucky to do that. Hardly like today when a foreign service was numbered in months, and one had to volunteer for sea service to get qualifying time in for promotion, as all promotion was dependent on having the necessary sea experience.

It was while home on leave, that Mother visited brother Glen in Roehampton Hospital where he had been moved from the Naval Hospital at Haslar near Portsmouth. Fortunately I was able to contribute a little towards her fare, and it was decided that only Mother should go to Roehampton Hospital. Needless to say, Mother was quite upset when she returned as Glen was almost blind, although the doctors did hope and were optimistic about saving his sight. Returning on board *Marlborough*, we learned that soon we should be sailing for the Spring Cruise to Gibraltar. This was a sign of the times, for the Spring Cruise the Home Fleet and the Mediterranean Fleet did their exercises in the Atlantic and then all ships would rendezvous at Gib after the exercise. However, before this happened almost the whole complement of boys on the *Marlborough* were unexpectedly given another week's leave. It was not realised then, that this would be our Foreign Service Leave. Not that I was unduly worried just where I would be going. What it did for me, was to give me a week with Glen before I went abroad. That week's leave was never so short, for although Glen could not see, I was able to take him out daily for walks despite him wearing thick dark glasses to hide his accident damage. It seems that he was working on some smoke making apparatus, when it exploded, sending the chemicals up into his face and eyes. The staff at Roehampton, Mr McIndoe and nurses had to take skin from various parts of his anatomy to make new eyelids and repair the facial damage. There is a funny side to this skin grafting, but I will refrain from repeating it here to save any embarrassment to Glen, even though he still makes a joke of it all. I was more than pleased that I had been able to see him and help him about, and Mother was most grateful to me. Glen had to continue attending Roehampton Hospital for several years and it was many operations before his sight and face was anywhere near normal, and today he leads as nearly a normal life as the average person.

With the return from leave, the ship stored and provisioned and away we sailed. Just what our part in the combined exercises was, I have no idea. Then, one morning we entered Gibraltar Harbour with bands playing and guns banging. This greeting was not for us as we may have thought, but of one admiral saluting another as is the Naval custom when Flag Officers meet for the first time. Everything was a novelty, particularly the surrounding landscape. From our berth, we looked out on Algerciras Bay, with Algerciras and La Linea in the distance, overshadowed by the towering Rock of Gibraltar, and further out to the south was Morocco just across the Straits of Gibraltar. In the harbour itself, were the numberless ships of the combined fleets, totalling in all, some three hundred, from submarines to sloops, and cruisers to battleships and aircraft carriers. There were over one hundred destroyers alone in the pens as they called the destroyer berths. Our berth was alongside the detached mole, so that there was little fear of our getting ashore, at least for the present. We did however, get on to the mole, in fact we were obliged to go onto the mole for the toilets. It was from this vantage point that we were able to watch the Spanish Gibraltarians fishing for the large grey mullet. These could quite easily be seen in the clear water and the fishermen were catching them in fairly large quantities. The fish would later be sold in the local fish market. Although quite a few of us tried our hand at fishing for the mullet, not many were successful. Being only boys in the service, our leave would in any case be restricted to the afternoons and evening until about 1900 or 2000 hours. Then again, what on earth could a boy do with only a few pence pocket money each week? Thus hardly any of us visited Gibraltar on this trip. After only a few days, orders were posted on the messdeck notice board that all boys would be leaving the ship at the weekend, for destinations that would be made known later that day. In the meantime bags were to be packed ready for instant moving. As it turned out, I was being drafted to a cruiser, the *Calypso* of the Third Cruiser Squadron. Some of the lads had struck lucky and were being posted to the large County Class Cruisers like *London* and *Sussex* or to battleships. We all noticed that in this drafting every one of us were going to ships of the Med Fleet. It was then that we realised just why we had been given the extra leave. My pal Stimpson had struck extremely lucky for he was being posted to the Med Fleet Flagship, *H.M.S. Queen Elizabeth* a battleship. At last our ways parted but I did see him a couple of times after that but only passing visits when on shore which for me was very seldom.

H.M.S. CALYPSO

On the Friday, I received my marching orders for *H.M.S. Calypso*, one of the smaller 3,000 tons ships although I suspect that their displacement was more than that, but not much, and with a top speed of about 32 knots.

Although *Calypso* was small, being a light cruiser, she certainly looked very business-like and very smart. If memory serves me correctly, the Captain was The Hon. G Frazer D.S.O., a tall smart and very impressive person. Whether this was correct or not, well, it's only a boy assessing his Captain of several years seniority, so he probably is not exactly correct. I also remember that on board *Calypso*, we had an officer in the torpedo department by the name of Christmas whom everybody referred to as Santa Claus, but not in his hearing. In fact, in the few dealings that I had with him, he was always very helpful and fatherly and I must admit that his real name and his nickname really suited him. I apologise if perhaps I am leaping ahead of myself, but these are the things that most reminded me of the *Calypso* at the moment. The reason for my joining the ship on a Friday (late) was that the ship only arrived in harbour early that morning, having been detained through bad weather damage in which a man had been lost overboard and quite a lot of structural damage had been made. These events had caused her to return to Malta Dockyard for immediate repairs, and she had eventually caught up the fleet at Gib. However, I, with about half a dozen other boys, was transported to *Calypso*. We were now joining a real ship of the navy and those that greeted us on board were not slow to inform us of such. We were all to be accommodated in the boys mess where the Boys Instructor was none other than the P.T.I. (physical training instructor) that we had known from Ganges. His first words were, "Just because you know me, don't expect an easy time," but it was nice to know that he recognised us. Fortunately, I as a Signal Boy did not have an awful lot to do with the seamen branch as we signal staff were always employed on the bridge with the Chief Yeoman to watch over us. Quickly we had to settle down, for the ship and most of the fleet would be sailing on the Monday. The Home Fleet ships would be going back home, while the Med Fleet ships would be leaving Gib for their various exercises en route to various destinations in the western Med. Although it was fairly late, us few signal boys had to read the usual nightly flashing exercise that was transmitted from the signal tower. The C.Y.S. thought that it would be a good idea to see just what we could do in respect of reading the Morse code exercise. Just how he would check our results, I do not know, for the returns would normally be sent to the squadron flagship for checking and then be returned to the ship for the signal boy concerned. When we had finished the exercise the C.Y.S. collected them in and looked through them. We were all probably too excited to have done very well so it is not surprising that the Chief later sent for us and told us that in view of our poor returns, he was not sending them for checking. Of course, we did not know any different so that when he told us to buck ourselves up and do much better we accepted his version without question. We later found out that Chief had made us read the exercise so that his right to control the Signal Boys would not be disputed. Also, it saved us from mustering with the seamen and getting non-signal jobs to do. I must emphasise here that this ploy on the Chief's part, was not in any way setting us against the seamen, but as ever in the navy, there is always a requirement for more bodies and the signal branch was no exception. After all, as we were told, "A signalman is a signalman and nobody else can do his job." In fact the whole communication branch considered themselves to be the elite of the lower deck. On the ships staff of Signalmen were the C.Y.S., two yeomen, four leading hands and about eight or nine signalmen, plus of course, us three or four boys, who after a certain amount of training, would be a big help to the signal staff. Chief was determined that we should start helping as soon as possible.

On the Saturday night after supper, a cinema show was held on board. The majority of the ships did the same, as nearly all ships were so equipped with cinema gear. Of course the cinema did not always perform as it should do, so that the ship's company off-duty and watching the film would get a little boisterous in their remarks and comments. One could always count on the wit of the ship to be present on these occasions to add his remarks to the fun. Such films would be passed round the fleet in succession, from ship to ship as the whole idea was apparently something new, being instituted by the then Fleet Signal Officer Lord Louis Mountbatten. Obviously, with the number of ships in the fleet, and considering that each ship would endeavour to carry sufficient films to last the cruise or until the ship would arrive back in its base, in this case Malta. It was usual for the films to be shown on week day nights for the ship's company, and on Sunday evenings for the Officers. The films themselves ranged from cowboy, to comedy, to cartoons and occasionally the good film would creep in, although most of the films were a little ancient. This was understandable as the films had probably been shown round half or more of the fleet before any particular ship got a particular film. Also, on week day nights but not at the same time as the film show, Tombola would be played for a modest fee per ticket. There was however a great deal of difference in the game to that played in civilian street. Almost all numbers had their own designation, such as four and nine the valentine, all the eights garden gate, all the fours pompey ladies. In fact it was almost a language on its own, so that anyone playing the game had to have their wits about them, for in addition the rules were very strictly enforced by every ship. The prizes were always in money with about ten per cent being reserved for the Ship's Benevolent Fund and the remainder going in prizes of about two pounds for the line and five for the house. The amounts of the prize money would depend on the numbers playing and the numbers in the ship's company, so that the bigger the ship the bigger the prizes.

To return to the signal staff and the duties inflicted on me. To start off with, new staff usually assumed the duties of "daymen." This meant that they were responsible for the cleanliness of the signal bridge and the running repairs of flags and other equipment. This was besides being on duty from early morning until late at night. If a dayman worked after about 2130, it was usual to be awarded a "Steerage Hammock." This meant an extra half hour in one's hammock on the following morning and being excused the bridge cleaning in the morning. I being a signal boy, was classed as a dayman, until such time as I should prove my ability at reading signals, for this was the main purpose of the junior signal staff. If one could read signals and obtain one-hundred per cent, one was a definite asset to any signal staff. From this, one can rightly assume that signal boys would not be left to read signals on their own but would read signals under the charge of a leading hand or yeoman of signals. This in turn meant that signal boys would be reading the nightly flashing exercise until they obtained a percentage over ninety and then they would read the exercises according to percentage gained. If one should obtain one-hundred per cent one was excused officially from the night signal exercise for a whole week. The reader will possibly remark that if it was one's job, one-hundred per cent should be quite possible. This is not so, for one must take into consideration that the signals are made at fleet speeds (22 WPM) and that disruptions like smoke, or pedestrians moving in front of the reader, were a common and everyday hazard. Needless to say that yours truly had not developed that experience yet so that it was nightly exercises for me.

By the end of February, and into March, the ship arrived back at Malta, having completed a cruise of various Spanish ports including Barcelona and several lesser places that are now holiday resorts along the southern coast of Spanish Costa del Sol and such places. We arrived back in Malta, much the same weather accompanying the ship as when she sailed in early January. It was the tail end of the Gregale season and quite rough weather was experienced. The wind was so strong that every ship had a tug in attendance as she entered harbour and went to her berth, which was at a buoy in Bighi Bay under the shadow of the Naval Hospital. Not many ships were seen to make use of the tug that was in attendance, as no doubt the Captain would consider it a slur on his ability to accept the use of a tug except in an emergency. What we did notice was that the Grand Harbour was just about full up with battleships and cruisers and that each ship had in attendance a gondola shaped native craft called a "dghaisa." The strange looking craft were adopted by each particular ship and no matter the time, be it day or night, the dghaisa would be available if required by that ship. One did not even have to hail or signal the boat if required, as the native boatman would know all the signs that people might be requiring his services, and he would be waiting at the gangway for his passenger, ready to transport the person to where ever the passenger so desired. If I remember correctly the fare would be about three pence to the shore, (one-and-a-half pence today), from ships to shore. That would be the official fare so that one usually put a little extra for the inconvenience, unless several people were using the dghaisa at the same time when of course it would be a mass contribution and the boatman would receive considerably more than just the official fare.

In all fairness to the naval folk and the native boatmen there was very little attempt to over or undercharge for the use of the ship's dghaisa. If one got into the boat and found that one did not have sufficient money for the fare, it was common practice for the boatman to tell the unfortunate sailor that it did not matter as the sailor could pay next time. This would be left to the sailor's honesty, but the boatman would remember and tackle the person at some later trip. For myself, I found that the boatmen were friendly and cheerful and there was always that willingness to help if at all possible. This was found to be the case when a few years later, brother Jim was a C.P.O. and had his wife living ashore in Malta, I often used to visit them and stay until late in the evening; there was never any question of dishonesty in their dealings. It was probably all due to the fact that the Maltese folk in general were dependent on the Navy for their livelihood in many ways, so that any infringement in the unwritten code would be made known through the boat fraternity in a very short time.

By this time I was becoming reasonably good at reading the signals and as I had passed the exam for advancement to Ordinary Signalman at seventeen-and-a-half, the Chief of the signal staff started to grill me to be ready for the signal exam that would finally qualify me for the promotion. This meant that I had to do a little more swotting than I had been doing. In this swotting, I was greatly assisted by two of the leading signalmen whose names I am not sure about. Daily during the lulls in the signal work, if they were on duty, I would be grilled by them asking me questions and helping prepare me for the examination. Before the exam however, we were to sail on the next leg of the cruise to the Greek Islands, as it was here that we should be holding the squadron regatta. Our Boy's Instructor, the P.T.I. that we had at Shotley, having obviously remembered me as having been stroke oar in the divisional cutter, promptly installed me as the stroke oar of the boys' cutter in the squadron races. During these practice sessions, I one day developed boils on my bottom, which did not help with the boat pulling work. With this affliction bothering me, I informed the P.T.I. that I would not be able to pull in the big race because of the boils. Of course, I had to offer proof that I was not sprucing, so that when I showed the boils to the P.T.I. he remarked that it was nothing and that it was not sufficient to stop the rowing. On the day of the race, we manned the boat and were towed to the start line. During this relaxed period, I was not happy about the boils and when I suggested that I again dropped out, the answer was the same. Boils were nothing in the Navy according to the P.T.I. With all due ceremony we slipped the tow and slowly paddled to the start. Our rig for the racing was a coloured jersey of the ship's colours, and white shorts, no socks but plimsolls. As soon as the boats were in line, the starting gun was fired and away we pulled, the boils temporarily forgotten in the excitement of the start. Much depended on the start for it would be a twenty-minute pull roughly to the finishing line. We pulled like the proverbial Trojans, eventually winning the race by several lengths. At the finish, the coxswain of our boat ordered, "Toss your oars." This to anybody in the ships present, was a sure challenge to all, that we were the BEST. Having just won the race, there were no challengers and when we were ordered to stand and cheer the next boats in, I found that I was unable to move for the pain of the boils. I was stuck to the seat, for my shorts had ridden down during the pulling and I had been pulling on my bare bottom. Now the boils were discharging on to the seat and had congealed to fasten me like glue, so that to move was very painful. The P.T.I. seeing my plight, extended his hand to help me, so that with a pull and a yell that was heard round the squadron, I stood up, leaving a boil from each cheek protruding from the seat like two ice cream cornets upside down. Pleased to relate, I have not suffered boils on my bottom since and I am in no way anxious to renew that experience. One thing good came out of it all. The ship's gunnery officer had apparently placed a large bet with another ship backing us to win. This we did to his advantage, so that we lads were each rewarded with a model silver cutter's oar to mark the occasion. Each oar was appropriately inscribed with the date and the occasion, to be a treasured souvenir and memento of two boils.

The return to Malta, our base, was completed with the carrying out of various exercises. Again we returned to our billet in Bighi Bay, where I was soon engaged in the examination for advancement. This involved reading everyday signal traffic, reading a special transmission exercise of semaphore and Morse, and of transmitting exercises for the other ships in company. It was during these duties, that I heard somebody referring to the ship as the *Pyso*, so making a few enquiries (unofficial), I was surprised to learn that almost all ships had a nickname. Ours was a mixture of the letters and the deletion of others. The *Royal Sovereign* a battleship for instance was called the *Tiddly Quid* for she was always so smart looking that Tiddly being a Naval word for smart, and Quid being the old term for a pound in money or sovereign, it was easy to see where the name came from. Another one of interest was the *Cocoa Boat* being the nick name for the *Curacoa*, another cruiser. All these confusing items certainly served to keep one on the alert at all times. I do not suppose for one moment, that Admiralty, when they allocated names to ships, ever intended that the names should be reconstructed and abused. Many a senior officer no doubt, would gnash his teeth in disgust and dismay at hearing the ship so irreverently referred to. To return again to signals examinations. It was while preparing myself for these that I found one night that I had no partner to write down the signal flashing exercise for me so that I did as I had seen some of the senior ratings do. That is to read the signal and at the same time write it down for oneself. A bit difficult to start with but one soon gets into the habit and becomes quite efficient at it. To be truthful, from that time on, I would prefer to read and write down for myself. The only snag was that one always had to be prepared to receive signals, be they short or long messages. However the day of the examination came with the squadron signal officer supervising the exams and to my great relief I had managed to pass O.K. This meant that I could now be promoted to Ordinary Signalman, which in turn meant some extra pay and that I had finished being a signal boy and was moved to the signalmens' mess. It also meant that I would be eligible for being a signalman of the watch. Looking back, it seemed an enormous step up, but with today's knowledge, it really did not mean anything much. However I was delighted to be able to write to Mother and tell her of my promotion, such as it was. One other thing it allowed me to do, was that I no longer needed to attend school classes as we had to do as boys. Here I promised the schoolmaster that we had on board, that when possible, I would attend school with the object of more promotions. Schooly, (this is the naval term for school teacher), was most helpful and ready to place his knowledge at one's disposal, for he would usually be one of the deciphering officers as well as an assistant navigating officer, and in both these things I wished to improve my knowledge. By now the Chief had decided that I was fit to assume watch duties and by good fortune I was allocated to one of the leading signalmen that had so helped me before. In harbour, if all was quiet, particularly during the night watches, I would literally be bombarded with signal questions. These questions would cover a vast range of signal subjects so that at times I was somewhat bewildered by the variety and depth of knowledge required. For all that we pressed on, and before long the C.Y.S. got to know of my progress and ability so that further promotion was mentioned. Unfortunately, as has already been related, I needed to have more sea experience before I would even be permitted to sit the examination. Being a "watchkeeper," I was permitted, if not required for duty, to go on leave when my watch was completed. This was a great advantage, for one could go sunbathing on the rocks that surround Bighi Bay and the adjoining Calcarra Creek, to be brought back to the ship about 1600, (4 p.m.). This I often used to do in preference to going on short shore leave. For one thing, money was not over plentiful as being on a small ship where one did one's own catering on a mess principal, and the mess bill would be payable each month, (called canteen messing), as one purchased one's requirements from the canteen to be paid for at the end of the month. One could also obtain one's cigarette requirements from the canteen but at that time I did not smoke so that there was no problem attached to that pastime. With swimming and sun bathing between watch duties, and fitting in a few hours at school, time soon passed and it was almost time for the autumn cruise. This was not to be for more important matters were in the offing.

Just before we were due to sail for the autumn cruise, the ship was ordered to go to Cyprus where trouble was beginning to disturb the peace of the world. Arriving off Famagusta where apparently the British in general were not welcomed, *Calypso* landed a party of Royal Marines and some sailors to ensure the safety of the oil tanks in the vicinity. Just what the real trouble was, I had no idea, except that the ship was there for the safety of the British population, and the safety of the oil tanks. Just before we were supposed to land the shore party and the signal station crew, one of the signalmen of the landing party was taken ill. As I was on watch, I was detailed to act as his relief for the time being. Hastily gathering my equipment and revolver – a Webley Scott 45 – and about six rounds of ammunition, these were more for show than anything, at least I thought so. Eventually we landed, with very little idea of what we should have to do, but displaying lots of swank and tons of "bull." The signal station was set up on top of the oil tanks, and I established communication with the ship as I had been taught. All so very easy. The marine detachment and the sailors of the landing party marched off leaving Fred as the sole occupant of the oil tank and about sixty feet in the air. About half way through the morning, I noted that there was a crowd of natives gathering in the streets below. At first not much attention was paid to this gathering, until I noticed that some of the natives had climbed over the fences. Being quite new to this sort of thing, I was preparing a message to send to the ship telling them of this incident. It was then that I noted that a couple of the natives were endeavouring to light a fire-brand. Realising that this could be dangerous, I drew my pistol so as to be ready for possible bother. Then, to my alarm the natives with the fire-brand moved toward the oil tanks and as I thought started to attempt to ignite a bonfire at the base. This was sufficient for me, so that without more ado, I fired two shots into the air. It seems that the saboteurs had not noticed that I was on the top of the tanks, so that at the shots those inside the fence hurriedly withdrew. A few minutes later some ten seamen and marines entered the compound and ascended the ladders to the top of the tanks. I was immediately questioned by a Lieutenant or Sub Lieutenant and instructed to report the matter to the ship. This I would have done in any case. The two empty rounds of ammunition were retrieved from my pistol by the officer and I was given further instructions as to future actions. That afternoon, I was relieved as had been arranged and on return to the ship, I got the impression that I was the saboteur from all the questions that I was asked. I was also questioned as to my feeling and reactions when I fired my revolver. Needless to say, I informed all that having a 45 revolver did not give one all the assurances necessary under the existing circumstances. I was also asked if I had any ideas of what could be done to improve matters, and being a very young and junior O Sig. I thought it best to keep my ideas to myself. I did however mention that I sincerely objected to the thoughts of being toasted for the pleasure of a few natives. Some few days later the *Pyso* was relieved by a county class cruiser which I think was the *Sussex* probably: my memory is a little hazy. By that time the thoughts of toasting and the reports had almost been forgotten by all concerned apart from the signalmen who wanted to know all the ins and outs of the affair. I was glad about this, as I began to feel that somewhere, I had not been doing what I should have done and that trouble was brewing. Nothing more was heard of the incident, very much to my relief, except that I was verbally admonished for unofficially using two rounds of ammunition without authority. Needless to say, the story got round the ship that I had been responsible for shooting many of the natives which was quite untrue. That is the result of "mess deck rumour." After a pleasant couple of days, we rejoined our squadron somewhere round the southern Greek Islands, with each ship going to a sheltered bay of another island. I should imagine that each ship was only a few miles from her neighbour but out of sight because of the intervening land and hills. How great it was going to be on our own with no signals to bother about. Again the navy had a shock for us for we received a letter from our admiral saying that the ships of the squadron would play chess by signal and that the signals would be made by using the large signal searchlights and reflecting the Morse signals from convenient clouds. This meant that we were no longer on our own on a pleasure cruise. The chess game did not bother me for I had been taught to play chess in my spare time at school. When the Chief got to hear of this, I was removed from watchkeeping so that I could be available during the night for consultation about the chess game. When word got round the ship about the games of chess, it seemed that a large number of sailors would like to take up the game, as the officer in charge of the entertainment on board would put out a daily report on the progress of the current game. Obviously the moves were not timed, as in competition chess, for we had to depend on the cloud state for making our moves. Also, I was in great demand by the signal staff and here I redeemed myself from the Famagusta fiasco. The game of chess that was started in the Greek Islands was never completed for we moved on with the cruise arrangements before there was any decisive conclusion. Another game that was played on board was "uckers." This is played on similar lines to the game of Ludo but the rules are quite different and definitely more complicated. The board itself would be painted on the deck and would measure about six to eight feet square, while the dice would be about eighteen inches cubed and the shaker would be a dustbin. I feel confident in remarking that there, any similarity to the ordinary game of Ludo, promptly finished, and the terms and language was completely alien. The term "blob up," was most common and meant that counters could be piled on top of each other to any number of the counters being played. To disperse or get past this "barrier" required the throw of a six to challenge it, then a succession of sixes as for the number of counters "blobbed." Hence if four counters were "blobbed," it would take five successive sixes to disperse or pass by the "barrier." Much fun was obtained by this game, and messes would compete against each other, then divisions would do the same, finally at times making ship versus ship. In some ships, an entrance fee was necessary to enter the game with the final proceeds going to the ship's favoured charity. At one time the *Pyso*'s charity was St Dunstans and many of the lads would conjure up schemes for that charity. Then at the end of the commission, any spare money in the ship's funds would also be donated to the favoured charity. This practice is still carried on today in the navy, for sailors are very good hearted and perhaps a little soft hearted. So much for some of the recreational pastimes of the navy that are played on board ship. The cruise that we had started on went as planned by the Admiralty, we, calling at many places ranging from the Greek Islands, Constantinople, the Black Sea ports and Palestine. During some of the ports of call the ship would entertain various officials from various countries. Ours was no exception for we, on that cruise alone, entertained King Boris of Bulgaria, King Carol of Romania, and many lesser dignitaries. Never a dull moment, despite the fact that many of the kings have since been deposed. In fact many of the countries have disappeared from the map or been renamed.

Christmas came and went with the usual Naval festivities and ceremonies. At 0001 (midnight, Christmas morning), the holly garland would be hoisted to the masthead, no unnecessary work would be carried out, all messes were expected to decorate to the best of their ability. This could be anything from bunting to crepe paper decorations and of course flowers if available. After church service (carols) the Captain would change places with the youngest member in the ship, who would don the captain's cap and jacket and the whole of the mess decks and living spaces would be inspected by the new captain. This latter would only be exercised should the "Exigencies of the Service" permit. This, would after the inspection, be the time that the Officers appreciated their C. & P.O.s by inviting them to share a glass of something. It was also the time that the C. & P.O.s could demonstrate their appreciation for the officers of their department or division by inviting them to the mess to sample the specific gravity of their tot. All good excuses which did not effect the lives of the junior ratings, or the folk that were on duty. During the inspection of the messes, it was expected that the Captain would sample the various culinary delights that were conjured up by the messes, and would wish all the compliments of the season. The whole of the Christmas events would be undertaken with spontaneity and much good will on all sides which was great for morale.

January came and stores were loaded while everything was made ready for the spring cruise and the combined fleets exercises in the Atlantic. This time when the fleet's exercises were over, the entertainment's officer organised for the junior ratings on the ship to visit Gibraltar and the excavations, plus of course the Barbary Apes. The climb up the rock was done as a party under the charge of a military officer and then we were escorted through the tunnels and caves with the varied histories being explained to us. The stalactites and stalagmites proved most picturesque and interesting for these formations grow at only a few millimetres a year and some of them were many feet high. With this visit over, we were escorted to the Palace where we witnessed the Changing of the Guard ceremony and then back on board for supper and our duties. After a few days' rest and recuperation in harbour the Med Fleet sailed eastwards while the Home Fleet made tracks for their home ports. While we of the Med Fleet sailed eastwards various exercises would be carried out. For this, we of *Calypso* were to act as escort to the aircraft carrier *Glorious* being stationed some half mile on her starboard bow. The *Glorious* would be flying off her aircraft which would be attacking the various units of the fleet, while we would be acting as part of her defence against the same aircraft. All went well and most of the aircraft from *Glorious* were airborne as we steamed along at about twenty-five knots. Our position made the whole of the flying operations most accessible to viewing of the flying off and on of the machines. With some time into the exercise, FOG, quite thick developed, causing much consternation for the powers that be, for at that moment there were some thirty aircraft in the air. Some of those aircraft had already been airborne for the allotted fuel endurance so that there were many fears for their safety. To add to the consternation of the Captain of the *Glorious*, some aircraft reported that there was a merchant ship heading straight for the ships. Already the sirens were sounding for the warning to any vessel to keep clear. Without the slightest warning, a huge merchant vessel appeared out of the fog, well away on our port side. There was little that we could do other than to ensure that we kept well clear. Frantic signals were now being made but the accident of collision at sea now happened. The merchant ship, *S.S. Florida* collided with the *Glorious* on her starboard bow, tearing a great hole at the waterline at the bows. *Florida* was badly holed just before the bridge so that there were fears of a major calamity. However both ships remained afloat and our immediate problem was the safety of the aircraft and their crews. Many of these aircraft had to ditch in the sea near any ship that was in sight, while some continued to circle such ships as were in the vicinity. Some of the aircraft were lost completely with their crews and many aircraft were lost with the crews being rescued. I remember that we picked up some crews, who would remain on board until convenient transfers could be arranged later. The transfers were completed later that day when it was established that the carrier and the *Florida* were in no danger of sinking. The exercise was immediately cancelled with all ships remaining in the area after the fog lifted. As is usual in these events all signal staff were busily employed making and answering the different signals. As we were employed near the *Glorious* we acted as a signal link between her and the various other ships for almost the whole fleet had something of importance to report or ask of the *Glorious*. There were requests for information of relatives who were serving elsewhere in the fleet, reports from ships that had picked up survivors, in fact everybody's signal was more important than anyone else's, or so it seemed. With the transfer of any flying personnel back to the *Glorious*, the fleet later dispersed to their destinations for the cruise. If memory serves correctly our ports were based on Italy's west coast and Sardinia. Here we would work up as usual for the coming regatta, which actually we never took part in.

On return to Malta, I was selected for the course at the local signal school, Fort Verdulla, for promotion to signalman if I passed. This was a course of about six weeks where one started to delve into the intricacies of fleet manouevres, coding and decoding, and all the other seemingly strange practices of the signals world. In addition to this sort of knowledge, there was the usual reading of the flashing and semaphore exercises daily where one had to obtain at least ninety-eight per cent. This meant that out of a fifty-word message one was only permitted one error. Life became a whirl of signalling, for even at the meal tables, some wit would find a method of asking for the butter by signal, which was not really difficult with the knowledge and expertise that we were fast obtaining. The last week at Fort Verdulla would be taken up by the actual exams, where the various qualified Signal Officers of the fleet would examine one with every question possible. Whether one passed or not, one was a far more knowledgeable signal rating than when one joined the school. On completion of the course and exams, one waited or tried to wait patiently for the results, until with fingers chewed down to the elbows, the results would be published as a fleet memo. No matter how I tried, I could not find out the results in advance, as seemingly these results were equivalent to state secrets. Eventually, I was included in the secret results, with a good pass mark, which was soon celebrated in the usual way when I was promoted Signalman. A little more pay was the prize, and the opening of the channels for further advancement.

It was not many weeks after my advancement to Signalman, that rumour started to go round the ship that *Calypso* was to go home for paying off. Within a short while this was confirmed by certain staff in the ship ordering the paying off pendant which would be made on shore in the dockyard. The paying off pendant replaces the commissioning pendant and is supposed to be a foot for each day in commission. This may have been in the old days, but since *Calypso* had been in commission for over two years, this would have meant that the pendant would have been about nine hundred feet in length. I would imagine that our paying off pendant would have been in the region of 250 to 300 feet long which would still make it very awkward if one started manoeuvring while the pendant was flying, bearing in mind that the ship itself was somewhere in the region of 250 feet long. In any case the pendant had to be supported by balloons filled with hydrogen or compressed air, so I was given to understand. The day of paying off arrived and with the daily hoisting of colours and its attendant ceremony the paying off pendant was hoisted and the commissioning pendant came down. Then, about mid-morning after certain official calls and ceremonies had been completed, *Calypso* slipped from her buoy while the seamen's band of *Pyso* played the traditional tune of *"Rolling Home to Merry England"*. Proudly the little ship steamed out from Grand Harbour while any ship that was passed raised three rousing cheers for shipmates that were going home. Once clear of St Elmo Light, we changed course to the westward and started the long trip for Gibraltar and home. Speed for the Home run was about twelve knots, as these were economic times and high speeds were frowned upon. At Gib., we stayed for a few hours, just long enough to replenish fuel and necessary stores and also to allow the ship's company a few hours leave in which to purchase any souvenirs that they wished, for here it was customary to purchase duty free goods for friends and relatives. It is pointless to remark, that when the ship sailed, there were no absentees. On leaving Gibraltar and then altering course to the northwestwards on the evening of the first day from Gib., notices were posted on the general notice board, that certain members of the company would be required to recommission the *Ceres*, another "C" class cruiser and sister ship of *Calypso*, after arriving at Chatham, our home port. As I had not completed the full commission, (two-and-a-half years), in *Calypso*, my name was on the list for those to go to *Ceres*. This would be my first home-coming from foreign service of any sort and I felt that the safe arrival of the ship at Sheerness was entirely my responsibility. Accordingly, as I was on watch the night that we entered the Channel, I was very alert to spot the various lights on our way to Sheerness. The first light that we saw, was that of the Lizard I believe; and then it was a succession of others until I was relieved of watch. By that time we were in sight of the Needles. As ever being a watchkeeper one adapts one's body to sleeping whenever one can so that in spite of my self control, I was drawn to my hammock where Old Man Gravity rapidly took charge of me, so that by breakfast time we were almost entering the Medway for Sheerness. Here, as is the routine with all ships going into dock at Chatham, we de-ammunitioned and destored as we should be going alongside in the Chatham dockyard. Here also the customs men came on board to check for illegal goods or over dutiable goods. I did have a few things, but these were brushed aside as being of no consequence. That evening not wishing to go on shore, I had no inclination and as I would be going on leave when we arrived at Chatham, I volunteered to do another signalman's duty, as he lived in Chatham and could get home that evening. This was not unusual, as one often swapped duties as a point of favour to those that could get home. These favours were normally returned at some later date when it was convenient to do so. However, as I should be going on leave the next day, I postponed the return of the favour until some years later. Next day I was given leave of some fifteen days before I was to rejoin the *Ceres* direct, which I did about the end of March.

H.M.S. CERES

Joining the *Ceres* presented no problems for she was berthed not too far from the old ship *Calypso*. In fact it was quite convenient, as many of the surplus stores from the signal department had already been transferred to *Ceres*. In this, I was able to help considerably, for I had known many of the people that were still on board and they were only too pleased to see excess stores going to a ship that would at some future date be referred to as a "chummy ship." It is quite possible that those responsible for the stores would be highly annoyed if anyone suggested such things, but it was far better than being wasted. Many of the stores so improperly transferred were always usable. The stores usually consisted of items that would in any case wear out and consisted of such things as flags or ensigns. Although such transfers were not officially sanctioned, a blind eye was usually turned on the matter. The stores so transferred were usually referred to as "rabbits" and this originated from old navy times when a rabbit was counted as food, which if poached, was counted as stolen. Also, much of the system of stores keeping originated from the times of Samuel Pepys who was the instigator of accounting for the various stores supplied to ships. Many is the time that one may hear of the stores staff condemning Mr Pepys to the nether regions of eternity.

By mid April, the ship was beginning to look like a ship with most of the stores already on board for we were due to commission in early May. In the meantime, huge bundles of flags would be seen on the dockside and the signal staff would be busy sewing flags on to three lengths of wire. The three lengths of wire were for the Dressing lines that had to be made to fit each individual ship. These stretched from the bow, over the masthead to the mainmast head and down to the ensign staff. It was not just a question of sewing the flags on in any old order, as this had to be done according to a set plan so that looking from the front, all ships would appear to be the same. At least, as near as possible, depending on the length of the ship and the heights of the masts. The dressing lines would be used to "dress ship" on such occasions as royal birthdays and anniversaries, all of which would be notified by admiralty orders. The task of making the dressing lines by the signal staff caused the use of bad language, especially when one got one's fingers in the way of the needle as it was forced through the wires, and many fingers were punctured and torn in the process. The lines were made and ready for use by the end of the month and a trial run was arranged. All went well. During these weeks and between getting all equipment ready for sea, the normal signal work would carry on. Not by flags, flashing, or semaphore but by telephone, as the ship would be connected to the dockyard system of telephones. There never seemed to be enough time to get everything ready for the sailing date which was all too rapidly approaching when we should sail for Gibraltar and our "shake down cruise." The term "shake down" is possibly derived from our American cousins, for this term is used throughout that Navy. For the British term, one usually refers to "working up period," which means more or less the same thing. Ours would take us a month at Gibraltar and would be far different from when we called there on the way home.

The middle of May saw the *Ceres* pushing her bows through the swells of the Atlantic and the Bay of Biscay en route for the Rock of the Apes, or as is sometimes known, "one of the Pillars of Hercules", Gibraltar. Here, the ship's company would immediately go to work, as first the paintwork had to be renewed and all working parts of the guns, torpedoes and signal equipment to be overhauled and the other one hundred and one things that make for efficiency were attended to. While en route, much of this previously mentioned work would be attended to, weather permitting, while the signal staff would signal any ship encountered. This would be done by using the international code of signals and using the appropriate method of signalling according to the time of the day or night. It was always done with some idea of competition in mind, for the Admiralty published periodic returns, stating which ships had communicated with the most merchant vessels while on passage. As the ship approached Gibraltar from the west, one would pass by Cape Trafalgar and the scene of the famous battle. On passing this spot, as reckoned by navigation, the ship would sound the "still" or pipe, as a salute to the memory of the Battle.

Entering Gibraltar Harbour, the ship (Captain) would request permission to salute the flag of the Admiral, unless there were more senior Captains in company. On this occasion, *Ceres* was on her own and we saluted the Flag Officer Gibraltar with a salute of thirteen guns, which denoted the rank of the Rear Admiral in Charge. Immediately, scores of seabirds would take flight, and if one was caught napping, the result could be an unholy mess all over the ship. The salute would be accomplished by firing blank ammunition and the salute would be returned by an eleven gun salute from the shore battery. With the bustle and din of the saluting over, the harbour would become alive with small boats from the local traders who would bargain for the supply of fruit and vegetables for use by the ship. Also coming on board would be the proverbial dhobying woman (local laundry maid), but much older and hardly a maid, as most of them had large families and were quite aged. These dhoby women would wash dry and iron one's clothes for a pittance and return the washing the same evening or the next morning. Quite a service since washing machines were unheard of. Much the same thing as regards the dhoby women would occur through the Med and further east. Gibraltar is usually reckoned as the first stepping stone to the East.

The working up period now really started in earnest, for on completion, the ship would be inspected by the port Admiral and his staff. We now went to sea almost daily for gunnery exercises and torpedo firing, and both of these would be at a target towed by a tug. The tug which was quite a powerful ship, would tow any type of target from small to over large, or as the Navy would say, a B.P.T., (battle practice target). Taking part in this was quite exciting, for if there were any mistakes, one could quite easily receive a practice shell close to one. The tug and target, with a special crew and signal and wireless ratings on board, would leave harbour several hours before the ship would leave harbour, so that by the time the ship was ready to open fire, the target would be in its correct station.

If all was ready, a very large blue flag would be hoisted in the tug, then as soon as the ship was ready, she too would hoist a large blue flag. From that moment on, the signalman of the tug and the signalmen on board the ship would not take their eyes off the blue flag. Any movement of the flag in either vessel would indicate that firing should cease immediately, for some reason or other. The main reason as already mentioned, was that the shells were not falling on or round the target but were too close for comfort. I must add here, that the shell as fired by *Ceres*, both live and practice ammunition, weighed about seventy pounds, so that if accidentally hit by one of the shells, it would cause one hell of a dent to say the least. Some of the signal and other ratings strongly objected to being sent to the tug during practice shoots. This meant that one invariably got detailed to go. For myself, I always thought that it was good training having one's own command so to speak, so that sometimes I would volunteer for the job. For one thing, on board the tug, one was one's own boss and apart from obeying signals and orders there would be very little routine discipline, so that the whole event became a kind of treat and all arranged by courtesy of the navy. In addition to that, it meant that I was classed as a dayman, so that I did no night watches and that my time if not on the tug, was pretty well my own apart from the daily signal exercises. For the shooting, first we did what was and maybe still is known as sub calibre shooting, where a special barrel would be fitted to the guns so that instead of firing a six inch projectile, one would fire a smaller shell and this would require almost the same drills as the larger shell, which was the whole point of the exercise, and the range of the gun would be reduced accordingly. The full calibre shooting would be done during the last week of the period, and when the Admiral came on board for the inspection. All these things and the firing of the practice torpedoes went according to plan, with the Admiral apparently being satisfied with the performance of the crew. With a few days left in harbour the time was taken up by 'paint ship', as during the exercise firing the smoke from the guns and other non-mentionable rubbish from the seagulls had to be erased. For the 'paint ship', the whole ship's company would be involved, as would most of the officers, so that the ship would be "out of routine" for the period of painting. The painting was all finished by the Friday dinner time when a general clean up followed and leave was given to many of the ship's company, if they wished.

On the Monday morning about 0900, *Ceres* sailed for Malta and to join the squadron, which was accomplished without incident of importance. During the trip to Malta, the ship would stop each evening, and the ship's company would be permitted to bathe over the side at a certain time. The time would be so arranged so that if one happened to be on watch at the commencement of the bathing period, then one could by making haste, catch the tail end of the bathe, as the bathing usually lasted about an hour. Although some sharks had been reported in the area, this did not stop most of the crew from taking the bathe, as a marine sentry was always posted with rifle and ammunition in case it was needed. The majority of sharks in the Med are generally small ones and of the HammerHead variety. In due course, we arrived at Malta and being the only ship present able to salute, we, with due ceremony, saluted the flag of Vice Admiral Malta (V.A.M). This followed much the same routine as at Gibraltar, except that here we fired a fifteen gun salute, V.A.M. being one grade higher than the officer at Gib. It was part of the signal staff's duty to know the various gun salutes that are given to different dignitaries, be they British or foreign, as the salutes are all contained in the books of reference that the signal staff had to have a comprehensive knowledge of. In this as well, one had to have an excellent knowledge of the flags that the various dignitaries were entitled to fly. In short, the senior signal rating had to be a walking encyclopaedia as well as a signalman. Being the month of May, it was gloriously hot, so that bathing from the rocks that surrounded our berth was the daily pastime. Incidentally, our berth was the same one as that had been used by *Calypso* whose place in the squadron we had taken. Again it was the old routine of the daily signal exercise at 0930 when all ships of the fleet would compete against each other. Although we were the only ship there, the exercises were still conducted by the Naval Signal Station at Castille, which is well-known throughout the world. Since I was now a signalman of some standing, I was given some privileges that are not normally given to junior signalmen. Also, there were again a couple of leading signalmen that were very helpful and also keen to help their juniors along, especially if that junior showed a desire for advancement. Again, I was fortunate in being in the watch of one of these leading signalmen. During the night watches, if signal traffic permitted, all the signal books and some others, would be laid out and questions fired at me to answer, or quote from the books. Unfortunately, I was not permitted to take the exams for promotion, as again one had to have a certain amount of sea experience before one's name could be submitted for the list of candidates. Although it seemed unfair at the time, it was so arranged to prevent some uninterested person standing in the way of a person that really wanted to make headway. It will be remembered that even the course for signalman took four weeks to complete so that the course for leading signalman would be correspondingly that much longer. When the time came for the squadron to be joined by *Ceres*, it was again the routines of exercises of all sorts until the efficiency of the ship reached its peak, and then come what may it had to be maintained. By the time the year was out, *Ceres* had visited many more ports on the Mediterranean's northern shores and a few on the southern shores. At one of the ports on the southern shores, I believe it was Mersa Matruh, not too far from Alexandria, one morning while on watch, we heard what we thought to be the sound of bagpipes coming from the shore. This had us all puzzled, for we knew of no Scottish Regiments in that area. Soon, coming over the sand dunes away from the town, came a camel corps or even a battalion who were lead by a bagpipes band mounted on camels. I have a feeling that the bagpipes were not the same as the bagpipes of Scotland, as they did not even sound the same. Even though we watched through telescopes we could not establish just what the instruments were. One lives and learns, and I was certainly learning fast. It was just one more peculiarity to add to one's store of knowledge, for we had already heard the drum beats at sea of a Turkish fishing fleet when fishing at night. There are some things that bedevil the mind. This latter took several signalmen quite a long period on watch to establish just what that was, even though it was in one of the signal books. As a little point of interest, when I did sit for the leading signalman's exam some time later, that was one of the questions that I was asked, so that I was able to answer with confidence. On return to Malta, at the end of the autumn cruise, I received a letter from Mother telling me that brother Jim had been posted to Malta for *H.M.S. Egmont*, which was the shore depot for Malta. Some few weeks later I was able to meet him at Egmont where he informed me that he would shortly be getting his wife out to Malta, as soon as he could arrange a passage for her. By the time his wife arrived, we were again at sea for the spring cruise and on return to Malta, Jim was living in a flat at the bottom of Calcara Creek. This was most convenient for me to visit, as Calcara Creek was at the bottom of the creek where we were berthed. Later on, Jim and his wife moved to St Julien's Bay which was the other side of Valletta, so that I had quite a trip to visit them. It was also about this time that another young signal rating and myself became friendly. When he suggested that I should write to his cousin in London, I agreed, and after some period of delay and waiting I duly wrote to the young lady. After some weeks' waiting, I received a reply from the young lady and a good correspondence quickly developed. It was shortly after the first letter arrived from this young lady that I was selected for the course for leading signalman. This was the ultimate or so I thought, so that I went into the swotting as never before. In the meantime also, I had been in touch with the schoolmaster that we had on board, and it was agreed that I should attend the classes for eventual promotion to Warrant Rank. This meant taking certain stipulated subjects such as Navigation, Mathematics, English, General Knowledge, History and Geography. With the possibility of doing the leading signalman's course, I devoted most of my time to the signal side, but reserved a couple of mornings each week to the school work. By the summer when the squadron returned to Malta, I was posted to the signal school at Fort Verdala, the same place as before, and with much the same routines, except that now, the whole course was more intensified. For six whole weeks, we again lived and slept signals, so that by the time the exams came one's mind was one constant whirl. As before, all the examining officers were specialists in their particular field of signals, and these officers were headed by the Fleet Signals Officer, "Lord Louis," who was a Lieutenant Commander at that time. He would personally vet all results. Again, it was a very impatient wait for the results for much depended on this examination. Yes, I made the grade, as a result of which, by having passed, I became what was known as a V.S.3. or Signalman 3rd Class and would be paid as such, but not as a Leading Signalman, yet. That grade came a good bit later after a couple of years' patient waiting. Whatever one did or achieved, by way of examinations one was always rewarded by some increase of pay, even if it were only a few coppers. This examination gave me the equivalent of just over 1 penny a day, or near enough 10p per week. Those were the days, or were they? Through all this seemingly endless study and examination period, I continued to correspond with the young lady, just informative and newsy letters of pen friends, and it was to be nearly two years before I eventually met her. Time passed very quickly and soon it would be time again for paying off and our going home. Counting the time that I had done on the *Calypso* and the *Ceres*, it amounted to just over three years' foreign service with just a short break before I recommissioned the *Ceres*, hardly any comparison with the length of foreign service that is done today. Of course there are many factors today that make for such differences, and I suppose that it is a little bit of jealousy that make for resentment, at the more human treatment that all the services today experience.

In the late autumn of that year, *Ceres* nosed her way home so that I wrote to the young lady, Eileen, that we should soon be arriving home at Chatham and could we please meet somewhere in London on the date that I would be going on leave. Not knowing London very well at that time, I suggested that we met under the clock at Liverpool Street Station. Eileen agreed to this, and as we had exchanged photographs I knew who to look for. As arranged we met and moved to a restaurant for tea where we chatted for about two hours as I had to catch the train Home, having arranged another meeting some few days later. So the letters became more frequent and perhaps a little more personal. It was during that leave that I told Mother about the friend, so that she wrote to the young lady and invited her to stay with us for the weekend. This was agreed to, so that I duly made the trip to London and met Eileen at Liverpool Street Station to escort her home. It was some time later when again Eileen came to visit Ipswich that I had several days' leave and was able to show her round the district. From then on everything went extremely well. It is sufficient here to say that romance blossomed until eventually the young lady became my wife, but that is advancing a bit too far.

With the end of my leave, I returned to Chatham Barracks, where by a little "string pulling" I managed to get to the signal office for a posting. Here I was working with other signalmen on a twenty-four hour watch system, so that being near London, I visited the young lady when off-duty. The meetings invariably took place in London where the young lady worked near Cannon Street Station. Before long I was making Plumstead, where Eileen lived, my second home, or it could just as easily have been my first home. By the spring, Eileen and myself were by now firm friends and spoke of engagement so that in the May of that year, we became engaged to be married.

H.M.S RAMILLIES AND VALIANT

For some several months this happy state lasted until My Lords of the Admiralty decided that they would soon have to commission the battleship *Ramillies* that was refitting at Devonport Dockyard. By now I had been home some fifteen months so that I expected a posting at almost anytime. This was about the general time that one spent at home between foreign service commissions, so that I was not surprised when I was informed that Fred was for *H.M.S. Ramillies* and that I was to report for further instructions. The essence of these instructions was that I should report to *Ramillies* at Devonport in a few weeks' time. This was not the good news that I had hoped for, so as ever, one just goes where one is sent. The same applied to a couple of other signalmen who were to accompany me to the battleship at Devonport. Packing our kit bags and hammocks we entrained for Plymouth and after a long exhausting journey we arrived in the evening just in time for supper at the Naval Barracks Devonport. Hurriedly we settled in and made it known to those concerned that we were for *Ramillies* as were several other naval ratings that were already in the barracks. The next morning we were marched with the others out to the ship which was berthed near the river and alongside the dockyard. I suppose that it took about fifteen minutes to walk (march) out to the ship each time so there would be ample exercise. In the ship's signal office, a telephone connected the ship to the shore telephone system and it would be our job to start getting the signal logs and files in working order. Between ourselves we suggested that it would be better if we could sleep on board, particularly as the barracks were a bit crowded, and that we would at least be ready and on our working positions. Whether we proved good talkers or our logic was most persuasive, I do not know, except that our request was approved. From then on, we did not have to march to and from the barracks as we arranged that we should be there in good time for all our meals. In fact we did not really want a lot to do with the barracks routines, so that our leave was entirely up to us to arrange, so long as one of us was always available. If money permitted, two of us would make the trip to London at the weekend where by means of a little "juggling" we would arrive about four o'clock on the Friday afternoon. Then we would catch the midnight mail train back on the Sunday night arriving at Plymouth about six in the morning and walk to the ship, having enjoyed the benefits of weekend leave. However the date for the commissioning was eventually made known, but this would not be for another three or four weeks. During this time, we had been joined by another signalman whom we used to call Cabbage who was quite a scatter brain for he did the wildest things imaginable. One of our favourite pastimes in the evenings was to go on a "rat hunt" for there were several on board. From somewhere Cabbage produced a length of rubber covered cable, about two foot long and about an inch and a half in diameter. This was to be used as a cosh for hitting the rats, as they would usually run along the overhead fittings. At some vantage point, Cabbage would hit out at the animal which, if hit, would squeal wildly as it fell from overhead, to be immediately clubbed by Cabbage. That was good fun until one evening, Cabbage being on his own, decided that he would go on his own rat hunt. During this hunt, he must have struck some obstruction, causing the cosh to rebound back and hit himself. This was only realised when about 2100 when we should have found Cabbage busy in the office, we arrived to find NO Cabbage present. Putting our best detective brains to work we decided that we should look for Cabbage as we guessed that he would probably be ratting. After descending several decks we eventually found Cabbage laid out on the floor with a whacking big bump on his forehead where the cosh had caught him. On another occasion, Cabbage was known to slide from the "Fighting Director Top" about half way up the foremast, down the triatic stay, this runs from the foremast to the upper deck, just to prove that it could be done in a hurry. He was also a keen opportunist, for while we were discovering our way about the ship, Cabbage discovered that if one put a circle in chalk and placed in the circle the diameter, the drillers when they came round with their equipment would drill a hole that size in the metal work. Getting the idea that this could be to his advantage, he organised several of these holes to be drilled so that he could install positions for his Hammock to be slung. This was good until Cabbage thought that it would be a great idea to have a ready billet, just forward of the flag deck, ready for when we reached the sunny climes of Malta. The driller did his job as he came round, or at least tried to but unfortunately, he was attempting to drill into about eight inches of armoured plating. No wonder the man was puzzled as to why the drill would only make a small impression. Cabbage was a great guy who volunteered for the submarine service, and I believe that some years later Cabbage was lost when the submarine he was serving in, was sunk somewhere in the Baltic. I pass these comments so that one may realise that even the thoughts of serving abroad for two years or more did not always dampen one's sense of humour, as I am sure that nobody in the navy, unless of lunatic tendencies, would relish the thoughts of being away from home and all that it implies. Most sailors accepted this as part of their life and was included in the pay that they received. With commissioning completed, the ship stored and provisioned, a few days' leave was granted to some of the crew that had joined early. This was greatly enjoyed by those who had the leave and was taken in good heart by those that had been at Chatham having leave while others were on board the ship at Devonport. The day for sailing approached and the ship was moved to the Plymouth Sound for ammunitioning which took several days. This was because the huge shells for the 15 inch guns weighed approximately one ton each and had to be handled carefully. Not that there was fear of explosion, but rather that if one of these monsters broke loose, several people could be severely injured. While this part of the ammunitioning was in progress, other munitions were also being taken on board and the obtaining of the cordite containers were the explosive problems. No smoking was the law as were the wearing of rubber soled shoes or plimsolls. Smoking would only be permitted when all the ammunition had been stuck down to the magazines and locked away for the night. Although most sailors were smokers, I never heard of any of them breaking the rules for obvious reasons, they themselves would have been included in any casualty list. Not a very pleasant thought perhaps, but a thought that was always present on these occasions. Soon the ship had left Plymouth and the Eddystone Lighthouse far behind as we made our way again for the Mediterranean and "the land of hells bells and rotten smells" as the sailors termed Malta. The weather on the trip to Gib. was grand and while on duty one morning, we received a distress call stating that a merchant ship, was on fire somewhere to the south of us and not that far away. Soon the blue sky was tinted with columns of black smoke and before the hour was out, we were in sight of the burning vessel, being hull down on the horizon. As we approached we were able to see her signal letters flying from the halyards of the triatic stay. She was also flying the signal to state that she was not under control. The Captain and some of the Officers held a hurried conference the result of which depended on the vessels needs. Fire fighting crews were organised and equipment brought to the ready on deck. As we approached the ship, *S.S. Methilhill*, we signalled her to ask what assistance she needed. To our astonishment the reply was, "none, thank you." In reply to our asking what cargo she was carrying, the answer came back, "Esparto grass." This caused a hurried attack on the signal books where we found that her cargo would be used in paper making. It seems that the fire was caused by spontaneous combustion of the cargo which had some dampness or water in the hold. Such are the hazards caused by paper making requirements. Viewing the burning ship, from the safety of our signal deck, I felt more than pleased that I was not on board *Methilhill*, although I must admit that nobody on board her seemed to be unduly worried. It was possibly of some great assurance to know there were ships standing by in the near vicinity, as two more merchant vessels had now arrived on the scene. Even though we were about half a mile from her on the windward side, one could feel the heat and could also smell the acrid smoke from her burning cargo. We learned later, that she was helped into one of the ports of Portugal by a tug that had come out to her. I have a feeling that the merchant skipper was reluctant to accept help for fear of involving salvage money. Once a line is passed on to a ship under these circumstances, salvage claims are started and can involve considerable sums of money. *Ramillies* being on the main shipping lanes to Gib. and the African Ports, considered that the *Methilhill* was adequately assisted and, signalling to all ships present that we were resuming our journey we altered course to the south and soon left the burning ship behind. This action, I think was taken in view of it becoming dark and the burning vessel was clearly visible for many miles. There was very little fear of another vessel running into her through not seeing her.

Again the grand weather made it a pleasure to walk the deck during the evening recreational hours. Here we were entertained almost all day every day, by schools of dolphins and whales of which there seemed to be an abundance. The dolphins in particular would play and tumble in front of the bows, and yet never seemed to harm themselves. Of the whales, I am not sure of the species, for they were certainly fairly large creatures and they would dive and surface for air, sometimes quite near the ship. The only snag with the whales entertaining us was, that when they surfaced and "blew" near the ship, there would be an awful smell for some considerable time afterwards. However, there were several fishing boats in the area, so we assumed that the whales and dolphins were sharing the food for which the fishermen were after.

Pressing on, we again soon altered course to the eastwards and soon were to pass Cape Trafalgar. This time the Captain ordered the Royal Marine Band and the Guard to parade so that full honours were given to the memory of the dead of that battle. Each Captain will decide what he will do in this matter and some have been known to hold a short service and even drop a wreath over the side. The next morning, Gibraltar itself was in sight and silhouetted against the rising sun. All was made ready for entering harbour and the usual salutes would be fired. By the time we had secured to the detached mole, the normal berth for ships that are "working up," it was long gone time for colours and the usual morning ceremonies. As ever the signal staff were kept busy reporting the endless stream of dignitaries that came on board. These would include military and diplomatic officers of varying ranks. When one talks of military ranks, this is a very broad term, for it included Naval and Air Force Officers as well, while other officers would be grouped under diplomatic and consular authorities. If there were foreign Officers, these also had to be placed in their correct order. Even though we were in Gibraltar, and many of the dignitaries were already catered for by the Flag Officer Gibraltar, that did not absolve any ship from giving the proper respects to those concerned. Woe betide the signal staff if one of these persons slipped past the ship or worse still, came on board without being observed by the duty signal staff. These ceremonies were something of a nightmare in foreign harbours of some importance, where many of these officials were accommodated. While much of these ceremonies were being carried out, the proposed "working up" programme would be discussed and arrangements made by the various officers of the ship, which would take at least six weeks. In the meantime the normal daily routine would continue. As the date was mid-June 1934 every person on the ship would be in white tropical rig, unless of course doing dirty work like attending to engines etc. The following morning started with the ceremony of "Colours" which is the normal ceremony for hoisting the colours at 0800 daily. The signal ratings having the "forenoon" watch would be required to be ready to parade at 0745 when they would prepare and lace on the ensign and jack to the staffs. This is rather an intricate job ensuring that the ensign and jack will go to the top of the staff without bellying in the wind. All preparations would be completed by 0755 when the signal, "Prepare for Colours" would be hoisted in the flagship. At that, the signalman would report, "Five minutes to colours sir." In the meantime the marine guards and band would have completed their marching and counter marching and would be facing the ensign. At the signal from the flagship, the signalman would call, "Colours sir." At this the colour party (signalmen) would unfasten the ensign from its straps at the ensign staff, no touching the ground for this, the guard would be ordered to present arms and the band would play the National Anthem. Should there be foreign warships present, then the anthem of that nation would follow ours. All this would be quite impressive and spectacular, but, if there were several foreign Naval ships present it would be a long and even very long programme. I have known there to be as many as eighteen to twenty national anthems played at these ceremonies, and that takes quite a time if one assumes only four minutes per anthem. Once the Guard is called to attention, there is no further movement until the "carry on" is sounded. For those that consider this is nothing, may I suggest that they try standing perfectly still for only a quarter of an hour. I wish them luck in their endeavours. With the ceremony completed the guards and band will march off the deck with all the pomp and ceremony possible, while the signalman will hasten to take over his watch which should have commenced at 0800. Here, one could expect to hear subdued murmurs of, "What a load of bull." Call it what you will, but I defy anyone to stand through such a ceremony without feeling that little tingle of pride that unconsciously arises in one's body, especially when the whole ceremony is carried out with punctilious precision, as is done by the Royal Marines.

The normal "work up" programme would be carried out in a similar manner to that described for other ships with the main difference being, there would be two batteries of six inch guns to be fired and also the eight, fifteen inch guns. For this, there would be two B.P.T.s instead of the one as before, remembering that each battery of six inch guns was more than the number of guns carried by *Ceres* or *Calypso*. The whole if fired together with the fifteen inch guns would possibly dispose of some ten tons of shells. This could and does cause the whole ship to move bodily sideways through the water for several feet. Before firing such a weight of shells, the ship would fire one turret at a time, that is, two fifteen inch guns at the same time. It was while doing such a shoot on the *Ramillies* that I was on duty in the Signal Distributing Office, (S.D.O.), that we were tensed for the roar and rumble. When the guns fired, there was a bang in the office so that we thought that there had been a misfire or such like. This was followed by an almighty roar of rushing water, and the next moment we were wading knee deep in salt water. The first thing that we thought, was that we were exercising "Fire drills" and that somebody had forgotten to tell us about it. It is a well known thing that in an emergency whole compartments of the ship can be flooded at the press of a button. We need not have bothered for within minutes the Damage and Control Parties were crowding the office to block a water main that had broken under the strain of the firing, as the main had broken at a joint where it had flexed to the power of the explosion. Needless to say, by the time it was repaired, there were many wet shirts in the office. Oh yes, it caused a good laugh afterwards. One thing that did evolve from this mishap, was that the whole ship was warned to "always expect the unexpected" and in a way that became the ship's unofficial motto. On another occasion, during a day shoot of the fifteen inch guns, I was on duty on the flag deck when the guns fired. Apart from the smoke and flash the most striking thing that some of us noticed was, that we could actually see the flight of the huge shells from just after the shells left the guns. Provided that one stood almost directly behind the gun, one could see this phenomenon whenever the guns were fired. This fact was much later established, as was the fact that one could observe the shells coming if just off the flight line of the shells. Whether the gunnery experts realised this, I have no idea but, it was a point worth remembering. The only snag with standing near the guns was, one usually got enveloped in cordite smoke and the stink of explosive. There seemed to be so much that was surprising particularly the night shoot of the big guns. Extreme care would be taken to ensure that everything went according to plan. All hands would previously have gone to "Action Stations", as for the real thing, so that when all was ready, the only warning that one might get would be the "ting ting," just like the bus conductor's signal for the driver of the bus to move on. The small tinny "ting ting" would be immediately followed by the shock of the guns being fired. If one had been smart, a wad of cotton wool would have been screwed into the ears to take the initial noise. No such things as ear defenders in those days as it was not readily realised that one could speedily become deaf against gunfire noises. This small point, was only too apparent by the increase in one's volume of speech. With the guns being fired, a temporary blindness would afflict one, but this would only last for a few seconds before one returned to normal sight or anything resembling that state. Witnessing these glimpses of scenes from Dante's Inferno, I was determined that one day I would witness the firings from the inside of the turret. Years were to pass before that happened. With all the firings and the inspections over, we returned to harbour for the night, knowing that on replenishing fuel and stores the next day, *Ramillies* was now ready to join the squadron that we assumed waited for us at Malta. At approximately 0730, before the "colours" ceremony, *Ramillies* left her berth and headed eastwards into the Mediterranean for Malta. The voyage en route was not a pleasure cruise as may be imagined by many, but it was a repetition of the many exercises and drills that we had already undergone with many additional ones as well. Each evening about 1600, (4 p.m.), such drills as stopping to rescue a man overboard, or rig the ship for paravanes. All these drills would be completed against stop watch timing, until everybody could more or less do the job blindfolded, and possibly somebody else's. All this exercising carried on even after we had joined the squadron. If anything, it intensified as with the squadron in company, there was always the competitive feeling that one must be the best in the squadron.

We had just about reached the peak of efficiency, by the new year, 1935, when rumour and gossip went through the ship that there was to be a big fleet review at Spithead in the coming summer. Hardly a day passed but that one heard of confirmation and denial of this event, or whether or not *Ramillies* would be there. Then, with the coming spring cruise and the combined fleet exercises rumours became more persistent that *Ramillies* would be at the Review. To counter this, there was the fact that only months ago, *Ramillies* had sailed fully expecting to complete the 2½ year commission. From the combined fleet's exercises we sailed as usual, for the Med. spring cruise, when we should visit various French ports. Returning to Malta after these places seemed very dull, especially for the signal staff, who daily did their exercises. Within a few days, we heard on fairly good authority, that we should be going home for the fleet's review at Spithead to celebrate the Jubilee of King George the Fifth and that this event would take place in July. This would also mean endless scrubbing, polishing and cleaning until the proverbial specks of dirt were banished. For about two weeks more the "clean ship" routine was paramount, then it was homeward bound. The weather during the trip home was glorious and all hours not on duty were spent in developing a good suntan. On arrival at Spithead, we assumed the billet that we should occupy for the review, which was third in line, behind *Queen Elizabeth* and *Royal Sovereign* to be followed by *Revenge, Resolution* and finally by the battle cruisers *Hood* and *Renown.* Each day following would find more ships arriving from all over the world. Ships from the China Station, India, Australia and New Zealand and the West Indies. Between the arrival of these ships, there would be ships still arriving from almost every Navy in the world. Some would seem a little ancient, while others were even more modern than some of our own ships. The ships of Germany were of outstanding beauty for ships, and looked most efficient. Here one found that at "colours ceremony" each morning the number of foreign anthems grew daily, until as mentioned earlier, there were eighteen to twenty foreign men of war of different nationalities. This meant about an hour was taken up by the "ceremony of colours." Even so, there was never a moment when something of intense interest was not happening and in which the signal staffs were all on their mettle. There were always boats passing with admirals of some sort on board, and these HAD to be saluted with the appropriate salutes, be it gun or musical fanfare. The royal yacht *Victoria and Albert* arrived a couple of days before the review, and took up her berth just ahead and to port of the *Queen Elizabeth.* I would like to point out to the reader here, that the *Queen Elizabeth* does NOT refer to the merchant liner of that name but to the battleship. The liner *Q.E.* was not then in being and it would be another four years before she would be completed. The day before the review, the royal yacht *V & A* moved into the harbour at Portsmouth alongside South Railway Jetty so that Their Majesties could walk from the train to the *V & A.* They would then proceed out to the fleet for the review. The yacht itself passed down the starboard side of the line of battleships and down the lines alternately allowing the maximum coverage for the inspection, the whole of which lasted some two hours or more. On completion, the usual signal for these occasions was made to the fleet, "Splice Mainbrace," so that those sailors in the fleet that had elected to draw their rum received an extra issue. For those that did not draw the rum ration, they each received a glass of lime juice. The rum issue was withdrawn from the Navy some years later, much to the dismay and disgust of many of the old timers, for no matter what is said, good or bad, about the issue, future events would prove its value.

However, with the completion of the review and the dispersal of the ships, another great surprise awaited the *Ramillies*. She was ordered alongside in the dockyard, just astern of the battleship *Valiant*, and here, we were to exchange ships completely. This meant for us, the ship's company, a lot of hard work, for although we were both battleships, there the similarity ended for we were of a different class of ship. For several days it must have appeared to the casual observer that the navy had gone mad, and the appearance was like that of an ants' nest having been disturbed by a playful schoolboy. Eventually things straightened themselves out and both vessels became ships of the Navy again. For the review there were about two hundred ships present and I think that it must have been the largest number of ships of the Royal Navy to be assembled except for perhaps the occasion of the surrender of the German fleet at the end of the First World War. This total of ships was later to be exceeded by some ten to fifteen times that amount but not for some years and under completely different circumstances. To return to the *Valiant* to which ship I was now assigned, we were each given a few days' leave before sailing again for the Mediterranean, for we still had some twenty months to do, to complete our commission. I believe that I am correct in saying that this was the first time in modern Naval history that two capital ships had exchanged crews in the middle of a foreign service commission.

Although we stayed at Gib. on the way back, it was only a quick visit with no working up to do. I expect that the powers that be considered the crew of *Valiant* was already in a high state of efficiency. Quickly the ship's company settled themselves down to the routine that we all knew so well. At about this time, the population of Palestine decided that they were being unfairly treated by each other, so that the result was that Arab and Jew came into conflict with each other over this matter. I have a nasty feeling that the Lords of the Admiralty had already decided to let "Fred" sort these things out for by early 1936 the *Valiant* was sent to Haifa (Palestine) to protect British interests and property. The trouble had been brewing for some time before we arrived, so that with the usual Navy manner, platoons of sailors and marines were landed to take over many strategic points. This also included the driving of the armoured trains and being readily available to stamp out bother in such places as the Jordan Valley and other check points. On several occasions I attended lectures on the overall subject of Palestine as it was then called. From what I gathered, these troubles had been in existence since just after the end of the First World War when the legendary figure of T.E. Lawrence was operating with the peace keeping forces of the allies. Almost daily it was a question of somebody somewhere, being ambushed and shot up by the opposing side. How so much like today's problems as both sides declared their right to the land. Daily one would hear of school kiddies and young women or girls being involved in bombing or shooting incidents and for carrying arms when on their normal shopping runs. The poor British sailor and marine took the brunt of all the arguments; truly a "piggy in the middle." During the quiet spells, it was customary to spend the relaxation time bathing in the sea from the harbour wall for there was very little else that one could do unless one had an armed escort. This situation lasted some several months and it was during one such period that I learned that I had been promoted to Leading Signalman. Not that it really mattered, apart from the extra pay of course, as I had been doing the duties for some time. This meant as far as I was concerned, that I should be leaving the ship which is usual when one is promoted. However, I was retained on board and no reasons were given. This suited me immensely, for I knew everybody on board especially the senior officers and I suspect that they may have had some hand in the matter. Many of them offered their congratulations on my promotion which was quite gratifying. Perhaps as I had been an assistant editor of the ship's daily newsheet, it may have helped to persuade them in keeping me. On the ship being relieved by another, we returned to Malta to replenish provisions and stores and then were off again. This time it would be to Alexandria.

I think that we only stayed a few days there before we were again shunted on to Haifa as events had again changed from semi-peace to open hostilities. Soon, they got fed up with the monotony of being hostile to each other and an uneasy period of peace ensued. During this period of so-called peace, as many as possible of the crew were permitted to visit some of the places of interest that we had been trying to look after. The only thing was, that we had to go in organised parties and with a guard as escort. On this trip we visited Jerusalem, Gethsemane, the Mount of Olives, the Church of the Holy Sepulchre and the Sea of Galilee. Being given a guided tour one could not help but compare the guide's stories with what one had learned at school. Most of it compared favourably and rang true to teaching, but there did seem many unanswered discrepancies. If one questioned too closely the answers given, one would be told that it was all due to the misinterpretation of the ancient scriptures. Who was there amongst us to dispute such philosophy, which in any case was the answers given by the guides. For all that, it was most interesting to experience, and one that I would not have missed. I do not wish to discuss here the facts or fiction of the guide's stories other than what has already been said; like most stories, they have been handed down from generation to generation, and one must interpret the stories as best suited one's individual beliefs. I understand, that today tourists are given almost identical stories to those which we were told. After this, the *Valiant* sailed for Port Said where we were to act as guardship for the canal and its traffic. The reason for this was, that the Italians were getting very aggressive towards Ethiopia at the far end of the Red Sea.

Day after day, we had to make detailed reports of all vessels entering or leaving the Canal, what type of deck cargoes, an estimate of whether fully loaded or otherwise, and an estimate of the numbers of troops if any were on board and a description of the badges if it were possible to gather the information. Some may remark that it was rather like spying on one's neighbours, but that was the job we had to do. During this spell of duty, I was loaned to the Port Authority Signal Station that stands at the head of the Canal, (Suez). Here one learned of many small things that would assist the authorities in assessing the attitude of Italy, for much of the traffic was destined for Italian Somaliland next to Ethiopia. For several weeks we enjoyed our lone vigil of the canal and it gave us a good opportunity to study the local folk. It was at Port Said one day when I was enjoying a cup of coffee in a local cafe when an elderly native suggested the he cleaned my shoes. This is the old trick, of being in a position where they can grab one's trousers, produce a razor blade from apparently open space and then threaten to cut one's trousers if "bucksheesh" or cigarettes were not immediately forthcoming. Naturally, I was very wary of this ploy, so I determined that if this was to be the case, I would in the ensuing bother, tip the marble topped table onto him. I need not have worried for he was quite genuine, so that I gave him a few pence for the shoe clean. It was then that he mentioned to me that I had recently received promotion and that soon, I would be making a very fast journey to a far away place. He also told me of some other things that have since come true in almost every detail. Giving the old man a few more coppers, I thanked him and went on my way, little dreaming of the dramatic events that were to follow, after I had returned permanently to the ship. It must be remembered that the Suez Canal was jointly owned by the British and Egyptians and, that at a moment's notice the canal could have been closed to all traffic. That is probably one of the reasons that *Valiant* was so handy for the entrance. Again it was thought necessary to move the ship back to our temporary base at Alexandria, where to our surprise the bigger part of the Med Fleet had mustered due to the impending trouble with Italy. This was not very long in coming, for with very little official warning, Italy declared war on Abyssinia (Ethiopia), with the intention of making it part of their new found empire.

ITALY'S WAR: AUSONIA

One morning, quite early, about 0700, a large Italian liner was seen approaching the harbour, and just before the colours ceremony. Being on watch, it was my duty to see that the ensign and jack were all ready for the 0800 parade. It was also my duty to see that the ensign was readily available for dipping to merchant vessels, even before the Ensign had been paraded. With these facts in mind I dispatched a young signal rating to the ensign staff so as to perform this task. This was not needed for the Italian slowed down considerably and the colours ceremony went ahead as routine. We could now see the name of the Italian ship quite plainly, AUSONIA was easily readable without the aid of telescope. Just as the Ausonia got abreast the fleet flagship, a large booming explosion came from the Italian. Immediately flames spread along the cabins and before long the whole ship was ablaze from stem to stern. Since she was visibly carrying civilians, we thought tourists, all ships were standing by for rescue operations, for word of the disaster had rapidly gone through the fleet. Had the *Ausonia* with the explosion, happened a few minutes earlier, there was grave concern that the fleet could have been bottled in the harbour for several days. I understand that the explosion occurred in the engine room and was purely an accident. Suggest that to any sailor that was present and one would be awarded with a very large "horse laugh," no matter what the Italian official reason was. As it was, the *Ausonia*, was grounded just clear of the exit channels to the harbour, much to the relief of the Admiral in charge of the fleet. The ship eventually became a complete wreck and lay in a position of absolute dejection for several months. I do not think that the real reason for the explosion was ever found out, which in many ways was a real pity for the *Ausonia* was one of Italy's modern ships. The Italian - Ethiopian War did not last very long, as Italy with superior forces and aircraft, rapidly overcame any resistance offered by the ill equipped Ethiopians who had little or no aircraft and very few modern weapons. While the countries of the League of Nations dithered over the affair, the Italians completed and secured their conquest. The Emperor of Ethiopia, "Haile Salasie," (I apologise if I have spelt it wrongly); and family were later taken to Britain for accommodation and were exiled for several years. There is no telling just what may have happened had the *Ausonia* explosion happened in the exit channels close by *Queen Elizabeth*. It would have taken many days to clear a passage for the fleet, during which time, the fleet could have suffered intense aerial bombardment and possible fleet bombardment, for the Italians had the ships and aircraft if they had needed them. No doubt the diplomatic communication channels were well and truly overworked as a result of this ship disaster. Whether as a result of this "accident" or not, *Valiant* was again dispatched to Port Said for the supervision of the canal traffic. Most of the Italian traffic went through at night after having made the journey during the day, when just deck cargo was visible. At the north end of the canal, two large arc lights had been installed, so that when the ships entered the canal at night, any troops on board would come on deck to take the air. It would be a common sight to see three or four transports passing into the canal, as though in convoy, with scores or perhaps hundreds of troops enjoying the cool night air. All this information was noted as before, and there must have been thousands of troops, hundreds of aircraft, tanks and guns. During this latter spell at Port Said, the cruiser *Emerald* made a hurried passage through the canal from south to north, having on board the Emperor and his family. I said the cruiser *Emerald*, it may have been another of that class, but *Emerald* was known to be in the vicinity at that time. Shortly after this the ship returned to Alexandria again.

It was here that I learned from the Commander of the ship that my mother was seriously ill. It was somewhere around 2100 that this news was given to me and Commander Glover asked if I had the means of getting home. To this I replied that I was a member of the Ship's Emergency Passage Fund, which catered for such events. It had probably been some sixth sense that had prompted me to join the scheme when we first commissioned. The idea of the fund was that members paid a small subscription from their pay each month. This would be kept in a special fund by the paymaster and, in any emergency such as my own, the fare home would be met by the fund. It was certainly a good idea, for one usually had the resources of the ship and her officers behind one. In my own case the Commander arranged for the issue of a passport through the consular authorities, he also arranged the passage and fares so that in roughly forty-eight flours I was on my way, having experienced no bother, apart from posing for a passport photograph. Two days after seeing the Commander I boarded the French *S.S. Champolion* bound for Marseilles where I should catch the train for Dieppe via Paris. From Dieppe, I caught the cross channel ferry to Newhaven and thence to Chatham barracks, my home port. Reporting there early in the morning, and presenting the papers that had been supplied on the ship, I was, with very little delay, sent on two weeks' leave with instructions to report to barracks as affairs progressed. Wasting no time, I arrived home just a week after having first visited the Commander.

This probably does not seem a very remarkable achievement by today's standards of travel but, then there was no air travel for the average person and then I think that the longest journey would have been London/Paris. All this happened in the June of 1936. Arriving home, it was agreed that I should sit by mother during the nights, as I should be able to sleep at daytime, while sister Win and any others of the family, should split the daylight hours of looking after Mother. During the night watches I took up as a hobby, rug making, and surprisingly enough, in the time that I was home, some four weeks, I managed to complete the rug. One other important thing that I should mention. Having told the young lady of my unexpected homecoming, and the reason for it, I arranged for Eileen to visit my home for a few days. Where she and myself became engaged. Mother was very pleased at this news and Eileen and myself spent quite many hours chatting with mother about various things. It was also here during the quiet night watches that Mother told me of much about her childhood and early years. Mother died on 14th July and was buried in the Ipswich Cemetery after a simple funeral which was carried out to her wishes. Again, I reported to the Chatham barracks where after a few days I was sent to Devonport to join a cruiser on passage to rejoin the *Valiant*. To my surprise, the ship that I was joining was the *Curacoa* the flagship of the old Third Cruiser Squadron that I had left some couple of years ago.

The disadvantage of joining a ship as a passenger is that nobody really wants much to do with one, except to make an extra hand for working and cleaning the ship. This is understandable, for passengers cannot really be considered when making out the various stations such as action, abandon ship, damage and control, with many other minor requirements, as the ship organisers cannot count on the person being in the ship when the need arises. As a consequence of this, I was used as a kind of general dogsbody in the signal department. By the time we arrived at Gib. for the cruiser's working up period, I had almost forgotten what it was like to be a signal rating and the powers that be realised that in me they had a ready made answer to their problems of supplying a signalman to the tug during the shoots. Hey presto! That person was me. Little did they realise that I rather enjoyed that sort of job. There again, was a small snag, for I had no old clothing with me so that I was allowed to purchase from the stores an overall suit to wear on the tug. Things then went along grandly, for was I not helping them out? During that stay in Gib., one morning when nothing much was arranged for me, I was surprised to see coming round the Europa Point, (a promontory at the seaward end of GIB), an older type of battleship, escorted by a fairly modern cruiser. Our surprise did not rest there, for they were both flying the Spanish colours. The battleship was definitely established as *Jaimie I* and the cruiser was one of the Lepanto class. No, they did not enter Gibraltar harbour but made tracks straight for La Linea, the Spanish town just across the Bay. I estimate that when the ships were about three miles off town, they suddenly opened fire. It was not until the shells burst in the town itself, that we realised that this was something entirely off the cards. The shelling continued for about half an hour, with little or no opposition from the La Linean people. Yes, it was the beginning of the Spanish, "Franco Civil War," which was to last for a few more years yet, and, as usual the sailor and the Navy would become involved, although it was to be some considerable time before I personally became involved.

At the time, I was much too engrossed in wanting to get back to the *Valiant*, where all my belongings were, to be over interested in other people's squabbles. Eventually we arrived at Malta after all the usual working up trials. This would have put us into the month of October or early November, so that we were not surprised to find that the bulk of the Fleet, including *Valiant* were in harbour. Without making any official signals, I let it be known that Fred had returned to roost in the *Valiant*. This is easily done, ask any signalman that is worth his salt, and he will communicate by what is termed "the short arm method" of semaphore to any other known bunting tosser, (Signalman), and he will make at such speed that all except a bunting tosser will be left in a daze. I managed to catch the eye of the fellows on watch in the *Valiant*, and it was not an hour later that a boat was sent to collect me. The real reason, was that *Valiant* was now a leading signalman short, through sickness, and that Fred was required. With grateful thanks for the ride, I said farewell to the signal staff of *Curacoa* and journeyed home to *Valiant*, where I was more than welcomed. Rumours were already going round that *Valiant* was due to pay off sometime in the year 1936, but this at the moment was all high in the air and with little substance. I rather think that somebody was getting their facts twisted, for without warning, the rumours changed to, "*Valiant* will pay off in the year 1937." In fact the fleet was again under orders for a review at Spithead, but not just yet. In the meantime it was back to the old routine of daily signal exercises and of going to sea on odd occasions for gunnery, torpedo and paravane drills. At the end of 1936, *Valiant* was told officially that she was to go home for pay off. By early December *Valiant* made her way towards Gibraltar and home, where we arrived in the January. This movement caused a mild panic in the ship's company and there was much letter writing and telegraming to various young ladies at home, arranging weddings and all that went with those arrangements. Banns had to be called and such similar matters, such as dressmakers and tailors, receptions to arrange. The calling of the banns also included my own which were read on board the ship, the last reading being while the ship was at sea on the way home, between Malta and Gibraltar.

With the arrival of the ship in Plymouth, there was much work to be done for the ship had to be emptied of all ammunition and stores before going alongside in Devonport Dockyard. They do say "as busy as beavers." I have never seen beavers at work, so I would suggest that the saying be altered to "Let the beavers see the Navy at work," for I am sure that they would be able to learn a few tricks.

The big date for our wedding was February 6th 1937, when Eileen and myself were married in the local church at Plumstead, Kent. Fortunately for us we had made good friends with the builder of a small estate at Bexleyheath Kent. Having paid a deposit of £25, on the semi-detached house of our choice, we approached the building society for a mortgage. Here we were informed in no uncertain terms that the society did NOT make house loans to service personnel. Dejectedly we returned to our builder friend, (Mr Grubb) and explained the story of our loan refusal. Telling us to leave the matter with him, it was just a question of waiting and being patient. Mr Grubb met us next day, all smiles, and told us in a few words that he had arranged the whole mortgage transfer. Briefly it meant that he would stand as part guarantor for us and he would put up the necessary extra cash for the loan. Within a few days before the wedding, all transactions were completed and we took possession of the house, number 5 Winchelsea Avenue. There would be no honeymoon, for with the little furniture we could afford and the repayments on the mortgage, there was a strange absence of working capital. As was the case, nothing mattered but that we had our house and we were married. Our ages were just twenty-four, quite old for some of today's couples. It did mean, that although we were legally married, we were not officially recognised by the Admiralty as being old enough, and no marriage allowance was available. This meant very careful budgeting for everything, at least for another twelve months when we should be eligible for the Admiralty Marriage Allowance at the age of twenty-five, or in other words in 1938. For the time being stringent economy was the order of the day.

FLEET REVIEW; SCOUT

On 10th March to be precise I was drafted to the *Scout*, an old destroyer from the First World War. This had its compensations, for she was based at Chatham, and would belong to the Chatham Defence Flotilla. This meant that each day, she would sail as required from Chatham and return each night. Also the weekends were from Friday evening until Monday morning. For these occasions, I would cycle home each night and return to Chatham in the mornings for the ship would normally sail about 0830. As a little point of interest, the cycle cost £3 brand new, a three speed gear machine that eventually did me great service. The distance from Bexleyheath to Chatham was just over twenty-four miles each way, and for the first few days it was a tremendous effort. By the end of the third week, I was really into my stride and was making the trip in about one-and-three-quarter hours, depending on the weather conditions. Yes, I was in great form physically, and before long I was finding that I was able to devote some spare time to the garden and other household chores, for the financial state of affairs required that Eileen carried on working. It was a case of helping out wherever possible even if it meant getting home and starting on the washing straight away. No such things for us as washing machines, but we did have a gas copper, which was supplied with the house, and proved a great help. No such spare jobs as stoking up the copper fire and cleaning away afterwards. We were quite happy to accept the situation as it was, for we knew that whatever we attained we should have to work for. Another little point of interest, the house that we had purchased cost £550 with repayments of approximately £3 per month. That was a lot of money in those days, at least for us, and this in today's money would be about £36.00. We managed, for I would invariably cycle to Chatham with two pence in my pocket in case of necessity. The two pence would usually be in the pocket at the beginning of the next week, ad infinitum.

One of the duties of the *Scout* was to sail from Chatham to Shotley once each month, to act as sea training ship for the senior boys classes. Somebody in authority must have been psychic, or at least very far seeing, as later events soon proved. While on one of these trips to "Ganges," I was surprised to find that one of the instructors that came on board was one of our Yeoman of Signals from the *Valiant*. All signals were placed in abeyance while we two reviewed old times in the *Valiant*, and of sharing my tot at the appropriate time. It was also when we returned from one of the local trips one day, that, making my way home by cycle I was overtaken by a Fyffes banana lorry. Having overtaken me, the driver pulled in to the side of the road and beckoned me to climb on board. On this particular road, there was only two places that he could pass through to suit me. One being Dartford and the other being Bexley. Either of these would suit me fine so with a smile of pleasure, I almost threw the cycle on to the lorry and climbed in beside the driver. The first question he asked, was for my destination so that on telling him Bexleyheath, he suggested that I got off at Danson Park. Since Danson Park was only five minutes riding time from home, I readily agreed. Almost like getting on a tram or bus. On arrival at Danson Park, the driver helped me down with the cycle and at the same time presented me with a stalk of large green bananas telling me to wrap them up in a towel in a dark place or drawer so that they would soon ripen. This we did, and shortly the bananas helped to supplement our daily fare and the weekly budget. Of course the local neighbouring kiddies benefited to some extent from the lorry driver's kindness. Unfortunately I never did see the gentleman again for I was quite prepared to offer him cigarettes in exchange for more bananas. With the lorry lifts that used to happen, one just took a chance with the destination of the lorry as one could not ask the driver to make detours in his route. After all, I had the cycle and was prepared to cycle the whole distance, but any lift of any distance was thankfully accepted. The tour of duty on the *Scout* did not last for long, at least for me. Soon I was recalled to Barracks for drafting to the *Skipjack*, a fleet minesweeper of the Fist Minesweeping Flotilla.

SKIPJACK; SPAIN'S WAR

The *Skipjack*, a vessel of some 700 tons displacement, was berthed at the Dockyard in Chatham, having been undergoing repairs and refitting for further service in the flotilla. At first I felt disappointed in the change of ships, knowing that it meant an end to the almost unrestricted leave that I had been getting. However, on reporting on board the Skipjack I found that I was the senior signal rating and would be in charge of the staff such as it was, two signalmen. After I had met them, I found to my delight that they had both been on the ship for some time before the refit, and consequently knew something of the routines and signals appertaining to minesweeping. I must point out here that although when one passes an examination for higher rating, one gets a smattering of the signals used in different types of ships, but the intricacies of the particular types of signals have to be learned on the job. For instance an aircraft carrier uses certain signals that are only applicable to carriers, while minesweepers have their own particular codes. By having two signalmen that presumably knew the job, it would make a short cut in my obtaining the necessary knowledge required, for once the ship is under way only the rating on the bridge is responsible for knowing the signals made, and some captains can be short of patience when signals are made. The two signalmen gave me a quick crash course on what was required. This meant learning many new and strange terms connected purely with minesweeping of which I had little previous knowledge. Such terms as kites, oropesas, floats, dan buoys, and arming of sweeps, all added to the temporary and mind boggling confusion, for they are peculiar to sweeping vessels only. In this, it should be explained that in the event of any war, minesweeping would be done by many smaller vessels such as fishing trawlers and they would consequently have many of their own signals. To return to *Skipjack*, which was only about half the size and tonnage of a destroyer, would have no protection from bomb or shells of any size, her top speed would be just over fifteen or sixteen knots and her maximum draft would be in the region of seven feet. Not a very stable ship in any sort of seaway. Her captain, whom I should be seeing plenty of, was a Lieutenant Commander, a

Navy rugby player of some repute, standing over six feet and from appearances just as broad. Certainly not a person to argue with at any time either on or off the rugby field. The ship's armament consisted of one 3 inch H.A. gun mounted on the forecastle, (pronounced FOLKSAL), that deck where the anchors and cables are worked. This term originated from the old days when ships had a castellated tower at each end, hence forecastle and after castle, (abbreviated FXLE). There were also on board a couple of machine guns (antiquated) and a supply of half a dozen rifles. These latter were chiefly used for exploding any mines that we swept up particularly in war time. Oh, yes, we did have some practice at that and it's not so easy as it looks. Of course lots of the practices that we got were only on dummy mines that in any case would not explode. In all the crew numbered some seventy plus persons which included the four officers, and the whole were really one happy family. No such thing as union rules, for if a job wanted doing one just got on and did it. If expert knowledge as required, one just helped the expert where one could. The leave that I enjoyed here was similar to that which I enjoyed in the *Scout*. Here also I had the benefit of finishing work at 1600 daily when I would cycle home and back in the morning. It was then that a leading torpedoman made himself known to me and as he lived at Dartford, we had company each morning and evening. This person and I would usually meet at Dartford just after 0500 and it then became a convoy run to Chatham so as to be on board by 0730. Funnily enough, the weather never seemed to hold us up, so the weather clerk must have been sympathetic towards us. This was certainly early morning exercise for the trip had to be completed in uniform. Civilian clothes were not yet allowed to ratings. One had to leave and arrive at the ship or barracks in uniform and an inspection followed each occasion. It appears that today, the old disciplines have deserted the Services, for one has only to stand outside any Army or Naval barracks to witness the comings and goings of the unkempt looking service people entering and leaving the barracks.

All this spell of leave came to an end much sooner than was hoped for, as we were ordered to sail in company with *HMS Harrier* for Weymouth which was to become the home base of the First Minesweeping Flotilla. From here, we daily were at sea exercising getting in and out sweeps (nicknamed Brooms), and taking up different sweeping formations. In this flotilla, there were eight ships, all of the same class and design, so that we were organised into two divisions and four sub-divisions, each of two ships. This meant that each sub-division would form a pair for most of the minesweeping formations, or when actually doing any sweeping. If a pair of ships were required to act as mine laying vessels then the sub-division was normally detailed as a complete unit. In the course of time, I got to know Portland and Weymouth quite well especially from the seaward side, and it was not very long before I was able to anticipate most of the signal requirements both in sweeping and in the signal sense. One point that I will make here; although all officers of the Navy have some knowledge of signals, depending on their personal interest in the subject, it is usually left to the wisdom or otherwise, of the senior signal rating, to advise the captain and the necessary officers of the contents and meaning if necessary of any signal made. One has only to stand on the bridge for a short period during manoeuvres to realise that the signal rating is an integral and important member of the bridge staff. Although it may sound like a bit of "own trumpet blowing," most captains will accept precisely what the senior signal rating tells them of the signal interpretation. Very seldom is this trust betrayed and most certainly NEVER intentionally. I have only ever experienced one exception to this statement. That was by the renowned Lord Louis Mountbatten when he was a captain, he being an old Signal Officer, would more often than not read the signals himself. That however did not absolve the Chief Yeoman from reporting the signal to him in the usual manner.

But, back to *Skipjack*. The flotilla having worked itself up to a frenzy of efficiency we returned to Chatham for summer leave. This passed without incident and we again returned to Portland, forming the flotilla as before. Now, it was off to Scotland and the Kyles of Bute where we would exercise sweeping and laying mines for all we were worth. These practices would be done with dummy mines which would later be swept up and recovered for further use. During these trials and practices, we would encounter several whales or basking sharks, which would if caught in the sweeps, inform their chums most loudly in whale language, that they were in trouble. This would set of the alarm signal on board so that we would assume that there was a mine in the sweeps. At the ship slowing almost to a stop, the unfortunate whale would either free itself, or its pals would surface near the ship and "BLOW." If the freeing efforts should prove unsuccessful, the other whales would BUMP the ship in their annoyance. It would be then, that one would hear the whales crying their anger and frustration at being so treated by these foreigners in their home grounds. These creatures were enormous being some fifty feet long, and weighing anything, we estimated, up to thirty or forty tons. These estimates were only really guess work, as the rough size would be estimated and this would be converted into tons displacement using meat weight from the store as a means of calculations. All this was done by one of the officers who had an interest in all sea life, and for the remainder of the ship's company, I would suppose it was a matter of passing interest. I got the impression at times that these creatures were playing games with us, for at times they appeared to lead us to the places where the mines had been laid by some other ship. Most of the time, it was a question of putting up with the intense fishy smell of the whales, especially when they "BLEW" or came to the surface and slapped their sail-like tails on the surface near the ship, giving everybody on the upper decks a good wash down and showerbath. This event was particularly noticeable if the ship had stopped to clear the sweeps or get in kites which would take several minutes. When this happened, it seemed that the whales would surface and appear to laugh at our discomfort. That could have been their natural expression. When I remark that the whales playfully did these things, I am probably very wrong, but that is how it appeared to me and several others on board. No doubt the oceanic scientists or the whaling experts can explain this in a few simple words, and although I have since read numerous books from libraries, I can still find little explanation for the whale's conduct. When we were the acting mine layer, there were no restrictions placed on the actual laying for it would be done out of sight of the sweepers. The only restriction was that we laid the mines in a specific area. Everybody else would then try to find the elusive needle (mine) in the hay stack, (specified sea area). The successful recovery of the dummy mines would depend largely on the craftiness of the ship laying the mines, which was quite entitled to use any ruse to prevent the quick recovery.

Little did we realise at the time, that all the successes of the laying and sweeping mines would soon be put to more grim uses. Before passing from the Kyles of Bute, I must comment on the grand beauty of the entire landscape. Many of these comments could equally apply to the friendliness of the local inhabitants, who whenever we had occasion to set foot on their domain, gave us the most cordial of welcomes. In a way, it was all like a working holiday. As we are told, "all good things must come to an end" so that we eventually returned to Portland for storing and leave.

On return from leave, I was informed that I had been recommended and selected for the signal course at *Victory* for the rating of V.S.2. Should I pass this, it would mean an increase of sixpence, (two-and-a-half pence), per day on my pay as well as meaning that I had passed for Petty Officer and Yeoman of Signals. It did not take long for me to spread the news and almost daily I would expect to be called to *Victory* at Portsmouth for the signals course. There were however, quite a few days and incidents before I was to get to the signal school of the World. Early in the New Year, Skipjack with most of the flotilla was ordered to Gibraltar to help form part of the International Non-intervention Patrol that was being established there. This was because there were many countries trying to "cash in" on the Spanish Civil War, where anything that may have been of use to or assist one side or the other, could be used to some cash advantage. Such dealings would make a very profitable cash benefit for some ship owners. Not much knowledge of anything like this was available to any ship of the patrol, for never before had there been anything like an International Force trying to maintain peaceful commerce. One just had to learn the hard way and by experience, so like on all those occasions, one learned very quickly indeed. Arriving at Gibraltar, we were informed of our patrol areas. Being small ships and of shallow draft, we were ordered to patrol from Algerciras to Guardelquiver in the west, at the entrance to the river that leads to Seville. Up and down this stretch of water, just outside territorial waters all the time, as the Insurgents (Spanish) would let one know in a most unfriendly and unceremonious manner if one got too close to their territory. As I have previously commented, the sailor and the Navy got involved, not voluntarily, and soon many Navy ships were patrolling, and were evacuating civilians from the many trouble spots. A couple of incidents will display the Navy's versatility.

One of the small ships evacuating refugees, took on board several women and children for passage to safety. In accordance with orders, the numbers of evacuees were signalled to the Flag Officer Gib., who was in charge of the operation. This was to allow for the preparations for their arrival to be made in good time. Somewhere en route to the designated port of arrival, the ship concerned made an additional signal referring to her previous message giving the number and details of the refugees, "Please add two more." This when investigated turned out to be that some of the women on board were in a pregnant state, and that two of their number had produced additional offspring during the journey. It was quite a common sight during some of the patrols to see sailors playing nursemaid to several young children, and even changing the nappies. These latter would be supplied by the crew buying towels and cutting them into suitable size squares. That is why at times in later years, one would find a Spanish adult with a name closely resembling the name of a Navy ship that rescued them during this period of civil war.

Another little incident, not like the previous one, that happened to us while patrolling our area near Huelva, during the night. A darkened ship, totally blacked out, was seen making towards the estuary. Immediately the signal was made asking, "What ship?" No reply was forthcoming. Again the signal was made and still no reply. This was too much for the Captain, for the vessel was quite a large one, so that he ordered our only gun to be loaded with blank ammunition. At the same time I was instructed to make the signal, "HEAVE TO OR I WILL OPEN FIRE." No sooner had I made the signal than back came the reply, "This is German warship *Deutschland*." To this our captain ordered the signal "Thank you, goodnight." This was how some of the nations did their patrolling in the non-intervention area, for without further signals she entered the river bound for Huelva. No wonder there were people like "Potato Jones" a merchant skipper, taking immense risks to get their cargoes to those that paid them most. He, Potato Jones, became quite an outstanding figure during the Spanish Civil War, particularly on the Bilbao coast, and at one time there was a considerable price on his head. Eventually, General Franco's forces ably assisted by various non-belligerents overcame the opposing forces and Spain became a republic, after the destruction and ruination of many towns and villages and countless casualties. Soon, *Skipjack* was ordered home, and during the trip, the Captain would do a standing morning watch, 0400 to 0800, there being only three officers on board apart from the Engineer Officer. Since the signal staff were similarly situated I also did the standing morning watch. As the Captain had obviously read my personal documents, he would have to sign them each year, he allowed me to perform some of the officer of the watch duties as I had passed the initial navigation exams. Always while on watch with the Captain, I would be under his supervision and guidance. This practice was quite common in small ships as it gave many prospective officers the chance to improve their knowledge of navigation and ship handling. In short for a few days on the trip home, I thoroughly enjoyed myself.

H.M.S. VICTORY & VINDICTIVE

After our arrival in Chatham, we were pleasantly surprised to learn that for our troubles and trials of being in a small ship, we should be awarded what was termed "hard layers money." That was another sixpence a day as some form of compensation for the missing comforts and amenities of larger ships. I was also to hear of my drafting to the signal school *Victory* at Portsmouth. Once again we should eat, sleep and breathe signals, where even going to the toilet was signalled as "pump ship or bilges." This incidentally is a genuine signal from one of the naval codes of signalling. The course at Victory was very intensive and no let up in studies was permitted by any person on the course. During all this, there was one redeeming feature, that was, we were permitted each Saturday noon to proceed on weekend leave until the Monday morning. This meant that I would return from home on the midnight train on Sunday evenings as the instruction started at 0800 promptly. Once each month, we were permitted a long weekend from 1630 on the Friday, when the signal for "disperse" would be given by the instructor. One just had to know all the more common signals in use in the Navy. The train that we returned to Portsmouth by, would be the mail and paper train, going on a very circuitous route so as to cover all the outlying villages, and would arrive at Portsmouth somewhere about 0430 in the morning, where a friendly porter would go round and rouse all sailors from their slumbers. Most of the sailors would leave a couple of pence on the seats for his troubles.

It was while on this course that I met another leading signalman, Jock Strachan, pronounced Strawn, who although being a first class signalman, was the wit and comic of the class. If ever a comic cum prankster-cum-tormenter, was permitted to join the R.N., then those honours must go to Jock. One of our studies was to individually represent destroyers screening ships of the fleet against submarine attacks. For this we were spread across the parade ground in an inverted V formation. As we were signalled to advance Jock immediately started to chant "Bingggg- Boooooppp." Chaos reigned for just at moment when we were signalled to stop by the bewildered instructor, who wanted to know just who the idiot was. Jock straightaway stepped forward and informed the instructor, that if he represented a ship on an anti-submarine sweep, he must at least work his asdic gear and that the "Binngg Booopp" was the bridge repeater gear signifying that the asdic gear was working. As Jock explained, this note would change if submarine contact was made. Jock had just left a modern destroyer that was so fitted with this equipment. Needless to say, the duty signals officer who had been watching wanted to know what the bother was about. Explanations followed, and soon the senior signals officers of the school were in attendance, listening to Jock's detailed explanations, to which they all agreed. Unfortunately, Jock's idea was not accepted, as being too noisy and distracting to other signal classes on the parade ground. This was after a full scale demonstration by our class of about twenty leading signalmen. On another occasion, during an advanced coding session, when we were in individual cubicles, we were transmitting messages for the benefit of other classes. After some minutes into the lesson, we were all astounded to hear that a ship had been severely bitten by a love bug in its rear section. For a breathing space only, there was silence then complete uproar. Everybody wanted to know who the practical joker was. Jock again rose very nobly to the occasion when he explained that the message should be interpreted as, "Have been severely damaged by explosion in the rear section or stern compartments," which sounded reasonable. He also explained that the signal had been para-phrased in case of interception by the enemy. Well done Jock. There were quite a few more such hilarious jokes of which he was the instigator. For the moment, enough of Jock and his methods of signalling in the lighter vein, which really did enlighten the many days of hard studying. The course lasted just over twelve weeks during which there had been no let up, so that it was with considerable relief that we finished the last exam. These examinations were supervised, conducted, and marked by long course qualified signal officers, who gave no marks away for any reason, knowing that someday, it may be their misfortune to be "saddled" with an inefficient person that they had allowed to pass the examination. That theory was predominant throughout the communication branch of the Navy. There was no use pleading an attack of examination nerves, one was not expected to have nerves. That was probably why so many Yeomen and Chief Yeomen usually stand their ground when discussing signals. One could not adopt the attitude that one could bluff one's way through a signal exam, for the bluff would be called in a very short time. With the end of the course and the examinations, we and our instructors had a party of celebration, which did us all credit, so that we eventually bid each other farewell and good luck for the future. Little did we know that soon many of us would need that good luck. One thing I would remark upon, that during the exams each candidate would be called upon to give a lecture on a subject agreed by the Senior Signal Officer. If one was lucky, one might get an hour's warning to prepare for one's lecture which would be addressed to the class and an audience of all signal officers. No two candidates would be given the same subject, so that one could not purloin even a few phrases from another lecturer. The lecture or talk, would normally be scheduled for twenty minutes duration after which one was expected to answer any questions raised by the audience. If the speaker knew his subject, the talk might be cut, but still the questioning and cross questioning.

Returning to Chatham, after a few days of peace and quiet, if being in Jock's company, could be called quiet, Jock and I decided that we should endeavour to complete the school work necessary for officer rank. I did not realise until on the train back to Chatham, that Jock was of the same division as myself. Daily we would haunt the signal school for any possible news of our exam results from *Victory*. In the meantime we made our acquaintance with the School Master Officer, who was none other than our old teacher at Shotley, Mr Middleton. As I had already completed some subjects, a couple of additional subjects would not come amiss, or making an improvement on previous subjects. Schooly was of course delighted to see and have us. I have a feeling that we could have been his star pupils, for he was already talking about us taking the London University Examinations. All these pipe dreams were suddenly brought to naught, for within a few weeks I was posted to *H.M.S. Vindictive*, the cadet officers training cruiser, while Jock was posted to another ship in the Home Fleet. Before I lost sight of Jock, he did manage to offer me his congratulations at having passed the V.S.2 signal examinations, the same as himself. Where he got the information from is anybody's guess. This was great news, for it meant that we were both in line for promotion. I did not hear officially that I had passed until I got to the *Vindictive* some days later.

The *Vindictive* being based at Chatham and in the dockyard, was quite easy to get to, so that I hurriedly got my gear to the ship and was briefed for my duties. These would involve giving certain instructions to the officer cadets and for helping maintain the signal traffic in the ship. In other words, it was to involve a little bit of all things. Not that I minded, for although we should be cruising most of the year, all the staff would be getting leave at Easter, mid-summer and Christmas plus any extra time spent in dockyard. The cadets themselves came from Dartmouth Naval College at each of the leave periods. The senior entry of cadets would leave the ship at the end of their third term, so that it was a continually changing population over the course of twelve months. Although it was a cadet officer training ship, the cadets had by no means an easy life, which was probably based on the training of the boys at "Ganges". Each morning the cadets would be called at 0600 and would be scrubbing decks by 0630 in all but very bad weather, and at most times, it would be in bare feet. Cadets would go to breakfast at 0800 and by 0900 they would be parading, ready for the day's instructions and work involved in the running of the ship, signals, navigation, gunnery, electrics and engine room duties. In fact the cadets had to do all sorts of duties, no matter what their chosen category, and this included the work normally done by seamen. The cadets were always under supervision the same as any one under training. Punishment for the cadets was also meted out by the Captain and the First Lieutenant. It was quite a common sight to see a cadet sitting up the mast as a punishment for some minor offence: cadets had quite a tough time while on the *Vindictive*. Amongst the cadets were the sons of admirals and generals, nobility and princes, some of them from the Commonwealth and foreign countries. The cadets were generally a fair section of the officer classes and many were to become admirals themselves in the years to come, whilst most of them would distinguish themselves in the not too far distant future. One of the more notable of the cadets was Prince Philip of Greece, now H.R.H. Prince Philip Duke of Edinburgh. For the cruises, it would usually be to the West Indies for the spring cruise, the Med. and the Baltic for the other two cruises. Here the cadets would indulge in plenty of boatwork and boat sailing plus any other of the multitudinous pastimes enjoyed by young officers of the Navy. All the cruises would be arranged well in advance by the Admiralty, as most of the places visited by the ship were either politically or diplomatically associated with the welfare and the careers of the cadets in mind. Under no circumstances must one think that the naval cadets were wrapped in cotton wool, for I rather suspect that most of the instructors would treat the cadets as they had been treated at Ganges if it were at all possible. These cruises were a very pleasant interlude for the Naval crew and it certainly gave us Naval ratings a good insight into the intense training that Officers in the making went through. I think that as training, it compared most favourably with the training that we had received at Shotley, although obviously there were many differences. During the spell on *Vindictive*, we survived the war scare of 1938 when Britain and Germany almost went to war. That episode did blow over, but from that moment on, the training of everybody in the Navy went ahead with far greater intensity than ever. That autumn, since we should have gone on the Baltic Cruise, this was cancelled, owing to the international situation. The ship cruised instead in home waters so that we returned to Chatham a little early. At Chatham we gave Christmas leave and in the New Year sailed for the West Indies. Here, we visited such places as Tortuga, Kingston Jamaica and many other places. At each place visited, the ship would be inundated with gifts of oranges, grapefruit and bananas by the local population. This was possibly some of the residue of the kindly feelings that the natives have for the British Navy. It must be remembered that it was just over a century ago that Nelson had his base in these islands, and that it had been from these islands that the Naval TOT had been instituted in appreciation for the services rendered by the Navy. It should also be remembered that the Navy had played an important part in helping to end slavery. In short, the cruises were always intensified history lessons if one cared to take the trouble to pay attention to the local historians. Another event that we enjoyed on this cruise was the catching of very large crayfish from the clear water of the rock pools. All one had to do, was obtain a large forked stick, search the pools until the prey was spotted, then a quick lunge, and the crayfish was caught in the cleft of the stick. The only difficulty now was to remove the Crayfish from the forked stick without getting one's finger badly bruised in the process. The crayfish, some as big as two feet long, would slap his bony tail over the offensive hand. A slap on the fingers at school was just a tickle compared with the unexpected whack of this tail. This was overcome by wearing a stout leather glove to remove the Crayfish from the fork. The natives also taught us to kill clean and cook the creatures which when cooked by our chums (the cooks) were most delicious and made a grand tea or supper.

Before I get too far ahead of myself, I must comment that while in Antigua (West Indies) I heard the good news that my wife (Eileen) had given birth to a son and that both were progressing well. Keith was born on 19th May 1939. Rumours were in the air that Mr Hitler was being troublesome in the Baltic State of Poland. Everything suddenly went from rosy red to black. This time the war scare was not expected to pass over, so that defences were hastily being constructed in all manner of places. In the parks and fields, even in people's gardens there were signs of intense activity and preparation; for what? Everybody was guessing what might and what might not happen. Trenches were being dug, sandbags by the thousand were being filled, air raid shelters were being hastily constructed. There was even talk of gas masks being issued. Needless to say, we again arrived home early in *Vindictive* for she was not a warship in the true sense of the word, but rather a floating school or collection of classrooms.

Soon it was home and special leave again, and then at the end of May, due to the threatening international situation, (Mr Hitler again), the summer cruise was greatly curtailed so that by mid-June we were back in Chatham. Here the ship was unexpectedly taken out of commission and to be sailed to Devonport for refitting. All cadets were distributed to the various ships of the fleet as were most of the crew, but leaving just a skeleton crew on board to take the ship to Devonport. Here incidentally I was the senior signal rating on board and there was much work to be done. In the event of trouble, the *Vindictive* would have been a liability with little or no armament. Destoring and de-ammunitioning was carried out at full-speed so that nobody in the ship was excused. The de-commissioning went ahead at a very fast pace. Somebody wanted us back in Chatham barracks in a hurry. I suspect that it must have been the drafting authorities, as every day that passed, saw ships of all sorts commissioning. Any of our stores that could reasonably be disposed of were given to any of the ships that cared to collect them. I only hoped that when the time came for me to get another ship, some other ship's yeoman would be as generous to me as we had been, for having been the cadet training ship, we had quite a lot of what were termed consumable stores. With the clearing of the ship and placing her into Dockyard Control, the few remaining of old *Vindictive*'s crew, returned to Chatham barracks for further drafting.

JOB NO. 535

As I was already a Petty Officer, I was accommodated in the P.O.'s Mess, which meant that I was permitted to go ashore if not required for duty. This I quickly did, for I had left my cycle at the Sailor's Rest, and to my relief and pleasure I found that the cycle was still there and that nothing had been removed. Without more ado, I cycled home to Bexleyheath and returned the next morning for the 0730 musters. No company to share the trip this time and no friendly lorry driver to assist with the journey. On return to barracks I was informed that I should report to the drafting office at 0900. This sounded most ominous. The normal custom was for a messenger to deliver the draft order, with the indication that it was for several days ahead. From this information, it was obvious that I had been earmarked for some ship, so that I was left with many unanswered questions. Hurriedly completing my breakfast, I cleaned myself up and reported to the drafting office well before the time required. This was just as well for I was able to glean from the office staff that I was being drafted to Job Number 535 building on the Clyde. So, it was to be a new ship, but what sort was anybody's guess, and nobody could tell me. Perhaps it was that they really could not, as job numbers were only given to ships that had NO name, or were waiting to be named. Was this to be one of the mystery ships that one heard of being rumoured round the barracks? Although I asked everywhere possible for information, regarding Job 535, I was unable to glean any knowledge other than some remarks like, "you must have volunteered." These kind of remarks only proved that which I already guessed, "they just did not know." All that they could tell me was that it was a ship, and this I already knew. I returned to the mess in case I should be required at any time. I also ascertained that I could go on ordinary night leave until the date was known, when further instructions would be available. It was while in the mess that I met again, friend Jock who had also been promoted to P.O. I also enlisted his aid in trying to find some information regarding Job 535. After all Jock was a Scot and he may have had friends on the Clyde or even in the Drafting Office. This state of affairs lasted several days during which Jock agreed to do any duty that might be allocated to me, so that I could get home. As we both said, there would be no duties for me as I was officially nominated for Job 535. Sounds like one of those "X class railway engines." Jock informed me one evening that he was duty P.O., and that if I arrived in time in the morning, he would arrange for my breakfast rather than for me to wait in the mess.

That morning, I duly arrived as usual, before time, and Jock had as promised, arranged for my breakfast. Before accompanying me to breakfast, Jock suggested that I went with him to call the ratings, and this I did. Before calling anybody, Jock lead me to a hammock in which was a young signal rating. He was uncovered, it being quite warm and his legs were draped one each side of his hammock. Without more ado, Jock unwrapped the small parcel that he was carrying and placed the contents between the lad's legs. The contents I noted, were the intestines of a rabbit that the cooks had been preparing for the day's meal. Jock then promptly called the ratings to get moving; then going back to the young signalman, he shook his hammock so that he woke up. In his best Highland dialect, Jock drew his attention to the mess between his legs, remarking at the same time that he had previously on several occasions warned him that if he slept like that, his insides would drop out. Filled with alarm, the lad asked Jock just what he should do. With a perfectly straight face Jock replied, "just push them back." Coward that I am, I vanished before I burst out laughing, while Jock calmly offered the lad a pencil to assist in the probably impossible task. Jock returned with me to the mess, and we suspected that it would not be too long before his laughing chums told him of the joke promoted by Jock. One could not help liking Jock, even though some of his pranks were sometimes a little "off beat" so to speak. Shortly after this event, I was called to the drafting office one afternoon and was told that I would be joining my ship the next day. This meant that I should leave barracks that evening to get to the Clyde by the following morning, as for all that anybody knew, the ship could be sailing almost at once. That is called a "pier head jump" in anybody's language. I did manage to obtain leave for an hour or so to get my cycle to the Chatham Sailor's Rest for safe keeping. I also tried to get off a note to the wife to inform her of the latest movements but I was unlucky, so that I should have to try on the journey to the Clyde. Any telephone booths that were passed en route seemed to be out of order, so that there was just time to catch the night train to Glasgow, where I arrived in the early hours of the morning and reported to the R.T.O., (Rail Transport Officer). The post offices were as yet unopened, and again the telephone booths were seemingly out of order. This may have been intentional on the part of the telephone company or by orders of the government to prevent troop movements etc., being given over the telephone, security in all aspects being the watchword. I was here told that as it was just 0700 I could get a breakfast at the forces hostel close by and that there would be transport going to Job 535 at about 0800. Again I enquired as to the type of ship that was Job 535, and again all I was told was that it was building at Govan Shipyard by Messers Fairfield. This was a little helpful and hopeful as it seemed that I should at least have time to get off some sort of letter before we sailed, if indeed we were sailing that day.

MY ADDRESS: - Job 535

C/O GPO LONDON.

I can readily imagine any woman's feelings at getting a letter from somewhere called Job 535. It would be an immediate case for the hospital treatment of shock at having suddenly taken a convict number 535 for a husband. However, arriving at Fairfields Shipyard at Govan, I duly reported to the Contractors Office, where a kindly elderly gent of typical Scottish origin escorted me round the ship yard until we came to a grey painted hull that to me appeared to have a certain beauty and purpose included in her lines. As she was not equipped with guns or torpedo tubes, just having the bridge works and the funnel (one) in place, she certainly gave one the impression of speed and business like proportions. "There," he told me, "is your Job 535." To my question of what the name of the vessel was he pointed to another much larger ship of two funnels that I would have classed as a merchant liner, saying, "that is Job 534, and like yours she ain't got a name yet." My apologies for not being able to write it in the dialect of the Scots, but it took me some little time to interpret his meaning. It was not until a while later when I met some more of the crew of the 535 that I fully comprehended just what I had been told, for Job 534 was destined to become quite famous. I certainly found that during the stay at Govan, the Scot in general is a most likeable character and also quite generous in spite of tales to the contrary. Most of those tales are jokes, and more than likely are the tales of meanness of Scots about themselves and by themselves.

Meeting the staff of 535 was quite an experience, for like me, they were some of the crew of an anonymous ship, and each one represented the head of each department of that ship. In addition, this was to be my first ship as a Yeoman of Signals so that I would have nobody that I could turn to for advice regarding signal matters. In the normal way, there would be the Squadron or Flotilla Signal Officer to offer advice or assistance, so that since we had no name or knowledge of what we were supposed to be, one just had to adapt to the idea that one's decisions could effect the well being of the ship until her identity became established and her name known.

For the moment, the most that I could gather was, the ship was a destroyer of the latest class. That, I could understand from her lines and construction, for her one funnel was elliptical and with a pronounced rake, a rather shortish mast forward, and with four gun mountings. Two of the mountings were already in place and waiting for the guns, which it was understood were shortly to be installed. With a couple of other P.O.s, we commented most favourably on her lines and anticipated with some pride and pleasure just what she would look like on completion. For the rest of that day, I was busy getting myself into some lodgings for there were no barracks or such like that could accommodate us. The lodgings that I eventually choose, were not too far from the shipyard and were sponsored by the contractors. The landlady was an elderly widow, a Mrs MacDougal, and the lodgings were not far from the Ibrox Park Football Ground. No doubt, I could have caught a tram to and from work in the yard, but decided against this as the walking would afford some valuable exercise at least. No, I was not trying to imitate the Scots of the jokes, but rather to continue my fairly good state of physical fitness.

The next morning, I reported early to the yard so that I might have a good look round the ship, (535), while all was fairly quiet, as some work had been progressed overnight. Yes, she certainly was to my liking, although it would have made little or no difference if it had been otherwise. She was being built for a real job, and not just to please Fred. While looking round, I encountered another P.O. from the Torpedo Department, and from him I learned that we should be equipped with TEN 21 inch torpedoes, being a bank of five each side. The P.O. turned out to be "Shiner Wright," who became a good friend from the start. I hope that I have the name correct because we also had another P.O. called Knight and it is quite possible that I could have mixed them up over the passing years. Together we wandered back to the office which was quite large, having to be used by about eighteen of us as our only office. My first real task was to travel to St Enoch's Hotel, which had been taken over by the Navy as a sort of local Admiralty, to collect some signals for the ship and some for the Navigating Officer with whom I should be working closely. The signals were already parcelled up and addressed to Job 535 so I was still no wiser with regard to the name of the ship.

For all that, I started as I had been taught, to get my signal logs working for these would be the correct record of the ship's movements and employment at future dates. It was while checking some of the signals and signal books that I noticed that Captain Mountbatten would be the Captain "D" of our newly formed flotilla. Carefully remembering this little tit bit, I spoke in due course to the First Lieutenant, (1st Lieut.), as opportunity offered. It was then that I was enlightened as to the name of our ship and also the name of the Captain that was appointed to our ship, for this information had previously been unknown to me. Also, the Captain would be arriving very shortly and he would enlighten me still further if he thought fit. The Captain did arrive a while later, while I was in the office with a couple of other C. & P.O.s. A tall person, well built, and with the looks of a disciplinarian. The First Lieut., (otherwise referred to as Jimmy or No 1), dependent on one's rank, introduced those present plus the only other officer, the Engineer Officer, as no other officers had as yet joined the ship, but were expected soon. The Captain with No. 1, then went on a tour of inspection of the ship, while the rest of us busied ourselves with our respective tasks, but mostly with discussing what the new Captain was like, if anyone knew him. Little was known that could help us assess the Captain, so that we just had to wait and see. Of course, it made little difference just what we thought, and to be absolutely correct, we should not even have discussed him. But, like all crew matters this was a matter of supreme importance, as this was the person that literally had the power of life and death over us, for on his decisions rested the ultimate safety and fate of the ship, and that meant us the crew.

Most of our time spent in the office, termed the Ship's Office, was in suggesting and studying the plans of the ship, for our respective departments, each one hoping that he could make some improvements. None of the improvements would be major ones that would effect the construction of the ship. Just minor items such as positioning of cupboards for signal books, repositioning lights, the best positions for the flag lockers and various little things that would add to the comforts of the crew and their living quarters. Just how these little differences made for comfort, we were to find out within a few weeks, and then with a vengeance. The passing of each day brought remarkable changes to the appearance of the ship as the workmen seemed to be working day and night to get the ship ready for sea. The crew was being augmented daily and very soon stores and all the impedimenta that goes to make a ship ready to play its part in the fleet, arrived, especially as we were rapidly nearing completion. The torpedo tubes and the guns were now in positions according to the plans. Ten torpedo tubes, five each side and the four twin guns really set the ship off . Soon it was to be all hands in overalls and paint ship a peculiar light grey. This was later to be called "moonlight grey," when the purposes of our duties were further known. It was during this preliminary painting of the ship that those of the crew that were there, were let into the secret of the ship's name. We were to be named after a national celebrity and a person from the Glasgow area, "Lord Kelvin." This person was much-better known in the sea going circles for his inventions which greatly assisted the navigation of all ships. In fact the local people thought that highly of him that they named a whole district of the city and the University after him. Thus was the ship, *H.M.S. Kelvin* born, without fuss, pomp, or parade. Some of that would come later, then the ship would be officially named at what would be termed the "reading in," when the Captain would officially take over the ship. In the meantime, it was on with the work of getting the ship completely ready for sea and trials. Due to the acute diplomatic state of Europe, no efforts were spared in this task, of being ready. This was especially so, when we received a message from Captain D 5, (Captain of 5th Destroyer Flotilla), giving us a brief indication of his expectations of the ships of the flotilla, together with the flotilla motto, "KEEP ON, KEEPING ON." Just what that implied we were to find out later on.

WAR DECLARED, PATROL

On Sunday 3rd September 1939, at 1100, when all was quiet on board, with only the crew's radio breaking the silence, it was announced by the Prime Minister, Mr Neville Chamberlain, that as Germany had not agreed to withdraw her invading forces from Poland, Great Britain was to be fully considered "AT WAR" with Germany. There was no joy over this dramatic announcement for one and all expected the worst. I remember recording in the signal log shortly after this announcement a signal received in plain language, "COMMENCE HOSTILITIES AGAINST GERMANY." This was a general signal to all naval ships in the world from Admiralty, I have put the wording in heavy type as these were the actual words used in the signal, and they still stand out in my memory. A very sombre bunch of fellows inhabited the office from that moment. We each had our own thoughts, and whatever they were, we were all well aware that much would now depend on ourselves. I heard later, that just after the announcement by the Prime Minister, the air raid sirens were sounded in earnest for the first time. Most folk went to the shelters as they had been instructed to do, but many stayed on the street just to see what would happen. Fortunately NOTHING did happen.

During the period at Govan, I did manage to get home for a couple of weekends, but with the price of fares and my home financial commitments there was not much spare cash to allow the luxuries of weekend leave. The greater part of the time in Govan was spent on board attending to getting the ship ready in all respects for war. The area round Govan was hardly the place to spend some hours of enjoyment for the area was typically a shipyard building area where the workmen of the shipyard would enjoy their glass of drink and then sweat it out for the next few hours. Tough people but great hearted. During some of the emergency storing etc of *Kelvin*, we would occasionally get some stores for Job No 534, whom we learned was the new Cunard liner *Queen Elizabeth*. When these stores were returned to the rightful ship, we were jokingly told that it was quite O.K., as we were being built from the odds and ends of the *Queen Elizabeth*. If that were so, then it was later proved that the odds and ends were of good material and that the workmanship of *Kelvin* was every bit as good as the *Q.E.*

It was also learned that the following ships would form the Fifth Flotilla under the command of Captain Mountbatten, *Kelly Kelvin Kashmere Kimberly Khartoum Kandahar Kipling* and *Kingston*. What an illustrious group of ships and led by an Officer who was a signalman at heart and in ability. These ships were soon to make themselves known to the public at large, and in particular the areas where they had been built, chiefly on the Tyne and in the Glasgow areas. Our sister flotilla were the "J" boats, being *Jupiter Javelin Jaguar* etc who had or were just completing just ahead of us. More of these ships later as they were eventually to intermingle with the "K" boats.

At last, with the full crew on board and everybody moving at great speed, the preliminary basin trials were completed successfully. It then became the accustomed thing to see an armed sentry at the gangway, and also to be stopped at the dock gates by a policeman checking one's identity. With the completion of the Basin trials, the ship was moved by tug to the river where further tests were carried out which included compass swinging and certain radar tests, although it was not then called radar but RDF. After that, it was time to take on ammunition and fuel and move to a buoy at Greenock, on the Clyde, a place that was called "Tail of the Bank." Here final checks were made and at 1100 the hands were piped to fall in aft and the Captain "read himself in" just as captains had done for centuries past. It informed one and all that the person reading the article informs all that he is in command by appointment of their Lords of the Admiralty. The actual document then refers to the Articles of War that are in reality the Captain's instructions for various actions that he may take under varying conditions. This was the first time that I had heard the Articles of War read with such seriousness of purpose. The parts that I had previously heard referred to such things as somebody being deprived of badge for overstaying leave. After this all hands returned to the work of ammunitioning and storing and of getting in the torpedoes which are quite cumbersome things. This meant that for several days the members of our mess saw very little of one another, each being busy with their own department. For us in the signal staff, of myself and a leading signalman and four, we were all to be at full stretch and extremely busy for now we had to be on the ball for every thing to do with the signal world. In all this turmoil, many high ranking officers of the dockyard and presumably the Admiralty came on board making their inspections. Then, with a completed crew and stores on board plus an unknown number (to me) of dockyard workmen and officials, we sailed for the "Tail of the Bank" just off Greenock. Here, all last minute checks and tests were made, to ensure perfection if that were possible, and away we sailed for the Combraes and Ailsa Craig where the trials would be carried out. Within a few minutes of leaving Greenock, the ship was doing about seventeen knots with the asdic gear already working. It was now that I realised just how good Jock had been with his imitation (Binggg Boop), for here it was, just as he had shown us. This was not just a show exhibition, for submarines had been reported in the area, and I don't mean friendly ones. In fact, the Royal Oak, a battleship, had been sunk in Scapa Flow only a few days earlier. We were taking no chances, and everything now was to be on a war footing. Off Ailsa Craig, we carried out gunnery and torpedo firings and also depth charge trials, where some half dozen depth charges were fired as tests. Having successfully completed these trials we returned to Greenock to replace the expended ammunition and to top up used stores. The next day was to be the turn of the engine room, for we were scheduled to do "full power" and "full speed trials." Leaving Greenock about 0915, we started to work up to full power and before very long were speeding along at almost thirty knots and still we increased speed by about one knot at each period of satisfaction. Soon we were making some 33 knots until with a whispered word to the engine room the Captain gave the order to go for full speed. With that the ship seemed to jump forward as speed increased. I suspect that we were in excess of the contractors' estimates, for there were many smiles and thumbs up from engineers and workmen alike. All the while that this trial was going on, we flew the appropriate flag, (a white flag with a blue swallow tail), to denote to other shipping to keep clear as we were doing speed trials. With that trial completed the captain made the signal to various authorities stating that H.M.S. Kelvin had been accepted into Admiralty Service. During this last trial of full speed, we twisted and turned until we were all confident that we had broken every piece of crockery on board, it's just as well that we had known of these turns and twists at high speed so that we had made the necessary arrangements for securing anything moveable in advance. As a little point of interest, while doing the speed trials we had reached and possibly passed the makers estimated speed and were doing about 45 M.P.H. or the equivalent of 36 knots. I mentioned that the ship would now be known as *H.M.S. KELVIN*. This is quite true but nobody ever wore a Kelvin Cap Ribbon until at least after the war, probably 1947 or even 48, as all ships were just simply known as H.M.S., at least to the general public.

From Greenock, we sailed for Portland to join the rest of the flotilla, at least, as we thought. It was not all that easy, for again we were given exercises to do and told to practice firings of gun and torpedo. After a couple of weeks' preparation we were sent to join the fleet at Scapa Flow. Again this was no easy matter for the fleet was on constant alert against another submarine attack, and being a very new boy so to speak, we were detailed for all the odd and so-called errand boy work. There was little time to spend in harbour for if it was not guarding the ships at sea it was anti-submarine patrol in the harbour. I do not know the exact records, but I feel sure that at no time while at Scapa did the ship revert to normal notice for steam. The powers that be, certainly meant us to earn our keep as there never was, and I suppose never will be enough destroyers in the Navy to meet the demands of the Navy, for escorts. However, time passed and we were sent to Greenock. Not for leave, that was a thing of the past; and the only people that got leave in those early days of the war were "survivors" from ships that had been lost. Then it was only for a few days until another ship was ready or a replacement was required for a dead man. At Greenock we refuelled and provisioned and were ordered to stand by at a berth near "Tail of the Bank." This was to be an escort job of which we would know nothing until we got to sea again. If I remember correctly there were to be five destroyers, under the command of one of the tribal class destroyers. As we neared Ailsa Craig, we were formed into an inverted "V" with the tribal in the centre, at point. This was a definite screen formation so that we guessed that before long the convoy would show up. Sure enough, just before dark, a huge shape was spotted astern making fair speed. Our speed was now reduced so that the shape could take station on us, which she did, somewhere about half a mile astern of the tribal destroyer and a little on our port quarter at about the same distance. From the shape of our convoy, I guessed her to be the new Cunard Liner *Queen Elizabeth*, and this was later confirmed both by the

Captain and at daylight when we could see her properly. Rounding the North Coast of Ireland we headed westward at about thirty knots. What a sight and one which I doubted would ever be repeated. This Liner of some 80,000 tons was heading westwards with five small destroyers keeping pace and station with her and at high speed. After some exchanges of signals with the *Tribal*, the *Queen Elizabeth* started to close on the *Tribal* so that the signal was made to increase speed to 32 knots. Again we intercepted some of the signals between *Q.E.* and the *Tribal*, and again we were signalled to 33 knots. This happened a couple more times, until eventually some of the older destroyers began to loose station, until soon it was only the *Tribal* and *Kelvin* anywhere near in their correct stations. Observing this, the *Queen Elizabeth*, while steaming at approximately 36 knots, made the following to us and the *Tribal*, "Thank you for your company, Good-bye and Good Luck." For a few moments longer we held our course and speed, as the Liner steamed away from us into the path of the setting sun. What her speed at that point was, I would not like to estimate but, from the moment of bidding us good-bye, she appeared to make further increases of speed. We learned later that the "Queen" had made a record run of the east to west crossing of the Atlantic, and had docked in New York there to be employed, with several other large fast liners for transporting troops round the world. I did not see or glimpse the *Q.E.* again until after the war ended some years later. Meanwhile the escorts reformed and headed back to the Clyde and Greenock. Arriving off Ailsa, we were informed of a submarine in the vicinity which should not have been there, and *Kelvin* was to investigate. On reaching the position of the supposed U-BOAT we dropped a couple of charges. Several times the operator reported contacts but each proved to be false but the search continued through the night. In the morning as we entered the Clyde, we picked up several dead bodies, all German, which we took on board for later handing over to the Authorities and burial in the local cemetery. It fell to volunteers to remove any papers etc that may have been on the bodies, under the supervision of an officer. Their identity discs were not removed as these would be required by the Red Cross organisations for informing the relatives. On arrival in harbour, a tender was already waiting for the bodies and I am sure that everybody was glad to see them go. This was not a question of hate or irreverence for the dead, but rather this was our first sight of the enemy and they were not a pleasant sight, as some of them were cut and bruised, possibly when they escaped from the U-Boat. As time went on, and we had got used to the sight of bodies, enemy and our own, we gradually became quite hardened to these things. Also, it was not going to be so very long before we saw our next dead. Just a matter of months. After an evening in harbour, we were ordered to proceed to sea again, this time heading south after clearing our familiar landmark of Ailsa Craig. Down through the Irish Channel with just a glimpse of the Isle of Man as we passed. Speed would have been about 22 knots. We were apparently off to Portland again to complete more trials. This break was to be short lived for we had received a signal telling us to proceed to a certain position in the Atlantic where a tanker had been torpedoed and was in need of assistance. Away we went again, life was certainly never tedious. For one thing, in that first winter of the war the weather at sea was atrocious, and it was often as much as one could do to stand up straight for a few moments. For those of us that had been in from the start, we certainly found our sea legs, this was because most of the crew were regular navy and had some experience somewhere of life at sea. We pushed on at best speed to find the tanker, just as it was getting dark. Yes, she was in a bad way, listing heavily and down by the bows, she had been hit forward on the starboard side. When asked what assistance was required she told us that she had had a fire on board and that there was a certain amount of gasoline on board which could have made things for her very interesting, if not disastrous. However, she also informed us that the fire was now out and that no assistance was required. Since we were not far off the local patrol boundary, we escorted her almost to the Ailsa Crag before leaving her to the care of the local escort trawlers, by the coming light of day. Immediately, we returned to Greenock to refuel etc at much better speed. Passing through the boom defences and taking up our assigned billet for oiling we noticed a wreck where we should normally have been. While taking on the oil, we learned that the wreck was that of a French destroyer. She had been on some operation and had been unloading one of her torpedo tubes, when for some unknown reason that we did not know, the torpedo had been fired from its tube, careered along the upper deck to explode aft, almost blowing the complete stern away. Being in harbour, various compartments would have been opened up, so that the waters of the harbour had just flooded the ship. It would seem that there had been many casualties amongst the French crew. This was quite an introduction to what the newspapers referred to as, "The Quiet War." This incident as far as I know, was never reported by the newspapers, or they would not have suggested "The quiet War." No sooner had we refuelled and reprovisioned, and with the expended depth charges replaced, we were soon off again on escort and patrol duties.

This time it was North and still we kept going. Hourly it became colder, and still the course was northwards, until with really freezing weather and huge seas running, we found ourselves off Iceland and not too far from Greenland. We surely were seeing the world, but hardly "Cook's Touring." At this stage of the war, one was lucky if one got a balaclava helmet and a pair of gloves from the parcels of clothing that the ladies of various societies knitted and sent to the ships. Possibly the idea of clothing comforts had not really got going, but later on, towns, cities and villages adopted a ship and the ladies provided many comforts for their adopted ship. Through the gap between Greenland and Iceland, the enemy would try to sneak their commerce raiders into the Atlantic. Certainly the enemy had their early successes for it was almost impossible to prevent submarines getting to their assigned station on the merchant shipping routes. All they did was move on the surface until they saw any vessel, then submerge and either attack the vessel or if a destroyer they would just wait until it had safely passed and then surface again. It was all a question of learning the hard way, at least as regards the U-boat war. Already at home, certain items were already being rationed because of the losses of merchant ships and in the course of time, before the navy got into its stride, the ship losses became calamitous, so that the nation was almost starved out of the war. We were not the only ship to do this patrol. We were only backing up so to speak. The main ships of this patrol were the armed merchant cruisers that consisted of large liners of about ten or fifteen thousand tons and with a speed of about twenty plus knots. These vessels armed with six inch guns of perhaps an old make and although quite adequate against a small raider of perhaps three or four thousand tons, they were no match for anything bigger, of which the enemy had quite a few. Nearly all his bigger ships were built with the idea of commerce raiding such as the pocket battleships, which had a turn of speed of thirty plus knots and twelve inch guns. It was to this environment that we were assigned as a stop gap, until the Navy, like the other services could get their breath back.

Having started to find the places where all these depressions from Iceland originated, there was little that we could do but remain constantly alert and patrol up and down an assigned stretch of water. For quite a few months this was to be our lot, but we never did find a depression from Iceland, for the simple reason we lived with them all the time. I will endeavour to give a small word picture of these patrols, entirely as it appeared to myself. One more heave and twist, and the ship will have been whirled round in a complete circle, that has neither been vertical nor horizontal, but a devilish combination of both. With the simulated agility of a cat, the swaying light movement of an expert ballet dancer one shuffles, glides and staggers in turn in an effort to dodge the various loose objects that are being hurled about with a shuttle-cock like precision. To fail in this grim game of "RUNNING THE GAUNTLET," can easily and often does result in a broken leg, perhaps a rib and at the worst, your ruddy neck. A fast game to be sure, with either no stake, or the maximum stakes. There are no middle bids. It will either mean, breakfast in the morning or at least a cot in the sick bay. There is never a dull moment, and for those that are bored or just want a bit of fun, try this treatment. Suffering such joys, one pauses for a moment by a small blue shaded light, peers intently at the dial of one's watch and notes with dismay and disgust that it has only been five or six minutes since the same procedure was used. The time is 0120, time when all self-respecting folk are in bed. A tired arm movement as the watch is brought to one's ear. It may have stopped, but no such luck as the time piece ticks merrily on in defiance of one's longing. The owner resigns himself to the simple fact, and resigns himself to several more weary minutes of the long and weary watch. No wonder they called it the graveyard watch from midnight until four in the morning. With a final sigh of relief and another glimpse at his watch, our hero, if such he may be called, passes on through a canvas screened door. Lifting the canvas flap, he passes inside. The lone walker no longer half-frozen with the biting wind and flying salt spray, is very thankful for the brief warmth. This joy is to be short lived. From under a pile of coats, a stern weary voice questions the intruder. "One twenty-five, Sir," replies the lone walker, "the ship is due to alter course at one thirty, Weather is filthy, All is correct, Sir." The voice had the pleasant schoolboy ring, like that of a lad in his teens. It is definitely a voice that would be more appropriate on the cricket field reading out the scores of last man in, before calling the tea interval. It is most unlike the voice of a very young Naval Officer, calling his captain somewhere in the Arctic Circle, and spoken in the blustering full gale in the month of January 1940, or the fifth month of the Second World War. Shuffling and gliding, this young veteran mounts the sloping steel ladder which threatens to jerk from under him at any moment until he reaches the bleak comfort of the weather drenched bridge. For a moment he stands, getting his eyes accustomed to the night and the impenetrable darkness. Then, turning round, he speaks to a second oilskin clad figure, whose face is faintly visible in the murky blackness. "Any Ki (cocoa) yet Yeo?" The words are scarcely audible in the roaring of the wind and sea. Together both figures make a neat quick courtesy and remain down, not with any feeling of humility, like some might experience in the presence of some great personage. Some sixth sense has warned them as the little ship pitches and plunges, that closely following this mad gyration of the ship, an avalanche in miniature, of icy green sea that will drench all that have defied that instinct to seek some brief cover. The Midshipman, it was none other, now quotes, "Oh to be in England, now that April's there." To his question about cocoa the yeoman replies as he straightens up, "Yes Sir, it should be here any moment now. I expect that the O.D., (ordinary seaman), messenger is stopping for a smoke in the galley." At last there is a grunt, and with a sigh of great feeling and a job well done, the O.D. arrives with a fanny, (small kettle), of steaming hot cocoa. Cups of steaming hot liquid that is almost solid are poured out, to be immediately gulped down by those fortunate enough to catch this round. Needless to say, the Captain, the officer of the watch, the yeoman and himself are in the first round, otherwise it will be treated as most undiplomatic at some future occasion. The yeoman steps beside the Captain and reports that the ship is to reduce speed to 15 knots and to alter course together to two two five degrees at 0140. A mumbled word of thanks from the captain as he drinks deeply of his cocoa. A few minutes after what appears to have been the disclosing of state secrets, a rating moves from the bridge and soon a distant shrilling whistle is heard followed by an order warning all hands to exercise great caution as the ship will alter course one hundred and eighty degrees to starboard, and that the ship will roll heavily. Moments pass and anxious eyes that are stung and are sticky with salt watch the small illuminated clock in the corner of the bridge signal table. The Captain now moves to the centre of the bridge, peers intently at the madly swaying compass, then calls down a nearby voice pipe, "Starboard fifteen." This is answered from what seems miles away and is answered in a similar manner to the order that was given. Immediately, there is a combined move by all on the bridge to catch hold of something stable and secure. For a few brief minutes that seem like hours, the ship rolls, lunges, lurches, staggers and performs numerous nautical aerobatics that are entirely peculiar to destroyers. Those fortunate enough to have been holding something secure enjoy the not too grand sensation of being catapulted towards the faintly visible clouds, to be immediately flung down with a bone jarring crash. These nautical antics give one the feeling that the stomach has become a hat band as the ship squirms and corkscrews in a smother of whirling spray and foam. At last, the mad roundabout ceases, and after a short look round and a few words to the Officer of the Watch to ensure that the following seas will not swamp the ship (pooping) the captain makes to settle in his bridge chair. He knows, as do the rest of us, that there will be a signal in a very short while. That signal soon came from the officer in charge of the patrol line, reading "resume patrol course and speed 18 knots". The reduction of speed was because of the worsening weather conditions that were soon to be expected. Where did they get all this spare wind from? Surely it must run out at some time and we had now put up with it for the last ten days. Never mind, we should soon be due for a relief, as eleven or twelve days was our limit for patrol, and we were all eagerly looking forward to a few nights' sleep without having to bother with anything. Much of this period of relaxed sleep would depend on the operational requirements of the area that one was in. Namely if at Scapa, and few destroyers were available, one would be lucky to get one full night's sleep, but if one was at a small place, say Lowestoft, one could reckon on at least one night clear, as here there would be anti-submarine patrol trawlers to do the job. It was all the luck of the draw. But back to the present patrol.

The speed reduction and the course, means that the ship now takes on a bit more stability, instead of rising and falling thirty or forty feet and suddenly stopping, it would only be about ten feet. We in

H.M.S.K., are hopefully on our last day of patrol for this particular stint and again hopefully, we should meet our relief somewhere about 1130. Should the relief have been delayed on sailing for any reason, then a signal would have been made to us had the delay been of an appreciable length. There had been no signal to that effect so we all cross our fingers and hope for the best. Word has been passed that the skipper (Captain) has donated a tin of cigarettes for the one who first spots our relief so that by 1030 everybody not otherwise employed will be competing for the cigarettes. Certain of the ratings are excluded from the competition namely myself and the duty signalmen and the lookouts whose job it is to see the relief. By 1100, many hands are looking anxiously ahead hoping that by pure chance they will see the relief before anyone else. At the latitude that we are operating, the dawn should be just about breaking and there will only be about four hours of daylight, or perhaps in these weather conditions, it could be murky pale light that will be neither dusk or dawn or day or night. Powerful glasses are constantly sweeping the horizons and the guns are constantly moved about to prevent freezing up of the working parts. Between mouthfuls of scalding hot tea and corned beef sandwiches, a belated breakfast, now that the ship is much steadier, for before the turn it would have been sheer insanity to try to make tea or a hot meal for the ship's company. The most that one could hope for or do was to make hot drinks in a jug or fanny, (small kettle), heated by a home made electrical heating rod. Yes, life was full of surprises, and necessity was ever the mother of invention. Telescopes continue to sweep and search the foam flecked wind blown sea, as these are the ideal conditions for U-boats to attack. The Asdics are working but there is far too much sea mush, (sea noises from turbulent seas), for the machines to be fully effective. Men are relieved as others take their places, as it has been found that an hour on lookout duty is more than enough for any person to remain on the open bridges. At times it was found that even half an hour was the limit, as such things as frozen eyelids or even frozen eyeballs would cause extreme complications to the ship's efficiency. It must be realised that so early in the war there were no such things as protective goggles or anti-flash equipment and ear protectors. Suddenly a lookout stiffens at his post, rubs his eyes in disbelief, takes another look and calls, "Masts bearing Red oh five, sir". The Bridge becomes electrified with activity and the captain appears almost magically on the front of the bridge. Alarm gongs ring, torpedo tubes are brought to the ready, guns cease their rhythmic swaying and centre themselves as though waiting for further commands. The ship is at "Action Stations" in almost the catch of a breath. This is a well rehearsed drill, for who knows, this stranger can quite easily become a sneak raider trying to creep through our patrol lines. Signal lamps are flashing, eagerly waiting for the correct reply to the challenge, for the reply will be the correct reply or the flash of guns being discharged. Course is slightly altered to bring the stranger almost dead ahead so as to give a possible enemy as small a target as possible. Gladly the reply is interpreted as correct and we are informed in the same signal that it is our relief *H.M.S.K.*, another of our flotilla mates that has come to relieve us. Quickly we pass by signal lamp, the course and speed that he will need to remain on station on this patrol line. Also he is informed of any relevant information that the captain feels he will require.

Another light from the other side of the bridge starts to flash and is immediately answered by the signalman standing ready. This signal tells us from the officer in charge of the patrol line to "Proceed in execution of previous orders." We need no second bidding for the captain orders a new course to the southeast and pushes on the speed a little, as though testing the ship's ability to manage his directions. In truth, this is what is happening, for with the state of the wind and sea one has to nurse one's charge and also provide as much comfort as possible for the crew. Already there has been the pipe for messdecks to be cleaned up which will be done with a will, so that hopefully by the time we arrive in harbour everywhere will at least be clean and tidy, for although we are released from patrol, all living quarters are to be kept clean. Grumbling about the weather, the signalman reports to the Captain, "signal from "K," please bring steam roller when you return." "It has been ordered, have a pleasant voyage." Our captain replies, thanking him for his good wishes. As we pass each other, not so very far apart, caps are waved to friends, cat calls are made and replied to, only to be lost in the noises of the weather and the increased roaring of the ship's engine room fans, as we slowly work up to our best manoeuvring speed of about 24 knots. In the engine room the grinning engineer smiles at his crew, as the turbines start their tuneful humming note and all settle down for the long trip home where we shall arrive, if all goes well, on the day after tomorrow. At the end of the foaming wake, will be hot food, dry clothes, a wash-up and shave, for we are all looking like the gentlemen of the road with our half and three-quarter grown beards. Shaving has been forgotten almost from day one, and now we shall smarten ourselves ready for harbour. For two or perhaps three days we shall be able to relax in peaceful quiet, to read our books or the mail and then we shall again be off to relieve the next ship on patrol. Oh, no, we shall not be permitted to rusticate as other unfortunates must be considered. Incidentally, we never did find the source of the weather mens' pet; the depression from Iceland, but we shall look again on our next trip that way. When that might be is anybody's guess as next week or even tomorrow, we might find ourselves heading for the sunnier climes of the West Indies, or even further afield. It all depends on the whims of the admiralty, which controls our destinies for the present. At the moment we were steaming up the Clyde for Greenock where before settling down to a well earned rest period, it would be restore, oil and in general prepare for immediate return to sea if required. These routines would do the keen trade unionist very much good, and it would be no use complaining to the Captain, as he as well as us, has to take it and like it. With the oiling and storing completed and being in all respects ready for sea service again, the word is passed for all hands to relax, so that the ship virtually becomes a dead thing except for the unfortunates on watch who must maintain their vigil come hell or high water, as even in harbour one is not safe from attack by keen enemy saboteurs who, without coming on board, could quite easily attach an explosive device to the ships side, but for the folk on watch to spot them and challenge them before they get near to the ship.

MORE PATROLS

Blackout in its most strict sense, complete impenetrable darkness, that almost engulfs and most certainly clings to one. Long silent weary hours of it spent in the cold that really bites into one despite many layers of thick heavy clothing. That is a little bit of the Arctic night. Add to this, the homely comforts of the continuous bucking and rearing of a rodeo pony, the plunging, rising, falling and jolting along at high speed, then add a liberal dose of a moderately fresh north westerly gale and a bucket full of freshly whipped spray, and one has the ideal mixture for Arctic Patrol.

The knowledge that even a glimmer of an unscreened luminous wristwatch, may cause anything to happen, perhaps a ton of high explosive in the form of a slithering black torpedo will smash into you, and so finish the recipe for you. You may now realise just how the word "blackout" almost leaps from the pages of the dictionary, to hit you between the eyes. Such were the conditions that we found ourselves sampling in the late winter of 1939/40. For some fifteen days had the ships company of the little ship, *H.M.S.K.* known the full meaning of that word. The comforts of bathing and shaving had long since become an historic fact, in those cold, dreary, uninviting, uncomfortable and God forsaken parts of the world, until even the crew themselves seemingly formed a part of that detestable word.

One hundred miles of westering, a wide sweeping and staggering turn and then another hundred miles back again from whence we had come. Some fifteen miles away on either beam (side) known friendly escorts are sharing the same simple joys, if such they can be called. Somewhere, anywhere, and perhaps who knows nowhere at all, there is a blockade runner endeavouring to sneak her way in or out of German waters. Enemy forces are about somewhere, and this is not guesswork, for only a few days previously an ill fated armed merchant cruiser had been attacked and sunk by a pocket battleship, believed to be the Deutschland. Thus, for self evident reasons were all our nerves and senses very fully alerted, and likewise the blackout just as fully detested in every way. The Deutschland would have been about five times our tonnage and size while her armament would have been about the same 5x in effective fire power, while her speed would have been a little short of our own maximum speed. The only comforting thought in this sea of woe, was the fact that somewhere, not too far away, were several of our own ships, that would at least have been able to assist us in our need. Those hours, when life is at its lowest ebb, between 0100 and 0300, at least so the medical profession informs us, were the hours of watch still being kept. A strange sense of wakeful weariness seems to overcome everything. Even the little ship herself groans in sympathy with the crew, and the shuttle-like gyrations of the ship. Eyelids move with a strange slowness, in an effort to shake off some of the sticky stinging clinging remains of the salt spray. We and the little ship seem to be at one accord over these strange pleasures that only those peculiar creatures they call "sailors" are supposed to enjoy. Why not ask him yourself at sometime, he may disillusion you.

Suddenly, one of the heavily muffled figures on the bridge straightens, tenses, cocks his head forward and listens to some peculiar noise apparently coming from the port bow. Half uncertain, perhaps doubting his own keen sense of hearing, he whispers something to a similarly clad figure near to him, whom he addresses as BUNTS. Together they stand, each adopting his own particular most restful and attentive attitude, hardly knowing just why or for what they are listening. Moments pass, and slowly they resume their own places again, having muttered something about "imagination." Yet, they are still convinced that something has been heard by one of them, for they know and trust each other's senses.

Violently the little ship lurches as a heavy sea punches hard at her side, then slowly she regains that drunken-like stability. Now, both the whispering conspirators are alert as again they speak quietly together. Yes, they are convinced now that the low sullen and distinctive rumble was gunfire, and from their own limited experiences, they think it to be of fairly heavy calibre. Such a decision on their part calls for no further hesitation and clearly above the noise of the wind and sea, a young excited and eager voice calls "Gunfire on the port bow Sir." Immediately heads bob, figures move abruptly, alarm gongs ring, sharp necessary questions are asked and answered, as the whole bridge becomes alive. Questing fingers move in the dark, they pause, fumble and move again as the switches are made for the power to be supplied to various action instruments.

Within minutes, the whole crew are assembled at their ""Action Stations." Some are heavily clothed while some have brought their heavy clothing with them, having come from their off duty "hide aways." None of the romantic rigs as some story tellers relate when the hero appears in a howling blizzard in shirt and trousers. Although the war has only been on for a relatively few months, these youthful veterans have learned by bitter experience that one is always dressed ready to meet the weather. To the casual observer, it would appear that the ship has gone mad as canvas covers are pulled from the guns and the crew seethes and writhes to and fro in apparent disorder like a disturbed ants' nest. Hatches and doors are slammed shut while others are flung open, pneumatic pressure pumps commence their clanking as shells are hoisted from the magazines. From this apparent panic and cacophony of sound, busy business-like quiet ensues. Well drilled men are executing orders with incredible speeds for men that have just woken from their sleep. Shells and cartridges begin to appear in little stacks at the foot of each loading shute, mess tables are removed and folded away, to make room for the casualty clearing stations that are being rapidly prepared. Metal clangs on metal, as shells are rammed home and gun breaches are slammed shut, torpedo tubes are trained outboard and brought to the firing positions. A young doctor passes in to the messdecks and prepares his operating table while an assistant lays out the tools of his trade. All this in the centre of an already crowded space and heaps of cordite containers.

On the bridge there is an air of alertness that is almost terrifying in its intensity. All available eyes are trained in the direction of the gunfire noises and the blue grey snouts of the guns follow the roving eyes of the gun control officer, weaving patterns in the night as the various controls are operated. Again the little ship rolls and lurches with a sickening corkscrew motion. This time the whole bridge staff hears the low sullen rumble somewhere on the port bow. Swift calculations are made, brains race at maddening speed, nerves tingle with the expectancy of the unknown, while course is altered slightly so as to bring the object of attack into a dead ahead position. Speed is increased slightly and a coded message is prepared ready for transmission. The ship's position is checked and rechecked ready to warn the world that the little ship is about to commit herself to its Admiralty assigned task of DESTROY OR BE DESTROYED. The finger of the yeoman is curled round the trigger of his signal lamp, he checks and mutters the challenge and reply to himself. If he does have to make that signal, there will be a definite reply, either in the stuttering blinking of another signal lamp giving the correct reply or the flash and rumble of enemy shells approaching. For perhaps twenty minutes the ship glides and plunges on, while every moment one might expect to hear the ripple and see the belch of flame that heralds gunfire. Now we have arrived at the position where the enemy were calculated to be and still there is no sign of a ship. Can it possibly be a U-boat that has dived? Time and again those deep rumblings are heard and each time one expects to hear the whine of a shell approaching. Thoughts and questions arise. Is the enemy using some new flashless explosives while attacking a ship as surely by now those intent watchers on the bridge should have seen some indication and as we are in the area calculated we should at least smell the smoke from the gunfire. Surely the ships that were being engaged would have sent a report of attack, or had the enemy's first salvo of gunfire destroyed the victims radio equipment so that transmission was now impossible? All the questions were asked but there were no answers. Carefully the ship is turned first one way then another as though trying to sniff the enemy like some gun dog sniffing his master's bag. Tired eyes continue to search for the mysterious enemy. Again we are facing the original direction and again we hear that dull rumble. This is too much for the bridge staff whose nerves are now bar taut with unknown expectations. Someone now suggests that perhaps a shell has gone loose from its rack and is rolling about with the movement of the ship. 'This starts a string of investigations so that the damage and control parties are told to make a thorough investigation of all possible causes below decks. Moments pass, a muffled figure hastens to the bridge and speaks quietly to the captain. A few words are spoken and a quiet laugh is heard. Orders to relax are rapidly given and the ships hastens to resume her normal patrol position. Below decks a repair party is busy plugging and shoring up a buckled plate that had shed a rivet with the seas heavy pounding and almost constant jolting and jarring. Fortunately, this plate was not on the outside of the ship but on an inner skin. As the ship had rolled and jarred in certain directions, the plate had buckled and then straightened giving the effect that we mistook for gunfire. I guess that none of us will ever make the same mistake again and it was just as well that the ship's company had been alert. No doubt, the young lad that reported the incident felt a little sheepish but as ever, "better safe than sorry." Should the offending plate have split with the constant flexing and bending, (it's called metal fatigue today), water could have seeped in causing a certain amount of flooding and consequent instability of the ship. Thus did H.M.S.K. do battle with the mystery raider. The alertness of the one young fellow prevented the possible loss of ship and men, and he of no medals, just a pat on the back as it was no more than his duty. In that type of engagement, the elements are equally as merciless as the enemy as one cannot appeal to the elements for quarter.

On return to base, when the captain had made his report of the incident, the ship was ordered to Liverpool for emergency docking and repairs to the buckled plate. While in dock at Liverpool, opportunity was taken to clean boilers and inspect and clean the remainder of the bottom of the ship. Opportunity was also taken to give a few days leave to the ships company in two lots. For this small mercy the ship's company was truly thankful and especially those fellows that lived in the immediate area. To carry out the tasks of docking and repairs and of cleaning the ship's bottom, H.M.S. K. was docked in Gladstone Dock the day after our arrival at Liverpool. As was noticed at any other docks, the workmen and the locals were only too pleased to make all members of the ship most welcome in all respects.

LORD HAW HAW MENTIONS
"K" IN HIS DESPATCHES

Arising from the docking mentioned in the previous chapter, the following incident is worth noting, if only to prove that so early in the war, spies or fifth columnists were not something new. As previously mentioned, the ship was docked down for bottom cleaning and inspections. The day dawned that the necessary work had been completed so that all arrangements for undocking were made. At about 0830 on the morning arranged, everything was ready and with steam raised for the undocking programme. This was because during the docking the ship was on shore supplies of electricity and water and the steam was necessary for our own power.

The captain and officers and the necessary bridge staff being already on the bridge and as the saying goes, "Raring to go." The dockyard staff and the pilot were also on board for we were to move to another dock, (possibly called Bidstone Dock), where we should be able to take on the necessary stores replenishments. With a blowing of the Dock Master's whistle, sluices were opened and the water started to flow in. Soon, the shoring timbers were starting to be released by the flooding of the dock. It would not be very long now before we should be waterborne and the ship in her own element.

Without warning, there is a frantic calling from the upper deck. The ship is not rising with the flooding of the dock. Quickly the dock master calls for the flooding to cease and at the same time an engineer officer reports to the captain that the ship is taking in water quite fast. Again the dock master calls for the timber shores to be replaced and the dock to be pumped out. This is quite a lengthy process. At last the flooding of the ship is checked and soon reduced. As soon as is possible, the engineer and his staff enter the flooded compartments to find that the flooding cocks were still open. This is an impossible situation, for the engineer officer himself had only a short while previously closed and secured the flooding valves. At the moment the main concern was to empty the partially flooded compartments and get the ship floating properly. Fortunately all the shoring timbers were either still in place or secured by lanyards to the ship. Dockyard workmen toiled like Trojans to rectify this apparent mishap by replacing the main shoring timbers as quickly as possible. In the meantime, armed sentries had been placed at each end of the only gangway to the dock side. Strict instructions were given quietly to the sentries that NOBODY was to leave the ship or come on board unless approved by the captain or first lieutenant. We were a Navy ship again, no matter the dock regulations.

Urgent inspection of the flooding valves, urgent questions by the Captain and the Engineering Officer of various ratings whose duties took them anywhere near the flooding valves. From the immediate answers it is apparent that no naval person had committed an act of sabotage, for that is the only name for this outrage. It now rested on the docks authorities to check the workman, which I believe that they did as efficiently as was possible. It would seem that the culprit had already got clear of the ship, or that the person responsible must have been a skilled agent of the enemy, and also a good actor.

However, the floating and undocking programme went ahead even if it was a little delayed, and we then moved to Bidstone Docks according to programme. That evening as we were sitting in the mess having our supper, the radio was on and tuned to the programme that was used by the German News Agent, Lord Haw Haw, who always announced his programme as "GARMANY CALLING." Some of the items that he commented on were at least based on truth but most were enemy propaganda. In any case it was always a good laugh to listen to, for at that time there were few Home comedy programmes to entertain one. On this occasion, Lord Haw Haw announced that H.M.S. Kelvin had been sunk while in dry dock. Somebody somewhere, must have moved very fast, for it was then less than twelve hours since the incident had happened. The Lord Haw Haw was British subject that had defected to the enemy from the first day of the war, and he carried on broadcasting until the time of the German Surrender in 1944. At the Nuremburg War Trials, he was convicted of being a traitor and was executed after the trial.

The person who was responsible for the Kelvin's dilemma, was never found at the time, but we did hear unofficially that a fifth columnist was arrested in the dockyard several months later. Whether this was the person responsible or not, I have no means of confirming. It was certainly a clear warning to us to watch very carefully the workmen that came on board.

"HEIL & FAREWELL"

Clear skies, a pleasant summer sun over a calm glassy sea, with just sufficient breeze to disturb occasionally the sea's bright scintillating surface. Almost perfect peace. So it seemed to those on board H.M.S.K. in the summer of 1940 on a glorious Sunday afternoon. There was only one thing missing, a deck chair, a good book, and then for anyone who wished, it could have been a pleasure cruise. Sunday in the Navy, although it is often impossible, the powers that be do try to give the day, particularly the afternoon, over to general relaxation. Make and mend is possibly the general rule, or as the sailors themselves interpret it, "Make bed and mend sleep." Thus it was, with the ship's company making and mending in the afternoon sunshine.

Without warning, there echoes through the little ship the urgent and strident notes of the alarm bells, summoning the ship to ""Action Stations." Pillows, beds and sweet dreams are immediately forgotten, and there is a hurried racing of all hands to their various stations. The ship's special instruments (ASDICS), have detected a lurking U-boat. Speed is reduced slightly so as to allow the asdics to operate at their full efficiency and the big search is on. It is "Hunt the needle," only this game is a bit more difficult, as in this pastime, the haystack is a very large ocean and the needle is moving in various unpredictable directions. Should the hunter not be fully alert, and the hunted be a little smarter than the hunter, then, the roles can be reversed with dire consequences for the loser.

After much apparent idling, and the exchange of strange talk such as "extent of target," "Left or right cut off," or something that sounds like "no doppler effect" or hopefully "classified." The latter is entirely nothing to do with the latest racing results, but signifies that the target is definitely identified as being that of a U-boat. If the latter is called, then there is a sudden increasing of speed and the destroyer will surge forward with impatient and malicious intent. From the bridge comes the orders for the depth charges, settings for depth that it is intended that they shall detonate, also the type of pattern to be fired. All this jargon is carried on while everybody is intent on their own particular job. The signal staff are busy signalling the latest information to the ship's consorts who now will have joined her in the hunt. The setting of the depth for the depth charges is done by the simple turning of a key, something like the winding of a clock. This depth is something that must more or less be guessed at, one must just guess and hope that you are right. The charges will be either released from their racks, or thrown out from the sides of the ship by the "throwers." Actually they are fired by a small charge, to about fifty yards from the ship. Also the charges are released on orders from the bridge when the Captain considers that the U-boat is under the charges when let go.

As the ship approaches this position, when the charges will form a triangle and the submarine is in the centre of all three, if the Captain has calculated the depth correctly, or guessed correctly, the result will be a kill and the U-boat will be destroyed. Things do not always go as they should for the U-boat will hear the charges being fired and also the noise of the ship going overhead. The noise although indescribable is not easily missed for the ship will increase speed just before firing the charges. It is in these moment, when the charges are fired and the ship passing overhead that the Submarine may alter course or speed or both. He may even go astern, hoping to get back into the track of the attacking ship, or he may increase or decrease his depth and this is only limited to the depth of the sea. At the time of writing, the ASDIC set will not predict the depth of the U-boat or just what the enemy will do. This must be done by the captain using his own experience of submarine attacks. All that the asdics will tell the captain is that the submarine is there and that he is going on a certain course and at a certain speed. This information like any other computerised information takes time to be formulated into language that the captain can quickly interpret.

From the bridge, as the captain orders the release of the depth charges, a small flag will be waved for the charges in the racks to be released. The charges themselves give the appearance of dirty green painted oil drums, the only big difference is that these drums contain very high explosives. As the charges are dropped, the ship will reduce speed and start turning so as to try to keep the target clear of one's own wake. Ideally the hunt for a U-boat is carried out by two or sometimes three ships if they are available. Then one ship will attack the target, and the other will hold it on asdics until the explosions, when they change round, in their respective roles. When the first depth charge is dropped, a small calcium flare will be dropped over the stern to mark the position of the original attack, so that if the target manages to elude the ships, they have a point from which to start the next search. With a sweeping turn under almost full rudder, we shall be in time to see the charges exploding as the sea boils and heaves and then erupts in a giant fountain of spray and solid water. Other explosions will follow at intervals as the charges explode at various depths. Should there be any thing, including fishes, within the range of the explosion, it will surely be destroyed and if at a little further distance, the concussion from the explosion under the sea will either destroy that body or render it completely unconscious.

The little ship shudders and staggers as the explosions follow one another in succession or together. A patient wait for a few moments while the spewing tumbling sea settles again. The small spiral of calcium smoke from the smoke float that was fired at the first charge, is not too far away, and it is on the surrounding area that we concentrate our observations. As we pass back through the violently disturbed water, one sees countless fish floating, silver bellies up, but we are looking for bigger and more deadly fish. There are no signs that the attack has been successful, so that we make ready for the next attack. Speed is again reduced and the asdic operators again commence their mystical chanting. Yes, the U-boat is still somewhere beneath the ocean, for again we relive "Jock" famous BINNNG BOOOOP. The ship forges ahead again and rushes in to repeat the attack but with slight changes in depth setting and the numbers of charges to be dropped. If this attack is any where near successful, we shall see on passing through the area of disturbed water, perhaps a thin streak of oil, or even a big slick, denoting that we have at least damaged our adversary. Yes, we have been lucky in this attack for as well as the oil slick, there are other miscellaneous objects such as a life jacket, or a sailor's cap, perhaps a letter from the messdeck of the U-boat. We again mark the spot and at the next attack we drop an increased number of charges to ensure the completion of the task. We must not however be duped by the old trick of the U-boat discharging debris to confuse us and so make his escape. Turning quickly, we again pass through the floating wreckage and again we drop a couple of charges just to make sure that our adversary is not trying to fox us.

There is not much fear of that, for as we again try to observe the results, the sea where the charges exploded is broken by a black barnacle covered shape, almost like one of the navigation buoys in some dirty river. The black weed strewn shape soon shows as a submarine being forced to surface in a hurry. From our deck, a ragged cheer breaks out but is soon silenced by the discharge of one of the 4 point seven guns opening fire. The shell burst not too far from the U-boat, and soon men are noticed evacuating the now floating motionless U-boat. Firing ceases immediately but the guns remain at full alert and the upper deck is prepared for rescue operations. Some dozen of their crew manage to get clear before the U-boat finally shows signs of sinking, so that we move in at very slow speed, keeping our bows toward him all the time as we have no wish for a torpedo from him as a last defiant gesture. Scrambling nets are lowered ready and heaving lines are prepared for getting the men from the water. As each survivor reaches the ships side many willing hands reach out to help while some of our own crew go down the scrambling nets and immerse themselves waist deep in the cold water ready to help any unfortunate that just has not the strength to pull himself up. A couple of armed sentries are quickly organised to greet the survivors and there is no bother except from one silver braided individual who, as he steps on board, gives the Nazi Salute and calls out "Heil Hitler." To one of the seamen standing near by, this is too much so that he quickly dashes forward and in his eagerness to help one of our own rescuing seamen back on board, he brushes, or perhaps barges, against the haughty individual and knocks him over the side. At least that is his story when the incident was investigated, and the seaman that he had helped back on board strongly supported him, in all his testimony. Of course the incident called for very strong protests from the offender which were reported as his protests but the Geneva Convention does not cater for accidents, that are genuine in every way. As we leave the scene of the rescue, the Asdic operator reports that there are very strong breaking up noises coming from his instruments as the U-boat slowly disappears completely. Soon the engines are pushing the little ship at 25 knots, while the enemy have been given clean dry clothing and placed under armed escort below decks. All the clothing taken from the prisoners is bundled up and labelled ready for inspection at a later opportunity after they have been landed and placed in the care of the military. For the crew of the "K" it is just another occasion in which to drink their tot with much relish and good humoured bantering from those who have witnessed the whole affair.

H.M.S. Glorious and S.S. Florida, after colliding

S.S. Florida

Ramillies at Gunnery Practice

Egyptian Mail

The Daily Round
The Common Task

The Route

Italian S.S. Ausonia

Job No. 535 H.M.S. Kelvin
Leaving the Humber for one of the North Sea Sweeps

H.M.S. Euryalus 1947

Launched 6.6.39 and completed 30.6.41. Joined Mediterranean Fleet until 9.43. 22.3.42 Second Battle of Sirte, 13.12.42 with others sank three enemy supply ships off North Africa. 10.7.43 invasion of Sicily. 9.43Salerno landings. Returned to the Clyde for refit 10.43 - 6.44. Home Fleet until 12.44 then joined British Pacific Fleet for operations agains Japan. 11.1.47 left Singapore to retun to the U.K., arriving at Sheerness 17.2.47. Mediterrenean Fleet 1948-53 then South Atlantic Station 3.53 - 8.54. In reserve at Devonport 9.54 - 7.59. 18.7.59 arrived at Blyth to be broken up.

(see page 218)

H.M.S. Barham
Sunk by S/M Torpedo

'Sinking'

Battle of Sirte 22 March 1942
Keeping one eye on the object

The Battle of Sirte

Attack with Torpedoes

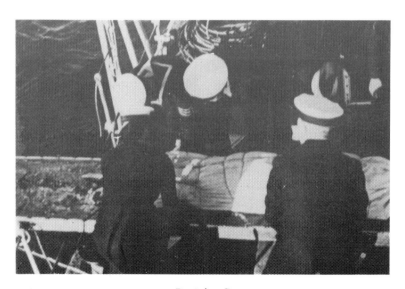

Burial at Sea

Old Friends of War Days, Ganges 1948
Grandad on left

H.M.S. Ark Royal is sunk after a convoy
run and within a few miles of Gibraltar

*Field Marshal Rommel and others visit the Afrika Corps
(taken by a German Prisoner)*

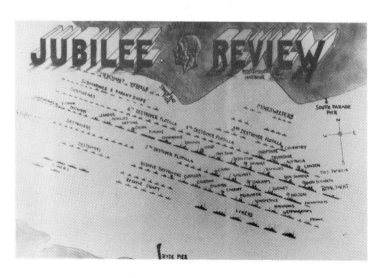

Fleet Review Spithead 1935

WAR OPERATIONS

THE MIRACLE: DISAPPOINTMENT AND DISASTER

In May of 1940, the forces of Germany broke through the allied defences and fanned out towards the ports of Ostend, Calais and Dunkirk, causing the Allied forces to make a "strategic withdrawal" as the newspapers called it. In other words it was a retreat in the most common of languages. The causes for this debacle are now history and the story of this retreat is obtainable from any library.

When it was fully realised that there was no stopping the enemy forces, the Navy was called on to evacuate what they could of the army. This meant endless days and nights at sea between Dover, Ramsgate, Margate and the beaches of Dunkirk. The small town of Dunkirk is flanked on either side by sand dunes stretching for miles and rising from the sea to a height of about eight or ten feet or more in places. It was to these beaches that the Allied forces retreated ready to be picked up by any Navy and civilian craft that could be mustered. I do not recall or even know the date that the civilian boat population was recruited to assist. All that we in the Navy Ships knew, was that civilian motor yachts, Thames Barges, and even lifeboats were used to get the army from the beaches. About the 20th May, we and all possible destroyers were ordered to sea and to report to the Flag Officer Dover for instructions, regarding the duties of the Navy ships. On arrival at the Dunkirk Beaches, the dunes were already covered in a seething mass of Allied troops, the great majority of whom were British. Daily the destroyers steamed at high speed with their cargoes of soldiers that had been rescued from the beaches. In the first few early days of the evacuation, the destroyers would steam in as close as possible to the beach and with the aid of boats, would take off numerous soldiers until they were almost dangerously loaded. While this operation was being carried out, air attacks by German dive and high and low level bombers would be endured. Eventually the damage and loss of destroyers made the beach evacuation direct to the destroyers, most hazardous and the losses could not be sustained. This meant that the soldiers would be loaded into the boats and barges, and ferried out to the destroyers waiting at sea where they could at least manoeuvre and keep on the move. During this time of about ten days, casualties slowly mounted each day.

It was daily expected that the German Navy would make some attempt to interfere with the evacuation, but they did not, amazing as it may seem. Most of the Navy ships were kept going purely by the grit of the crews, who more than usual stood up to the unequal strain, of several days without sleep, or most probably snatching a few moments while standing up. Several were the medical cases of sailors suffering "battle fatigue," which became a new term in the language. In all, two hundred thousand troops were successfully evacuated from the beaches and surrounding areas. This salvage of the Forces was to form the basis of the new army that was to be formed as the saying goes, almost from scratch, for many of the rescued had nothing but what they stood up in. Some forty to fifty destroyers were lost through those few fateful days, in which the Navy and civilians wrote a brilliant page in the nation's history.

During the operation of Dunkirk, the Navy was constantly on patrol of the sea areas approaching the beaches and the only moments of relief came when one or another ship was ordered to bombard some place or assist with the resistance somehow. There are even records of the Navy ships engaging enemy tanks while carrying out their evacuation tasks. Also, the rescue of heads of state and bullion of the countries being over run by the enemy. It was just as well that the enemy had neither the will nor the means to carry on his advance from the continent, for there would have been nothing very much to stop him. In truth the army at home was very poorly equipped in all ways and the reserves, if any, were supplied with sporting guns and in some cases pitch forks with which to repel the enemy should he come at all. This was to be the testing period not only for the British people but for the enemy, for whose nerve broke first was bound to go under. As Providence would have it, the enemy was to crack first after some twelve months waiting. Meanwhile other events had been taking place.

Just prior to the Dunkirk debâcle, the powers that be decided that we should invade Norway and accordingly the Navy was to play its part, of which the start was as is related next.

"NORWEGIAN INTERLUDE"

This is a brief account of the loss of the aircraft carrier *Glorious* and her attendant destroyers. At the start of this operation, the *Glorious*, *Ardent* and *Acasta* were some forty miles to the south east of us, operating aircraft in support of some operation off Norway, and covering some of the forces that were still operating in the Narvik area although Narvik had been terminated a few days earlier, Britain having lost any foothold in the Scandinavian peninsula because of a speedy enemy occupation, mainly due to fifth columnists. It was extremely important that what forces could be evacuated, should be. Our immediate job was making a patrol line with other destroyers, off the northwest coast of Norway. This was to prevent any enemy forces, and there were several, from interfering with the evacuation. The *Glorious* with her escorting destroyers were operating off Narvik embarking what was left of the Fleet Air Arm aircraft. These consisted of Gladiators that were manned by Fleet Air Arm and Royal Air Force personnel. Also from the shore defences there were some Hurricane aircraft of the R.A.F. still to be collected.

The *Glorious* was an elderly ship, originally designed as something entirely different and converted to an aircraft carrier somewhere about the early 1920's.

Immediately the aircraft had been landed on, *Glorious* and her escorts withdrew to the southwestwards. At about 1600, two enemy heavy warships were sighted to the east. One of these was most probably the *Hipper* and an escorting cruiser, *Hipper* being a so-called pocket battleship. *Acasta* and *Ardent* were immediately ordered to lay a smoke screen in an effort to confuse the enemy force. Although the enemy fire was only between breaks in the smoke screen, *Glorious* was hit in one of the hangar spaces, and fire quickly spread to the retrieved aircraft which were still being struck down. At any time, even in peace time when aircraft are being struck down or ranged on deck, this is the most precarious time as aircraft movement is severely restricted or there is the fire hazard of fuel being transferred. *Glorious* had only four point seven guns as opposed to *Hipper*'s eight inch guns so that *Glorious* was hopelessly out gunned and out ranged.

Also, *Hipper*'s speed would have been equal to or more than *Glorious*'s best. By 1645, the *Glorious* was blazing fiercely, and some ten minutes later, an enemy heavy shell hit *Glorious* aft, destroying her steering gear. With the aircraft and the petrol blazing furiously, the Captain had little option but to order "abandon ship," and about 1720 *Glorious* sank.

Meanwhile *Acasta* and *Ardent* were engaging the enemy as best possible. The *Acasta* having fired off both lots of her four salvoes of torpedoes, was hit severely and was soon sinking. The *Ardent* was still valiantly attacking her enemies with her guns and torpedoes, one of which was reckoned to have hit the cruiser. A few moments later a shell from the bigger enemy hit *Ardent* amidships so that she sank about 1800. British forces were hurrying at the maximum speeds to the area but by the time they arrived the enemy had vanished at high speed back to their bases.

The loss of these ships was confirmed the next day by a German broadcast saying that the ships had been sunk and that prisoners had been taken. Numbers and names were not given. The fires in the hangars had made it impossible for the life rafts to be freed so that there was no option for the crews but to jump overboard and trust that they would be picked up. It was later made known that the enemy ships taking part were the *Scharnhorst* and *Gneisenau*, both of which were more heavily armed than the *Hipper*. We of the patrolling destroyers knew of these ships for it had only been a couple of days previously that we had been engaged by them. These two ships were known to the Navy as "Salmon and Gluckstein" or "S & G" for they always seemed to work as a pair. In our ship we realised and were soon to implement the old saying that "all things come in threes" and also to reinforce the introduction that "truth is stranger than fiction." As the newspapers reported almost daily, this was the period of the so called PHONEY WAR. For my money, it was just as well that it did not develop seriously, or perhaps the news casters had got it wrong as Dunkirk proved.

Just before the battles for Narvik, which were rather intense, for this meant steaming up the fjords of Norway, not quite knowing just what might be round the next corner, and it was a good guess that the enemy would have the whole fjord ranged. It was the plan for one ship to go in at moderate speed and hopefully draw any fire that might be intended for the ships.

If the decoy did not draw fire, then the remainder of us would steam past with all guns ready for instant action. One could never be sure. If the enemy did open fire, then the remainder of the force would give the target a fair pasting. All this may seem a little tame, but, believe me, there was little that was tame about our or the enemy's intentions. In short the first Battle of Narvik was fought mainly by destroyers of the "H" class, *Hardy*, *Havoc*, *Hyperion*, and the rest of their gallant band of "H" Class boats.

The second battle was fought by a mixed force of destroyers and the battleship, *Warspite*. It was known that several enemy destroyers had holed themselves up in Rhombax Fjord. Hope I have spelt that one correct but I doubt it. That's how it sounded. The fjord has several channels leading into it or from it, and the water in the fjord is quite deep with mountains on either side. The whole place was an ideal position for an ambush if the enemy wished to make it so. The drill was much the same as before, with one ship doing the decoy work and the others following and with the *Warspite* in company. It was a question of holding one's breath as we passed each channel entrance. Then, at last it happened we were warned by radio from the decoy that about five enemy destroyers were in hiding round the next bend. This was it. Target Identification orders were given and the guns loaded with H.E. and S.A.P., (high explosive and semi armour piercing), shells. Speed was increased to pass the opening of the fjord, then with a tremendous crash that echoed and re-echoed round the fjord, *Warspite* opened fire with her fifteen inch guns. This was followed by the destroyers opening fire with every gun that would bear on a target. The echoes gave a peculiar drum fire effect that seemed to almost shake the whole fjord as the noise reverberated round and round the hills. Soon the four or five destroyers that had been hiding in the fjord were just masses of burning and blazing wreckage. In all, seven enemy destroyers were written off that day before the Warspite and her escorts withdrew at high speed, knowing full well that enemy aircraft would be on their way for revenge before very much longer. Yes, the enemy had already installed himself on the surrounding airfields, and it was most prudent not to linger. Our force returned to base without loss.

CHANNEL OPERATIONS

A CHANGE OF DIET

Having completed our operations at Narvik and Dunkirk and the adjacent beaches, we returned to Immingham so that we were available for convoys, escorts and protection for North Sea traffic. Normally destroyers would not have been used for coastal convoys, but it must be remembered that between Narvik and Dunkirk, the Navy had lost some fifty ships that were difficult to replace. All this meant extra work for those ships that remained in service. From Immingham, we would sail in pairs and patrol an area somewhere between the Tyne and the Yarmouth Roads. This, I would imagine, was supposed to be a period of relaxation after the strenuous efforts that had been made by the navy during those last weeks. I suppose that we were not expected to be used for the convoy close escorts, but rather the outer defences of the convoys running north for the Tyne and Scottish ports, or south for Yarmouth and the Thames and southern ports. Any convoy that met trouble or needed assistance, we would obviously assist, otherwise it seemed to be a roving patrol to meet the requirements of the local officers in charge. In any case there was always the possibility of attacks by enemy E-boats, (fast gun and torpedo boats). It was the enemy's favourite trick, just to drift with engines stopped, in the path of a convoy, or as was known, to tie up to a navigational buoy until shipping went by and then attack. One learned very quickly.

It was 30th August 1940. H.M.S.J. and H.M.S.K. proceeded in company to their patrol area where they were on station by 0800 that day. The sea was smooth, the wind light, just ruffling the water's surface, visibility was very good with a clear blue sky with perhaps a few traces of summer haze caused by the heat. In short it was a typical summer's day and intended only for the holiday maker. Up and down the two hundred or so mile stretch of patrol with only the coastal convoys ploughing their smoky ways in the distance to the westward. Occasionally one would catch a glimpse of the coast of

Norfolk, Lincolnshire or elsewhere as we moved up and down our stretch. This situation lasted all through the night and into the next morning without incident. Then the peaceful monotony broke when an urgent signal was received, in both ships, at about 1400. This signal being in cypher was quickly translated to plain language by the medical officer. Reporting to the bridge and the Captain, (Commander J.A. Allison. D.S.O.), both ships soon altered course and at increased speed were soon making tracks for the Humber and Immingham, at about 28 knots, which was not reduced until we were off Spurn Point. On arrival it was to go straight alongside for oiling and any other urgent stores. Here, we soon found that our duty was to act as covering force for some minelayers that were operating off the enemy coast.

This gave rise to much speculation as to where the ops might be, for the enemy were in occupation of the whole coastline of Europe from the North of Norway down to the coast of Spain. By now it did not really make much difference to the ship's company for we were getting used to surprise jobs as this was one of the dubious pleasures of being one of the Navy's maids of all work. By 1700, we had oiled and were proceeding down the Humber ready for whatever awaited us. Soon it was Spurn Point again on our way out, to be passed by a group of M.T.B.S., (motor torpedo boats and gunboats), going, as they termed it, out for their NIGHTLY PANTOMIME. With Spurn Point well clear of our starboard quarter, the huge turbines increased their purring hum and the engine room extractor fans increased their high pitched whirring. The two ships now headed almost due east at almost maximum speed leaving long boiling wakes trailing back to the Humber. There was only one place that we could be going in that direction and that was Holland. No, not even France as that was too far to the south. Terschelling Banks was our destination. That long curving line of islands off the Dutch coast, and we were to rendezvous with the fast minelaying destroyers *Express*, *Esk* and *Ivanhoe* of the Twentieth Flotilla. These destroyers had been especially adapted for minelaying so that in fact they were old friends, at least in the ship world. Having identified ourselves to Captain D.20., (Captain Bickford D.S.O. D.S.C.), and informed him that we were his escorts for the evening, just like escorting a young lady on the prom on a summer's evening, but hardly as dainty.

With all the minelaying ships in their positions, orders were given to commence the lay, (mines). For about twenty minutes the lay continues, the quiet of the night only being broken by the dull plops as the mines were dropped over the sterns of the laying vessels, for mines can only be dropped at a slow speed. This meant that "K" and "J" were soon some distance ahead of the layers, when "J' spotted some suspicious vessels away to starboard. "J" immediately gave the alarm, by radio telephone, and went to investigate at high speed. "K" forgot her intentions and wheeled round to assist "J" if necessary. The mystery vessels must have been enemy gun boats judging from the size of the wakes and the speed that they made off, disappearing in amongst the shoals and islets of the Terschelling Banks. The mystery vessels soon altered course and were making for Texel, probably their own base. By now, both "K" and "J" would have been some twenty five miles from Captain D.20. In the meantime, the minelayers had ceased their operations and were moving towards K and J, as it was obvious that they had been observed, which would result in aircraft attention at first light. This would have been in some three hour's time it being summer time.

During the ensuing half hour of the little ships chasing, *Esk* struck a mine which must have exploded more or less under the centre of the ship. *Esk* disappeared almost immediately. In almost the same breath, *Express* and *Ivanhoe* fouled what was thought to be floating mines. These were probably dropped by the disturbed and retreating enemy vessels. It was then that there was an explosion under the bows of the *Express* which destroyed the forward part of the ship as far back as the bridge. *Ivanhoe* had meantime been snared in the moorings of other mines which exploded fore and aft leaving *Ivanhoe* completely helpless and a floating wreck. It was small wonder that *Express* and *Ivanhoe* were still afloat. "J" and "K" are now in the close vicinity of *Express* and both are making ready to attempt rescue work. "J" is left to attend to *Express* after we had transferred some of the badly injured to "K." One of the badly injured was Captain Bickford, and they are all placed in the sick bay to receive what attention is possible. *Ivanhoe*, is by now some fifteen miles distant so that "K" proceeds with great caution fearing that more unsecured mines may be about. It is quite evident from the look of *Ivanhoe* that her back has been broken as the result of the explosions under their bows and stern. As "K" closes still nearer the stricken *Ivanhoe*, there is a sudden heavy clanking under our stern. We wait for the bang, but no bang happens, so that thankfully, at greatly reduced speed we investigate our own situation. It takes no more than a quick look over the side to establish that some wires have entangled the screws and rudder. Meanwhile signals are being made to *Ivanhoe* to establish if there are any crew left on board as she seems deserted, like Marie Celeste. Some friendly M.T.B.'s now join the rescue work. These I think were the same ones that left the Humber when we did, and they had rescued the survivors of the *Ivanhoe*. We inform them of our predicament so that they circle us at a safe distance while we make every endeavour to clear the offending wires from our rudder and screws. In this we are partially successful for with a shout from the working party working on the wire they inform the bridge that the wire has cleared the screws. At least we shall be able to move and steer the ship by using our engines. With great urgency, the Captain calls for a quick conference on the bridge and all available officers attend. The main ones being the first lieutenant and the engineer officer whose advice is most important. After some deliberation it is decided to sink the *Ivanhoe* by torpedo as to attempt salvage would be too dangerous with the approaching dawn and the proximity to the enemy occupied coast. By the time we have sunk the Ivanhoe by torpedo we make to catch up with "J" and *Express* which we do at best possible speed, all the time hearing the clanking under the stern. "J" now takes over the towing of *Express* and slowly make to the west and Immingham while we do our best to keep in her company. Now the alarm bells are ringing, and we have sighted an unknown ship approaching from the north. It could be an enemy out from Texel, hoping to make a quick easy sinking, but no, it is H.M.S. *Garth* come to help us in our efforts to get home. *Garth* is dispatched to assist "J" with her towing operations while we do our best to shake off the offending wire or obstruction, for the engineer officer has established that we have something dragging on the shaft of one of the engines, and this is confirmed when another engine room rating is lowered over the side hopefully to spot the trouble. This attempt is unsuccessful but we can still steam at a reasonable speed. By 1600 that day, we again sight "J" and *Garth* towing *Express* and are shortly joined by a couple of other destroyers and M.T.B.'s that have been sent out from Immingham to assist us.

Leaving the towing of *Express* to our new friends from Immingham, we push on at our best speed and make straight for the dock where we go alongside. Ambulances are already waiting to take the casualties from us, for news of our mishaps has already preceded us. The dry dock is made ready to take us and within a couple of hours we are docking down and getting ready for the inspection of the shaft and rudder. When sufficient water has been pumped from the dock, and engineers can see what has been bothering us. Yes, it did bother us, and I am sure that there were quite a few badly bitten finger nails to prove it. For myself, I know that I smoked far more than I would normally have done. When the shaft examination was completed, it was found that a length of mine mooring cable had been wrapped round the shaft and as the shaft turned the loose end was banging on the rudder post. Thankfully we had sustained no damage. The time was now getting on for 0800 on September 2nd. For the last forty-eight hours the whole ship's company had been at "Action Stations" so that when a general "pipe down" was made at dinner time, I feel sure that the whole of the ship's company decided to make up for lost sleep. I decided to call on some friends in Immingham just across the field from the docks.

Idle talk and gossip had already preceded us, and according to my friends the "K" had been lost with all hands. They were in a terrible state mentally, and could hardly believe their eyes when I showed up, for their dilemma was, how could they inform my wife of the supposed tragedy. Also, I sat in the armchair in the dining room and promptly fell asleep, waking up some eighteen hours later.

Captain Bickford died on September 9th 1940. I later learned that Bob Wix, the Yeoman of the *Ivanhoe* and friend from Shotley days, and also Bill Hood from Bexleyheath and *Ivanhoe*, were safe, having been rescued by the M.T.B.'s.

ANTICS IN THE CHANNEL

Some four weeks after the episode of the minelaying, just as we were getting accustomed to the routine at Immingham, Captain Mountbatten, (Captain D 5), considered that the flotilla had been sufficiently long enough at standing by for invasion threats that we should get in some real destroyer exercises. One Monday morning all eight boats of the flotilla were in harbour, a most unusual thing. I had just been to see the Captain when I spotted the Flotilla Signals Officer on the jetty looking at the ship. Knowing each other, I dutifully saluted which, after returning my salute, he promptly pitched a black bundle at me, saying, "for the captain with Captain D's compliments." This was not a present in any way for the whole flotilla knew by now just what the black bundle meant. It meant that Captain D, would be transferring his command to the unfortunate ship that received the bundle. The bundle contained just a wide black canvas strip, just long enough to go round the funnel and denoting the ship of Captain D. No time was lost in telling the Captain, (Commander Allison) the good news, which spread through the ship like fire. This was no secret to be kept from everybody. Quickly arrangements were made to receive "D.5" and also to start preparing for sea again. With the black canvas band round our funnel, the captain ordered the flotilla to be ready for sea at 0945. By 0930, Capt. D was on board *Kelvin*. In vain I looked for my old friend Jan Bottoms, but to my disgust he was having a "holiday," at least so I was told by the Signals Officer. This meant as far as I was concerned that the flotilla from a signal point of view, was to be entirely mine, as this task usually fell to Jan who was the Chief Yeoman of the Flotilla. Without further waiting, I instructed my four signal staff, that today they would earn their keep, the same as I would do. At precisely 0945, Captain D, arrived on the bridge. If one remembers from previous chapters, Captain Mountbatten was once the Fleet Signals Officer of the Med Fleet, so it was not surprising that I felt a little apprehensive at him being on the bridge. Of course he had every right to be there, and who was I to deny that right? Quickly he ordered the flotilla to SLIP AND PROCEED. In the same breath he ordered the speed and the formation to be taken up. Remembering my responsibility, I ordered the signals to be hoisted and reported to Commander Allison exactly what I had been told. At this Captain D remarked that he too was on the bridge. Nothing lacking, I promptly replied that my responsibility was to my Captain. With a laugh, Captain D replied, "Well done Yeoman, I am only here as a visitor," so that I felt that I had done the correct thing. I also realised that as well as being Yeoman of the ship, I was also doing duty for the Flotilla. This was no great extra burden so that we soon settled to the task. It did however mean that the ships signal staff had to work that much harder as Captain D would have had extra staff which he had not brought with him. No sooner were we clear of Spurn Point, that, we cracked on at 25 knots and doing various manoeuvres, that I would term "straight stuff" which were what we had done as boys at Shotley and other parade grounds. Now came the finger nail biting exercises, for speed was increased to 28 knots, (about 35 MPH), and the signal was made to reverse the sides of disposition. This, in signal terms, was called the "Grid Iron Movement." The two columns of ships turn inwards and race at each other at about 70 MPH, and each ship was only 500 yards apart. This meant that at the point of crossing in the middle there would be about two hundred yards between each ship. Sounds easy and sounds like plenty of room. Try it with approximately four thousand tons of ships racing at each other at 70 mph. It has been known for some junior officers to leave the bridge when this manoeuvre has been attempted even at much slower speeds. I won't say that fear made them leave but it is a horrid thought of what could happen. The whole idea of the exercise was to test the nerves of the controlling officers. We did eventually do the manoeuvre at 30 knots. Of course there is far more to doing the manoeuvre than has here been related, as the signal book devoted almost a page to the instructions for this manoeuvre. This exercise has been done since, but I very much doubt if it has been done at thirty knots. Shortly after the last period of manoeuvring, two of the ships were detached for patrol duties and two more were detached for some other purpose. This was to be the last time that we were to see the flotilla together, as many events ordained that we should amalgamate with other flotillas. On return to Harbour, the Captain was congratulated on the ship's performance, and I was given a, "Well done Yeoman."

MORE ANTICS IN THE CHANNEL

Once more the flotilla was to move, so that hastily I said my farewells to the Nicholls. I could not stop, for I had only been to the base to pick up some last minute signals. No, I did not tell them that we were off, I did not know at that time, I just left word for them to be on the harbour bridge about sailing time and they would be able to wave us out. This they did and as usual I flicked the signal light to them as we left. Clearing the usual turning points, this time we altered course to the south and kept going, at high speed. Soon we were leaving even the Yarmouth Roads behind and were making for the Thames Estuary and the Goodwins. Yes, we were going to make the passage through "Bomb Alley", that little stretch of water between Dover and Calais. This was quite evident when "Action Stations" were ordered and battle bowlers were much in evidence, for at Calais the enemy had several very heavy guns installed. It was more than likely that we should attract the gunners' attention as we passed through. We were not to be disappointed, for watching the French coast one noticed a sudden flash and then with a roar and a crash the shell would arrive. During the time of the flash and the arrival of the shell, it was prudent to alter course radically so that hopefully one would not be in the place where the shell landed. Some half a dozen rounds were fired at us but with no effect, other than perhaps to cause the sea to be turbulent which at our speed would cause us to roll a bit in passing. On we steamed past Ramsgate, and then later an alteration of course to the westward so that soon we were passing the Seven Sisters cliffs and making for the Needles and Plymouth Sound. Here we were to form the Channel Night Striking Force, not that the imposing sounding title meant a lot, for we did much day work as well.

Again after a short rest period, an overnight halt, we got into our stride again. On the occasion in question, date of 23rd October I believe, *Kelvin* and *Kipling* were idly swinging at their moorings in Plymouth Sound after a night of channel patrol. Suddenly the peace and tranquillity of the day was rudely shattered by the clack and rattle of the signal lamp. The time was shortly before 1100, as it was while reading the signal to raise steam with all dispatch that the pipe, "Up Spirits," was made. Nothing must stop the sailors' RUM ISSUE. For that was the spirit referred to, and I was as keen as anyone to get my issue. Quickly all concerned were informed of the raising of steam requirement, and the faint haze at the top of the funnel soon thickened and the forced draught from the engine room fans made quite an appreciable cloud. Orders would shortly be arriving by fast launch and, watching beyond Drake's island, one could see the white wake of the launch rapidly making its way out to us. The Captain, already rigged for sea, with binoculars slung round his neck, was waiting at the side ladder. As the launch came alongside a young WREN officer smartly saluted the captain and handed him a package. Quickly he glanced through the orders, gave a receipt to the WREN Officer, and hurried to the bridge. Here he called for certain officers and held a quick conference, then turning called, "Yeoman make ready to proceed." Successful anticipation in these matters is most satisfying, for scarcely had he said the word "proceed," than the flags denoting that message were fluttering from the masthead. The signalmen were on the ball. *Kipling* had also reported the same message to the Flag Officer Plymouth, who quickly acknowledged it. This was very shortly followed by, "Proceed in execution of previous orders." With the sharp clang of hammer on steel, the slip holding us to the buoy was removed and we slowly made our way through the breakwater to Cawsand Bay to await the rest of the ships that would be accompanying us. We had only a short wait before a city class cruiser, (*H.M.S. Newcastle*), and the *Emerald* appeared moving towards the Sound. These two six inch gun cruisers were followed by *Jersey*, *Javelin* and *Kashmir* from our amalgamated flotilla.

Putting two and two together one would arrive at the answer that something reasonably big was afoot, for under normal conditions the "J and Ks" were quite capable of coping with the normal run of enemy traffic in the Channel. *Newcastle*, the officer in charge of this operation, signalled the destroyers to proceed ahead and take up screen formation while the *Emerald* was stationed astern of *Newcastle*. Soon we were clear of Eddystone Lighthouse and heading southwest. Four large enemy destroyers had been reported as leaving Brest and making up the Channel. This was to be our prey, so that before long we were pounding along at a speed of some 26 knots on a course 235 (S.W.), the destroyers being told to take station on the starboard beam at one mile from the cruisers. This would put the destroyers on the side further from the enemy ships. At least that was our reckoning, which later had to be amended as we altered course several degrees to the eastwards. Speed was increased to 28 knots and at 1550, a slight smoke haze was seen distorting the horizon ahead. This was shortly followed by the sighting of mast tops of vessels coming towards us at speed.

At that time the sea was delightfully calm and there was only the smallest ruffle of wind caused by the passage of the ships. Just after 1600, four enemy destroyers are distinctly visible and are identified as MAAS class. These are more heavily armed than us, so that it is now clear why the two cruisers were brought along. The enemy appears to be steering a north westerly course as though anxious to meet us. We were already at "Action Stations" as were all our ships, as *Newcastle* had already signalled "enemy in sight." This was readily amplified by *Newcastle* and *Emerald* opening fire with the six inch guns, and by breaking out their "battle ensigns." Immediately, we in the destroyers did the same, as in those days of the war, one always had the Battle Ensign handy. At least we were trying to conform to the Geneva Conventions which state that ships shall identify themselves nationally before opening fire. The range was now about ten miles for us, so that we held our fire. *Newcastle* being away to port, and opening up from us, was that much nearer the enemy. The *Newcastle* had also flown off her aircraft for spotting the fall of shot. It was not long before we were being informed that the enemy, having come under fire from the cruisers, had turned away and were heading back the way that they had come. We were informed also, that a squadron of bombers from a Cornish base were on the way to bomb the enemy. The signal "General Chase" was received which relieved captains from strict station keeping and allowed the destroyers with their fast speeds to close the enemy. For all ships, the best course and speed to intercept became the rule of the day. The two cruisers had in the meantime altered their course towards the east, in an endeavour to get between the enemy and his French bases, in the Brest area. This meant that the distance between us and the cruisers was rapidly opening. The five "J and Ks" were not long before they came in extreme gun range, so that it was no surprise that we heard one of the destroyers open fire. Observing the fall of shot in the aircraft, they signalled that we were in range, so that before long, all five of us were firing ranging shots. Occasionally, one would glance astern, looking for the bombers, as from the way the enemy were going, the aircraft were the only ones that could slow them down for us to deal with. Soon we in *Kelvin* were firing every minute or so in the hope of getting a lucky long shot to slow them down. It would be a long and stern chase, and all the time we were getting nearer the occupied French coast. Soon it would be a question of enemy aircraft having a go at us and then we should be the hunted.

At last our own aircraft as expected, were sighted low down on the horizon astern. To our joy, there were about twelve aircraft, (probably Wellingtons), coming up astern. At about 1725, I believe it was *Javelin* that sighted smoke on the horizon to the westwards and was told to investigate. This left just four of us steaming hell bent for the four enemy ships, now about eight or nine miles ahead. Our own aircraft were now almost overhead, and at this critical moment, *Newcastle*'s aircraft signalled that the enemy had fired torpedoes. This was expected and caused us to take avoiding action by altering course from time to time, thus losing more valuable distance in this chase. Torpedo tracks were spotted away to the eastwards. It was also noticed about this time that the aircraft were assuming a threatening attitude as they were diving on the destroyers of our own force. Needless to say the Navy lads were disgusted and dismayed when we had to take avoiding action to dodge our own bombers, so that it became quite hopeless to continue the chase especially as the enemy destroyers were now almost hull down on the horizon ahead, and definitely out of range. One of the pilots approached to about a thousand feet before dropping his bombs which luckily fell some thirty yards clear of our bows. We on the bridge had a very cheap and unexpected shower to cool our tempers and ardour.

This must have all been a mistake, or was it that the enemy had somehow managed to secure some of our aircraft with which to bomb and use as a ruse of war? I suppose it could happen, but then again, such things only happened in boy's magazines of pre-war days. It was just as well that there were other ships present to witness this act, for I am sure that our yarn would not be believed. It was just incredible.

Having lost so much distance, (range), and with the fading daylight, plus the fact that we were nearing enemy airfields, Captain D.5. ordered us to concentrate on *Newcastle* as submarine and A.A. defence. *Javelin*, that had been sent to investigate the smoke on the horizon, was again on her way to rejoin us. Apparently the vessel proved to be a Spanish trawler, which was supposed to be neutral. Soon, having rejoined *Newcastle* and *Emerald*, we altered course to the northward and retraced our steps for Plymouth, having been robbed of our prey.

On arrival in harbour D.5., (Captain Mountbatten), immediately went to the *Newcastle* to lodge this complaint. It is believed that later they both went together to the Admiral in charge, who was apparently most annoyed about the whole affair. It would appear that some of the pilots, after attacking us, had realised their mistake and fully reported it. D.5. had also seen some of the offending pilots and crews of the aircraft, so that knowing D.5 as we did, we could well imagine the telling off that was awarded to them. They had seen four destroyers moving at high speed towards Brest and the two cruisers nearer the land. Putting two and two together and making six, and especially as they had seen both lots of ships firing which they assumed to be at each other. They had disregarded the four enemy ships or had not seen them. *Newcastle*'s aircraft when it was recovered, was quite badly shot up from the enemy destroyers and the pilot was apparently badly injured. From photo reconnaissance later received, two of the enemy destroyers had been hit during the operation, as the pictures showed them being repaired at Brest.

On his return to the flotilla, D.5. informed us by signal that the pilots of the "friendly" enemy bombers offered their most sincere apologies for the mistake that had been made. The whole problem had been one of mistaken identity and bad ship recognition by the air crews.

All of us would learn from our mistakes before very much longer.

ANTI INVASION 1940!

On the morning of 9th September 1940, four destroyers; the second division of the Fifth Destroyer Flotilla, steaming at high speed, turn sharply to port just south of the Eddystone Lighthouse, and make a bee-line for the harbour of Plymouth. Most certainly an inspiring sight, but few are interested in the spectacle of keen bows slicing through the green waters causing their creaming wakes to ruffle the water round the Eddystone Rocks. The crews of those four ships are certainly not interested, for this has been their umpteenth consecutive night of routine patrol as the Channel Night Striking Force.

The German Ships *Scharnhorst* and *Gneissenau*, (Salmon and Gluckstein), were then based at Brest, and it was the task of the "FIGHTING FIFTH" to ensure that they did not venture out without warning. These two heavily armed and armoured ships had been a source of intense annoyance to the Royal Navy and British shipping in general. So, it was hoped to keep them bottled up in Brest. Today was no exception as the routine patrolling had been going on far too long to cause any of the crews a flutter of excitement or even pride, although each crew had infinite pride in the flotilla and more so in his own ship. The next night and day would be a repetition of so many others gone before. Reducing speed, the four destroyers enter harbour and secure to a waiting oiler, after which they will anchor in various berths, ready to weigh anchor and go on the next patrol.

By mid day, all is peaceful and the crews have settled down for a quiet afternoon of sleep in readiness for the night patrol, in perhaps a rather boisterous Channel, for the wind is already increasing. About 1330, all hopes of sleep that afternoon have vanished with the receipt of a special secret signal by fast boat.

The whole of the Fifth D.F. under the command of Captain Mountbatten, together with the battleship *Revenge*, are ordered to keep steam for full speed at half an hour's notice. Surely the "S and G" as the German ships are called, were not trying to break out from Brest, as according to latest reconnaissance they are still docked down under repairs. If they were coming out, then why not let us be going and get the job done with?

That was the question that all the crew were asking of anybody that might supply an answer. However, patience is a virtue, and one must wait for the orders. Meanwhile, gun's crews and various other parties are ordered to exercise "Action Stations." This is most irregular, for while this is happening the magazine crews have been ordered to put on deck, the supply of "direct action impact" shells where they are to be fused. These shells are jokingly referred to as champagne bottles because of their similarity in shape. The two clues do not make sense, as this type of shell would be no good against the armour of "S and G". Something special must be afoot. That we guess but are NOT to know just yet. On the signal bridge, we are besieged with questions of "What's Happening?" The Gunners Mate, Nick Carter, stops to pass the time so that I ask him, "Why the special shells?" He did not know except that these kind of shells were normally used for bombarding shore defences. That, with what little I did know, gave me a bit more food for thought. Then, at 1600 when all the work is normally finished, we were ordered to revert to the normal notice for steam. At the same time, we are informed by word of mouth, (not piped or broadcast), that the usual nightly jaunt will NOT now take place. This was because of the apparent worsening weather conditions, but even that did not make sense, for never before had we had the night's operations cancelled because of bad weather. Believe me, we had experienced far worse conditions on the northern patrols earlier in the war. The crew then adopts the attitude of "why care?" for with a stroke of luck, we shall spend the night in harbour and get a good sleep. So it was to be, for we did not have an air raid alarm to disturb us. The powers that be were relenting for keeping us on the go so much. How simple can one get, thinking things like that? But what a wonderful thought!

Next morning, the 10th, the *Revenge* moved her berth to Plymouth Sound and the 5th D.F. comprising *Jupiter, Jackall, Jersey, Javelin Jaguar, Kashmir Kelvin* and *Kipling* all again refuelled and took up new berths near *Revenge*. All ships are ordered to remain at immediate notice for sea. Mid-day, and the weather is typical of the late summer in Devon. The sea is now almost flat calm, and at 1600, news is passed that the operation will take place that night. Early suppers are arranged and at 1900 *Revenge* and the eight destroyers weigh anchor and move towards the harbour entrance and out into the mine swept channel. Off Eddystone, the force is joined by several motor gun boats, (M.G.B.'s), who will accompany us. This is obviously going to be no routine patrol. After clearing Eddystone, the force alters course to the southeast. Again, complete consternation for the crew, as we normally go the other way for night patrol.

Now that we are at sea and out of sight of land, word is passed that we are off to bombard the port of Cherbourg, where intelligence has reported large gatherings of troops and various small craft and destroyers ready for the threatened invasion of the British Isles which had been long awaited. The bombardment is scheduled to commence at 0200 on the 11th September. This will be preceded by a small diversionary air raid on the town and docks, commencing at 0130. Time for a couple of hour's sleep in two watches before going to "Action Stations" at about 0015. The second watch of sleepers will be relieved at about 2200. At midnight all ships will assume "First Degree of Readiness" for we shall be off the French coast heading in the direction of Cherbourg. Time moves with irritating slowness as the crews assume their battle stations at midnight. About 0115, from the northwest, comes the faint thrum of heavy aircraft engines. The R.A.F. is arriving on time, and at precisely 0130, the first flares go down over Cherbourg. Soon we can hear the distant thump of bombs exploding and before long we see that there are several fires which light up the target area. Next, we see and hear quite a large explosion which must have been an ammunition dump or petrol store, most probably the latter, as now the town is clearly silhouetted and all ships are able to plot their positions with accuracy. It is still not quite time for us to take part, so that we while away a few moments watching the inferno and recording the positions of various explosions. This information will be required for "Intelligence" so that they can check the accuracy of any information that they already hold, or to add to the store of new information.

From our own local knowledge, it appears that even the smallest piece of information, be it good or bad, positive or negative in content, will all form part of the giant jigsaw that the "Intelligence Boys" are building up. We in our blissful and simple duty, are happy to assist in any way possible.

The destroyers are now in line ahead on the starboard side of *Revenge*, as we steam into our bombarding position. Nerves suddenly tense that little bit more as from somewhere on the starboard bow a low thrumming hum is heard. It is that of high powered motor boat engines. Fingers tighten on the triggers and firing mechanism of the guns, but it is a false alarm. It is our own M.G.B.'s forging ahead to patrol close in shore by the harbour entrance, ready to intercept any enemy boats that may attempt to interfere with our intentions. We now alter course slightly to the eastwards so that all the guns of all ships will bear and be able to fire on the targets, as by now we are only about four miles from the harbour, and *Revenge* is about one mile to seaward of us. One officer, the leading signalman and two lookouts are now detailed to go to the darkened chart house. The only reason for this is to ensure that there will be at least some control party in the ship, ready to take charge without being temporarily blinded by the gun flashes. This is termed "preserving one's night sight."

Each ship has previously been allocated a selected target area and ours is that of one square mile in the centre of the dock area, possibly where the landing craft and barges are berthed. Fire will be opened on receipt of a signal or at the opening fire from *Revenge*. All ships will be using flashless cordite in the guns. At 0159, just as we tense ourselves for the last minute before opening fire, *Revenge* shatters the stillness of the night by firing a full broadside. That is about eight and a half tons of high explosive to be delivered to some unfortunate. Immediately there is a rippling line of fire from the destroyers firing rapid salvoes. That is another sixty-four guns firing rapidly with a probable weight of explosive of just over one ton being spread around the harbour and the approaches. The din is terrific, especially on such a dark night, with the addition of the surprise opening of fire before it had been anticipated. Apart from that, the smell of burning cordite and explosives seems to make one's heart and breath race a bit more than normal. To those in Cherbourg it must have been one hell of a shock to find that the harbour was being pelted with roughly thirty-five tons of H.E. every minute. It would seem that the surprise is so complete, as it takes about ten minutes for them to realise that the causes of these explosions are coming from seawards, for the aircraft had departed some ten minutes previously. Every gun, rocket or other weapon is directed skywards as the enemy defences believe that this is a large scale air attack. Suddenly this excellent display of pyrotechnics becomes eclipsed as a shell hits an oversized ammunition dump. With a roar that deafens, and a brilliant flash that blinds, the whole place seems to dissolve before our eyes. The display is now augmented by several smaller explosions and flashes which confirms our thoughts of ammunition dumps. In the glare of the explosions and burning, we see shells blasting streets and houses. Whether they were our shells or from the blazing dump we did not know, but we continue to pump our shells at our allocated targets. If there is any sympathy for the locals, then that is dwarfed by the fact that this is enemy held territory. In fact I felt no sympathy at all for I was too busy watching the *Revenge* for signals. Not only that, but the French forces had deserted us at a very bad time and to my mind were greatly responsible for the debâcle of Dunkirk.

For another eight minutes the bombardment continues with the guns crews sweating and singing, (not too loudly), as shell after shell is loosed off towards the target. There appears to be keen rivalry to see which gun on board, and I suspect each ship, shall fire the most rounds at their individual target. I do not know what it is like to be on the receiving end of a fifteen inch shell exploding, and I am sure I have no keen desire to sample it. We had seen just what it could be like when we were at Narvik, and that was sufficient for me. The sound of the broadside from *Revenge* firing over the top of us was enough thrill, if that was what was required. The whining and rumbling of the huge shell in flight is sufficient for those on the bridge to instinctively duck as the huge shells pass over. Now, we receive the order to cease fire and the course is altered to the northward so that the destroyers would be screened from their targets. *Revenge* continues to oblige with a few more broadsides. The shore defences have now recovered their wits and are endeavouring to return our compliments with as many guns and batteries as is possible. We are now carefully watching for the M.G.B.'s as they have been told to return to their base. Our speed is increased as we move away. As each shore battery opens fire, the position is observed for future reference. They are getting our range and their shells explode and plop in the water round us, but no one is hit. The most damage that the destroyers received was from shell splinters and these were not too many, also there are no casualties in the force. As *Revenge* observes, the shells are falling close to many of us, we are ordered to withdraw from the range as quickly as possible. Due to the heavy firing and the shaking and jarring of the rapid fire salvoes, only a few of the destroyers receive the signal because of radio breakdown. Those that did receive the signal did not move from their positions on the screen formation, as it is the prerogative of the flotilla senior officer to order the destroyers to do what is necessary although each individual captain is still responsible for the safety of his ship.

Forming up in close screen round *Revenge* we steer a north westerly course for Portsmouth and to replenish stores and fuel. Arriving at Portsmouth in the early hours of the morning we busy ourselves clearing up the ship. It is then that we notice that there are several jagged holes in the funnel and on the upper superstructure. These were soon repaired with the aid of the dockyard. A patch here, a patch there, add to this a touch of paint and the ship soon looked as good as new.

The newspaper reporters made much of these events. Here is an extract and I apologise for copying it.

NELSON TOUCH IN THE NAVY. HEAVY BLOWS STRUCK AT ENEMY SHIPS.

Brilliant actions by the Navy during the last few days have shown that the Nelson spirit is still very much alive, both in the ships at sea and at the Admiralty. Day after day we have been thrilled to learn of smashing blows upon the enemy occupied Channel Ports and of actions in which enemy warships and supply ships have been chased and sunk in the North Sea and Mediterranean.

There are signs that these actions are but a prelude to a still more vigorous offensive by the Navy, since the collapse of France. By the German occupation of the continental coastline and the consequent dispersal of their naval forces, this has presented the British Navy with opportunities which it has not been slow to accept.

MED CONVOY RUN

HITTING HARD

Taking the offensive, both in waters near home and in the Mediterranean our warships have;

Sunk a complete German convoy of five ships and damaged another vessel of 7,000 tons.

Followed the shelling of Cherbourg with a similar bombardment of Dunkirk.

Sunk three Italian destroyers in the Mediterranean.

Chased four enemy destroyers from off Land's End to Brest and sunk a big enemy trawler near the French coast under the noses of the defences.

I apologise for not being able to append the date of the news cutting, but it must have been some time later, because when the Cherbourg raid took place, Italy was not in the War.

"OPERATION SPRING CLEAN".

While sorting out some old papers during a period in dock for boiler cleaning, I came across some old letters and on the backs of some of the envelopes were the following notes. (Sorry I am unable to make it sound a bit romantic, but the notes were obviously scribbled during some operation or they would not have been on the envelope.):-

Jan 28th 1941. More periods of escorts and patrols.

April 18th. Fifth Destroyer flotilla detailed to cover Minelaying operation off Ushant. The operation started at 0200 and lasted almost two hours. Ushant Lighthouse clearly visible. There were no incidents.

April 20th. The first night of the Plymouth Blitz. *Kelvin* at anchor off Mount Wise. Hundreds of incendiaries and High Explosive bombs dropped, several just missing the ship. Many large fires started on shore. The whole city brilliantly illuminated by the fires. Bombing lasted five nights. Day patrols maintained.

21st April. Fifth D.F. ordered to sea with all despatch. Thought that *Scharnhorst* and *Gniesennau* plus cruiser *Hipper* attempting to make Channel dash. Many larger units ordered to sea. The affair came to naught.

April 25th. *Kelvin* and *Jackal* rescue five airmen from sea. They had been adrift for over two days.

April 27th. More night work. Minelaying off Brest, etc.

It is just as well that all times are not full of excitement and action. I doubt the human frame and body would stand up to it. So it was, long periods of monotonous routine tempered with short periods of intense activity so that the mind sometimes wonders if the things ever did happen ....

I note at the end of one of the envelopes that there are remarks regarding October 1940.

On this occasion *Kelvin* with other forces was ordered to concentrate on Gibraltar. This was to be a new field of operation, for here, as we arrived there was a considerable fleet of ships of all sizes were gathering. None of this sort of thing was entirely new to us. As ever the destroyers were required for almost any task and were always on the go, be it submarine hunting, fleet duty or convoy escorting. Being a new ship of just over twelve months old, it seemed that the next job to be tackled would be including the fleet at Gibraltar. Nobody guessed wrongly, for we were employed on anti-submarine patrols on most nights. The job meant patrolling up and down the Straits of Gibraltar and crossing from La Linea to the Moroccan Coast, at about 15 knots. The enemy at that time were trying to reinforce their friends the Italians, who had recently entered the war. Any submarine of the enemy would try to break into the Med at night and the object was that we should hope to stop them. Not as easy as it sounds, for at the entrance to the Mediterranean there are numerous cross currents and layers of water of differing temperatures. This small matter affects the hydrophone effects of the listening ship, for where the water changes temperature there is very much disturbance. This helps the U-boat in its efforts to dodge the destroyers.

At dusk on the particular night that *Kelvin* was patrolling somewhere off the southern tip of Spain, we received a cypher message to the effect that about a dozen Allied escapees were somewhere adrift in the Straits, and that we should keep watch for them. As was usual on these kinds of stunts, everybody was expected to keep their eyes peeled for the object of the hunt. We had been informed by the ship's broadcast system about these unfortunate escapees, so that everybody, even those taking the air on deck for recreation purposes would cast their eyes about them as they walked the deck. All eyes would be on the lookout for an open or drifting boat, with several people on board. Many of the ship's company had by now, become quite expert at spotting odd objects from the upper deck in the dark. It was no surprise when sometime later, about 2130, somebody on the upper deck reported that they thought they had heard sounds like being hailed, as though from another very distant ship. Carefully we altered course and made our way with extreme caution in the direction from where the sounds came from. Soon, we were able to see from the bridge through binoculars, an open fishing boat, similar to those used by Spanish fishermen and indeed there were several people on board. Closing in on the boat we circled it and then called for the Captain of the boat. To this there was no reply, so that again we hailed him in language that almost any seaman would understand and we also admonished him for messing about without lights. To this he replied, "Don't you know there's a bloody war on!" There was no mistaking this northern accent, so he was told to come alongside. One had to be careful on these stunts, as the enemy was up to all sorts of tricks. They were then told that an officer would go on board and that if there was any trickery, the boat would be sunk on the spot. This was no empty threat and to ensure that the message was understood, an armed guard was already covering the fishing boat. In the boat were some fifteen very dishevelled men who were all chattering away. As they came on board, they were met by an armed guard, for we still had no knowledge that these people were those that had been reported to look for. Fourteen people came on board, so that we were again suspicious until it was explained that the person remaining was the Spanish owner of the boat and would be taking it back to harbour after he had been released from us. After many questions and answers it was established that these folk were indeed the escapees that we were looking for. They were all British army or air force escapees from the Dunkirk debâcle so they had travelled quite a way to make their escapes. We did hear a little bit of their trials as we fed and clothed them with what we could scrape up. They had apparently all made tracks to Andora and there as a party had crossed into Spain where they had been passed on by various friendly folk to eventually get a boat from just west of Almeria. It was very fortunate that *Kelvin* had been in the vicinity. Amongst the escapees there was at least one high ranking officer and I am sure that on return to Gib. the next morning they were all happy to be taken by the Military authorities for onward passage arrangements. These were probably quite lucky for they were some of the first escapees to make the journey through Spain as later on, Spain became very pro-German and German agents were widely scattered over Spain. Yes, we did do the oddest of jobs.

For some twenty-four hours we were permitted the luxury of remaining in harbour, not required for duty. This was sampling luxury to the limit, so the ship's company enjoyed their favourite pastime, that of making up for lost sleep. One never knew just when the need for sleep might arise. This need very soon arose, for during the late evening a secret envelope came on board from the Commander in Chief. Yes, your guess was just like mine. We had to raise steam for some operation which was not long in coming. We got to know the signs. By early morning we were off to sea and steering an easterly course and with several other destroyers in company. Behind these came several cruisers. Most strange this for one seldom had cruisers as escorts. Looking further back, towards the Rock, one could see the ponderous shapes of battleship and aircraft carriers leaving the harbour, all to turn to the east. Something was obviously very big to need such a force, or perhaps we were just going to see if the Italians would like to play games with us, for they were not held in very high esteem by ourselves.

During the late morning of the 27th, information received from intercepted signals told us that some screening ships on the port side of the battlefleet screen, had sighted enemy aircraft but well out of range. Probably a snooper, (reconnaissance aircraft), so it was more than obvious that the Italian enemy knew that we were at sea, and were messing about in his pond as we called it. The snooper was driven off by one of our fighters from the carrier. Too far away for us to see anything of them. By late afternoon, the fleet was attacked by three separate groups of torpedo bombers, ample warning having been given to the fleet. The first group of aircraft came in low from the direction of the setting sun. As the first group came towards us from the distant horizon, the *Nelson* opened fire with her sixteen inch guns. *Nelson* did not need to hit them to put them off; the passage of the shells passing near them would be sufficient to really upset their formation, and if the shell happened to explode anywhere near the aircraft, that would be final. The carriers fighters were also being kept busy at high level as Italian high level bombers made repeated attacks on the ships. In this small skirmish, at least four torpedo bombers and one fighter were destroyed. Many near misses were experienced in the fleet but nothing really serious. Later on that day the *Nelson* was reported hit forward so that her speed was reduced by a small amount. There were no casualties in the fleet. During these operations, it was also reported that the Italian fleet were at sea. Wherever they were, they managed to avoid contact with us and it was later learned that we had been delivering a large and important convoy to Malta. These must have been well away to the south of us for we never even saw them.

After dark, the convoy, with a special escort left the fleet to pass through the narrows of the Pantellera Channel while the rest of the fleet stooged around until nearly daylight when we altered course again for Gibraltar. The convoy would by then have been under the protection of the aircraft from Malta. On this occasion the *Kelvin* did not engage the enemy other than aircraft, which was and indeed did become the common lot of the Malta convoys of the future.

The return to Gib. was uneventful as far as we were concerned and after ammunitioning, refuelling and provisioning we were soon again ready for sea. Within forty-eight hours we were again to be at sea, steering westwards with another "J" or "K" class destroyer. This again was to be a convoy job, but of a different kind, for by noon the next day, we were somewhere off the Azores. Here we spotted a convoy of which we were to be the escort for passage to the Clyde. This was great news, for we all expected to get a few days' leave when we got in.

The following is a retype of the signal made to us following the Malta run.

To All ships from Flag Officer Force "H". (Admiral Somerville).

The following is a brief summary of yesterday's (28th Nov.) action.

1   After the enemy was reported, convoy was detached and ships from Gibraltar and Eastern Med concentrated.

2   After concentration, closed enemy at full speed. Enemy force consisting of two Battleships, including one modern 45 thousand ton ship, 4 eight inch cruisers, 3 six inch cruisers and about 12 destroyers. Our force consisting of Renown, Ramillies, Ark Royal, 1 eight inch and 4 six inch cruisers and nine destroyers.

3   When sighted, enemy turned away and when fire was opened made smoke. Long range chase continued for nearly four hours until within thirty miles of enemy coast. Enemy had the legs on us, observed. Chase was discontinued in order to close convoy, now 60 miles away.

4   Subsequently enemy starboard wing ship damaged by gunfire.
    a) 1 cruiser;   8 inch hits at cruiser, on fire aft burning furiously.
    b) 1 destroyer GREGALE class stopped, down by stern and listing heavily.
    c) 1 destroyer stopped and listing slightly.

5   Fleet Air Arm attacks resulted as follows:-
    a) 1 torpedo hit on Littorio class battleship.
    b) 1 torpedo hit on BOLZANO 8" cruiser.
    c) 2 very near dive bomb misses on 6" cruiser.

6   Only damage to our force, 2 eight inch hits on Berwick.

7   2 enemy aircraft shot down by fighters. 1 Fulmar lost.
    TOO = 1743/29/11/40.

The above is a copy of the original signal as made by Flag Officer Force "H" after the action off Calabria.

THE CHERBOURG RAID

Another snip of paper has just revealed itself regarding this.

Subsequent reconnaissance showed that the port was finished for several months. The docks were left in a shambles and almost every vessel in the harbour was destroyed or severely damaged. Two of the M.G.B.'s whose job it had been to patrol the harbour entrance, being dismayed at their own inactivity, went INSIDE the harbour and beat up by gunfire anything that happened to be in their way, causing the enemy to think they had been invaded. I suppose they were in a way. Several newspapers reported that many bodies in German uniform had been washed up on the southcoast beaches. Some few weeks after this incident it was reported in the papers that the enemy had made an attempted landing. All I can say to that is, we never saw any signs of a landing by the enemy, and since we were handy and already in the channel area, I feel that this was a lot of propaganda. If it was put out by the enemy it must have been for their own consumption and to boost the morale of the German people at home. The whole point was that so far, the only people to oppose the enemy and seemingly to be holding them, was the British people with the aid of the English Channel.

To put the raid in the words of one of the air observers that took part in the diversionary raid, "Southend on Gala Night was like a damp squib compared to Cherbourg."

I remember writing on a piece of paper somewhere, "Farewell Cherbourg, until some later date. We shall return." I am not psychic in any way but that remark was to come true a lot later.

"EXTRACTS FROM NEWS OF THE DAY"

Clash off the Isle of Wight; say Berlin. (New York reporting.) According to telegrams from Berlin, it was officially announced in the German Capital today that there had been a heavy engagement between a U-boat Squadron operating from an undisclosed port and British Naval Forces in the Channel. The Nazi announcement added that "(preliminary) reports indicate that some British Destroyers and torpedo boats have been torpedoed." -- Reuters. No comment on the Berlin report was available from the Admiralty in London yesterday.

"This does riot necessarily mean," states the News of the World Naval Correspondent, "that there has been no clash between British and German Naval Forces. There may be very sound reasons why no statement should be issued by Admiralty at present. Frequently reports are issued in Berlin, with a view to attempting to obtain information through Official Channels from this side, which the Nazi High Command could not secure otherwise."

It may be noted that the German claim follows upon the bombardment of Cherbourg by British Naval Forces.

"IGNORANCE IS BLISS"

OR

"PLENTY HASTE - LESS SPEED"

Almost complete blackout with a chill wind from the northwest to herald in the 24th December 1940. Save for the occasional flicker of a torch on the quayside and the impatient demands and orders from the lockgate men, it could have been anywhere else than at Liverpool Docks. Suddenly the inky blackness is stabbed by an urgent questing finger of light. Muffled up in a teddy bear coat, thick wool lined leather gloves, all enclosed by a service issue oilskin, the figure reports in a loud voice that the stern is clear of the lock. Now another commanding voice is heard, "let go forrard, let go aft," and then in almost the same breath, "any signs of *Javelin* yet Yeoman?" Promptly comes the reply, "about five cables off the starboard quarter, Sir" (just over half a mile). "Good," he tells him, "Lets go. Follow father." Again the lights flicker from the bridge as the signals are passed. Back comes the reply, "Lead us gently father lead us, o'er the world's tempestuous sea."

No, it is not meant to be irreverent as one might think when first hearing it. It is just the friendly signals between friendly captains before getting out to sea, where no signals will be made unless vitally important, and with the emphasis on the VITALLY. In fact no signals at all will be made by any means, for radio silence is in force and will only be broken in dire emergency. Then, faintly to the ears comes the distant sound of the engine room telegraphs as the Captain orders half speed ahead both. Immediately the engine room fans take up their comforting whine, and so it is that "K" and "J" head out in to the Irish Sea, to meet the gentle waves that give a rocking horse motion. Clearing the Formby Lightship, (no light working) both ships increase speed and course is altered to the north. Increases of speed and alterations of course have already been agreed to by the Captains before leaving harbour, so that one keeps a careful watch on the movements of one's consort for any undeclared alteration of course or speed. By 0100 they again alter course to the southwest, and *Javelin* jockeys herself to a position about one and a half miles on the starboard beam of *Kelvin* leaving them in a line abreast formation. This formation is assumed so as to give a wider field of vision for sighting anything and for offering the best support to each other. Daylight, and the ships are gently rising and falling to the atlantic rollers, while the mild wintry sun gradually drives away the chill of the night. By 1000 the weather is glorious, considering it is mid-winter in the Atlantic. The lookouts are able to see considerable distances which helps tremendously now that the rendezvous is approaching. The two ships are to meet a medium-sized convoy homeward bound from South America. At approximately 1020, the so far unbroken horizon is smeared by several blobs which soon materialise as the convoy. Men are now released from "Action Stations", as always when meeting blobs on the horizon one has to be prepared for the unexpected. The Yeoman counts the ships as they appear.

Again and again he counts and calls for another signal rating to check numbers, as there appears to be one short according to convoy orders. Surely the convoy has not been attacked within the last hour when the latest news was received. The missing ship is a county class 8 inch gun cruiser, H.M.S. K.... that the two ships had purposely come to escort. On realising this, the bridge of *Kelvin* becomes a hive of activity. The navigator checks all his latest information and reports that it is up to date. The yeoman is now told to contact the Senior Officer of the escort, (a naval ship) and ask him the whereabouts of the cruiser. A signal rating rattles out the signal to the Escort Commander. Almost an immediate reply is made to the effect that the cruiser left the convoy some half hour earlier on a southeasterly course at about twenty-five knots. The Captain then tells the yeoman to thank him and wish him a Happy Xmas. With this exchange of greetings, come other commands and a string of coloured bunting appears almost in a twinkle of an eye, which is answered by *Javelin* and the flags disappear almost at once. The two destroyers wheel round to the southeast and increase to thirty knots. The cruiser has roughly an hour's lead on them, which at twenty-five knots means five hours steaming at thirty knots. Quite a problem, for like any machine, the faster it goes the more fuel it burns, and destroyers are no different. For a short space the chase is on with no signs of the cruiser. It is then that the Captain consults different personnel regarding the breaking of radio silence and the sort of code to be used. The two greyhounds are still chasing the elusive hare without success and Commander Allison wears a troubled look, for the unescorted cruiser is ideal prey for any lurking U-boat. With consultation over, he tells the Yeoman to make a signal to the cruiser telling him to cease his intentions and retrace his course. This is a most unheard of thing, for a Commander to tell a Senior Officer to do such things. The signal had to be made by radio, which is breaking radio silence so that there were two unpardonable sins being committed. The signal is received in *Kent* but she has been instructed in the message not to answer. It is only to be hoped that *Kent* will understand the signal, especially as it was an order and not a suggestion. As the winter's night starts closing in, additional lookouts are posted, for we must sight the cruiser before he spots us. At about 2000, a blurred shape is spotted through the bridge binoculars and immediately the challenge is made to which the cruiser replies correctly. Hurdle number one successfully completed.

The cruiser is now moving at reduced speed as though reluctant to obey our instructions and at the effrontery of the signal that we had made. *Javelin* is now stationed directly ahead of the cruiser while we manoeuvre ourselves into a position just off his port quarter. There, we hail him through the loud hailer and apologise for our effrontery. At the same time the Navigating Officer tells *Kent* that he has to back track because of a secret minefield that had very recently been laid in front of his intended track. This information somewhat mollifies the Captain of the cruiser so that more information is asked for, and our Captain informs the cruiser that we will supply the necessary information first thing in the morning, when we will drop close by and transfer the signals necessary for a safe passage. From snatches of the ensuing conversation, it was gathered that *Kent* had hoped to spend Christmas in harbour, having just come from extended service abroad of nearly three years, and had recently been damaged in action in the Mediterranean. From that moment on there were no more signals except that we gave him a course to steer.

The signal staff and the Navigating Officer spent the next five hours making copies of all the relevant mining signals that Kent had not picked up for she had not called at Gibraltar where the information would have been available. Before closing the signal section down for the night, the *Kent* made to us, "Lighten my darkness Lord, and lead me to my green pastures," for the *Kelvin* had been named after a certain famous seafaring gentleman who had done much to help the causes of safe navigation and ship safety. The green pastures were those of home in *Kent*, where the ship's company of that ship hailed from. Finally, at about 0600 on Christmas morning, the Yeoman reported to the Captain that all signal matters were now ready for transfer. At the first signs of daylight, *Kent* was informed that *Kelvin* would transfer a package by line at 0830, and that this was to be considered as a Xmas Card.

At approximately 0820, signals were made for *Javelin* to take station ahead as screening vessel, while Kelvin dropped back to *Kent*'s lee quarter, (sheltered side aft), ready to effect the transfer. With both ships ready, and *Kelvin* steaming about fifty feet from the *Kent*, a rocket line was fired from *Kelvin*. With a "whooosh" and "bang," the line went straight to the *Kent*'s quarter deck. Here it was grabbed by seamen and the line hauled in board at speed. Attached to the line was a Canvas bag containing the secret signals that *Kent* was in urgent need of. This was hurried to the Bridge as the line was cast off and *Kelvin* surges away to rejoin Javelin and reinforce the screen. Some little time passes and they are a considerable distance south of the Southern tip of Ireland. As darkness falls, *Kent* flashes to *Kelvin*, thanking him for his kindly warnings and saying that now he expected to spend Christmas happily but belatedly in harbour, and wishes both ships a Happy Boxing Day to all. A few hours later without mishap or incident the little force passes in to the extensive and highly dangerous minefield with full knowledge of the positions of the mines. This could hardly have been likely had *Kent* not acted on *Kelvin*'s advice, but had carried on with so much haste and speed for in the little bag that we had transferred by rocket line, was the key to her safe passage home to Plymouth and on up the Channel to the Thames. The most rewarding part of this operation was that I personally knew the majority of *Kent*'s signal staff and the Chief Yeoman was a friend of mine from before the start of the war, so that our efforts and ultimate success amounted to a job at least well done. There was not much after this but to look forward to the next convoy, wherever it might be.

The next convoy was to be to go to almost the centre of the North Atlantic and return with another convoy. The trip out was no more exciting than the usual ones but the trip home turned out to be rather more hectic than usual; if hectic is the correct word to use for such occasions. On looking back at the dictionary term for hectic, it states that the word is used to describe something that is exciting with a sense of morbidity, or out of the usual. I think it fits to a fair degree.

The following poem was written by one of the merchant captains of one of the ships in the convoy concerned, and is a modest account of what that convoy put up with en route home.

SPECIAL ESCORT; POEM

1941 CONVOY THOUGHTS

Now way out on the rolling sea,
There steams a score of ships,
They're bringing home your cups of tea
And the food which pass your lips.

Now some folk never stop for thought,
As now we are at war,
Of the men and the ships with danger wrought,
Who bring all this food to the shore.

Onward and onward they steadily plough
While escort ships guard outer flanks,
A destroyer which steams up the line then and now,
Like a sergeant inspecting the ranks.

The Captain bawls out, "You're out of the line,"
So alter your course now to port,
If Jerry pops up, we'll probably find,
We're one damned good cargo ship short.

The weather has changed rather quickly,
The blue skies are now overcast,
The ships are now reeling quite sickly,
And the glass, is by now, falling fast.

The waves wash over and sweep them
As the wind increased to a gale,
The hatches, the men have to fasten,
The ships, to the waves, seem so frail.

The storm is now passed and is clearing,
The sun once again starts to shine,
For a calm after a storm is so cheering,
To the ships as they steam on in line.

The darkness is now coming nearer,
While the moon shines down from on high
Which show up the convoy much clearer
To a U-boat that's lurking nearby.

A deadly device cleaves the ocean,
And everything doesn't seem right,
When a sound like a muffled explosion
Then shatters the still of the night.

A ship has been hit and is sinking,
The escort sends out a lifeboat,
To the men in the water, who're thinking,
That while there is life there is hope.

Survivors are pulled in and taken
To a warship that's standing close by,
Who will take care of nerves badly shaken
Or to the wounded, a dressing apply.

The escort steams round dropping charges,
The raider has got clean away,
And at a ship, a torpedo discharges
At dawn on the following day.

The same operation's repeated,
And the men, at the submarine, are sore,
This surely can't go undefeated,
After dropping depth charges galore.

The danger from under is clearing,
The lookouts are watching on high
At four black spots they are peering,
Which seem to grow large in the sky.

Our ships are now slewing and turning
As the raiders sweep down from the blue
Which sink two, and one now is burning,
Up forrard are huddled the crew.

The guns from the convoy are blazing,
At the planes which are now coming back,
The seamen are cursing and raving
As they drive off another attack.

The men in the water are tended
When rescued from out of the sea,
The courage of all, is, well, splendid
And just as expected to be.

The ships are now steady and silent,
Their numbers decreased rapidly,
By the force of the drama so violent,
Which came from the sky and the sea.

NOW, remember when eating your dinner,
And all the while Britain is free,
You'll never become any thinner,
While there's sailors and ships out at sea.

I apologise for not having noted the name of the author who was in the convoy. This poem emphasises the every day life and action in those convoys of the early war days. In some months the figures for U-boat sinkings, reached the staggering totals of some half to three-quarter of a million tons of shipping. That is about TEN fair sized merchant ships each week. It was well in to 1942 before there were signs of beating the U-boats. As I recall, Mr Churchill, the Prime Minister of the day, referred to those battles as the LONGEST Battles of the War. Whether or not that is fact, one thing is most pertinent, as from the first day of the war the submarine menace was constantly with us, until the last day of the war. Just how near the enemy came to winning the Battles of the convoys is a matter that requires much careful thought, for if those battles had not been won, the outcome of World War Two would have been more than doubtful with disastrous and horrendous results for the Allies and the free world.   F.S 1941.

NOTE

Having re-read some of the pages at random, it is quite possible that one MAY get the impression that the ship in which the author served only went to sea on the occasions mentioned. This impression would be far from the truth. If memory serves me correctly, and this is not boasting, out of the first 365 days of the war, the author estimates that nearly 300 of those days were spent at sea.

It should be remembered that for every group of merchant vessels that moved at sea, an escort of some sort was provided, either for that particular group or on a roving basis. Sometimes a convoy would consist of seventy or more ships, while other convoys consisted of as few as two merchant ships. Very seldom was a vessel permitted to sail without escort unless that vessel had sufficient speed, (about 26 knots or more), as in the case of the *Queen Elizabeth*, or some other large fast liners. In the case of some of the Malta convoys, where the opposition was in great strength, the force of escorts was increased to the maximum number of ships available.

Also, it should be borne in mind that many of the operations carried out by named forces consisted of the same ships as did other operations. As for example, heavy units of the fleet bombarding Cherbourg; light forces of the Med Fleet engaging the enemy, or cruisers and destroyers in action off Brest. In almost all cases, some of the ships taking part in those operations took part in them all, as well as many other well recorded operations such as Narvik, Crete, Dunkirk. If there was any spare time during these historic and momentous occasions there would always be home bound convoys requiring escort. The only respite was when and if a ship was in dock for repairs or overhaul, and even then, if the docking period was not extensive, the ships company would be required to assist in the work where possible.

In short, sea-time was the order of the day and the accounts here recorded are what were *some* of the highlights, if they can so be termed, that the author can recall, when writing.

F.S. Feb. 1944.

HOME LEAVE; NEW SHIP

Just before the beginning of February 1942, the *Kelvin* put into Devonport Dockyard for some urgent repairs. As ever on these occasions, opportunity is taken to relieve certain members of the crew and to replace others. This practice is understandable for *Kelvin's* crew had been together for nearly two years and were highly trained and efficient. It was amongst these reliefs and replacements, that I found that I was to return to Chatham barracks. With much reluctance, I said my farewells to, those closes associates with whom I had shared so much but as has been said before, and many times, "Ours not to reason why, just do as you are instructed." So, Chatham barracks, here I come.

In the old days of serving in the *Valiant*, when at Devonport, it usually took us about four hours by train to London. On this occasion, it took almost twenty-four hours, for the air raids on this country had started to develop. Somewhere about Clapham Junction, the train was held up, not actually in the station but some way outside. Even when we did start moving it was at dead slow speed for we could still hear the aircraft overhead. We eventually arrived at Chatham, tired, hungry and dirty where the authorities promptly told us to leave our baggage until the morning. In the meantime we could go on ordinary night leave the time being about 1700. Nobody needed any second bidding to this invitation, and soon we were scattered around the Kentish countryside like the proverbial chaff before the wind. Some two years ago I had left my cycle at the Sailor's Rest in Chatham so that I thought I would call and see if it was there. Luckily I had my cycle pass with me and YES, the machine was still in the racks. I think it cost me somewhere about the equivalent of one pound and twenty-five pence to retrieve the cycle which suffered from flat tyres. Even the pump was still in position, so that after a quick inspection I renewed the valve rubbers mounted the machine and peddled happily home to Bexleyheath. My surprise arrival home was as complete as the surprise of my departure two years ago. A quick bath and some food, plus a good night's sleep with only the interruption of one air raid warning, and I was ready for the road again to Chatham by 0500 the following morning. Quickly I made my way to the P.O.'s mess. Luckily I met JOCK just coming off night duty. Jock you will recall was the fellow that was on course with me at Portsmouth and delighted all and sundry with his jokes such as his inimitable "Binnng Boop" on the parade ground. Breakfast for us was a lengthy affair, for we had much to talk about after two years. Obviously, Jock put me wise to all the latest news regarding the drafting of signal staff and the duties required of them while in the barracks, but first I had to report for my joining instructions. So saying, I left Jock to get some well earned sleep. Reporting to the joining section of the barracks and having given them all the information that they required I started my rounds of the barracks. Reporting as was usual to the leave office, I was delighted to be informed that I was to have a week of leave starting that day. Hurriedly I completed the rest of my joining procedures and then gathering the necessary ration cards and some pay I again mounted my cycle for the ride home. No friendly lorry drivers this time, and certainly NO bananas, for these were luxuries and only obtainable with special ration tickets such as for expectant mums. Again I arrived home with only my wife and baby to share the joys of being on leave. At the weekend, on the Friday afternoon, the three of us walked the three odd miles to Plumstead where Eileen's parents lived in Villas Road. That night we were disturbed several times by the enemy aircraft going over so that it was the air raid shelter for most of the night. On the Saturday night, being one of the few able bodied people in the area, I volunteered to do a spot of fire watch in the immediate area. One could not have slept in any case because of the noise of the A.A. Guns and the drone of the aircraft. During my stint of this duty, I was standing at the door of the house when a large bomb exploded, I estimated in the next street, the blast from which carried me off my feet, through the house and into the back yard. I had no recollection of either having touched the wall of the hallway or of my feet touching the ground until I reached the concrete of the yard. It was during this journey that the elderly gent from next door, Mr Bush, came running out from his house in nothing but a little short vest. Air raids never bothered him, at least that was his story. On further investigation of the whereabouts of the explosion, it was found that the large building, the Working Men's Club, had been completely demolished by what was then referred to as a land mine. This particular building was only some hundred yards in a direct line from where I had been standing. Fortunately there were a row of houses in between the bomb and myself. During the night several bombs also fell in the vicinity, the majority being incendiary bombs of small size and intended to start hundreds of fires that could very speedily get out of hand if not attended to. Many were the odd things that one did to extinguish these devices. The chief action was to put a shovel full of earth over the bomb and leave it until it could be dealt with properly. Another method was to give the bomb a hefty kick so that the shock of the kick would upset the firing mechanism. This again was the Blitz of Plymouth all over, and many were the towns and cities to suffer this treatment; Liverpool, Coventry, Birmingham, Hull, Portsmouth, to name a few. Looking out from the street one could see the fires raging in the docklands and up into the city of London itself. For many nights this bombing lasted until it seemed that the whole of the city must be burning. When the incendiary raid finished the main stream of bombers arrived to bomb the centre of the fires. Casualties were enormous and in some reported instances the bombs fell on communal air raid shelters. Nobody hesitated to help in the rescue work or the salvage of property from bombed homes. Everybody was expected to assist where and when possible, and to offer aid to those that needed it. Just what the strategic advantage of bombing on such a scale is hard to understand, or at least it was at the time, so that when one had a night's respite from the bombing one took the greatest advantage and slept if that were possible. After about five nights that respite came, at least for us as we went back home to see what damage had been done to our home. Again it was extremely fortunate that we had received no damage other than a few cracked tiles caused either by falling shrapnel or the shock of nearby explosions. What a wonderful leave, and to have to spend it in close proximity to an air raid shelter, where one would be for hours on end only leaving during the lulls to make a cup of tea or to grab a loaf and some margarine and if lucky a piece of cheese. All these things were on ration so that one really appreciated something extra, no matter if it were only what is today termed offal. Butter if available was at the rate of a quarter pound per person per week, with cheese going in much the same fashion. Depending on the success of the convoy operations and the Navy successes against the U-boats, so the ration went up, by an ounce, or very often down by a similar amount. At one stage, the cheese ration was cut to two ounces a week. Clothes also were rationed as one had a card with a total of so many points which had to be surrendered when making any purchase. It was quite a common thing to see a family and their friends give up their points allocation to some female member of the family in order that she may be able to purchase a wedding dress of suspected quality. No eggs were available and this was substituted by the issue of coupons for the purchase of dried egg powder. Some folk when short of fats for cooking, would resort to the use of medicated paraffin as this was more or less the remedy for many complaints. At least it was until the authorities rumbled the idea, so then it became a rationable item. Not many items escaped the attention of the rationing authorities, and soon even the kiddies sweets came on the ration. As for petrol, one just did not get any unless one was employed on special duties such as doctors and the like occupations. There were some cases of out and out blatant fiddling, and if caught the penalty was quite heavy. One just hitched the belt a bit tighter and hoped and prayed for better times. We survived, but it must have been by a very narrow margin at the crucial times. Even the children in their games were encouraged to help by keeping their eyes open and reporting lots of incidents, which all helped in the end.

ANOTHER SHIP, ANOTHER QUEEN

My leave finished and I was again on my cycle each day for the Barracks at Chatham. I say each day, that is, when I was not required for duty. In any case I was soon to be informed that I was to be drafted to a cruiser that was almost completed in the dockyard. This was to be the cruiser *Euryalus* of about 6,000 tons with ten 5.25 guns of dual purpose, (H.A. and L.A.). Yes, she was a beautiful looking ship, and in peacetime would have been quite comfortable as regards living space. However this was not peacetime so that every available space was utilised for war purposes. The day that I was detailed for *Euryalus*, nicknamed "Urinal" by the sailors, I made some excuses to visit the ship in the dockyard and to my amazement she appeared almost ready. Naturally on my next visit home I broke the news that the ship seemed to be almost ready. There are quite a few advantages of being detailed early for a ship. These are chiefly that one can get a good idea of what is required in the stores line for a particular department, one can at least select a reasonable billet for one's hammock to be slung, and most of all, be able to find one's way about the ship without much difficulty, and know where all places and offices are located. These sort of things, to the average person seem to be of little importance but, at some time somebody will ask where a certain place is and being a petty officer, one is expected to give the correct answer. In fact when passing the exams for higher rating, ship knowledge is part of one of the subjects and in this I refer to damage and control training.

However, knowing of my drafting to the ship, (*Euryalus*), I made some enquiries and "pulled a few minor strings" so that I was then officially drafted to the ship. I was not the first person to be drafted to the ship, as there were some few others that had been standing by the ship while building, but the main ship's company would not yet be accommodated on board. I think the reason for getting certain ratings out to the ship was, the barracks had so many to look after that they were only too pleased to be released from that responsibility. Apart from that, it meant that the safety of the ship was the responsibility of those people that were already on board, especially during air attack.

Reporting to the officer on board, the Navigating Officer also classed as the Communications Division Officer, I was informed that I would be the Captain's Yeoman, and would also be responsible for the ship's Signal Office. This I felt would be quite easy as I had had previous experience on other ships. It was not quite as easy as it seemed, for in this ship there were to be somewhere in the region of twenty departments, each with its own officer or officers attached. For example the Engine Room Department had about seven officers and a fairly large office, likewise the Gunnery Section. Soon everything was working to almost perfection, and would be in order by the time we commissioned, or to put it in easy language, "A Navy ship with a Captain on board." Until that day, I was to be much my own boss, with very few restrictions on my leave. The day of commissioning arrived with the majority of the ship's company already on board, and the Captain was to be Captain Bush D.S.O. D.S.C. R.N., a short dapper type that had obviously seen much active service. With all hands mustered on the quarter deck, the Captain "read himself in," as the ancient saying goes, that is, read his authority for taking command, read out the various Articles of War, then gave the ship's company a short talk on the history of the ship and its previous achievements, which were quite impressive. All these things we were now expected to live up to. Little time was left to wonder or ponder, for we should soon be forming part of the fleet in general. For two or three days the ship's company, now brought up to full strength, laboured and slaved getting in the numerous stores. The next matter would be to ammunition ship, but this had to be done outside the dockyard so that we knew that from there on we should soon be at sea. Various trials were completed and soon we were out of the docks and into the Medway for ammunitioning. Then it was down to Sheerness for all the final bits and pieces to be completed before we sailed for a northern port, I believe it was Rosythe. The sea was kind to us for our introduction to the elements so that we were able to exercise various pieces of equipment during the journey. A short stay here for various minor adjustments to equipment and then on to Scapa Flow.

At Scapa, where there was quite a fleet assembled, we took part in many fleet and individual exercises which included exercise "Action Stations." Here everybody on the ship was tried and tested to the limit so that I was thankful that I had a reasonably good knowledge of action conditions. During one part of the exercise, it so happened that I was left in charge of the ship, if only for a few brief minutes, while an officer, was summoned to take over command. Yes, Smudger's moment of glory, but only during an exercise, and a little more knowledge to the store of experiences that I was to gather. A few more days of final shake down before we became a full blown member of the fleet. Our introduction to these duties was hardly over pleasant for our first job was to act as anti-aircraft screen to some carriers that were covering the main section of the fleet that were covering a convoy to the Russian ports in the Arctic circle. Just how the carriers operated is beyond belief for at times the flight decks were rising and falling by an estimated height of some fifty odd feet, and still some aircraft were operating from the decks. For several days we moved around with the carriers until with a final signal we were ordered to return to Scapa Flow. We had not seen anything of the enemy for between us and the convoy, somewhere were the battle ships. Again refuelling, and a night in harbour at Scapa, we sailed in the morning for the Clyde. It did not need any official signal or even a word, to inform most of us that the Clyde was the usual place for the East-West-East convoys to gather, and we were not disappointed.

Refuelling again at the Clyde, we were surrounded by many ships of differing sorts and sizes. That evening, it would have been about the early part of July, we proceeded to sea expecting the convoy to follow us. One should not guess on these stunts, for one is invariably wrong. No ships followed us so that there were only us and two Hunt class destroyers as we passed Ailsa Craig at the extreme entrance to the Clyde. Making a southwesterly course at a moderate speed, we enjoyed a peaceful night somewhere in the Atlantic to the west of Ireland. By noon next day we had met and joined another convoy going in the same direction as ourselves. Destination, so far unknown, not that it mattered for we knew that this was no course for home. This had all the match stick navigators on board in a deep quandary for if we should hold to this course we should finish up somewhere in South America. As some wit later remarked, perhaps we were going to collect a special cargo of beef from the Argentine. During these days, the ship was still carrying out various exercises. Steadily we ploughed on day after day, each day becoming warmer as proof of our going southwards, and then almost without warning we turned eastwards. This at least answered many of the amateur navigator's problems. There was only one place that we could be going, Gibraltar and the Med, but hardly in the manner that we did go. On the evening of the 19th July the loudspeakers buzzed and, a voice that we were soon to become familiar with announced, "This is the Captain Speaking," followed by the news of our destination which as we had guessed was Gib. He also told us that we should be arriving after dark, that we should refuel and leave as quickly as possible. Nobody would be allowed to leave the ship and nobody was to speak to anybody from the shore. We had to be well clear of the land before daylight. All this went according to plan and by daylight we were again many miles out into the Atlantic, heading westwards. Here we soon found ourselves joining up with the convoy that we had left yesterday. The only difference was, they were now heading for Gibraltar. So that all the "Guess Merchants" were again caught out. Any newcomers had still not sighted Gib., and furthermore, Gib. had not sighted us except for a few folk who had helped to oil us. The same thing happened again that night for we steamed past Gibraltar without a light or even a signal. The coast of Spain had now become a hotbed of what the navy called "evily disposed persons" and the less that they knew of the convoy movements, the better it would be, at least for the convoy. By morning of the 21st, we were surprised to note that the convoy had increased in size from the Navy point of view, for with us now were the aircraft carrier *Ark Royal* and the battleship *Nelson* with some others that could not yet be distinguished. Also a large force of destroyers and a couple more cruisers were in our company. Now there was no question as to our destination, which the Captain soon confirmed as being Malta.

The speed of the convoy is that of the slowest ship, and ours was certainly slow compared with our dash of the previous night. By the evening of the 24th, approximately south of the Island of Sardinia, we had a strange and unwelcome visitor by way of a large Italian reconnaissance aircraft who we knew was checking our composition, course and speed. Not only that, but we knew that having been spotted by him, this would probably be the last few peaceful hours until the job was completed.

At about 1000 on the 25th, it was obvious that things were moving, for with a wide sweeping turn and an increase of speed, the *Ark Royal* drew out of formation and commenced flying off her fighter aircraft. However, we were getting over anxious, for we had roughly another two hours to wait before anything startling happened. The hands off duty in *Euryalus* had just gone to an early quick midday meal when the *Ark Royal*, who had now rejoined us, and was not far from us, suddenly disappeared in a huge column of spray and foam, with the accompaniment of exploding bombs. For a few brief moments, all on the bridge expected to see the *Ark* badly damaged and perhaps sinking but, to our amazement she came through the welter of spray and foam little the worse for her shower. The Italian high level bombers were putting on a display for our benefit. It was not very comfortable, for they were at extreme height where no Anti-aircraft gun could reach. However they were not getting off entirely, for the *Ark Royal*'s fighters were now getting amongst the bombers and they were starting to split up. To those of us that had not so far experienced the delights of Italian high level bombing, we might and did ask why not open fire, on the bombers. Those that had been in the know were well aware that it would have been a waste of ammunition, and at such height it was best left to the fighters, saving valuable ammunition which we were now aware, had to be taken to Malta, or anywhere else by convoy. Five times again that afternoon did we experience the helpless feeling of being bombed by the Italians and not being able to answer back.

On the morning of the 26th, the alarm bells rang and rattled in real earnest for the first time in the ship. The ship immediately became alive with seeming disorganised order, for the broadcaster had informed us that more enemy aircraft were on the way. Since early morning, we had closed with the convoy who were now only some eight or nine miles from us on our starboard side. Pantelleria was now dimly visible in the distance ahead of the fleet, and was probably about twenty miles away. This was approaching "E-boat Alley" as it became known, and this point had to be passed before the convoy could alter course to the south eastward to make for Malta some two hundred miles with our own aircraft from the *Ark* circling over us. There was a sudden burst of gunfire from the Northward. One of the screening destroyers in that direction had opened fire, not so much in the hope of hitting the target, but more probably as an instant warning to the fleet that attack was imminent, so that all would be ready for the reception. Again the *Ark* flew off more of her aircraft to support those already airborne. This time we were to be attacked by torpedo bombers in restricted navigable waters so that all ships would be subjected to some form of attack, for the high level bombers were still circling overhead. The torpedo bombers meanwhile had split into groups of about six flights, and each group was making off in a different direction but always towards our forces and the convoy. Before very long, the torpedo bombers had apparently achieved their desired positions and it seemed that on receipt of a given signal by the leader, they then came at the fleet and particularly the convoy, in waves from all directions. Low over the water, until sometimes it seemed that they were flying on the wave-tops. This was until they met the concentrated fire of the fleet's close range weapons. Then, it seemed that it was everyone for themselves, for they would jiggle and twist in an effort to throw the gunners off aim. In all this maddening din, came the bellowing roar of the foremost guns going into action against some bombers that had become more daring than the others. One could not possibly watch everywhere with torpedoes being released and bomb dropping having to be observed. In short, it was a bit like Dante's Inferno, that is, if the story is anything to go by, as there was flame, smoke and explosions all about one. There seemed little time to think properly so that one's movements and actions were being done automatically because of the long hours of previous training. If one had stopped to think in a logical manner, perhaps one's nerve may have cracked. However, there was no time to stop and think and one would also be constantly watching the newcomers to the ship for any signs of incorrect behaviour. Under those conditions it would only require a small incorrect incident to start the less well trained into giving way to their nerves and feelings. Fortunately, the signal staff were all far too busy to indulge in such thoughts, and here, I doff my cap to those young signal ratings who had only a few weeks before been civilians and more deeply concerned with getting to work, such as it may have been. Bombs were dropping all round the ship and torpedoes were aimed at whatever ship happened to be in the line of fire. Thinking back on these events it was just as well that we were kept really busy as it helped so much. It was fortunate that many of us knew the drill of the torpedo bomber attacks, for the pilot had to fly straight and steady for a short period so as to stabilise the compass in the torpedo. It would be in those few observed periods that the trained gunners would ensure an excellent reception for the aircraft. At that same moment, the ship would if possible, violently alter course in order to avoid the missile. For the high level bombing, it was a case of watching for the bombs to be released and then altering course drastically in the hope that the bombs missed the target. Some of the torpedo bombers would prove unsuccessful in their efforts to dodge the gunners, or even the waves, in which case there would be a flash and a splash and the aircraft would nose-dive into the sea to immediately sink, for the torpedo weighing about a ton, makes a fair anchor. All these antics of the torpedo bombers had been rehearsed countless times in peacetime practices. Quite a few of the attackers paid the penalty of their daring. If any ship were to be hit by either bomb or torpedo, then she became a target for the remaining aircraft. In one of these attacks, one of our battleships received a glancing hit from a bomb which slowed her down temporarily so that she became a choice target for the Reggio Aeronautica, (Italian Air Force). Some slight damage was caused in the ensuing engagement, but punishment was served out by the damaged ship for she returned to Gibraltar under her own steam and with only minor repairs required.

As soon as the convoy had altered course for Malta, the fleet that were not going on remained in the vicinity for some time until it was known that the Air Force from Malta had the convoy under its protection and that the ships and tugs from Malta were on their way to assist any damaged vessel. *Euryalus*, being equipped with special radar gear, would be returning to Gibraltar with the remainder of the fleet. It is hard to tell exactly how the convoy fared as during the night they reported themselves as being attacked by E-boats. By next morning, the first ships of the convoy were arriving off Malta but the air attacks on the fleet carried on from just after dawn until the fleet was almost out of Italian Fighter range. From there on it would be sporadic attacks but nothing like those of yesterday. The Italian air force had been badly mauled in their attempt to block the convoy. There were some casualties in the convoy and naval ships. Some of the battle-fleet moved at high speed to the northwards in case the Italian navy thought of coming out to help stop the convoy. I believe that the enemy were sighted and that fire was opened on them. As the enemy withdrew at high speed there was no conclusive evidence that any damage had been sustained. Eventually the battle-fleet rejoined us and we made our way westwards at our best speed, although it was not until we were somewhere off Algiers that we left the bombers behind. The damaged ships and their escorts entered Gibraltar harbour four days later. There, all the force refuelled and restocked with ammunition and was soon again ready for sea.

It must not be thought the undamaged ships left the damaged ones behind to sort themselves out. Rather it was a case of the whole fleet acting as a strong escort for their damaged companions, for as ever there was always the bomber and submarine threat to be catered for.

MED VIA CAPETOWN

Euryalus had meanwhile replenished with stores and ammunition, taken a couple of days at ease and then with two hunt class destroyers, we headed out to sea and turned westward. Possibly we were going home, but no such luck. As soon as we were clear of the land, Spain on the one side and Morocco on the other, and we were clear of all shipping and that meant fishing boats as well, we altered course to the south. I mentioned fishing boats. It was known that lots of the fishing boats in the area would inform the Spanish authorities, and that information would be passed on to Germany with very little delay. This could quite easily result in a U-boat waiting for us not much further on. Soon we were making a fairly wide sweep into the Atlantic after passing the Islands. of Tenerife and Madeira. By now, the weather had warmed considerably and the skies became spotless blue, just like the picture books. This was without a doubt, Dame Fortune's way of making amends for us not going home. All thoughts of home vanished when at 0001, (one minute after midnight), the broadcast announcement was made that *Euryalus* and her escorts would be crossing the line, (Equator), and that in accordance with ancient customs, King Neptune and his Court would be welcomed on board at 0900 that morning. This was almost going back to peacetime routine, except that every now and again there would be a purring noise from the guns as the turrets swung round and depress and elevate their long snouts as though still sniffing out the enemy. In fact, this is just what they were doing even though at this stage the enemy would not be aircraft but, perhaps a German commerce raider on the prowl for some unescorted merchant ship. However, nothing disturbed the peace and tranquillity of the nearly peacetime independent cruising.

Promptly at 0900, the ship was hailed from the fox'le head and King Neptune and his court came on board by way of the cable hawse-holes. The ceremony of "crossing the line" was about to commence. First the Captain was hauled, yes I mean hauled, from the compass platform and carried to a large canvas bath that had been rigged on the upper deck. With due ceremony, he was questioned and made to answer for his sins of being the Captain, and of endeavouring to seduce one of Neptune's concubines in the form of HMS *Euryalus*, for she was named after "the queen of the open sea," and for daring to cross into the realm of King Neptune without obtaining the King's permission. Much cheering followed as Captain Bush, DSO DSC RN. was pitched unceremoniously to the bears in the canvas bath. There, he was ducked, lathered, shaved and given a pill, as is the custom of the bears at Court. Next it was the turn of the Commander, who received identical treatment although the mock charges were slightly different. So it went on through the whole ship's company, except for those who were exempt by virtue of having previously crossed the line and had paid their respects to King Neptune. For this experience, everybody going through the bath would be presented with a certificate to the effect that, "the line had been crossed," the date, and the longitude at which crossed. This was all a very pleasant break from the normal war routines to which we had all been accustomed. Many folk will say that this was a lot of tomfoolery, but one has also to remember that where the ships were, there was no possible chance of entertainment or real relaxation other than that which the ship's company made themselves. This was also taken as an opportunity for those of the ship's company that wished, to bathe in the canvas bath before it was unrigged. As the ship had only been in commission some three or four months, such matters as small entertainments did very much to weld the company into an efficient unit, which was most probably the idea in the first place. Just as quickly as the ship had been rigged for the spot of fun, so it was just as quickly dismantled and by the late afternoon watch, the ship was back to the state of preparedness that it ever was to be in. If normal is the word to use, then we had never been away from normal, for the watches and state of readiness had never been relaxed. Course to the south was maintained, and that evening the Captain informed us, over the broadcast system that our next port of call would be Capetown, provided we were not diverted elsewhere. As we passed further south, the weather was still very fine as it was the southern hemisphere spring that we were going in to. About the 10th October, *Euryalus* arrived at Capetown and here, after certain formalities, we were directed to Simonstown, the South African Naval Base. Before arriving at Capetown, the ship's company had been lectured on the folk of the port and that here there was no blackout. It was a well known thing that the hospitality of the South African people was as found nowhere else in the world. The lectures that we received were addressed chiefly to the new young ratings that we had on board, for only a few short weeks ago, they had been working as civilians at various jobs. They were in truth "greenhorns" and the good people of Capetown were not to know that they were not veterans of the Navy.

As I had now been on board for some four months, and without going onshore, I decided that as a break, I would have a "run ashore" especially that we were berthed alongside at Simonstown. This would be after the arrival duties had been attended to. As previously explained, my duties were such that it depended greatly on the Captain as to when I would be required. This meant that I should always hold myself available if and when required. It also meant that I had certain privileges in that I did not take part in the normal ship's routines. Signals were that for which I was paid. No, it was not a job in a thousand, it was a job in a million for all signals went through me, so that I was a veritable gold mine of information on most signal matters. It was my responsibility to ensure that all signals went to the correct authorities in the ship and that action was taken on those signals. As is usual in any signals office, the place was a hive of activity at all times, day or night. Very few officers were allowed in the office, and then only if their duty necessitated such action. It was all strictly "business."

On this occasion of my going ashore, I informed all the necessary people of my intention, and accordingly went ashore at about 1800 intending to catch the 1830 train in to Capetown. This was some fifteen miles away and there were twelve stations in between so that it was a leisurely ride. Getting to the station a little early, I gave myself a walk up and down to stretch my legs. Here, I was suddenly confronted by the biggest dog that I had ever seen. Probably a Pyrenese Mountain Dog, that stood as big as a pony. This dog then attached himself to me for the trip to Capetown. When the guard came along I told him that the dog was not mine and that he had got on the train at Simonstown. He assured me that it was quite in order as the dog "NUISANCE" was allowed to travel at will on the Capetown-Simonstown railway and that he was a good friend to all sailors, especially if under the influence of drink. This I found out to be the case later on, as I actually saw the dog take a sailor's arm and drag him on to the Simonstown train. What's more, the dog made sure that the sailor got off at Simonstown by using the same method. The dog would not let anyone interfere with the folk that he had taken charge of. The tales that were abroad about this dog, were so numerous and hardly believable unless witnessed. True to his teaching or instinct the dog saw me get off the train at Capetown and then curled himself up in a compartment ready for the return to Simonstown. The Capetown press wrote many articles about him, and I believe that there is somewhere in Capetown, a plaque or small monument to the dog "NUISANCE." Just who he belonged to was unknown, but I am sure that he was by no means a stray. The sailors of Capetown would ensure that he always had a good home for several had already tried to adopt him.

Arriving in Capetown I had a quick look round the city just to make sure of my bearings so to speak, and then went into a restaurant for a beer and a meal. The place selected was very well known and was frequented by all the forces for there were several voluntary and forces welfare workers there to ensure that service personnel were not imposed upon by the local sharks. Having ordered my meal and glass of beer, I sat back to enjoy the friendly atmosphere and the local band. The place was quite large and the ceiling was painted and decorated like the sky at night with the Southern Cross prominent over the stage. Some time later, a young lady dressed in the uniform of the local W.V.S. asked on passing my table, if I was enjoying my stay, so that we were soon chatting. During this short talk, I offered her a cigarette, as English cigarettes were greatly prized by any South African. Having smoked her cigarette, she moved on to talk to others, but eventually came back to my table. This time after her smoke, which I supplied, I was invited to her home and to meet her folk. This I was a little careful about, so that I made excuses to chat to a couple of other fellows from on board. This invite, I found was the general way of thanking the British sailors for their efforts and nothing seemed too much trouble for them. Going back to the table, I accepted the invite to her home, which was in the select quarter of the city. Her folk, when I met them, were apparently well positioned in the local hierarchy and known by most of the Capetowners that I eventually met. However, I did agree to walk home with her and to meet her folk. These were most charming people and Jewish. Not that I have anything against the Jewish folk. It just did not seem right that these folks having suffered all that they had done in Germany and in Palestine, should now be offering friendship to me. That evening when I went to return on board, about 2230, 1 was told not to worry about getting the train out the next day as they would meet me at the ship, at a time convenient to me. On the way back to Simonstown, I witnessed the dog NUISANCE perform. Several sailors, some the worse for beer drinking, were actually grabbed by the sleeve and taken to the train where the dog put them all in one of the long compartments. There must have been seven or eight of the sailors who seemed quite happy in the care of the dog. Nobody made any attempt to interfere with them, such as go through their pockets, not with the dog on guard. On arrival at Simonstown, the dog hauled the sailors off the train and took them to the waiting room, where a naval police patrol was waiting.

The following day, I again went ashore after ringing the telephone number that I had been given and told them that I would be ready at 1600. Promptly at that time a large black saloon car driven by a chauffeur pulled up beside the ship. This caused quite a stir at the gangway for the duty officer and his staff thought that the car had arrived for the Captain and that perhaps he had forgotten to tell them of his going ashore. After some moment's delay the chauffeur went and spoke to the sentry, so that shortly after, a pipe was broadcast for me to report to the gangway. Not just knowing what sort of car was being sent for me, I did not connect the two. I straightway thought, that is, bang goes my appointment, thinking that perhaps the Captain required me. To my amazement I found that the car was for me, and I need not add that many quiet remarks were made under people's breath about the Yeoman and his Barons. Barons is normally the term used for folk who offer friendship and entertainment to Naval people. Sometimes it is referred to as, "Strangling the Baron." Obviously I had caused quite a stir. I stayed the night at my new friends' home and in the morning I was returned to the ship by the same car and chauffeur. I was also told to ring for the car when I was ready to come ashore although they did not use naval terms. Again on return to the ship, there was quite a stir, for it was another officer and staff on duty and I suppose that nobody had thought to mention that the Yeoman was ashore in style. When I took the Captain his signals at 0900, after he had read his signals and commented as necessary, he mentioned about me causing a stir at the gangway. To this, I expressed my apologies for any bother, at which he remarked, "That's alright, it helps keep people on their toes." I need not have worried, for the Captain had a good laugh about it. Actually it stood me in good stead later, for when I asked for a long weekend to stay with the new friends, my request was readily granted. I think that I was the only person on the lower deck to have weekend leave. During that weekend leave, the family and myself travelled hundreds of miles sightseeing and shopping. Yes, the shops had everything that the shops at home did not have, so that I made up a grand parcel for the folk at Bexleyheath. Talking of parcels, the folk at Capetown would send parcels to Eileen at Bexleyheath almost every week after they had questioned me about rationing. As far as I know, Eileen received all the parcels from those folk, and she was of course highly delighted at the contents. If I remember correctly, each parcel would be of seven pounds weight and consisted of anything that went in tins, butter, cheese, fruits, jams and sweets. There was not a lot that I could offer in return for their kindnesses except to supply English cigarettes each time that I went ashore. They were quite happy with the exchange. When the time came for us to leave Simonstown, the whole family came down to the ship to see us leave. From that moment on I did not go ashore in South Africa although we did remain in the docks at Capetown for a few more days replenishing stores and other necessities. Leave at Capetown was in any case very restricted, and as we were more or less under sailing orders, there did not seem much point. One had to re-settle at some time. In fact, apart from going ashore on signal duty, I did not go ashore for more than another twelve months.

Our eventual departure from Capetown was done before dawn and our two escorts came with us. Apparently there was some scare on about an enemy commerce raider being in the vicinity so that we were required to be vigilant on our onward journey to where ever it was to be. About twenty-four hours out from Capetown, the Captain informed us that our destination was the Eastern Med Fleet. Back to the old hunting grounds so to speak.

Soon we were off the port of Durban where we picked up a convoy that was going our way and for us to escort through the Madagascar Channel, which was known as a favourite hunting ground for enemy U-boats. The famous and ill fated *Graf Spee* had sunk several merchant vessels in that vicinity. We did not enter the port of Durban but carried on with the convoy until almost south east of

Kilindini. Here, our escorts and ourselves went in to oil which took a few hours before we were off again making for Aden and the Red Sea. By the time we reached Aden, the weather started to cool a little, for at Kilindini it had been unbearably hot, so that we were glad to be back at sea where we at least had the breeze of our own making to cool us a little. During this trip up from Capetown, we had exercised "Action Stations" to the limit, for now that we were getting into waters that were not entirely friendly, there was no telling what to expect. In the Red Sea, there were reported some Italian submarines operating, and whether Italian or German, the menace was still the same. The passage through the Red Sea was uneventful except that we passed many of the great liners of the world which were now operating as troop ships.

Arriving at Port Suez, we again refuelled, ready for the passage through the Suez Canal. It would seem that we were to be reinforcements for the hard pressed Mediterranean Fleet, which consisted of three battleships, some cruisers and some destroyers. From all reports and from the news items that were about we should be in for a busy time. It certainly was to prove correct.

Entering the Canal, we were ordered to wear lifebelts and to be in a state of readiness for anything, as only the previous day, the Italians were reported to have dropped mines in the Canal and its approaches. The Suez Canal is roughly ninety miles long and about two ships' width or about 120 feet wide at the narrowest places. That is from bank to bank. Speed through the Canal is restricted to about twelve knots, for fear of washing the banks away. In most cases the banks have been channelled through the desert sand. Patiently we waited for the daily mine clearance signal and then we were given a priority passage as it is usual for ships to go in rotation of their arrival. As soon as this clearance signal was received, we three ships started on our journey to Port Said at the other end of the Canal. Beyond being ready for any emergencies, the ship's company had little to do but watch our passage through the canal and look at the Arab villages that were on the banks as we passed. Sometimes the Arabs appeared to be quite friendly in their welcome, while at others, hostile in their greeting. It was very well known that the enemy had agents all along the canal and that their influence had spread to the Arab populations along the banks. Many times we had to slow down, almost to a stop, to avoid dredgers at work clearing the canal of sand that had been washed down by the passage of ships going too fast. The passage to the Bitter Lakes, about half way to Port Said, was accomplished without bother. At the Bitter Lakes, there were many more transports obviously having unloaded the troops for the Western Desert where the battles were in full swing. Some nine-and-a-half hours after leaving Port Suez, we arrived at Port Said where we anchored for the night. Several times that night our slumbers were broken by the sounds of aircraft going over, probably on their way for reconnaissance or trips for bombing the Canal. Since the defence of the Canal was not our responsibility against air attack, only part of the ship's company would be closed up at air defence stations. This did not prevent many of the ship's company from watching the huge liners of well known names, disgorging their military cargoes that had been brought to Egypt via the Cape route. From all this, we deduced that much was about to happen in the desert, where the allies had suffered some reverses in recent weeks.

Early the next morning, (the navy became quite expert at moving early, before sun up), our little force moved north into the Mediterranean proper, for this was to be our final destination. Course was soon altered to the west, for Alexandria, where the fleet had made its temporary base having been withdrawn from Malta some time previously because of the severe threat of air attacks. Entering Alexandria, we were directed to a buoy near *HMS Cleopatra* and *Dido*, who were to be our new squadron mates for the future. These two ships were of the same class as *Euryalus* with just a few minor alterations. How strange it seemed, that the ships of the ancient Greek and Egyptian names, should now be defending the ancient harbour and city of Alexandria. More than once through history, the ships of the ancient names had come home to duty, in the seas and places that had originally been the homes of the legendary Greek Gods and Goddesses, together with their legendary offspring.

The berth that we occupied must have been previously arranged for waiting for us were fuel and water lighters, stores and ammunition lighters and best of all, boats loaded with mail, for we had received very little since our departure from Gibraltar, and even that was not an over large amount being most probably official mails. As far as I was concerned, there were hundreds of signals referring to our joining the Fifteenth Cruiser Squadron under the command of Rear Admiral Philip Vian of "Cossack" Fame. This admiral had, early in the war, liberated some hundred British prisoners from the German ship *Altmark*, literally under the noses of the German ships in Norwegian waters. We guessed from this, that Rear Admiral Vian would not hesitate to take us into action, if need arose. Our surmise was most correct as later events proved.

Looking round the harbour in a spare moment, I noticed that there were four French cruisers, all of modern design, berthed not far from us. From this, I assumed that we should be working with the French Navy. This assumption was soon shattered when on talking to the Captain, he told me that these four ships had been interned and de-militarised and disarmed, so that they would be of no embarrassment to us. Again the French had let us down, and they had been there since the capitulation of France just over twelve months ago. They were supplied with just sufficient fuel for the supply of power and lighting. What a wonderful reinforcement they would have made to our naval forces. I am sure that I am not the only one to feel bitter and angry at the so-called French Allies. As far as I was concerned, the French had severely blotted their copy books. In any future dealing of any sort where the people were concerned, one should look for the worst, as to my mind, the French will only let anything work if it is to their advantage. These of course are only my feelings.

BARHAM SUNK

Admiral Vian allowed us a few days to settle in, and then it was to sea and exercises with a vengeance, with practices of all sorts. About the end of November, I think it was the 20th, the fleet was ordered to sea. As far as we were able to gather, this was to cover a convoy, although we did not see them. On the afternoon of 23rd, the cruisers were operating to the south east of the battleships. The signals had been made to the battleships to turn in succession to starboard. This was executed about 1600, *H.M.S. Barham* who was second in the line, and was just starting to turn, when an explosion occurred on her port side. It was soon obvious that *Barham* had been hit by torpedoes and she soon started to develop a serious list to port. Within minutes, *Barham* had heeled over further and there were more explosions. Whether this was the submarine firing more torpedoes or internal explosions is not rightly known. Within a very short interval, there was another tremendous explosion and *Barham* disappeared completely, with the loss of some nine hundred lives. From the time of the first explosion, to the final disappearance, was about five minutes. The escorting destroyers were quickly searching for the submarine, and I think that there was a certain amount of reluctance at dropping depth charges, for fear of killing any survivors from acute concussion caused by exploding charges. Whether the submarine was caught, is not known. The signal of the *Barham*'s loss was obviously reported to certain authorities and when I showed the signal to the Captain he immediately ordered a complete blackout regarding *Barham*. It was known that Egypt had many enemy agents installed in the country so that for them to know that a battleship had been sunk would have been vital information. As far as I was concerned the secret was completely safe and it was not until many months later, when the tactical situation had completely changed in our favour, that any news of *Barham* was made known. On our return to harbour, all ships restocked with ammunition and provisions and were ready for sea within a matter of hours. It was not so very long before we were to receive our sailing orders again, so that in a very short space of time, the three cruisers of the 15th Cruiser Squadron found themselves heading for the open sea. The order of sailing was *Cleopatra*, *Euryalus*, *Dido* with a screen of eight destroyers. By dark, all ships were steaming westwards at a moderately high speed. We gathered from the vast amount of radio traffic that the battleships were also going to sea. Was this just a make-believe exercise, to make the enemy think that we were at sea? The next morning gave us the answer, as our constant course was to the west. It was to be to Malta with a convoy which had left various harbours during the time that we had been at sea when Barham had been sunk. One can only surmise and marvel on the planning of these operations, for it must be constantly remembered that the enemy had spies in all sorts of places. The less likely the place, the most probable for a spy or agent, and many agents were locals who had been recruited for little or no reward, except to get them employed as dockyard coolies. For the enemy to know that a convoy was at sea, was top grade information, for it left him with that much more time to plan a reception committee. Throughout that day, we carried on steering west and at moderate speed, when at nightfall, the convoy was spotted about ten miles ahead. Rapidly we overtook them, when, at a given signal, the three cruisers placed themselves about the convoy. One ahead and one on each beam of the convoy. Judging by the brief signals of welcome that were made, they were extremely pleased to see us, for they were entering the area known as "Bomb Alley," in the not too far distant future. A continuous zig-zag was ordered for the night, and all who could, took the opportunity to store away some sleep, so as to be ready for what we knew would be some sleepless days. These sleepless days commenced at dawn the next morning with an air raid alert. This trouble was in the form of a large Italian aircraft that kept his distance just above the horizon and out of range of our guns. No friendly aircraft were available as the aircraft carrier *Illustrious* had been severely damaged during the last convoy operation, when we had gone with the fleet from the Gibraltar end of the Mediterranean. Also, the Fleet from the Gibraltar end were again taking part in the convoy running business as they were attempting to put another convoy through from their end. This gave the enemy two large bodies of ships from which to choose for making an attack on. At the same time it also meant that if the enemy concentrated his efforts on one of the convoys the other would be left unattended. It was to be that or else divide his available aircraft between the two convoys. We should just have to wait and see what the Italian air force chiefs would decide. It was their problem not ours, and we were content to leave it that way. Our own troubles would start soon enough for now there were two of these aircraft out on reconnaissance which if the radar indications were correct, it would be us. Soon our radar equipment detected a force of unidentified aircraft approaching the convoy so that the whole force was ordered to assume the first degree of readiness. This does not imply that we were only just getting ready, for ever since the enemy "snooper" had been sighted at daylight we had been standing by. If I may, I would liken these degrees of readiness to the civilian air raid colour system. Air raid warning "white" signified no enemy radars were expected, "yellow" signified that enemy aircraft were in the area and "red" signified that raiders were attacking or overhead. As the raiders were detected at some sixty miles distance, that gave us about five minutes to prepare our reception for them. The enemy aircraft were soon circling and dropping their bombs from quite a height so that we were all twisting and turning in an effort to dodge the bombs. Again, our instruments told us that more aircraft were on their way. They could only be enemy for we were now well outside the range of our own fighters from the desert air force. It did not take over long before we spotted the torpedo bombers getting into groups and taking up their positions ready for attack. These particular aircraft waited until just after the high level bombers had finished, so that we of the convoy had more or less ceased twisting and turning to dodge the bombs and then they would start their attacks from all different quarters. Our plan was to get them split up by firing the main guns at the groups, and then, when the aircraft were in range of the close range weapons, oerlikons, bofors and pom poms all sorts of smaller weapons then gave them all that we could. Different methods of attack called for different methods of defence, and the gunners soon found which method suited which attack. As for the dodging part of the programme, the navy ships were quite good for we had the speed and the power to turn quickly, but not so the merchant ships. Their top speed would have been at the best, eighteen knots and possibly some could not do that. The enemy did his best to give us an assortment of attacks, so that each ship had to take individual avoiding action but, remain in the umbrella of the fleet A.A. defences. At times with the independent manoeuvring of ships, many close shaves were experienced and fortunately no collisions took place. One must certainly hand it to the skippers of the merchant ships for the way that they handled their ships. In addition to the bombings there was always the constant threat of attack by submarine. At least, there was very little fear of anybody dropping off to sleep although we could have done with some. Throughout that day we suffered these attacks but sustained no damage or losses unless it was from near miss splinters. During the evening we heard by radio that the convoy coming the other way from Gib. had so far not been attacked so it looked as though we had been selected for the dubious honours of the Italian Air Force attention. Closer still we got to the southern coast of Italy and Pantelleria, so that now we knew that we might expect the attention of the E-boats known to be based on Pantelleria. The night's quietness was split at times by the staccato bark of the outer escorts guns engaging some targets which we assumed to be E-boats, although we never saw any of them. It was the Admiral's intention that we should not open fire at targets, unless directly engaged and in the immediate vicinity. This had two advantages for us, as it conserved our ammunition for we had yet to go back from whence we had come, and we did not disclose our positions to the enemy, for no good purpose.

Daylight came, with the usual stand to at "Action Stations" and with the light also came the shadowing aircraft from the north. Without air cover, we were sadly handicapped, so it was a case of having to rely on the ship's radar and the vigilance of the aircraft look outs. No large scale attacks were made on the convoy although there were continuous nuisance raids through the whole of the day. By mid-afternoon, we heard that the Gibraltar convoy was being attacked fairly heavily as they approached Cape Bonn in Tunisia. Once there, the merchant ships and certain of the escorts would push on to Malta. The main part of the Gibraltar fleet would then cruise round in the area of Cape Bonn, in case of interference by the Italian Navy. At approximately the same time we should leave our convoy, pick up the empty merchant ships from Malta and return to Alexandria at best speed. On the morning of the 28th, we were making good progress towards Alexandria, and presumably so were the Gibraltar convoy and forces, for we had heard nothing untoward about any of the forces other than intermittent air attacks. Soon we were only being bothered by the odd flight of bombers who did their best to inform us that we had not been forgotten. Then, at dark, we in *Cleopatra, Euryalus* and

Dido, and some of the escorting destroyers made a large alteration of course to the south. Something was afoot. The three cruisers with two destroyers each would split into three forces. Then moving at high speed, we soon lost sight of our companions, who although unseen were not so very far from us.

As soon as we were clear, the Captain informed us that we and the other two groups would be carrying out simultaneous bombardments of enemy held positions on the North African coast. All target areas were to be in the vicinity of Tobruk but not actually at Tobruk. Each of the positions had been established as possible supply posts for the enemy forces. The three groups, as far as I can recall, would open fire at a pre-arranged time and the bombardment would last for some fifteen minutes. At the time arranged, the first of our salvoes were fired, and then it seemed to me, that it was a question of each turret trying to beat their pals in the other turrets. From my place on the bridge it sounded as though there was one continuous explosion so that whoever was on the receiving end would not have a lot of time to dodge out of the way. Just what were the results of this bombardment I have little knowledge. The only thing that I can say with confidence is that we used an awful lot of shells so that it must at least have kept the enemy busy and alert. We noticed that there was some answering fire but we neither saw nor heard any resulting explosions. From that we could only deduce that the enemy had been thinking along the lines of an air raid. No damage was sustained by any of the three bombarding forces.

Having completed our task of livening up the enemy positions, we withdrew at high speed to the northeast, so that by daylight, we were in distant company with the remainder of our convoy, who were heading at best speed for Alexandria. Arriving at Alexandria, we automatically went to our previous berths where the oilers and ammunition lighters were waiting for us. Provision lighters were also sent, for the navy does not neglect the stomachs of the men. This may not always be "A la Ritz," but it is always nourishing and sustaining, and as the sailors are wont to remark, "The cooks can't mess up corned beef and sandwiches." As we secured to our buoys, we could not help but notice the spick and span appearance of the non-combatant French cruisers, who would have been an enormous help in our recent efforts. It made one wonder just what the French bystanders thought of their efforts, especially as there were already

Free French forces fighting with the Allies under General de Gaul. There was little time to wonder, for the oiling and ammunitioning required all possible hands so as to be ready for other eventualities as soon as possible. A couple of nights in harbour with perhaps the odd air raid warning to spoil one's sleep, and we were all set for the next requirement. No rest for the wicked, as the saying goes, and before many days, we were again swotting up for the Malta run with another convoy. This time, however, it should be a little easier, we hoped, for the army were advancing slowly until it looked as though the enemy would be pushed back. The weather at this time of the year in the eastern Mediterranean was normally quite pleasant, but with the possibility of rain and strong winds (Camsin) at very short notice. So, away we sailed.

The following morning we had met one of those strong possibilities of rain, low clouds and warm, sand laden winds. Although the weather was making it unpleasant for those on deck, it would at least help the convoy. With increased low cloud and rain the convoy was at least being hidden from the view of the Italian aircraft that might be lurking in the area, the prying eyes of the Aeronautica Reggia, (the correct name for the Italian Air Force). For three days, progress was excellent, and tomorrow we should be getting near the Island of Pantelleria and Bomb Alley as it became known. Still there were no snoopers either seen, heard, or indicated on our radar. The fourth day, which would be critical, saw the weather improving fast, so that air attack was more than likely. Nobody had any more thoughts of a free run with the convoy. Soon we were not disappointed when the first snooper arrived about mid-afternoon. Slowly, and in a huge sweep round the horizon, he made his estimations of course, and speed, formation and composition of the convoy and its escorts, which information he promptly yelled to his base. Within a couple of hours, the first air attack had developed, together with the usual twisting and turning of the ships in their efforts to dodge the bombs. It was then that it happened. One of the escorting destroyers was near missed and she became hidden in showers of spray and geysers of disturbed water. One would have suggested that she had received vital damage, but with the next breath, she emerged almost unscathed. It certainly had been a very near miss, for she had received some slight structural damage, and the temporary loss of the use of her rudder. One of the merchant ships had received a hit by a light bomb which started a fire on the after deck, and had passed through the deck to explode there killing several of the crew. In a twinkling of an eye, another destroyer from the escort, ran alongside her and moments later some of the destroyer crew were helping to fight the fires. While the destroyer was alongside, some of the more severely wounded were transferred to the destroyer. It was exceedingly fortunate that these very anxious moments and damage that had been caused, was at the tail end of that particular attack. By the time that the next attack had developed, it seemed as though nothing had happened to the merchant ship. We heard later by signal that the bomb had exploded in the compartment very near to the ammunition that was stacked just through the next bulkhead. This particular ammunition was required urgently by Malta, which was at that time under heavy air attacks, sometimes amounting to thirty raids a day. Extra efforts were made to ensure that this ship got to Malta, which it did. Even after dark the raids on the convoy continued, so the enemy must have known that he had damaged a ship in the convoy.

It was perhaps a question of good luck, and more than probable good planning, for we were shortly joined by the Penelope and some destroyers from Malta. A sure sign that we were within reasonable distance of Malta. Malta had also sent out a long range Blenheim aircraft, which was heard and later seen when recognition signals were exchanged. Things quietened considerably that night so that with an amended zig-zag we should be almost within sight of Malta. Signalling good-bye to the Malta force and the convoy, the cruisers and certain destroyers made off at high speed in the direction of Alexandria. There was only one more duty to do before getting home. That was as before, to divide our forces into three and carry out a bombardment on the way. Again we split after dark and moved towards the enemy-occupied coast of N. Africa, there to bombard various installations and store dumps in the vicinity of Bardia and Tobruk. These places were apparently key positions on the maps and in the plans of the Axis strategy.

ARK ROYAL SUNK

On return to harbour the next day, an intercepted signal told us that the convoy from Gibraltar, had also been successful but had been severely mauled between Cape Bonn and Sicily in the narrows. They had been under almost constant air attack for over two days. Worse news was to follow, for on the 11th November, the aircraft carrier *Ark Royal* had been torpedoed and sunk by a U-boat. Super human efforts were apparently made to get her back to Gibraltar but eventually the weight of the water taken in by the *Ark*, was so much that the tow continually broke. As fast as one tow broke, so another was ready and another destroyer took over the tow. With continuing power failure, the *Ark* was unable to cope with the water intake, until the *Ark* finally sank about thirty miles east of Gibraltar on the 13th November. By skilful handling and the most strenuous efforts of the crews of the Tugs and destroyers the loss of life was small. At last after many times being sunk by the German press and radio, and Lord Haw Haw, she had been sunk with very much regret by the Navy and British people. She had been the mainstay of many successful convoys from the day of her commissioning. Sadly many of her aircraft had been lost, but the crews of most of these aircraft had been rescued by the destroyers. From the many numerous efforts that the enemy had made to sink her, it was obvious that sooner or later they would succeed. Since the sinking had been so close to Gibraltar, the enemy was able to claim the success in the *Ark*'s sinking on more or less the same day. This sad loss meant that the fleet at Alexandria would have to wait a while longer before their requests for a Carrier could be met. When it was eventually met, it was to be in far greater numbers that even the most optimistic person could have envisaged.

Meanwhile, the army were doing their best to push the enemy out of North Africa from the eastern end so that Tripoli was the target. Nightly for the next few months, the cruisers and destroyers of the Eastern Med Fleet shelled the enemy anywhere it was possible to do so, along the coast. Sometimes great risks were taken to bombard inshore, for at many parts the coast line was very shallow so that the cruisers could not get close enough to help. At times it was most laughable to hear on the radio, that cruisers of the Med Fleet had shelled such and such a place or, that cruisers of the Fifteenth Cruiser Squadron had shelled so and so, or units of the Med Fleet had bombarded another well known place, like Sollum or Bardia. The plain fact was that all the forces were one and the same ships for the simple reason that, THERE WERE NO OTHER SHIPS. Its wonderful what a story can be concocted by a good news reporter. Incidentally, efforts were made to reinforce our squadron of three ships. On the occasions that we sailed for Malta, or anywhere else, with the object of picking up the fourth ship to make up our squadron, as that is the normal number of ships in a squadron, we failed. Each time the reinforcement was due, something happened to prevent the planning of their Lordships from being fulfilled. On at least one occasion the ship that was designated to fill the gap, was torpedoed en route to join us. On another occasion, when the fourth ship did join us, be it only for a brief period, one of the other ships would be sunk. Rumour went round after that event, that the Lords of the Admiralty would not in future try to build up the strength of the Fifteenth Cruiser Squadron. Strangely enough, the strength of the squadron never was made up to four ships. Whether the Admiralty did decide on the matter of three or four ships is NOT known, but once again the "Messdeck Telegraph" had at least proved correct. It was again, "Truth being stranger than fiction," for the Fifteenth Cruiser Squadron never did grow beyond three. They were a grand and most efficient team of ships, and almost knowing each other's minds, which I am sure they did.

By the middle of December 1941, things were looking really black for the Allies, when on 17th December, the Japanese bombed the American Fleet at Pearl Harbour in the Philippines, without warning. It seemed that the last straw had been added to the camel's back. Although the unproclaimed act of war was a devastating blow to the U.S.A., it proved a bonus for us, as it meant that the unlimited resources of the United States would be available to us. This was particularly so in the case of ship repair facilities, ammunition supplies and other war materials. All these things were previously available to Britain, but they had to be transported in British controlled ships, of which there were beginning to be fewer and fewer, as losses due to submarines were becoming colossal. Apart from that, the rest of the U.S.A. navy was able to supply some escorts for the hard pressed convoys. The Royal Navy ships were spread more than thinly all over the world, and each ship was doing the work of three or more other ships. In case you ask, that is why Daddy did not come home so often. As for a sailor having a girl in every port, as the saying goes - the average sailor was very lucky if he was able to spend long enough in port to get acquainted with a glass of beer, let alone with a female.

By the middle of February, it was obvious from the slow gathering of ships, that another convoy to Malta was being prepared. Malta was itself in dire straits from a food and supplies point of view. Very strict rationing of the most bare essentials and of a minimum quantity was the order of the day, and the harshest penalties for the breach of regulations were imposed. Rice was the main standby of the folk in Malta. The only supplies that were getting through were those that were taken in specially adapted submarines. Any navy ship making the fast run through would fill every available space with stores of some kind for the folk at Malta. On one occasion when we relieved a cruiser at Malta during the siege, we loaded bag after bag of rice into all the empty places that usually are the sailors cubby holes. Even while at Malta, the ship had competitions each week in an effort to find new ways of serving rice. It was pop corned rice, boiled rice, frittered rice, stewed rice and in fact any way you could mention. Meat was an unheard of luxury and even the common onion boiled with one's rice became a feast. The rationing in Malta at that critical period was far more acute than even that experienced at home. Any ship or submarine cargo carrier would be harried from the moment of arrival until its departure, or it was sunk in the harbour. During the periods of the siege, it was quite common for the island to experience one hundred and fifty bombing raids each day. This necessitated living in the air raid shelters almost the whole of the time. Some folk never saw daylight for days on end; a case of prehistoric existence, for the underground caves made excellent shelter. At night those folk that were required for work would emerge and help unload the stores from the ships or submarines that had made the passage. In addition to the air raids, there was always the threat of E. Boat attack or even the threat of landings by the enemy forces, for they were only some sixty miles away as the crow flies. In fact, from the Island of Malta, at the top of the Barracca, I have seen Sicily on a clear dry summer's morning, that is how far away it is, and that was just after 0400. Another little point of interest was that we spotted the mails steamer, "Knight of Malta" about half way between Sicily and Malta on her daily run. That was of course in peace time when I was a signalman at Castille, Signal Station. Enough of these diversions.

I mentioned a little while ago that attempted landings were one of the additional hazards of the folk of Malta. Yes, there were some attempts at landings but, whether these were for the landing of agents or the landing of occupation forces I have no knowledge. All that is recorded for history is that no landings were successful for occupation purposes. Also, almost everybody, except casualties and the aged, were employed during the day at clearing the rubble from bomb damage especially to the air fields. In addition to all these possibilities there was always the threat of a bombardment by the Italian Fleet. This was quite a large body of ships, and according to our knowledge at the time, there were some seven battleships, many of modern design, some fifty odd cruisers, and numerous destroyers and a multitude of small craft and submarines. All were capable of inflicting damage and destruction to the island. These were the main threats to the Island but the biggest threat of all was that of starvation, unless relief came in some form or other. Several attempts were made to raise the siege, for that was the situation at that time. I have read somewhere that there was even the possibility of "Surrender" if relief was not soon available, as it was estimated that only a few more days' strict rationing was left. Attempts were made to pass convoys through from Gibraltar and from Alexandria, either in unison or separately, but without over much success for the enemy were just as determined that the Island should be forced into surrender, as we were to render aid to the folk of Malta. This then was the decision to force another convoy through if at all possible. Every person in the fleet at either end of the Med knew just what the fall of Malta would mean and there were no illusions on that score. With the attempt of the February convoy which was turned back to Alexandria, because of far superior forces in opposition, we came to the March attempt.

THE BATTLE OF THE GULF OF SIRTE

Before one considers Sunday as a day of rest, and even in the Navy they try to make it so, we must have a week of work before us. After all, we must go by our example, for the Lord made heaven and earth and all that therein dwells, for six days shalt thou labour and do all thy work, and on the seventh day shalt thou rest. The Navy never misses a chance to quote examples if they are good, and I follow my teaching. For us of the Fifteenth Cruiser Squadron, under the command of Rear Admiral Vian, (Vian of Cossack fame), holder of the Distinguished Service Order and two bars, (equal to three D.S.O.s), and the destroyers under the command of Captain Poland DSO. DSC., the week started on Monday 16th March 1942. The work in question, was I suppose, nothing of unusual importance as, from day one of this war, it had always been a case of being prepared and ready for sea at the drop of a hat. By Thursday noon on the 19th, we knew within a little and by reading the signs that the usual "CLUB RUN" convoy was afoot.

At noon, the *Carlisle*, an old type cruiser of the previous war, hastily converted to an A.A. ship, with several hunt class destroyers and four large merchant vessels glided past us towards the harbour entrance. Moving into the mine swept channel, they were soon lost to sight after passing the Great Pass Beacon, a prominent navigation marker. That afternoon, such ominous signs as securing boats for sea, warned us all that leave would be cancelled that night. For myself, I felt sure that all on board *Euryalus* had decided that Malta was due for some more supplies, if at all possible. By 0200 on Friday 20th, such pipes as, "Duty watch fall in prepare ship for sea," and then the following pipe of "Rig Paravanes," (devices for cutting mines adrift and towed from the bows of the ship), dispersed all ideas of not going to sea. Some of us who had previously met some of the Italian Navy started to speculate on our chances of another meeting. There would be no question of the enemy not knowing that a convoy was scheduled for Malta, as many of the local inhabitants were pro-German, and would be only too delighted to inform enemy intelligence of the navy movements during the day or night. All of us knew for certain that it would be a case of continuous air attack almost from daylight on the 21st, as we should be in range of enemy airfields at Crete or on the North African side. There would be no air support from here on, until return to harbour, or near enough. At first light on Friday 20th, at dawn ""Action Stations"," everybody inspected most carefully his station and equipment and this included medical equipment that is supplied to each station, all of which had become a force of habit. Friday, in short, was a dull day and to put it in plain words, was, "the calm before the storm." Dusk on Friday evening found us in the Fifteenth Cruiser Squadron joining up with the forces of the Carlisle convoy. *Cleopatra* went to the head of the convoy, *Euryalus* went to the starboard beam, and *Dido* to the port beam. The whole force was surrounded by destroyers screening against U-boats, we being well within enemy controlled waters. Some wise guy said something about trailing one's coat in front of the enemy, to which the usual wit on the bridge replied, "I feel more like trailing my trousers just now." Maybe he did mean it, for there was no comedy in that which we were about to attempt.

Saturday came just like any other Saturday at sea, with all being quiet, so that, "Clean messdecks and flats was piped," the usual weekly clear up day, except that half the ship's company were closed up at their defence stations. It would take approximately one-and-a-half minutes to get to FULL ""Action Stations." About half-way through the forenoon, our radar instruments detected an enemy snooper about twenty-five miles away to starboard, and the keen-eyed look-outs soon had him in sight just above the horizon. By about 1030, the hands had discontinued the Saturday Clean Up and had replaced all gear and prematurely secured for action. This necessitated stowing all gear, both service and personal, in cupboards and lockers so that in event of damage or a torpedo making a hole in the side, no item of any sort would be floating about to block pumps or such like. At about 1050, hands were already at "Action Stations" waiting for the Italian seagulls to visit us. Just after 1055, a destroyer on the starboard side opened fire to engage enemy aircraft. It is a tiring job waiting for the enemy to come within range so that one could open fire, but as ever, we found that the Italians were reluctant to come too close to test our gunnery. This wait is especially tiring when the guns are already loaded and the gunner's fingers are literally itching on the triggers. We are not kept in suspense for long in reality, for with a faint "ting ting" of the firing gongs, the conductor starts the orchestra of our guns. Each man unthinkingly places his feet more firmly on the deck, and slightly opens his mouth. These are automatic reactions of the body and one has yet to offer an explanation for this subconscious act. I suppose it relieves the facial tension, as quite unconsciously one looks at one's chum only to find that his reactions are very similar to one's own. There is a crash, and the ship shakes and shudders as the various units of our anti-aircraft armament respond to the conductor's baton, "button." Hot, brown, choking cordite clouds temporarily envelop one, as a blast of scorched air passes us on the flag deck and bridge, making all feel dirty and thirsty. Flags flutter up and down, signal lamps are constantly clattering as they blink their message from one ship to another, normal speech becomes useless. One has to shout, and even then the chances are that one will lip read after a fashion. It is all one cacophony of noises and glare of belching guns as all hell breaks loose, but from which comes in an unnatural way, a disciplined sense, and above all if one is watching, some cheery smiles from those around one. This is in spite of the hideous screech of falling bombs and madly diving aircraft. Occasionally there is a wild burst of cheering as a plane is seen to be hit and goes crashing seawards in a funeral pyre, but one cannot stop. The hungry mouths of the orange brown and flame tinted guns need ceaseless feeding, for they are constantly spewing their one hundred pound shells skyward at some new target. Ships twist and turn, missing collisions by what seems like inches and then to disappear behind a column of spray and geysers of water caused by exploding bombs. Some of these ships re-appear like dogs coming from the water as they shake themselves free from the tormented columns of sea. Now and again, one will hear the whine of tortured metal as a splinter flies past to hit another metal object as it protests its ricocheted way along the ship. The amazing thing is, that the ships, both convoy and escorts, steam on with scarcely a ship out of station for there is safety in remaining in close company. There are moments of sanity in the form of breathing spaces between the waves of bombers, when cigarettes are produced as though by magic, or perhaps a piece of chocolate from someone's pocket, are shared without thought of selfishness on any person's part. Perhaps a dish of sandwiches will appear as though someone has completed a conjuring trick. These also are shared by anybody that feels like a corned beef sandwich. In any case they will not be left to dry off, for if they are not eaten by the bridge staffs, there will be a frantic ringing round to any position that is normally inaccessible such as the gun director, or even the gun turret just below the bridge, as hopefully nobody gets forgotten. Occasionally the brief spells are broken by the Captain or one of the bridge Officers giving a brief summary of the situation as it appears to them. Such information is greatly appreciated by everybody, especially if working in secluded spaces like ammunition magazines. The Captain is a great believer in everybody knowing the up to date situations, for who knows when one may have to take over control of one's station or even the ship. Nobody is immune, is the Captain's motto and as far as possible, that motto is implemented. The squawk box stammers and announces that some ship has had a near miss, or that some ship has been credited with shooting down an enemy aircraft, and so the circus goes on.

Night eventually closes in after a final fruitless effort by the enemy torpedo bombers. In all it is calculated that the enemy has lost quite a number of aircraft from the scores of planes that have attacked the convoy. Then of course, there will be those that did not make it back to their base, as quite a number were seen to be emitting black smoke and vapour fumes from their exhausts and trying to keep low on the sea. Each ship, on receipt of a signal, will proceed to its night station as quickly as is possible with safety. It is now that some of the crews such as gunnery and torpedo crews, signal and engine room staff, if not on duty will coil up on deck or where they can, and grab a bit of sleep until duty or "Action Stations" require them to stand to. The cookery staff will meanwhile be preparing emergency meals ready for the next prolonged action sitting. The decks are cleared of empty shell and cartridge cases, and the ship in general will be at the ready, for the night time is the time of the night prowlers, the E and U-boat. The Captain will make discreet enquiries as to the state of the ship and its efficiency and then will pull his duffel coat a bit closer round him and climb into his bridge chair where he may snatch a few minutes' doze, but whatever he manages, his senses will remain fully alert. The convoy must press on, for it is badly needed if Malta is to survive.

Time after time through the night, we count the fleet through powerful glasses checking each position with the convoy plan, just in case one may have wandered in the inky blackness. There is little sound to break the stillness, only the monotonous swish, swish, as the ship forces her way westward through the moderately calm sea. One learns to spot a ship by the white wash at night or the phosphorescent swirl of the passage of a ship. Submarines are the past masters at spotting this swirling of a ship's wake. Every ripple that breaks or seemingly flashes, is carefully searched in case it is the tell-tale mark of a prowling E or U-boat. It is hard to say which is the worse, the night when everything is suspiciously like an enemy, or the day when one can see and has to put up with the bedlam of hell going mad.

However it is with thankful hearts that we herald the daylight creeping over the eastern horizon for this is Sunday the 22 March and the day that the convoy will be in reasonable sailing distance of Malta. At dark, we shall leave them, and make our way back to Alexandria at high speed. Once more, it is the calm before the storm, and at 0930 with everything peacefully quiet, the Commander orders, "Hands not closed up, Lay aft on the quarter-deck for prayers." At 0900 our position had been plotted as 3404N 1917E. This position is brought up to date at odd intervals, depending on speed made good, in case of emergencies. Not so very far to go for Malta, with a course of approximately west and a speed of fifteen knots. At 0936 four Italian torpedo bombers are detected and sighted. "Action Stations" are assumed and prayers are suspended. By 0945 the guns of the convoy are again offering defiance to the Reggio Aeronautica. It was shortly after this torpedo bomber attack that a seaplane was spotted just above the horizon to the Northwards. This, to the knowledgeable ones, indicates that fairly large surface forces are at sea, as seaplanes are only carried by cruisers or battleships. This was all the more significant as we were so far from the land as to be outside the range of shore based seaplanes. Obviously, Italian surface forces were at sea to the Northwards, and knowing the Italians, they would not be at sea unless well supported. Yes, they are at sea and as we later find out, very well supported, and from all indications we judge them not to be too far away from us. At 1015, after much twinkling of lights and the fluttering of streams of multi coloured flags, the Captain broadcasts to the ship's company that the enemy ships are at sea and are endeavouring to intercept the convoy. Orders have also been issued regarding the Admiral's intentions in case of surface craft attack. No sooner had this information been passed than the whole fleet was engaged in driving off a very heavy air attack by some sixty plus aircraft, which was a mixture of low level and high level pattern bombers and as usual, torpedo bombers. This raid lasted until just after 1100. Most obliging of the enemy, and convenient for us, as it was tot time which was served during the lull. No damage had been reported by the convoy or escorts and we were all steaming along, most serenely. The enemy had left, leaving just three "snoopers," shadowing aircraft, to keep us company and report our every movement. At about 1120, more aircraft were detected and sighted. This time they are just torpedo bombers, eighteen of them in groups of three. This we do not seem to mind, as the fellows at the guns more or less treat them as shooting bottles at a fairground. Swooping in low over the sea at about one hundred and twenty miles an hour, they make very good targets. The *Carlisle* now in the centre of the convoy, fires a heavy barrage to break up the formation. Whoops of delight now echo through the ship as one pilot more daring than the rest comes right in close. He stops everything that we can throw at him. With frantic efforts, he tries to pull away, but too late, he is on fire and flames are already belching from his cockpit. The plane passes so close to us that one can actually see the pilots tortured features as he tries to beat out the flames with his gloved hands. At last, reeling like a drunken man, the plane loses stability and crashes into the sea beside us, about 200 yards away, to leave a column of dirty oily smoke rising from the disturbed sea. The attack goes on, until eventually all their torpedoes have been fired or they have decided that it can be too warm in the convoy's vicinity. This attack, as far as I am aware, was the last torpedo bomber attack that day, although other ships in the force were attacked by these aircraft later on. The enemy must be very short of ready use trained T/B pilots in this area as one pilot that was later picked up, reported that he himself had made four bombing trips on the convoy that day.

From previous signals, we knew that the Malta force of a cruiser and some destroyers would be coming to support us so that course was altered slightly to port to rendezvous with the Malta force. This force consisted of the *Penelope* and four or five destroyers. This was a very welcomed addition as after events proved. At 1210 approximately, the Malta force was met and the convoy formation slightly re-adjusted. *Penelope* and *Dido* would take position on the port side of the convoy, while *Cleopatra* and *Euryalus* took position on the starboard side of the convoy, while the destroyers formed up with the screening destroyers. The cruisers formed roughly a large square with the convoy in the centre. By 1240, the air attacks had almost ceased and apart from sporadic fire from the outer screen of destroyers, all was quiet. In this quiet spell, we all managed to pacify our hunger, thanks to the emergency feeding organisation in the ship, we also managed at different moments to attend to the wants of nature and, "spend a penny." This was one of the great snags of being at "Action Stations" for a prolonged period. It was while eating one's sandwiches that a casual observer noticed that high above us, almost out of sight, were some four or five aircraft weaving and making trailing patterns of smoke. First it would be directly overhead, then to one side of us and then the other side of the force. At intervals this smoke trailing would be varied by the dropping of large daylight parachute flares. These flares we mistakenly assumed to be markers for some future bombing force to indicate their target. One never seriously considered the possibility of large surface forces, as so far, the main Italian Fleet had never sallied forth to visit or contest our passages to Malta. It had been just perhaps the odd squadron out for an airing. Our presumptions were soon proved wrong. The Admiral signalled that from information he had received, an interception by surface forces was more then possible. Eight minutes later, with much roaring, the guns of the force were as busy as ever repelling the screaming and vigorous air attack, which lasted some half an hour.

At 38 minutes past the hour, a small string of gaily coloured bunting fluttered from the masthead of the flagship. These were the orders for the cruisers and their escorting destroyers to increase speed and to prepare to concentrate to the north of the convoy. The Fifteenth Cruiser Squadron with *Penelope* and our escorting destroyers, the convoy still had their own escort of hunt class Destroyers, departed from the convoy to take up our battle station about three miles clear to starboard. A few moments later, we were joined by the small but efficient force of destroyers under Captain Poland, our course being a little north of west, and speed was increased to twenty-five knots. Meanwhile the convoy was steaming as fast as possible for Malta, some two hundred miles away. An intensified lookout was now kept for surface craft, while the enemy aircraft devoted their efforts to the now poorly protected convoy. At 1412 the normal noises of the ship are disturbed as a keen-eyed signalman from *Euryalus* reports that there is smoke on the starboard bow. Immediately, *Euryalus* hoists the signal for enemy in sight on a northerly bearing. This signal is repeated by all ships. All glasses and gun turrets are trained on the bearing, the guns' lean grey snouts weaving a slow and deliberate pattern in the air, as though proclaiming their impatience to be at contest with the new menace. All available eyes and telescopes of the signal staff scan the glittering and shimmering horizon to the north. At 1426, the masts and funnels of two large and one small cruiser are plainly seen. *Euryalus* trembles slightly as she turns towards them, and the low drone of the engine room fans rises to a vibrant note as speed is increased again and the sea piles up at the stern. Spray fountains glisten and sparkle as the spray is flung over the bows. A cheer rings out from the ship, and glancing overhead to the crackle of wind blown bunting as we see an enormous white ensign unfurl from the masthead. Battle ensigns have been hoisted in all ships, there is no mistaking their intent or that of the ships. We race towards the enemy ships, which are now well in sight at about eleven miles range. The combined speeds of approach are that of an express train and the range rapidly decreases. Every one is keyed and tensed up. Suddenly this tenseness is broken by the sight of an orange capped tawny brown flame from the leading enemy cruiser. Still we hold our course in breathless silence, as the enemy shells start to land in the sea that we have so recently vacated. These are shells from an eight inch cruiser. To give them their due, they are quite good opening shots. We still hold our fire for a while longer as this range is just about our maximum range. Our Admiral is sparring well or so it seems. Suddenly, from overhead, there is a dull rumble and whirring noise shortly followed by several large columns of spray and geysers of dirty water appear about a quarter of a mile beyond us. The enemy shells have landed, so that we alter course slightly towards the enemy cruisers. Then, the bus conductor's starting bell is heard, "Tinggg tinggg," and the ship shudders as our first salvos leave the ship, to leave us enveloped in smoke and fumes. Our shells land a little short of the leading cruiser as we watch with bated breath, so that the enemy is quite aware that he has a shooting match on his hands. He alters course away from us in an effort to open the range. As our next set of shells fall round and over the enemy ships, the range is passed quickly to the rest of the force. This they will correct as necessary according to their positions at the time. As they receive our range, the rest of our squadron open fire with rapid fire. Sometimes, if one is watching, there appears in the distance on an enemy ship, a strange crimson flash quite unlike the rest, as a shell strikes home. It was while I was reading a signal from *Cleopatra* that I saw an explosion on the after end of the bridge close to where the Yeoman was standing. A temporary stop in the signal for the yeoman had vanished, so that I informed the Captain that *Cleo* had been hit on the bridge. Yes, Yeoman of Signals Fred Thorpe had been killed in action. The destroyers meanwhile had been laying a thick black and heavy white smoke screen to hide the convoy and some of the other ships from the enemy. By 1430 the enemy cruisers had sampled enough of our fire for the time being at least, and hastily retire to the northwards to rejoin his own forces as we surmise that by now, these three cruisers are not the only ones at sea. Without more delay the Admiral leads us round back towards the convoy, in case some of the enemy may have slipped through in the excitement. Back we race, past the smoke laying destroyers, happy to know that the enemy had been driven off, even if only for the time being, as we expected more attempts to be made. This sense of exhilaration does not last for long.

For just a few brief moments we are left alone to muster our forces in our race for the convoy. Just as we commence to form into battle order, there is some heavy breathing, for it has just been reported that two enemy battleships and a dozen or so destroyers are just below the horizon to the northwest and are hastening towards us. Four cruisers of about five thousand tons each and nothing bigger than a six inch gun between them, plus a handful of brilliantly led destroyers are all that stand between the convoy and the bulk of the Italian Fleet.

Can it be wondered if more than a few of us murmured some hurried prayers, not so much for ourselves but for the women folk waiting at home in blissful ignorance of the coming evening. The captain broadcasts, his words are eagerly awaited, and being received, there are no cheers, for each man realises that the future is in the captain's hands. To filch another great sailors words, or some of them, "We expect to do our duty," for there is not much else that we can do. We are already committed. Perhaps clammy hands will tighten the waist belt a bit to waylay that emptiness in the stomach that seems to come at such times. Some may have puffed with a little more vigour at their lifebelts, just in case, who knows? Some will probably run their fingers over the inside of their overalls, to reassure themselves that they will not remain unknown warriors through the fact of not wearing an identity disc. This is not fear, that moment has passed long ago when the enemy first opened fire on us. No this is just carrying out one's instructions of the precautions that should be taken and the putting into practice some of the drills that we had been taught. Last minute checks at one's equipment, a quick glance at the emergency medical kit to ensure that it is handy if needed. Every waiting moment an unending hour, every heartbeat seems like a death knell that sounds in unison to pulses that thud like giant steam hammers. Those last few moments of sane thinking when all heads are thinking their own most private thoughts before the next moment of Hell's own making. The loud speakers buzz and crackle again, this time it is a new voice, the captain being at his action position. With a sigh the voice informs us that the enemy is now confirmed as being two heavy cruisers and some destroyers. Hearts again feel lighter, but the grim job is on again for an exploding shell makes no difference when it detonates. It causes destruction but only on a differing scale to that of another size shell. We twist and turn, weaving strange patterns in the curling foam of the smoke filled sea. By 1500, (3 p.m.), enemy torpedo bombers and high level bombers are again hurled at us and heavy bombs scream down. Planes whine and scream as they dive and bank away. A mad chatter of noises peal from the ships pompoms and oerlikon guns, gone still further mad; yet men are coolly sane working the guns as though engaged at some prize shoot at some far away shooting range at home. The enemy is again within range as we have turned again to attack him. Tawny brown fumes and cordite smoke cloud the brilliant sun. White foam splashes reach towards the sky as shells have screamed harmlessly by to land with loud reports not far from the ship. The enemy must be firing at random in the hope of obtaining some hits, but he has an almost impenetrable layer of very dense smoke to pierce and we are not where he thinks we should be. Again and again we tear at the enemy to the north of us amid showers of spray and shell fragments. Eight minutes later, the enemy withdraws, so again we alter course for the convoy that is still beating off air attacks. So far they have beaten off the combined strength of the Axis air forces hurled at them, for we note as some of them pass by us at sea level, they have the Nazi fuselage markings.

Thick black smoke curls and swirls from the paint blistered funnels to envelope all in its comforting hiding blackness. We do not get a comforting break, for aircraft are seeking us out. To add to this unequal struggle, somebody reports a submarine periscope. It seems ridiculous that a submarine should be in the vicinity with all the ships speeding about. One cannot afford time to question the report as to the correctness, that emergency orders are given to avoid any possible torpedoes. The ship heels at an alarming angle as the rudder bites the madly churned water, turning at high speed. Two destroyers race to the spot, the sea is churned again as depth charges are dropped. Charge after charge explodes in an effort to destroy this menace from below. No one can spare the time to watch for the results. The action eases slightly, and a member of the galley staff brings round water to quench one's burning lips and throats. Hurriedly produced sandwiches are produced, and just as quickly disappear, for we all know that we are now approaching a critical period of the whole operation. Food must be eaten when and where possible, for there is no telling just when the chance will again occur. The critical period is round about midnight when we of the Alexandria force must leave the convoy and return to our base, for fuel is getting low, caused by the high speed steaming.

Again the enemy comes within range, so that before many minutes have passed, tawny brown fumes and cordite smoke almost obliterate the bright sunlight. Huge white foam splashes reach towards the sky as some shells scream harmlessly by to land with load reports some distance away from the ship. Again and again we tear at the enemy away to the northeast of us. Again and again we pass through the showers of spray and splinters from near misses. We lay thick rolling clouds of black funnel smoke, then dodge in and out of the smoke bank to pump off as many rounds as possible before turning back into the enveloping smoke screen. Eight minutes later the enemy withdraws and again we alter course back to the convoy which is still battling against the combined forces of the Axis air fleets. This we know, for we have seen aircraft with the Nazi markings winging back to Italy as they try wave hopping tactics. Thick black smoke curls and swirls from the paint blistered funnels, and having reassured ourselves of the convoy's safety, we again turn back towards the enemy. There is no comforting break for a breather or smoke, for the aircraft are again seeking us out.

At 1610, the enemy spotting planes, high above our heads are again weaving their strange patterns in the sky. White flares dropped directly over us point us out to the enemy, and multi-coloured smoke trails of varying lengths apparently mark the various positions of the enemy selected targets or units. Again we begin to understand their particular significance. This time there is no mistaking the huge grey shape that distorts the horizon to the north east. It is the Italian Fleet flagship *Littorio* a battleship of some forty thousand tons and equipped with fifteen inch guns. She is accompanied by six or seven cruisers of various types, some heavy and some light, and of course many destroyers. The destroyer *Zulu* well up to the front has made her sighting report, confirming these details, and by 1630 we are able to observe them for ourselves. This is it, at least we all inform ourselves, and we expect the worst. Again our funnels are belching thick black smoke, as we attempt to hide ourselves, but some how it seems that the Statue of Liberty is quite small beside us. One cannot completely describe the feeling, and the nearest that I can suggest is that of standing in the middle of a bowling green and trying to hide behind a blade of grass, in an effort to dodge some terrible attacker. There is no turning back as the enemy is between us and our base at Alexandria. Malta now seems the only answer, unfortunately. This is going to upset all plans for there is little enough fuel at Malta to spare for all of us. Providence dictates that we cannot run as the convoy at its best can only make about seventeen knots as compared to the Italians' thirty and they are not encumbered by any other slower units. In the midst of all this, there is a little heartening news over the squawk box. Malta is hoping to help us by sending some of her own too few aircraft.

The hand of fate strikes the half-hour, 1630, (by ship's bells), and a few minutes later we hold our breath as *Littorio* has joined in the contest with a full throated roar. Her sides seem to erupt with masses of orange flame and clouds of dun coloured smoke. We turn towards this colossus and speed on without pausing. Those that have stood on a busy railway platform and seen the great steam juggernauts tear past, unconsciously draw back to avoid the following stream of suction. They have also heard the whine and tearing, the hiss and screaming of escaping steam and the rumbling of the wheels, and they breathe again freely when the monster has passed. That is what we heard and felt as the one ton shells screeched and rumbled over our masthead. Still we hold our fire as the range is too great for our popguns to compete. Slowly the seconds, that seem like hours, roll by, each one filled with more suspense than the last. The Admiral sees through the enemy's plan to cut between us and the convoy. After that, it would be so easy to exercise a bit of long range gunnery practice to annihilate the convoy and ourselves. Admiral Vian decides that the moment to act decisively has arrived. The situation has become very precarious indeed, for our own small force. Once more in history the ancient mariner's signal flutters from the masthead. The order is for us to, "ENGAGE THE ENEMY MORE CLOSELY." To the rising whirr and whine of the engine room fans, we race to close the enemy at maximum speed, for the order has released all ships from accurate station keeping. Straight for the fire and flame spewing giant, with our destroyers striving to draw ahead so that they may be in at the finish, for that is what it seems to be. The convoy had meanwhile altered course to the south, so as to open the distance between them and what seems like certain destruction. All ships are ordered to prepare to carry out torpedo attack, and that to any one means that we must literally be able to spit onto the enemy's upper deck, for the most effective maximum range of a torpedo is about four miles. A herd of bulls appears to have been loosed in some china shop, for that is the noises that reached us, as gouts of flame billowing clouds of cordite smoke, the ceaseless rumble of madly efficient guns, and the roar of the following draught of air, as salvo follows salvo. The continuous rumble as the ship shudders madly, reeling from side to side as we twist and turn at high speed. Everywhere there is cool hard thinking seaman's efficiency, that impresses on one that this is no nightmare in the midst of this present day civilisation. "Is anything or anyone really civilised, one wonders?" At 1729, a valiant war scarred destroyer is hit but fortunately not badly damaged. She hauls off to effect emergency repairs, and has to reluctantly retire with great loss of speed. She is hit sorely in the engine room and is ordered to make best speed to rejoin and help the convoy. *Zulu, Sikh, Kelvin* and *Kingston* have now drawn ahead and are in line abreast between us and the ever present monster. By gunfire and by feigning torpedo attacks these four gallant and heroic destroyers hold the enemy at bay. Three times they make out to fire torpedoes and then sheer off at high speed. How was it done or by what sheer good luck, there is no answer, and only the ancient Gods of the seaman will know. *Cleopatra* is hit forward and aft, her great white battle ensign flutters down as her masts bend and spring to the impact of landing explosives. Instantly another large white ensign appears at her main mast. She is badly shaken, her after director is temporarily put out of action, her signal deck becomes a shambles from fallen radio aerials and signal halyards. Men are wounded and killed in the drawing of a breath, but still Hell's inferno does not cease. *Euryalus*, the ship astern of *Cleopatra*, swings wide to avert collision with her injured consort and assumes the flagship's responsibilities for signalling as calmly as though at class instruction. This was training at its best. *Cleopatra* steams on and resumes her place at the head of the line but is unable for the time being to use most of her signal equipment. *Euryalus* is lost in spray and shell splashes as fifteen inch high explosive shells fall and cascade round her. She bears the legend of "Goddess of the Open Sea" and in that mythological divinity's keeping, she passes through the gates of Hell. Not altogether unscathed though. A vivid flash from aft, a wild screaming of tortured metal as a shell from *Littorio* hits her after superstructure. The ship swings wildly off her course for a moment, wheels sharply, staggers drunkenly and then ploughs her way serenely on, shaking herself like a large dog coming from the water. No slackening of her speed, for that ship of the Gods. Is she not their own? Strips of painted canvas appear on deck as identification marks for our bombers coming from Malta. We do not wish to dodge our own bombs for it is sufficient to dodge and cope with the enemy. The signal ratings placing the strips of canvas, duck and twist in feverish haste to complete the work, as the guns bark and spit defiance only a few feet over their heads. One gun swings perilously close, belches flame and fire and the canvas is torn from their fingers, while the signalmen are scattered like nine pins in a bowling alley, but the job gets done. Dazed and shaken, soaked through many times from spray, they heave a sigh of relief and vanish from sight to report back to their proper stations. That gun has caused annoyance not only to those signalmen, but to the enemy, for as they stood there dazed and shaken, a fiery red comet plummeted seawards, as an Italian torpedo bomber hits the water in its own funeral pyre.

The Italian ships are now only five miles away, dimly visible through the layers of dense smoke screen. On we charge to attack with our torpedoes and guns. At 1805, the great blue-black torpedoes are ordered to be released at a range varying from two to two and a half miles. The destroyers leading, they turn and fire their torpedoes and then gallop off to rejoin us. Dame Mother Nature now starts to play for us as the wind starts to freshen to almost gale force. The sea rises and tumbles at the fore feet of the hurrying ships, to cascade back over the bridges in roaring white masses. A dull explosion vibrates over the sea, and if one could only spare the time to watch in the direction of the explosion, one would see a dirty brown and white water spout up from the port quarter of the enemy battleship. At least one torpedo has found its mark and gouts of flame appear where the torpedo had struck. The enemy has been badly mauled by these gallant and audacious few ships, but not until some of our own ships have been damaged. *Kingston* is hit in the engine room by a large shell, *Kelvin* stands by to assist her and aid her flotilla mate. No aid is needed fortunately, as by superhuman effort the fires are brought under control and the ship steams on, quite a lot more slowly to rejoin her comrades near the convoy. The enemy has meanwhile altered course away from the gallant band, as though they are reluctant to continue the action any further. By 1900, all the ships of our force have regrouped and are ready for further attacks by the Italians. For the moment these attacks do not materialise, so that the forces under Admiral Vian rejoin the convoy to assist in its protection. The enemy however have tasted their fill and are withdrawing to lick their wounds. Our direction is altered again to the westward and Malta, and we move with all the possible speed that we can muster. Nobody in the convoy needs any urging, for to delay would be to court trouble, and that we have enough of to satisfy the most greedy of customers. The wind is still increasing and it is now blowing almost a full gale. At 1925 when all seems too quiet for reality, scalding hot tea, bread, butter and corned beef sandwiches are served to the ship's company in their gale swept and sea showered battle stations. Only those who are working below decks are dry and free from the spray and wind, and even most of these are soaked in sweat, as they too have worked without respite to repair vital machinery that may have failed during the turmoil of the action.

Night falls on the gale-swept convoy which is now within the bounds and within a few hours sailing time of Malta. Providing that nothing untoward happens, the convoy will be safely in their berths in Malta harbour, even though it is to be bombed and blitzed for three more successive days and nights. Just after midnight, our task is completed and gladly we turn for the home base of Alexandria. It is now with lighter hearts that we speed on our way for now we have only ourselves to look after. Vigilance is not relaxed. It is with ever watchful eyes that we scan the spray drenched blackness of the night. One of our reconnaissance aircraft from Malta has reported that the enemy fleet that we had tangled with yesterday, has been seen steaming at quite a fast pace towards his home base and there were still smoke and flames erupting from his scars and some damaged ships, as something to show for his eagerness. I believe that on board some of the Italian Ships, there were some German observers. If that were the case I feel that they did not have a very favourable report to make to Hitler's Admirals. We push on at a merry pace for Alexandria, slowing down at intervals to collect some ship that has received some damage and need to make some temporary repairs. The next day is taken up with sporadic bombing and torpedo bombing attacks, but nothing occurs to mar our progress home. After the previous day's activities, it seems almost a holiday.

Tuesday 24th March sees us nearing Alexandria, happy in the knowledge of a job well done. We round the marker buoys of the Great Pass Beacon and enter the swept channel for home, at 1400. At approximately 1430 we enter harbour. Suddenly, a siren sounds, wailing forth its plaintive notes. Without hesitation, for we are all keyed up still, we start to dash to ""Action Stations"," not even waiting for the alarms. Something somewhere is again happening. Other sirens join in the mournful chorus and all is bustle and grim activity again, and within a few moments the ship is at stations for repelling air attack, for that is what we assume the noises to herald. A string of gaily coloured flags stream out in the breeze, signal lamps begin to wink and stutter, and then a distant cheering is heard, as Admiral Vian's ship passes the base flag-ship. Slowly it dawns on our action-alert minds that merchant ships are sounding the worldwide recognised sign for victory, Mr Churchill's "Vee." The ship's sirens and the strings of flags spell out, "Well done," and there are soldiers that are manning the harbour defences cheering wildly. Even the four French non-combatant cruisers have manned their upper decks and the reduced crews are cheering. This clears the battle instilled minds that have been tensed up too long, eyes become tear-dimmed and one's breath catches in one's throat. Never having before received a standing ovation, this was something new to us all, and I hope that under similar circumstances, I shall never receive any part of such an ovation again. It is far too overpowering and emotional.

That evening, the news bulletins gave a brief account of the action. The world of the Allies hailed us as heroes, but where are they, you cannot find them, some have gone to enjoy a glass of beer, some to enjoy the smiles of a dancing girl in some local cabaret. Others are busy reading letters just received from home and some are writing home, hoping to dispel the fears or to gladden the hearts and weary minds of mothers, wives and sweethearts at home. Whatever the choice of the individuals, one cannot blame them entirely. All men are not alike, nor have they the same strong ties or perhaps the will power. But as one, they had faith in their able and capable leaders, and after all it is faith, no matter what in, that will see us through any great trial.

To those who did not return to see and get their share of the congratulations, let us hope that the greatest of all writers has recorded their names for Courage and Supreme Sacrifice in large letters of gold in His Own Great Book.

That evening, the padre held a special service in the small chapel on board. It was not only full, but it was overflowing, and with all denominations, and with all ranks and ratings.

The original of this was written by F. Smith on 26th March 1942 after I had checked the main details from the signal logs of the time. *Euryalus* had certainly won her spurs, and an entry into the book of fame, if one is kept by the Royal Navy. Here is a brief selection of some of the messages that were received after our arrival in harbour on 24th March.

All Ships from Commander in Chief.

The following message has been received from the Prime Minister. I shall be glad if you will convey to Admiral Vian and all who sailed with him, the admiration which I feel at this resolute and brilliant action by which the Malta convoy was saved. That one of the most powerful modern battleships afloat, attended by two heavy and four light cruisers and a flotilla of destroyers should have been routed and put to flight with severe torpedo and gunfire injury in broad daylight by a force of four British Light cruisers and destroyers constitutes a Naval episode of highest distinction and entitles all ranks and ratings concerned and above all their Commander, the compliments of the British Nation. Time and date of Origin 1650/25/3/1942 ends.

To Cruisers and Destroyers from Commander in Chief.

Well done Fifteenth Cruiser Squadron and Destroyers.

Time and date of origin, 1240/24/3/1942 ends.

Euryalus from *Valiant*.

Heartiest congratulations from us all on your splendid achievement.

Time and date of origin, 1258/24/3/1943. (by light).

There were many more such messages, some from the 8th Army Commander in Chief, (General Ritchie), and many other high ranking officers, but space prevents me from copying them although the above messages are as made and taken from the signal log of *Euryalus*.

I mentioned on the previous page that the press made comments on the action which was later referred to as "The Battle of the Gulf of Sirte," and is so called in the history books. Here is a transcription from one of the London daily papers that was dated 26th March 1942, that we received on board some days later.

"COMPLIMENTS TO THE NAVY"
Premier's Tribute for Convoy Success.

The Prime Minister has sent a message of thanks and admiration to Admiral Vian for the Navy's fine work in getting another convoy to

Malta with the loss of only one ship, during which one enemy battleship was hit by torpedo. The message says:-

A repeat in toto of the Prime Minister's message to Admiral Vian which is in full on page 261.

Difficult Ocean Route.

Commenting on the engagement, authoritative quarters in London state that the strength of the Axis air forces in Sicily and Crete apart from those in Libya make the sea route to Malta very difficult. The loss of Benghasi and forward airfields in the vicinity meant that fighter cover could not be given throughout the whole passage.

Nevertheless, only one ship of the convoy was sunk, and that by air attack. The attacks by surface forces were driven off and a torpedo hit was secured on an Italian battleship, which a German communiqué states was of the "Vittoria" Class. The Italian claims, as usual, have been fantastic, and a broadcast from Rome last night gave the results as two British warships sunk and eleven damaged, and two transports sunk and five damaged. Malta during the last two months has been subjected to very heavy air attacks, and has been putting up a wonderful fight. The arrival of this convoy with important supplies will naturally strengthen the defences.

"Longest Fight Yet"

Berlin Radio broadcasting, Rome reports that the contacts between British and Italian Naval units lasted over five hours, this being the longest battle in the Mediterranean so far. The broadcast stated that the engagement was opened by an Italian flagship and referred to heavy gales and intense smoke screen manoeuvres by the British Naval formations. The reports add that the targets were hardly ever visible but that the Italian warship succeeded in approaching to a distance of six miles. Berlin Radio quoting further reports from Rome, states that eight British Destroyers made an attack under cover of fog, against an Italian naval formation. It stated that between thirty and forty torpedoes were fired, but all missed their targets. Two of the attacking destroyers were heavily damaged, it alleged. Today's

Italian communiqué says that in the Eastern Mediterranean our torpedo carrying aircraft yesterday morning attacked an enemy naval formation. One enemy cruiser of medium tonnage was certainly hit.

"Shell Grazed Littorio"

Confirmation that the 35,000 ton Italian battleship took part in the engagement in the Mediterranean is given by Italian News Agency. It denies that any Italian ships were hit, much less sunk, but adds "only a 12 mm shell grazed a turret of the battleship Littorio."

A couple of comments of my own. Has any person ever witnessed thick fog at the same time as heavy gales are experienced? The Italians claim that five transports were damaged and two sunk. I can only suggest that somebody was seeing double as there were only four merchant ships in the convoy. According to the addition totals of cruisers damaged, the Fifteenth Cruiser Squadron no longer existed. To this I can only suggest that the ship builders at home really excelled themselves for within a couple of weeks that squadron was again tormenting the Italian Navy and Air Force, in addition to carrying out some bombardments of enemy positions along the North African Coast.

"NO CHARGE FOR DELIVERY"

You can sink yourself in wisdom, you can think you're
doing fine.
Have you ever had a thirst you couldn't slake?
Have you ever seen a convoy with the good ships there
in line,
And the bullets singing stinging in the wake?

Have you ever seen torpedoes dashing straight across
your bows,
As you slew the ship around and miss 'em fine?
Have you ever seen fat bombers screaming down
like ugly sows,
And the ships, a-slick and steady in the line?

Have you ever seen the packets from the bombers as
they drop?
Have you felt them as they crack the deck?
Have you ever felt the choking when your eyeballs
nearly pop
As the blast comes back and nearly breaks your neck?

Have you ever seen a seaman lying dead across his gun
With the flames a licking round him quite a bit?
Have you ever seen the bodies burning when the ship
is done?
If you had you wouldn't ever loose your kit.

Have you ever seen the blood and sweat that thousands
pay in kind
To bring the stuff you're wasting day by day?
Have you ever seen the telegrams to those they
left behind?
The charge for which is not against their pay.

Have you ever seen.... well have you? Course you have
and quite a bit,
Can you see the stuff they're piling on the quay?
Can you see the price that's written? P'raps you can't
decipher it.

It was paid for twice, thrice over; as they brought
it through the sea.

Malta 1942.
The above was written by one of the combatants on one of the
Malta convoys. My apologies for copying.

F. Smith. 1942.

NAIAD SUNK

During the month of February 1942, as in other months in the past, the powers that be decided that a convoy to Malta was due to be arranged. In accordance with the planners' arrangements, the Fifteenth Cruiser Squadron, under command of Rear Admiral Vian, using the cruiser *Naiad* as flagship with the cruisers *Euryalus* and *Dido* in company, plus the attendant destroyers and the necessary merchant ships, duly sailed for Malta. The weather was moderate, a Gregale just having blown itself out, so that little bother was experienced in forming up the convoy, which the cruisers would join the next day. Air cover in the form of long range Beaufighters had been arranged, so that all was quiet and serene. Apart from the sporadic air attacks, which by now we were quite accustomed to, we eventually arrived with the convoy at the entrance to the swept mine channel for the departure of the Malta convoy.

We were just ourselves and the *Cleopatra*, which had joined us from Malta, she having run through from Gibraltar, with more ships and a convoy from that end. Hurrah, at last we were four ships and the squadron was now completed! The destroyers soon formed up in the screening positions and away we went for Alexandria. Only a couple of days away, for we had no convoy to impede our passage. The weather at this time of the year was remarkably good considering that this was the season of Gregales and Kamsins, where the weather can change for the worse in almost the hour. At the time only a moderate sea was running so that we were making excellent progress. On the evening of the second day from Malta, having made about twenty-five knots progress, we were approaching the swept channel for Alexandria harbour. Then from the *Naiad*, came the signal for all ships to alter course twenty degrees together to starboard. This presumably was to bring us closer to the buoy marking the end of the channel. Having passed on the signal, (Blue 2), to the ship astern, Dido, I patiently waited for the executive signal to commence the turn. Soon the tiny flashing blue light from *Naiad* started to blink through my binoculars, so that I answered straight away. One does not exhibit any light longer than is necessary, so that the signal rating on *Naiad* started to pass the executive signal. At that moment, there was a tremendous flash and an instantaneous bang about level with where the signal rating had been. Since I had started to report that the executive signal for the turn had been made, I followed it with the report that, "*Naiad* has been torpedoed." The ship was already turning so that we continued to turn to avoid colliding with the torpedoed ship. I do not think that there was any other explosion, as I did not hear any, so that *Naiad* had probably been hit in the engine room spaces which are normally the biggest spaces in the ship. Destroyers were immediately on the scene trying to scent the assailant. Other destroyers went alongside ready for towing and transferring of the crew, if necessary. None of this was necessary for the *Naiad* was already beginning to settle and heel to starboard. Some twenty minutes later, she heeled over completely and sank, not so very far from the channel leading home. This again left us with three ships in the squadron. Many of the crew were taken on board, the rescuing destroyers without even getting their feet wet, such was the speed and efficiency of the rescuing ships. The Admiral and the Captain of *Naiad* were saved as far as I can recall, and it was a very dejected squadron that entered harbour some time later. Since all four ships were of the same class and looked alike, *Cleopatra* went to the berth normally occupied by *Naiad* and the Admiral hoisted his flag on the *Cleopatra*. *Dido* and *Euryalus* went to their own previously occupied berths. We had gone out three ships, and we had returned with three ships, all of the same look alike. Little was said of the sad loss of *Naiad*, and for quite a long period, the enemy was totally unaware that he had sunk a cruiser. From that, we could only assume that the submarine, that had done the sinking, had not returned to harbour either. It is possible that the wrecks of the sunken ships are quite near to each other not far from the Great Pass Beacon.

F. Smith. March 1942

ENEMY ENGAGEMENT

December 1941 must have been a very bad month for the Allies. In fact the whole year had been one of continual set backs. On the 17th December the Japanese attacked the American Naval base of Pearl Harbour in the Pacific without warning or even an ultimatum. This resulted in most of the American Pacific Fleet being destroyed. The losses included several battleships and cruisers, also many destroyers were severely damaged. It would take months, if ever, to replace the losses. The only fortunate part of this sad debâcle was that the American Aircraft Carriers were not in harbour, so that no Carriers were lost. These Carriers were to render themselves worthy of the highest praise in the near future, when the Americans rallied themselves and eventually, by intense effort, the fleet was replaced or repaired where possible, so that almost a whole new fleet was brought into being.

I remember at the time commenting to many people that perhaps this disaster would prove advantageous, for it at least gave the hard pressed British forces over the world the knowledge that there were no more enemies of any substance to make, and that we had at least one more ally. My feelings at the time were that we, the allies, would definitely win in the end. It was no longer a question of whether we should win, but when.

Round about this time also, we were somewhere to the east of Malta, possibly having been on a bombardment run. About 1100 and I think it was on a Sunday, smoke was seen to the southwest, so that speed was increased by *Euryalus*, who was ordered to investigate. By noon approximately, we had left the other ships of the squadron far behind. Gradually we overhauled the vessel whose smoke we had seen. This vessel when we closed on her and signalled her to stop, was found to be a large Italian hospital ship whose course would have made her returning to Italy. Full details of the ship were obtained, but no boarding was made as apparently, hospital ships are non-combatant vessels according to the Geneva Convention. Her decks were quite well crowded with army personnel, so the probability of her being used as a troop transport was noted. These details were later signalled to the Admiral of the squadron when we again caught up with them. The next day or the day after, when we were again stooging around on our way back to Alexandria, we again saw smoke on the horizon. Again *Euryalus* was told to investigate. Soon the masthead of the suspicious vessel came in sight revealing the tops of a man of war. This could only be one Nation as we had no other friendly forces in the area. The ship's company were already at "Action Stations" when the smoke was first sighted so that it was a question of just waiting for the starting bell. The range, according to the gunnery staff, was somewhere about sixteen miles, so there would still be a wait before *Euryalus* got angry. On the bridge, a copy of the warship silhouettes was quickly available so that nobody was over surprised when it was announced over the tannoy that the suspicious vessel was either a battleship or heavy cruiser, which would mean that there were other forces in the vicinity. It was just being decided that the enemy, it could be no other, must be a heavy cruiser, when a whistling and a roaring noise filled the air. This was no cruiser at that range, so there was only one answer, a battleship. I think that later it was identified as a battleship of the Cavoire class, with fifteen inch guns. An enemy report of the battleship was hastily prepared for transmission when it was noticed that she was turning away from us. Just why? When she could have targeted us at long range without fear of retaliation. Realising that there must be accompanying forces of substantial size in the area we held on for a while, hoping that we might be able to shadow and report accordingly. Some more large calibre shells were fired at us so that we were forced to retire towards our own squadron, for it seemed that the battleship that we had seen was the foremost ship of a squadron, although no more ships were seen. Funnily enough, we saw or heard no more of the enemy. Just what was the subterfuge? Was the Hospital ship of yesterday a decoy for some operation or was the enemy of today genuinely covering some operation? It is most unusual to have even a cruiser of any size at sea without the appropriate escorting destroyers.

With our fuel getting to a low state we were ordered to return to the Squadron which was then en route for Alexandria. Returning to Alexandria without incident we arrived at the Great Pass Beacon just after dark so that by early evening we were secured to our berth not far from the four French non-combatant cruisers. It seems that the enemy were under the impression that our battlefleet were not far from us cruisers.

Other ships had been detached to the northeast of Malta to act as decoys particularly in a radio sense.

As it was dark by the time that we actually entered the swept channel and the harbour at Alexandria the absolute minimum of lights were shown, even when securing to our buoy. This is really a normal and insignificant matter, but as events proved, it was a most important point in the future of the Mediterranean Fleet. The crews of the cruisers and destroyers that had been on the Malta Run, were already turned in and enjoying a night's sleep, hopefully. I had already turned to my hammock in one of the small signal offices on the flag deck. This I used as a sleeping billet so that I could readily be available if needed at any time.

About 0340 on 19th December, I was awakened by the signal ratings of the watch, rather noisily reading some signals, so that I went out to verbally admonish them for their noise. This was because the Navigating Officer also slept on the bridge, where his cabin was situated, as he also made himself available at all hours. Apart from that, he had hardly had any real sleep for several days, the same which could be said for myself. I had hardly got outside the door when there was a very loud dull rumbling sound. Obviously, the first question that I asked was, "What was that?" only probably not quite as politely. Before the young signalman could offer a full explanation, there was a second rumbling that sounded more like an exploding torpedo. The noises seemed to come from further up the Harbour. Hurriedly, I pulled on my trousers and sweater, and I was just about to go to inform the captain of the strange events that were happening, when to my surprise, the Captain himself arrived on the bridge.

Again there was a dull rumbling of an explosion so that the hands were ordered to ""Action Stations." From there, the Commander immediately ordered a boat away and to drop small depth charges round the ship. Whether this was an exercise or not I could not immediately tell. However, any ideas of exercises soon vanished when lines were rigged to go under the ship, and these to be armed with snags, so that if anything were on the bottom of the ship, it stood a good chance of being dislodged. It was then that we on the bridge noticed that the *Valiant* was listing slightly and was down by the bows. Also the *Sagona*, a tanker berthed not so far from us, and just this side of the French non-combatant cruisers. I was very much awake, with the crew on deck very busy getting boats ready and other safety precautions. This was no time for exercises as one could now clearly see.

Ships in harbour were being attacked, but by what means? Obviously there must have been an explosion of some sort on the battleship *Valiant*, and now the *Queen Elizabeth*, another battleship was beginning to settle in the water, as was the tanker *Sagona*. My apologies if I have spelt it wrongly, only my notes of the time are a bit dog eared and discoloured with age. As many hands as possible were now working the bottom lines for all they were worth, as in truth their very lives may have depended on it. According to reports and verbal descriptions from folk on the ships concerned, it seems that they were attacked by "frogmen" who had placed explosives magnetically on the three ships. Whether this was by design, or the selection of targets was by luck, is not known, at least to me. I think that the idea was to damage severely the tanker so that her oil spilled out, and then by firing the oil, at least put many ships of the fleet, out of action. As for the *Queen Elizabeth* and the *Valiant*, fortunately one of the frogmen, surfaced and climbed on to the buoy to which *Queen Elizabeth* was secured. The frogman was noticed by the Marine sentry who raised the alarm. Unfortunately the damage had already been done for the explosives were in place, and with very short fuses. It has been said that Admiral Cunningham ordered the captive frogmen to be placed in compartments near the bottom of the ship. Whether that was true or not is unknown, but suffice it to say, the frogmen spilled the story to the Officer concerned so that some precautions had already been taken by the time the first explosion occurred. It was fortunate that the two battleships were berthed so that there was very little depth of water under them. When they began to sink, they rested on the harbour bed having sunk only some few feet into the water. Because of this, and the normal appearance of the ships attacked, the enemy was unaware that he had put the fleets only two battleships out of action, at least for some considerable time. As for the frogmen, they were taken prisoners and admitted to entering the Harbour defences, behind the cruisers and destroyers when they came in from sea. They were certainly very brave folk.

POT POURRI EVENTS

As was mentioned in the introduction, "Truth is ever stranger than fiction." The following few incidents will prove the above statement, and official Admiralty records will no doubt testify to the authenticity of these events.

HMS Euryalus, in company with several other ships was returning to Alexandria after what had been a reasonably quiet convoy trip to Malta. The precise time and date and year were 1810 November 19th 1942. The weather conditions in the sailor's own terms were "ruddy lousy." The other particular ship to which we are referring was *HMS Javelin*, a destroyer of the "J & K" class. This ship almost turned completely over as the ships of the convoy and escort turned on to the port leg of the convoy zig-zag. These events happened as the heavy seas and the full force of the weather caught us on the starboard beam. Many of the ship's crews were on the upper deck, presumably depth charge crews, as the ships were still at "Action Stations." In the circumstances, it is miraculous that only one life was lost, when at a modest estimate the ships heeled over to nearly fifty degrees from the vertical. Had the ship been at all top heavy she would have turned turtle completely. The huge seas swept inboard, half submerging the funnel and completely swamping all gun platforms.

Perhaps the most amazing incident of the many that happened that day, was when Able Seaman McCabe was washed overboard, striking his head against some object as he went. His inflated lifebelt brought him to the surface, almost beside a cork carley raft that had also been swept overboard, probably by the same wave. No one was even aware that a man had been washed overboard. Some few minutes later when we turned to face the heavy seas, the able seaman was sighted not so far from the ship, sitting on the carley raft making the hitch hikers sign for a lift, which he was given as we manoeuvred the ship almost to the side of the carley float and then hoisted him in by line. That was not the luck of the Irish, for he could just as easily have been missed had we not turned when we did.

Another able seaman was swept from the pompom gundeck and was eventually released from the remnants of one of the seaboats which had saved him from getting a free swim. Another able seaman by the name of Hezeltine was washed off the forecastle where he was working, and swept back inboard into the waist by the same wave. Here he was questioned by a leading seaman as to why he had suddenly joined up with his working party. Then there was the case of the torpedoman at the depth charge throwers seeing an extra large wave hovering near by, hastily fastened himself to the depth charge davit there to see the depth charges being torn from their racks, and torn from their securing chains, to be tossed overboard like so many match sticks. A Leading Stoker Colinson, was observed to walk up the side of the deck structure, being under the impression that he was still walking on the deck. We in *Euryalus* saw both of *Javelin's* screws and a fair portion of her midship bilges as we almost rammed her in our haste to get to her assistance, for we were certain that she had been torpedoed and was sinking. Many are the very strange stories that one hears and were it not for the fact that the events happened to the person themselves one could quite easily disbelieve them and when one sees these things happen for oneself there is no likelihood of exaggeration. There is one more instance of the stranger than fiction that I feel I must relate. Sometime after the Battle of Alamein, we in *Euryalus* had been on a night bombardment along the coast beyond Derna. It had been a quiet night in all respects with little or no opposition from the enemy. We were withdrawing at high speed and in brilliant moonlight, with only a very light sea running. Soon, our radar picked up the indications of an aircraft closing in on us from the North African shore. Everybody was again immediately alert for the air attack that we expected as a result of our bombardment. It was our general practice to wait for any aircraft to be identified either by radar or by visual means, before opening fire. This particular aircraft could not be identified so that we were all ready to give him a good welcome. Closer and still closer he came, until we could see him quite plainly and at about five hundred feet in height, there was no reason that he should not see us. We could see quite clearly the Italian markings and for several minutes he flew over us. To be quite candid, I thought he was going to try a landing on our decks. However, without much fuss to anybody he suddenly opened up his engines and flew off, back from where he had come, or in that direction. There seems little explanation for such conduct.

SEAGULLS AND OTHER BIRDS

Just a small corner of the daily news columns, consisting perhaps of six to a dozen lines at the most. Nothing exciting in the words, "Our light Naval Forces carried out routine patrols of the enemy's seaward flanks." At least that is what the news would convey but, behind those plain words is enough excitement to fill any man's desire for such a commodity.

Euryalus and her two attendant escorting destroyers are returning at high speed from what was called "a beating up run" of Rommel's coastal positions. Well and truly had their task been executed in the hours of darkness when all good folk are fast asleep, or at least should be. The slanting rays of the early morning sun were feeling with shortening fingers of silver, over the eastern horizon, soon to be followed by the blazing red countenance of King Sol himself. He would bid us a cheery good morning on this particular day, for it was ideal cruising weather for which wealthy folk would pay enormous sums to witness. The hour was just after 0430, for in the Mediterranean the dawn is early, and on this particular day, it was no exception. The day's indication by the calendar was August 28th and the year was that of 1942, with the "Desert Stakes" in full swing, for this was to be the working up period for the decisive Battle of Alamein which was still to come.

Dawn "Action Stations" were being exercised as a matter of common routine, for this is the time that one meets an unexpected ship which may open fire in the split second. One has to be instantly ready to answer such actions or to challenge or reply to that ship. Special watch was being kept for any low flying torpedo carrying aircraft that can always be expected in the early half light of dawn and dusk. All eyes and ears were keenly alert. Almost before they are shown, and fluttering clear in the breeze, the signal flags will be reported. The first flag seen will inform all, that aircraft are in the vicinity. Slowly drawing clear of the flag deck, and then streaming out in the strong wind of our own progress until, a whole string of colours are flying from the masthead. At once many eyes of the small force are turned to the signal, as even most of the gunnery staff will have recognised the first flags. Quiet voices will report to their respective captains that "Unidentified aircraft are approaching from the shoreward direction." Those few words mean ENEMY, for all things are such until identification is correct and complete. The news is immediately broadcast to all positions in each ship. This is not only to alert the ship's company, but to ensure that all positions in the ship are fully acquainted with the latest information as to what is happening, as suspense is never so agonising as when one knows next to nothing about what is happening. Suddenly a tense young timid voice, overflowing with excitement calls out that aircraft are sighted on the starboard bow and almost in the centre of that glowing red ball that so gracefully adorns the distant haze-smeared horizon. Long lean grey gun muzzles immediately sweep round to challenge the flying enemy, ready to spew flame and shells at the distant raiders. High powered telescopes and binoculars peer into the sun and soon the shapes are sighted and counted. One, two, three, four.... thirteen, fourteen. This is apparently sufficient to start the day with. How very graceful they look with their wings glittering in the early sun. Under these conditions, one is far from admiring grace and beauty. Gunfire is held until the last possible moment before the enemy breaks formation. Now a faint chuckle is heard from some of the watchers on the bridge, and this chuckle increases to open laughter. The ship's broadcast now informs all that, "The dawn patrol of geese has arrived." Orders are quickly passed to all stations to relax but to remain closed up at stations. How sweet is that relaxation, time for a quick smoke before the next alarm, after an all night vigil and much excitement of the bombardment. The ships are swiftly withdrawing from the scene of the night's activity and soon we shall be reverting to Day Action Cruising Stations. This means that some will go to breakfast and then get ready for another spell of being on duty, while the others will remain at their stations and breakfast later. Some of the really lucky ones will be able to snatch ten or perhaps twenty minutes' snooze, depending on their duty. The young lad that had reported the geese as aircraft was not reprimanded, just given a fatherly talk by the captain, as the lad had not very long been in the ship. Apart from that he had only just turned eighteen and this was his first taste of action of any sort. One lives and learns, and day by day we grow better and better. So the day passes on, with only the occasional air attack to disturb the peace, if there is such a thing.

Not far from us are more ships, these are our own squadron mates for they have been on a similar stunt to ourselves, that of enemy bombardments, so that again we are three cruisers and six destroyers. Speed is reduced to twenty-two knots as we journey eastwards. Only slight enemy air activity is sampled during the day, probably just keeping track of us. No sooner is it dark, than we turn, increase speed to almost maximum and divide ourselves up again as for last night. Yes, it is intended that we shall bombard the same places as last night. Each to his own, is signalled to the ships, so that we all know exactly what to do. Each small force diverges slightly from that of its consorts. Again we sample the long dreary hours with some excitement as the enemy belatedly realises that he is suffering from bombardment from the sea and not from air attack. The shells that landed are not in any way a danger to us for the nearest ones that landed were some fifty to a hundred yards short of us.

Just before the dawn, there is a shouted order of, "Alarm Starboard," as from the misty darkness ahead there is an unknown shape. The ship heels alarmingly as she turns to counter attack the unknown. From the murky darkness looms a squat, fast-moving craft. Enemy E-boats are prowling. From her side appears a dull red flash as a torpedo is discharged. A second or so later, keen eyes spot the speeding torpedo, betrayed by its bright phosphorescent wake. With a swift, maddening, avoiding turn, that throws everybody momentarily off balance, so that many find themselves on the deck. By the skin of our teeth, "Thank God," the torpedo passes harmlessly astern of us. During that mad heeling turn some of the pompom and oerlikon guns, where the gunners are strapped to their weapons, have opened fire on the enemy and one can see the projectiles penetrating the thin skin of the E-boat. Whether that boat made it back to base is uncertain, but I should hardly think so.

One of the escorting destroyers accounts for another enemy craft but unfortunately another of the cruiser force has been hit either by shell or torpedo from E-boats. We join forces as rapidly as possible to find that the destroyer is listing heavily to port. On the bridge the Captain is making momentous decisions, while every man in the ship is doing his utmost to save the ship. There are a hundred things to do but the Captain decides to try to get his ship home.

Various officers on the destroyer, chiefly the engineer officer, have made their reports to the Captain regarding the state of the damage in the different compartments, then with the decision taken the hands go speedily and willingly to work. After all it is their home and nobody likes to be thrown out of their home. As is well known, no captain likes to lose his ship, but the main concern in saving the ship is the depleted state of the fleet, so that no matter what type of ship, salvage and repair are of prime importance. Orders follow orders in rapid succession, men move at seemingly incredible speeds. Certain gear is moved to other positions to counter the list, while other gear is jettisoned to lighten the ship. Meanwhile, the cruisers and their escorts churn the sea to frothy white as they twist and turn at high speed, circling their damaged comrade. At odd moments there is a dull crash, or perhaps the stuttering bark of machine guns, just as warning to the enemy to keep their distance. The enemy has disappeared altogether, as he seems to have taken sufficient punishment, or maybe there are no other boats to reinforce the damaged ones. The stricken ship slowly rights herself, inter ship signals are passed and acted upon, another destroyer moves carefully alongside the damaged ship, steel cables are quickly passed and secured, while some of the crew from the undamaged vessel board the damaged destroyer and help with the preparations and transfer of some of the more wounded cases. At last, the securing wires are cast off and the towing wires paid out very carefully, and then begins the long tow home to Alexandria. Almost dead slow at first, as the bulkheads are examined against the water pressure of the damaged side. Then, a sigh of relief from the bystanders, as the pair begin to increase speed and now we can see a small bow wave mounting at the fore foot of both destroyers. Crazily she splashes and wallows, for all the world like a fish on a line that is being played by an expert fisherman. Speed is gradually increased by a few revolutions at a time, until later on they are making good about four or five knots. Eventually the speed that is convenient for both ships is about seven knots. Long before this we have prepared ourselves for the day's picnic, if these affairs cán be so called. The thin slice of the waning moon has long since disappeared, its place being taken by brilliant sunshine and clear blue skies with a placid blue sea. Too much like peacetime postcards, and to us it spells the inevitable setting for an air attack. Under these conditions the air attack is not long in coming, but the slow parade home goes on. That is nearly two hundred miles away, so that at the least, we can expect a possible ten hours of bombing of any sort. It will be a tough job in more ways than one.

Nobody is left very long in doubt as to what the enemy intends. Out of the dazzling sun, just like the geese of yesterday, swoop six JU88's. Straight for the damaged destroyer. With a terrific screeching roar they herald their attack, to be answered by every available gun. I am sure that amongst all the din, there was the unmistakable sound of rifle fire from the direction of the damaged ship. The enemy bombers pay very little attention to the undamaged ship, and it is their evident intent to complete the already half-completed job. The enemy pilots know only too well, that towing and towed vessels are easy targets, for their manoeuvring abilities are strictly limited. To their dismay they find that the amount of retaliation is hardly worth their risking so much. Already two of the six aircraft are streaking for their base and they are flying just above the sea with long black smoke trails behind them. More aircraft are now arriving, the great black crosses showing plainly under their wings. Shattering blasts of gunfire from all ships, as they shudder and tremble to the recoil of the guns. Ever closer the aircraft scream down and then roar upwards from their mad dive. There is a terrifying swish and whoosh as the bombs literally send up huge geysers of spray that cascade about all ships. The damaged destroyer is often lost in huge fountains of boiling water. Everyone is surprised to see that the two ships emerge still afloat and undaunted. That attack was apparently just an appetiser, for from that moment on until 1700 there were very few moments that were free from the thud and crashing of the duel. Again and again there are cries of "Stukas Diving" as all ships engage them with every possible weapon. Fast crisp orders are given from the bridge and there is always the calling of "Air Alarm" and a stream of figures indicating the bearing and ranges. Always the guns are spewing shells at the enemy as they attack in varying numbers, from pairs to twelves. Different tactics are tried by the attacking aircraft, but fortunately the results are in the ships' favour. Apart from damage by splinters, no ships are seriously damaged. As the destroyer limps and staggers with her lame burden, other ships are racing round in elongated circles, ensuring that there is no interference with the towing operations. All crews are ever watchful and alert, ever fighting, hoping, and praying and one must not forget, ever swearing, which is intended for the enemy. The latter at least allows one to ease one's feelings against the enemy, and in a personal manner. The one main concern now is that the ammunition will last out until this ordeal is over, so that orders are passed to all gun positions, to conserve ammunition by firing only at attacking aircraft. In any case the chances of hitting a retreating aircraft are fairly remote. Young veterans standing at their guns calmly sight and pepper the attackers, for the oerlikon and pompom guns are manned chiefly by boys in their late teens for they usually have good eyesight for open shooting. Not all of them are young, for there is a small number of older hands that have quite a few years' of war experience to their credit. These gunners at the oerlikons and pompoms, are usually identified by the straps that they attach themselves to the gun mountings, and the amount of toffee and chocolate papers that are deposited in the waste bins by the guns. Whatever their age the shells from their guns continue to burst in the sky until it has the appearance of a blue and white speckled carpet. The roar and stammer of the guns, combined with the battering from the blast, deafens and shakes one, until eventually, one becomes completely oblivious to the noises and the din. Decks are constantly being washed by the spray flung up by the bursting bombs of the many near misses.

Slowly but surely the small force is winning through. Every minute takes them that little bit nearer home and safety. A few miles further on, as the force hopes to cut the corner on their way home, the force is engaged by the enemy shore batteries but with no success. Even as this happens, more aircraft appear. The whole contest takes on the fashion of ships versus aircraft, and there is no outside assistance that we can call on. Soon we draw away from the range of the shore batteries, whose guns must have been replaced recently, for it was not so long ago that these batteries were pasted by the self same ships as were now on the receiving end. At last the evening is with us and the first real relief and break for food and drink. It is really amazing just how thirsty and hungry one gets when in action. Probably something to do with the body's making and replacing adrenalin. The food is plain and the drink is lime juice, for nobody has had time to prepare food, and we can still expect air attacks at any time. No doubt some hot food will be prepared as soon as possible, but even with that thought in mind, the corned beef sandwiches are as tasty as they can be made with some pickle if required. Again there is an air attack alarm, this from the radar, which soon shows that these are friendly and are moving westwards at about twenty-five miles range. Obviously some of our own bombers out for an evening or night operation somewhere. A little later we are informed by broadcast, that we are now in range of the Desert Air Force and that we are expecting fighter cover at any time. This gives us all time for a meal that will soon be ready, a wash and brush up just to clear the grime of the actions that we have now endured for almost three days non-stop, with only short breaks for any relaxation.

At least we are now well clear of the enemy opposition for we have circling above us six fighters which is enough deterrent for the enemy. We hurry on, knowing that by the next sunrise, barring submarine attack, we shall be nearly home. All ships are now instructed to report their fuel states, and for the next half hour, the signalmen are busy reading and intercepting the fuel reports from any ship that can be read. This information is required so that the Admiral may dispense priorities for refuelling and, if needs be, send in any ship that may be getting low on fuel. There is no fiddling the figures, as these can be easily checked when the fuel readings are made by the tankers after we arrive tomorrow. A couple of the destroyers will obviously be sent in to refuel early but that is hardly an advantage as the chances are that they will be sent out again to reinforce us, as others go in for fuel.

After an uneventful night, dawn sees us heading for the Great Pass Beacon, our home marker, and the welcome twinkling light beckons us on. As soon as we enter the swept channel, the cruisers will forge ahead and replenish as quickly as possible with all stores and ammunition. This will be a long job, for we have used large quantities of all types of ammunition in repelling the seemingly endless air attacks. Like the proverbial boy scouts, we will be prepared for the next operation as soon as is possible, and all hands will assist. Tugs are soon appearing to take the damaged destroyer in tow and the wheeling screaming seagulls circle the ships for any scraps that may be forthcoming. It is almost as though they are heralding the small triumphant procession to their berths after what has been some of the most fierce air attacks so far. As the sun's rays catch the spread white hovering wings, one gets the impression of guardian angels escorting their charges to a safe and secure harbour.

One may well wonder just why there was such a shortage of aircraft to assist the hard pressed Malta Convoys. For that one must thank the pre-war complacency of various governments and officials in cutting back the very forces that the governments now desired to defeat enemies that were well prepared long before any signs of war became apparent. Also, it must be remembered that by the middle of 1942 the whole world was involved in the struggle where our few resources were far from adequate, and insufficient to meet the requirements of modern warfare. However, things were soon to change for the better, when by sheer guts and determination, some convoys were forced through to Malta, which was readily recognised as the key to all future successful operations in the central Mediterranean.

I mentioned a couple of paragraphs ago, that the Great Pass Beacon was showing a twinkling light. Although all lights were forbidden after darkness, there were special occasions when screened low power navigation lights were permitted, and this occasion proved to be one.

Somewhere in the past pages of this memoir, one has read of the minesweeping pranks of the First Minesweeping Flotilla in Scotland in the days before the war started. These little ships of some seven hundred tons, carried on clearing mines in 1939 and onwards through the present struggle. The only difference is that the mines were of enemy manufacture, and liable to explode with a bang for various reasons. Some of the mines will explode as described before, while some will explode at just the sound of a ship's engine going by overhead. Some will explode after a certain number of ships have passed and then the unlucky one catches it. Other mines, known as magnetic, will be activated by the mere presence of a ship with its magnetic field. Many are the types and devices that make the mines function. There are some mines, I am told, that cannot be swept by minesweepers, but this is doubtful, as although I did a certain amount of time and instruction with minesweepers, I am not an authority on mines or minesweeping.

For the most, minesweepers are manned by fishermen, merchant navy men, RNVR and RNR personnel. Depending on its type and size, so are the tasks of sweeping allocated to these ships. It should also be noted that some types of aircraft are equipped with special apparatus for dealing with mines. Some ships are designed and built for the job, while many are just plain honest to goodness fishing vessels that have been taken over and adopted for the clearing of mines. Some are even relics from the previous World War. Whatever the ship, the task remains the same and as perilous as ever it was, and with the cunning of enemy scientists, if one likes the phase, "still as exciting," although I would not use the phrase in the company of any mine clearing personnel. They in particular do not appreciate the reference to being blown up while working, as being in any way exciting. To them, there is probably much more excitement in obtaining a glass of illegal spirit or some such simple pastime.

To the men of the minesweepers, it is they who are the keepers of the seas, and to deny this fact, particularly in front of them, is fraught with a certain amount of danger to oneself. Under the Articles of War, the following saying of which the average sailor is conversant, "It is upon the Navy under the good providence of God, that the safety and honour, and welfare of this Realm doth depend." These words are usually read or said at the church service that may be held on board H.M. Ships each Sunday. To our friends of the minesweepers the following will be added, "It is also upon the minesweepers that the safety of the Navy will depend." This may be a pun to many folk, but it nevertheless rings very true.

During the North African campaign, the sweepers were at sea in all weathers, clearing each stretch of water where larger warships and merchant ships were liable to ply their trade. Not counting the Western Mediterranean, the sweepers cleared some thousand miles of water between Alexandria via Tobruk, and Derna to Benghasi and then south until they could clear up the mess of Tripoli. Some time later they would be required to link up with their pals from the Western end when they reached Tunis. Even then, the task would not be complete, as there were other areas to be cleared of the mines. The main sea lanes were cleared in general by the larger sweepers and the harbours and the local surrounds would be cleared by the smaller sweepers, (ex fishing vessels).

The placid blue waters of the Mediterranean that in peacetime carried the carefree folk on their cruise liners, are now strange places inhabited by the locals and a strange mixture of foreigners in multitudes of varying coloured uniforms with each one armed and ready for trouble. As the charladies, (minesweepers), leave harbour, perhaps one will see a cabin cruiser of fair size, roaring past, complete with bikini-clad blonde reclining in a tantalising attitude on the upper deck. There will not be any wolf whistles from the sweepers' crews, for they will be far too intent on their lethal task. It's hardly an excuse to tell Saint Peter that you were distracted by an almost naked blond on the upper deck of a passing cabin cruiser. Perhaps one may also see on a neighbouring beach, a whole family happily sun bathing or sporting themselves in the water. So quickly and efficiently have these charladies done their work, that one may forgive them for forgetting the men who made their leisures possible. The sweepers' crews are accustomed to these sights. They have also discarded their uniforms for the work-a-day overalls of denim. It can be filthy and bloody work at times, such as when the mine goes up in the half retrieved sweeps to the detriment of those working the sweeps. Up and down, up and down, the chars will plough their allotted area and sweep it clean without a stop, even for meals, until the area can be declared apparently clear of the lethal eggs. You will also possibly see towing astern, over the stern, a silver balloon like some overgrown sausage, or a fat circus clown with fins, acting as some small protection against the ever possible chance of a sneak air raider. There will occasionally be some excitement on board as a huge round black barnacle and seaweed covered ball bobs up astern, so that the sweepers will slow and perhaps stop, while the mine is cleared from the wires and kites. This is the precise moment that is meant for holding one's breath, or even perhaps the impromptu production of a toilet roll and clean pants. These two hundred and fifty pound eggs, with their ominous horns like some loathsome snail, are quite capable of blowing away half a ship. The comparative small pop of rifle fire is heard and if lucky, the marksman will puncture the horn when the sea water enters. This will result in an almighty bang and roar as the mine explodes with much disturbance of water. If the marksman has not been quite so good, but much luckier for the ship, the mine will be filled with holes and the mine will sink, like an old tin can to the sound of gurgling water, like a bottle that has been freshly opened and the pouring is done by an anxious waiter. As the mine sinks slowly to the bottom, to rust and rot and become so much garbage, to reappear some long time later in a hapless fisherman's net. Should the mine have exploded, the whole local population will have heard and seen, and will have marked the spot in their mind, ready for when the sweeper has gone on its way. They will then race out to the spot and pick up the fish that have been killed or stunned.

These will make a ready market for the locals in the morning without having to trawl or fish for their profit. At night one or perhaps two will lay off shore, most probably rolling their innards out, as they watch for the enemy aircraft, and act as aircraft spotters or spotters for the mines that may be dropped. There will be no let up and the whole operation is repeated daily. Laxity in these matters can and does result in the harbour being bottled up by perhaps only one mine. No chances can be taken, for the army must be constantly restocked with everything from water to ammunition and food and this can only be brought by sea. Not by the lorry load, but by the ship load, of hundreds of tons, thanks always to the dirty little minesweepers that daily plough on their way regardless of all else. I would ask the reader at this stage to imagine, or try to imagine, the number of minesweepers that must be in use by the Navy, for not only were they at full stretch in the Mediterranean, but in home waters where the convoys were arriving almost hourly, and scores of other outlandish places. Then there would necessarily be the training of new crews ready for when the Allies made their attempts at crossing the channel or wheresoever.

In addition to the hazards already described, the crews have to be physically fit to manipulate the paravanes or other types of sweeps in all weathers. On the sweeping operations, one will constantly have to be alert to the dangers of stepping on the sweeping wires or just standing in the way as if the wire breaks, the whiplash of the stranded wire can just as easily cut through an arm or leg as through the mine mooring wire. One does not even have to be careless to be a classified hospital case, and many are the minesweeping sailors that walk about with fingers missing through trying to clear snagged wires. The signalmen of the sweepers will be the jacks of all trades as not only do they have signal duties, they are at times required to help out with the sweeps, when signal work permits. Not all the signals will be of a minesweeping nature, as note the occasion when in company with some other ships, and the half yearly promotions were being signalled. The C.O., (Captain), of one ship had been passed over for the last time, as all promotions are made in zones, and promotions are signalled twice yearly. This is at the new year and at the sovereign's birthday. Very similar to the Honours lists where footballers and jazz singers get O.B.E.s etc. The C.O. in question, also had a sense of humour for on realising he was now out of the zone, he signalled his friend, "Request the pleasure of your company at the feast of the pass over tonight." Promptly the reply came back, "With much pleasure, presume the dress will be sack cloth and ashes." Whenever possible, if larger ships are in company with the sweepers, it is customary to put the facilities of the larger ship at the disposal of the sweeper, especially on outlying duties or stations. The facilities would include bathing, cinema, tombola, if the inviting ship possessed them, as it helped ease the monotony for the sweepers.

A CHANGE OF DIET

After the convoy to Malta in March, which became known as the "Battle of the Gulf of Sirte," our time was fully occupied by bombarding the enemy coastal defences and where possible intercepting his convoys to North Africa and Benghasi. During this period we did a spell of relief for the Force K at Malta. Here, we had four destroyers to escort and back us up in any operation that occurred. During some of these operations, we would wait for the patrolling aircraft to report enemy ship movements. The aircraft used for this reconnaissance were generally Wellingtons with modifications. It was quite common to find that one had some R.A.F. personnel on board for some of our forays, and likewise some of the Navy personnel were given the opportunity to take a flight with the Wellingtons. These interludes were all too brief for very often all the arrangements had been made to exchange personnel for the night, when hey presto, everything was cancelled by urgent sailing orders. A convoy had been spotted leaving Tarranto or some such place, and was heading south for Tripoli or Benghasi. Our job was then to intercept and destroy. Sometimes if the enemy were in force, we would go close in support of the destroyers, or, if the enemy was only lightly defended, the destroyers would go alone. This was to economise in fuel, for it must be remembered every drop of supplies had to be taken to Malta somehow, and conservation of fuel was of prime importance.

Quite often we would meet the reported Italian convoy of perhaps anything up to half a dozen ships escorted perhaps by four destroyers. No sooner were our destroyers on the scene and opened fire than the enemy destroyers would perhaps make an effort and fire a few rounds just to save face, and then beat a hasty retreat. It must have been very frustrating for the enemy generals, sitting on the doorstep of Egypt only to find that he could not carry out his intention of attack because of lack of supplies, to sustain his forces. Sometimes it so happened that the entire Italian convoy and some of its escorts would be completely destroyed. There was only one snag to these mopping up operations, that was, that we had to cease all operations in time to be back in Malta by daylight so as to be under the cover of the Malta fighters.   Then without warning, we were ordered to return to Alexandria with the destroyers.

AGGRESSIVE ACTION

This is the short story of a sea trip undertaken by one of our war correspondents attached to the cruiser *Euryalus*.

Going to sea in a British cruiser expecting to go into battle, is a completely new experience to me. I did not know precisely what was afoot when we pulled across the harbour after dark in a motor pinnace. My jovial comrades shouting "PASSING" to the ships that hailed us, just to let them know we were not calling on them.

The first voice that greeted me was Canadian, somebody said he was from the backwoods. I immediately thought, "Here's a new sidelight on the British Navy," and I also found other strange seamen on board. Two solicitors for instance, who are now, to use the extravagant phrase, "treading in Nelson's footsteps." Down in the wardroom was the ship's Captain who might have sprung from a traditional sea story. A small trim dapper man, a figure like Captain Kettle or Sir Roger Keyes, wearing the ribbons of the D.S.O. and the D.S.C., who last year ran the Dover Patrol and did a lot of the organisation behind the evacuation of Dunkirk. He seemed to regard my arrival as good evidence that the battle was really afoot, a sentiment that I did not know whether to share or not.

The atmosphere was lively, and the only anxiety amongst these people was whether the exploit that day of our destroyers sinking two Italian cruisers would send the enemy scurrying back to harbour. Bringing the Italian Fleet to action has never been an easy business. Nelson found the same difficulty with his opponents. And again, like Nelson's orders, ours had a magnificent simplicity, TO SINK AND DESTROY. Would the enemy give us that chance? At all events we were all prepared for the best or worst, as you choose to put it, for the time was somewhere in the autumn of 1942.

I had been given what is called anti-flash gear, long gloves coming half way up your sleeves and a cotton helmet to cover your head and to tuck inside your jacket to prevent your clothing being stripped off you, by flash. Up on deck, I could hear a faint voice saying, "Watch fall in; prepare for sea." I was just sitting down with one of the engineer officers for supper, when he rose saying, "I must be off....

can you hear them, the engines have started?" Yes, we were certainly off but it was not all that dramatic. Another officer, remarked, "In the middle of battle, you will hear a voice over the loud speaker telling the men to take down all the washing from the drying room. Battle or no battle you will hear that order from the speakers."

At dawn next morning, I heard the Captain broadcasting to the ship's company in a brisk businesslike voice, "This is the Captain speaking. Tonight offers a fair chance of a scrap. Intelligence tells us." Here he gave some details ending with, "our chances of being attacked by air are pretty good." I could not help smiling at that, as though attack by air was a consummation devoutly to be wished, and two ratings standing near me said, "So that's that," and got on with their jobs. Later on, a young sub-lieutenant with a studious boy's face, he did not look more than nineteen, had been explaining to me some instruments for dealing with air attack, when he suddenly said, "You could not have come at a better time, here they come." Sure enough our guns began to crack, and not only our guns, as I got out of the cabin in time to see a column of water like a thick fountain going up, about half a mile off, where a bomb had dropped. One could hear the whistle of our shells as they left the guns. The ships are flying the red flag denoting an air raid in progress. Rain fell in silver drops and then ceased. Indeed the whole scene was full of colour, white flecked sea and our gun muzzles shining grey, lifting and turning and thrusting this way and that like blind fingers endeavouring to touch somebody. It was announced that a submarine contact had been made to starboard but I was not clear how far off or how definite the news was.

I climbed back onto the bridge, where the Captain was now wearing his steel helmet and a signalman was using a long telescope saying, "Signal flying, Sir, executive signal, Sir, carry out zig-zag...."

The Captain was saying, "Port ten, twenty, ease to ten, midships...." while the guns belched and the sky blossomed with black puffs as though a master conjurer were at work. Then it ceased, the aircraft sheered off. Then I had an opportunity to speak to some of the characters on board. There was a seaman who had already been a survivor four times, once with Lord Louis Mountbatten. Once too, he was in the sea for over a hundred hours, as numb as a bit of wood when he came out, and as they treated him, and he came back to life, and he shouted for two hours solid. As the blood came coursing back he could not stop himself from shouting with the pain. Even so, this did not stop him coming back for more when he joined this ship. There was also the young ship's doctor wearing the ribbon of the Distinguished Service Cross who had seen more than enough of action at the beaches of Dunkirk, Boulogne and Calais. He had sailed with the sailors at the time that they had had no sleep for five days and nights. He in particular, had his own views on making up emergency stimulants in tablet form. Time passed quickly and when about three-quarters through my lunch meal, "Action Stations" sounded again. Stewards pushed aside the couches and opened a steel door in the wardroom, put down a large thick mat, produced a long iron rod with semi circular shaped end, which reminded me of some ancient torture implement. When I asked what it was for I was told to rake the empty cartridge cases as they come down the chute. Without more ado, I put on my lifebelt. This sounded like a bassoon when I blew it up, an object of pure delight to all who hear it. I got to the bridge just in time to hear that aerial torpedoes had been dropped on us, our guns were thundering at the planes on the horizon and the ship was making a great curve in the water. A good deal of bridge chanting was going on; the loudspeaker was saying that we had four aircraft closing at seven miles, and the Captain was saying, "Steer one three five.... Mr so and so, I want you to spot any torpedo bombers, keep a sharp lookout to port...." while the six forward guns were pointing accusingly to the west. For the next three hours we had only brief intervals when aircraft were not closing or being driven off. On and off went the steel helmet which was two sizes too small. Up came a jug of tea for the captain, my legs grew weary with standing and my eyes grew sore with searching. There was the moment when the aircraft were overhead and a calm voice saying, "aircraft diving sir," and again the voice saying, "Bombs dropped sir," as though he were announcing that the vicar had called for tea. We looked up as our guns roared and their flash turned everything yellow. The Captain's face silhouetted in the flash was as though he was covered in gold leaf, his skin as yellow as a guinea or a sovereign. Now we saw the bombs falling in a cluster as plainly as I can see the pen that I am using. Our neighbouring cruiser had a near miss but we were well clear of them. About this time also, an object was sighted ahead near the horizon, that might well have been a submarine periscope. We flew a signal to warn the other ships. So, the party went on, aircraft closing, guns swivelling their muzzles belching flame and smoke, while the bridge ritual went on. "Starboard ten, twenty, thirty midships, steady on one two oh, what does the washing say?" - meaning the signals from the ship ahead. "Anything on the board?" meaning anything on the radar. The Gunnery Officer with G.O. on his helmet coming up to report to the Captain and the Captain turning to remark that the last attack was a pretty poor one. I was reminded of the remark the Captain was always reputed to make when off on an adventure, "Well, blow 'em out of the water," so it was with a sense of disappointment we all shared, and mine no doubt less marked than theirs, that we received a signal saying the enemy battleships and destroyers were heading fast for home, and that for the moment our operation must be postponed. The sun began to sink, and the sea first turning grey then lit with touches of silver then gold and next, turned dark. The red glow in the west became for an instant as vivid as an open furnace door, and then grew dim and was extinguished. The Captain then broadcast that some of our destroyers were going off on a submarine hunt. We had not brought the enemy ships to action, but we had prevented one of his much needed convoys from sailing. We had not sunk or destroyed on this occasion but we had helped reduce the Axis to its furtive shipments using warships to take supplies. In von Rommel's retreat to Benghasi we had played our part.

A ship bearing the name of this ship that I sailed on, led the frigates at Trafalgar, another landed the Lancashire Fusiliers at Gallipoli where they earned no less than seven Victoria crosses before breakfast. This ship and her Captain and crew are in the great tradition.

The foregoing was broadcast to the people of Britain sometime in the latter part of 1942 by J.L. Hodson, War Correspondent of Allied Newspapers. I believe he was from the U.S.A., but I cannot be sure. I make an apology for repeating this article more or less as it was broadcast since it referred to our ship, *H.M.S. Euryalus*.

F. Smith. 1943.

HARRY CROCKET

In the days before the war, Harry Crocket was a much respected reporter on the staff of a well known paper. If he wrote some of the scandal for which that paper was noted, I would not like to comment. When I knew him on board our ship in 1942, he must have changed his style quite a bit, for there was then very little scandal to write about in the Mediterranean. While he was with us he was the accredited Associated Press Naval Correspondent attached to H.M.S. *Euryalus*, of the Fifteenth Cruiser Squadron in the Eastern Med Fleet. As I was the Captain's Yeoman, it was my job to keep the Captain informed of all signals that came and went from the ship, many of which were highly confidential or secret. Harry, being the accredited correspondent was told that I would keep him informed to a very great extent of what the ship was doing or what was happening. Any censoring that was to be done, would be undertaken by the ship's senior officers. Harry became a great companion of mine during his stay on the ship. He must have been, for he became one of the very few people that was permitted to take "sippers" with me and my tot. This of course was unofficial and taboo.

The following is an official report as made by Harry Crocket on 23rd January 1943 on board the *Euryalus* off the port of Zuara, which is listed in the geographical directory as, "Zuara, Tripolitania; waterfront railroad terminus." (To this was added a bit by the British Forces, "Jumping off place for Rommel's back peddling forces). Zuara was rocked and blazed furiously early today after British warships showered it with tons of high explosives in a surprise close range bombardment. The full extent of the damage caused to military objectives in the Zuara area, was not immediately ascertainable, after this ear splitting dazzling attack, but obviously it was heavy. Great fires, brilliant explosions and palls of heavy black smoke silhouetted for miles against a background of silvery moonlight still clearly seen after we were many miles at sea again, bore witness to that.

All plans for this bold stroke against the forward Axis Forces, only a scant twenty miles from the Tunisian border, designed to destroy military stores and installations and to hamper transport by damaging roads, were naturally kept secret.

Not until we were well at sea were we informed of the nature of our mission which was the first of its kind in that area of the Mediterranean. Announcement of the plans by the Captain, set officers and men alike buzzing with eagerness to get on with the job of smacking the Nazis and their stooges. Once again I was the only American with the fleet and it is not at all surprising to me, after sailing on other ships in recent very successful attacks on Axis shipping, that all hands were eager to smash at enemy held shores, regardless of what unknown dangers might be lurking behind the darkened coastline.

The night was virtually perfect for a bombardment. A brilliant full moon rode high in the sky and shone so brightly, that one could read without difficulty the labels on the various gadgets on the bridge. For the first time in many days the Mediterranean, recently whipped by northwest gales, was dead calm and sparkling in the moonlight.

Ahead of us, another cruiser cut a majestic swathe in the moonlit waters and left a sparkling wake through which this speedy and powerful fighting ship sped, with almost a silken rustle.

Reaching a position west of Zuara we altered course, turning broadside to the shoreline, which was already faintly visible. Soon the outline of Zuara lighthouse came into view and then came the order of Rear Admiral A.J. Power, the first commanding officer of *H.M.S. Ark Royal*, to "Open Fire." With a blinding flash and rip rocking roar, a score of Naval guns blasted more than a ton of high explosive shells at the Axis target. Before our ship had time to recover from her first reactionary shudder, there came another salvo, then another.

In the distance, the whump, whump, whump, of exploding shells ashore, could be heard. Suddenly a brilliant sheet of flame, scarlet red, shot skywards from the target area and a tremendous column of inky black smoke curled upward and then levelled off, hanging low as it drifted westwards in the wind. Into the fairly wide area illuminated by the fires, these ships pumped round after round of screaming shells; more than four hundred of them, aggregating many tons; each of them seeming to leave a white crease in the sky as it hurtled towards its target.

The great billows of black smoke clearly indicated that gasoline for the Tunis-bound tanks and aircraft had been set on fire. From the great volume of smoke it appeared that a great dump had been set on fire and from the large amount of smoke that a great dump was ablaze. Then came a series of explosions as other shells hit. Some of them were sharp brilliant explosions, the type you would expect when an ammunition dump is hit. Others were dull red blasts, and still others seemed to sparkle as a cluster as though something very solid was hit, disintegrated and tossed willy-nilly into the air.

That the Axis forces busily engaged in the serious business of evacuation, never expected to be struck so far forward, almost at the Tunisian Border, while they were running away from the forces already marching in to Tripoli, was obvious. The withering shell fire from these ships brought forth not even so much as a single gun blast from a shore battery. The only firing from shore was red tracer anti-aircraft fire aimed at our star shells and clearly indicating the Jerries and Itis thought they were aircraft flares and that they, were being attacked from the air. Meanwhile from their almost completely evacuated airfield in the area, the Axis managed to get one aircraft skyward but it remained strictly non-combatant, circling us at a respectful distance and never firing a single shot.

H. Crocket

N.B.

Roughly a week or so later, Harry was ordered by his seniors to leave the ship, and to take up a posting ashore. Ironically in the Tripoli area. On that particular night, the Axis decided on an air raid in that particular area. Harry was killed in the bombing.

F. Smith. 1943.

The report by H. Crocket as was printed in the papers, was copied by me during a break in the operations some time later.

PREPARE FOR ALAMEIN

By the beginning of October 1942, the Battle of El Alamein had started and nearly finished, during which time we were kept on the move without respite. By the 5th October, the Axis forces were retreating westwards, all the time under heavy bombardment from land, air and sea. Meanwhile, at the other end of the Mediterranean, American and British forces were making landings at Oran and Algiers. If not actually at those places, they were not very far from them, and as I was not at that end of the Med, I cannot say with absolute certainty. Our main places of interest were Mersa Matruh, Tobruk and Derna for the time being. As the Eighth Army started to advance, so our share of the operations increased until we were shelling the roads well in advance of the pursuing Eighth Army. I sometimes think that the ships of the Fifteenth Cruiser Squadron knew their own way from Alexandria to Malta because of the number of times that we had performed the trips. When the American forces occupied Algiers and started to advance towards Bizerta and Tunis, we all started to expect a change of scenery in the near future. It became more pronounced as each day's successes mounted that before too long we should be able to hope for and possibly expect the Axis to withdraw some of his forces towards Tunisia. This he did do, so that it eased the pressure greatly on the Eighth Army and of course ourselves. By the end of October, ships were beginning to operate from Benghasi, as the army pressed on to El Agheila and Tripoli. This meant, that for the first time in our recent history, we could operate from Malta with the knowledge that air cover would be provided. It was a great relief to the crews of the eastern Mediterranean ships, to know that they were not now alone in their efforts to beat off the Reggio Aeronautica and their Axis companions.

Then came the season of winter when the areas of Tunisia and Algeria became quagmires so that the army could not operate as it wished and pursue the enemy. During this time it was the job of the cruisers and destroyers to seek out and destroy the enemy convoys endeavouring to run the short passage from Tunis to Sicily and Italy. For the record, I have little recollection of Christmas 1942 even passing, for this was a time of great activity for all naval units in the Mediterranean. I recall that early in December, the cruiser *Aurora* with some other cruisers and destroyers of Force "Q" found an AXIS convoy of four ships escorted by four destroyers. This convoy was immediately engaged and after a running fight, the whole convoy was sunk and also three of the destroyers. The fourth destroyer made off in the darkness at his best speed. For our own convoys we had ourselves and a couple of destroyers more or less daily plying between Bone, Bougie and Algiers with the merchant ships loaded with various stores. This we presumed to be the building up of supplies for the time when the army would again be on the move from its stalemated winter positions.

It was while in Bone one afternoon that I spotted some fellows on the jetty from the Royal Tank Regiment. I know that it sounds funny asking Army people if they knew a Smith in the regiment, but that is precisely what I did. After a few questions and answers I came to the conclusion that they both came from the 5th Tank Regiment, which was the same as brother Len was in. These two fellows were sergeants so I thought it probable that they would know him, as the last I had heard was that Len was a sergeant major. No, they had no Sergeant Major by the name of Smith, but they had a Major L.C. Smith. Brief descriptions followed and the fellows agreed with me that it could be Len who had apparently become an officer with the war time promotions. However, they went on their way, having promised me that they would inform Len that I was on the ship in the harbour, and suggested that he come down and see me. Unfortunately before Len could even get anywhere near the ship we sailed on an urgent assignment, (convoy again). It appears that when I spoke to Len about this at a much later date, the fellows had not even told him about having seen me. Hard luck.

ETHIOPIAN BREAK

It was also during one of these so called quiet spells that we were ordered to Alexandria. This would make a pleasant change, at least so we all thought. However before we got to Alexandria, the Captain informed the ship's company that we were going on to Port Said. The telegraph of the jungle tom toms just hadn't got a thing on the speed at which the rumours subsequently flew round the ship. First we were going home on the reverse route to that which we had come out. We were also going to the Black Sea to help reinforce the Russian navy. We were also going to the Pacific to reinforce the fleet out there. These wild guesses all proved extremely wrong so that there were many red faces in evidence of the incorrect forecasting and also quite a few "Gulpers," (a generous swig of one's tot, unofficial), were lost over this, when the real destination was known. It was probably at much greater odds than ever the football pools knew. To reach our destination, a passage had to be made through the Canal and the Red Sea to what was Italian Ethiopia. Most of the ship's company had never heard of the place, let alone previously visited it. It seemed that our destination was the port of Masawa which had been used as an Italian base for submarines and small craft, besides for merchant shipping. Here at Masawa we would effect a self-refit and boiler clean, for in truth the ship had been going with hardly a break, since commissioning and great praise was due to Chatham dockyard whose builders had also built *H.M.S. VICTORY*. It appeared that this was the only place where this refit could be done. On arrival at Masawa, inoculations against various diseases was the order of the day together with liberal doses of anti-malarial tablets which were taken under the supervision of at least a petty officer or Chief who ticked one's name off. Salt Tablets were also served out, for with the temperature standing at 110 Fahrenheit from early morning, one lost a lot of salt via perspiration, which if not replaced, would cause chronic illness. Yes, a truly wonderful place if one wanted a sun tan and even so, in spite of the ban on sun bathing, there were several cases of heat and sun stroke.

While at Masawa, the ship's company was organised into two watches, and each watch was detailed to take a three day break to Asmara the Capital. Asmara was situated a few thousand feet above sea level, and some 150 to 200 miles inland. If that distance is incorrect, one can only blame it on the ever winding road from Masawa to Asmara through the mountains. It was certainly a very interesting trip up to Asmara for we passed along the road that the British and Indian troops had fought for and won from the Italians. On the road up, it was nothing to see the local women working in the small cultivated patches of fields, working with nothing on except perhaps an old pair of discarded army shorts that were well and truly worn and torn. Some even had babies suspended from their necks by a kind of oversized medical sling. From time to time the babies would be fed while the mother worked on the tilling of the cultivated area. Obviously these sights intrigued some of the sailors who had not seen such natural things before, so that the whole trip became a nature lesson, particularly as there was a guide from the army with us to explain everything as we progressed. On arrival at Asmara the sailors were accommodated with the army of occupation, but were given no duties. This was really going to be a short break from the Navy. I was accommodated in the Sergeants' mess of the Military Police, which was quite cosy and comfortable, and all that any naval person did was to comply with the army rules for meals, whilst the rest of the time was our own. Having made temporary friends with the sergeants, I was invited to go with them on their routine military patrol of the city. This was indeed a conducted tour and for this tour I was issued with the belt and armband of the Naval Patrol. In other words I was helping them to keep the Navy in order. It saved some of our own people doing the job, besides which I being in the M.P.s company was allowed wherever they went even to the native quarters of the town. Here, one could see the locals smoking their hooka pipes and from the smell, it was Hashish, which I am sure was cultivated locally. Obviously some of the sights encountered cannot be printed even if I could sufficiently describe them. After about six-thirty in the evening, when it became cooler, I was again invited to accompany the evening patrol, which I agreed to do, as one went and saw so much more of the local environment when going in a semi-official capacity. As far as the army was concerned, I was one of them, although I was informed that if there were any naval offenders I should be the one to deal with the bother whatever it may be. This was because, as they said they were not so well acquainted with the Navy Regulations. All went well with no incidents to mar the evening until about 2130, (9.30 p.m.), when we were called to the local red light district. I must explain here that there were two of these places, call them what you will, one termed the white house and the other termed the black house. They were identical places as regards activities, except that one employed white girls and one employed black or coloured girls. The place where the bother was occurring was the white house, so away we went, four burly M.P.s and myself. On reaching the white house, we all entered, to be met by the female proprietor, (the Madam), who informed us in quite good English that a sailor was being bothersome in one of the rooms. There was an immediate cry from all the M.P.s, "Away you go Fred, this is a Navy job." One of the M.P.s agreed to accompany me to help sort out the offending sailor. Madam opened the door to the room and we both entered to find a Royal Marine's clothing spread over the floor, and the offender was quite unashamedly and without interruption, pursuing his pleasures. Of course, one cannot just openly arrest a person without knowing why, so the Madam informed us that the sailor, (to her knowledge), would not come out, having been there some considerable time. "Oh yes, he had paid but just would not come out," so she informed us. Taking the bull by the horns so to speak, I tapped the marine on the shoulder and told him that it was time to go. To this the immediate reply was, "I've paid my money and want value." Here there was a consultation between the Madame, the sergeant and myself, so that we eventually agreed that he should have more time and then go. Fifteen minutes was the allocated time, so that taking off my watch, I held it in front of him, at the same time telling him just what we had agreed.

"O.K. Chief, that's fair enough," he replied and resumed his activities. At ten minutes to zero, the Sergeant told him that there was five minutes left. The gymnastics were energetically renewed, until at the agreed zero hour, I told him that he had expired his time, to which he agreed without bother. As he got dressed fully thinking he was being arrested, so that his female companion rapidly disappeared. Sheepishly he came and reported to me so that when I told him to get on his way he just simply said, "Ta chiefey, don't forget to come round for gulpers when we get back to the ship." I never did go round for Gulpers or even Sippers, but I did often see him, round the ship at various times and got a conspiratorial grin from him. The affair may have been embarrassing to a degree, but it was certainly entertaining, and enlightening into the oddest of jobs that befall the Navy at times. Certainly my oddest job to date. Returning on board we all had much to do to get the ship back to it's proper state and about a week later we sailed from Masawa heading north for the Suez Canal and the Mediterranean again. The passage north was completed in good time so that by the time we got to Port Suez and collected any dispatches we were given priority passage through the whole length of the canal. This was completed at about eighteen knots and is probably one of the quickest passages of the canal ever to be recorded. For all that I know, it may have been a record passage, for the native pilot whom we had on board, seemed to think so. I can only state that we caused much consternation and embarrassment to the many natives that were on the canal banks, either fishing or dhobying, (washing clothes), for without much warning, they would be swamped by the huge waves caused by the ships passing in such confined water. Perhaps it was wrong of us to proceed at such speed, but higher authorities had apparently sanctioned our priority passage. No sooner were we clear of the canal at Port Said, than we dropped the pilot and speed was increased to about twenty-five knots as we hastened to Malta. This trip was made without incident and we were pleasantly surprised to be able to oil and replenish stores without the proverbial air raid that we had previously been used to. From Malta, we hurried on again to Algiers, there, picking up some extra special V.I.P. to be returned to Malta. It was during this trip in broad daylight, that one of the look-outs spotted what he thought was a school of porpoises or dolphins frolicking in the water some miles ahead. In truth, from the look of the incident, it was just that, and we assumed that they were racing towards us in order to enjoy the frolicking that they all seemed to enjoy at our bows as we speed on at about thirty knots. It was not until one of the signalmen on duty, had studied them for a while through his telescope, that he decided that the porpoises were far more lethal animals in the form of torpedoes. These had apparently been fired at extreme range by a submarine. The depth setting had not stabilised so that the torpedoes were acting in the ways peculiar to the porpoises. With bated breath, we altered course slightly so that the bows were dead on to the torpedoes so as to reduce the target area. For what seemed hours we watched as the torpedoes came towards us about sixty feet apart. Our combined speeds would be in the region of seventy knots, (about 85 MPH), so that the helmsman was ordered to steer very carefully, in naval language, nothing to port or starboard. As we watched the torpedoes, one on either side of the ship and only a few feet away, one could quite clearly read the markings on the torpedos, which in Italian indicated that they were magnetic torpedoes. It was a very narrow shave and we were all thankful to have got away with the incident. Just what the V.I.P. said about the incident when he was later informed of it, will not be known, for at the time he was below decks. Just who the V.I.P. was, I did not find out, for this was apparently a hush-hush job. Obviously one did not stick one's neck out and ask who it was, that we had taken to Malta. It was all part of the job, and very shortly we were on our way again for some minor operations like bombarding the enemy shore bases or defences for he was going to get very little peace.

It was during one of these minor operations of bombarding some shore defences in some remote place that I had not previously heard of, that as we approached the target area, we watched hundreds of heavy bombers passing over head. It was literally wave on wave, and as they approached the shore they appeared to extend themselves into a series of long lines of perhaps some thirty or forty aircraft in each line. At what was apparently a given signal by the leader, each wave would drop their bombs in what was later called "Carpet Bombing." Hundreds of bombs of all sorts would hurtle down on the target area, completely obliterating everything. Dense clouds of brown tawny smoke would rise up several hundred feet. Suddenly the young signalman beside me was very violently sick at the sight of such destruction, and the tears came without effort or restraint. I don't think it was out of pity that the tears came, but rather out of revulsion at the sight. Of course he may have been reminded also of folk that he may have lost in the blitz bombings at home. I do not know, but it was certainly a sight that I shall not forget, like many others that were witnessed during this war. For myself, I felt intense pride in the fact that we were at last on the winning end and were able to dish out some punishment to the enemy forces, who were now beginning to receive what we had taken for so long.

RETRIBUTION

Almost a year after the eventful convoy to Malta, when we had to fight almost every inch of the way against untold odds, the tide had really started to turn. By early April 1943 the Eighth Army had fought its way through to Libya and the ports of Benghazi and Tripoli were in our hands. This meant a daily task of ensuring convoys of stores for the army were uninterrupted, while the continuous task of harassing the enemy from seawards fell to the cruisers and destroyers. Each night, somewhere along the coast of Tunisia, some ship or ships would be employed in hurling shells against the enemy defences. Although this seemed an easy task, there was always the chance of the enemy sending some of his still numerous cruisers and destroyers against our ships. In fact, on one particular night, a force of four enemy destroyers escorting some merchant ships was encountered. The result after a very brisk and lively half hour was that three enemy destroyers were sunk; the fourth sneaked away in the darkness and all the enemy convoy was destroyed.

From Malta we were operating at full stretch along the north and eastern shore of Tunisia for it was here that we expected the enemy to attempt to evacuate his forces. By now the British First Army had started to advance into Tunisia from Algeria thus effectively closing the pincer jaws on the enemy forces. Would they attempt a Dunkirk styled evacuation, which apparently they were quite capable of doing? Meanwhile, the Allied Air Forces were hammering the retreating enemy along the whole length of their front line while we of the Navy ensured no interference from Enemy ships. As far as I am aware, the enemy made no attempt to send his Naval forces in to assist the hard-pressed troops.   Soon it was obvious that it must be a complete surrender of his forces in Tunisia or else evacuation from Tunis and the surrounding areas.   Hundreds of guns and tanks were left behind as the enemy hurried towards the Tunis area, so that the only evacuation that could take place was during the night by aircraft. This was attempted on at least two occasions, when massed formations of troop carrying aircraft were set upon by allied fighters which caused havoc and great losses to the enemy.   Soon the allied forces had squeezed the enemy into a small pocket in and around the city of Tunis and Bizerta. By the second week in May, the enemy had been cut off from any possible hope of relief. By the middle of May the enemy could no longer offer resistance, so that the Eighth and First Armies accepted the surrender of the Axis forces in North Africa. Almost a quarter of a million men surrendered, together with some dozen generals and thousands of guns, tanks and vehicles of all sorts. When I had later spoken to some of the army chaps in Bone, they told me how they had actually seen Axis troops, driving themselves in horse or ox drawn carts, to the prisoner of war cages. Whether this was true or not, I have no way of knowing, but I can quite believe it.

Through this final operation, we of the Navy were operating at full stretch from Malta which was only the proverbial stone's throw from Tunisia. The operation was officially designated "RETRIBUTION" and all ships in the operational zone were obliged to display a huge bright red canvas over the quarter-deck to identify itself as Allied to the Air forces operating in that area. It was at the end of this operation that we actually received the signal from the Commander in Chief to paint out Retribution Red signifying that the end of the operation and that the Allies were successful. Again we returned to Malta to replenish stores and get ready for the next target. This was to be the invasion and capture of the island of Pantelleria, roughly midway between Tunisia, Cape Bonn and Sicily which had always been a place of trouble in the earlier convoy attempts. The Capture of the island of Pantelleria was perhaps a rather damp squib compared with the other parts of the campaign for although the island was fortified, most of the movable items of defence had already been removed. After some hours of heavy bombardment by Air and sea, Pantelleria surrendered so that the passage to and from Malta was comparatively easy. Apart from Submarine and air attack all eventual journeys to and from the eastern and western Mediterranean were practically uneventful.

SICILY INVADED

Once the powers that be had decided on the invasion and where on the European mainland, various ships came and went in mind boggling streams. As far as we were concerned, it had to be Sicily or Italy, although we had no knowledge for certain, as at times, there was talk of invasion at the south coast of France or perhaps the islands of Sardinia and Corsica. In any case, we all knew from our own experience, that we being dual A.A. and L.A. cruisers, should be somewhere near the front of anything that was going, as close air defence for the landing forces was a definite requirement. To a certain extent, our guesswork proved correct but hardly to the extent of the reality. Before the invasion, there would obviously have to be some softening up of the defences at the landing beaches and surrounding areas. The task of the softening up procedures would be allocated to the cruisers and destroyers. Again it was obvious that much of the bombardment would be carried out by the R.A.F while the sea bombardments would be our job. No sooner had the North African coastline been cleared of the enemy forces, plans were started for the invasion. Here it was necessary to keep the enemy guessing so that as many places as possible received some attention from us and the R.A.F. From the middle of February 1943, nightly probes by various ships were made. Sometimes just a few rounds would be fired while at other times a fairly large bombardment would take place. To my knowledge, which was restricted to the ship's activities, at no time did we visit the same place on successive nights. Always it was into the coast of Sicily at high speed, carry out the bombardment, then away again at high speed. Always there was the threat of enemy gun or torpedo boats being met, for they were always within easy distance of where we were bombarding. Some nights it would be a double bombardment where we would complete our firings in quick time, tear off somewhere else and do a few more rounds of quick fire. That at least kept the enemy on the hop and guessing the next target.

On one particular night, an intercepted signal was received to the effect that the battleships *King George V*, and *Howe*, would be doing a bombardment on the western side of Sicily. For this occasion,

Euryalus and two destroyers were to patrol about forty miles to the northwest of the battleships and act as outer warning screen in case enemy forces of any sort should be in the area of Favignana. Just what the target would be, I had little knowledge, but one can judge the importance of such a target by the allocation of two battleships to do the job.

On the same night the cruisers *Dido* and *Sirius* shelled the port of Masala, our target that night was to be a small port a little further along the coast. Other cruisers would be pasting other places in adjoining areas. With *Euryalus* at the centre of an inverted V formation with a destroyer on each bow, we steamed at high speed for our allocated target area, and with the ship's company being already closed up at "Action Stations." At precisely zero hour, all three ships opened fire on pre-selected targets which could be clearly seen in the moonlight. After some minutes of intense shelling, one of the destroyers left our immediate company and proceeded towards the harbour entrance. Then, she blasted the port at very close range with very little active opposition from the enemy. On the withdrawing of our small force to seawards we were able to see the fires resulting from our bombardment and from a small enemy ship that had exploded when fired on by the destroyer that had closed the harbour. These operations were most spectacular even in the most macabre sense and likened to watching fireworks displays during some pre-war carnival. Withdrawing at high speed, we made for our base at Malta to prepare for the next operation.

In addition to many of the operations similar to that just described, there were always calls from the army to help soften up some bothersome position that was causing a delay to the advancing troops. Whatever it was, it caused the enemy some delay of a sort, for he was constantly having to move troops or supplies to either protect them from the allied advance or to supply troops afresh from his reserve stocks. Many of the targets that we were given to destroy or demolish were ammunition dumps, columns of supply vehicles, gun batteries or troop movements, for most of the good roads of Sicily are near or actually on the coast. The bombardments each day increased as the army progressed across and northwards on the plains of Sicily. The climax of these operations came just before and during the battle for Catania, which would be the key to any further operations in Italy. Some of the bombardments were made during daylight hours and the ships often approached the shore to within five hundred yards for additional accuracy.

Some of the ships were from the Allied Nations such as Greek and Dutch. During the early days of the landings, on the southeast side of the island and along the east coast after the troops had landed and consolidated their positions, the fleet under Admiral Cunningham, were patrolling up and down the coast not too distant from the land, and caused Admiral Cunningham to comment to one of his staff, after about some sixty hours of the monotonous patrol, "that he would be greatly relieved to get off these blasted tramlines," referring to the continual churning up of the same stretch of water.

ITALY INVADED

Throughout the whole of the operation, called "HUSKEY," there was always the strong possibility that the Italians would come out in force to contest the landings. This obviously meant that there had to be at immediate notice, a strong force of battleships in the area. After all, they only had to come through the Straits of Messina as a short cut from Naples, one of their main naval bases. Another large base was at Taranto on the heel of Italy. That they did not oppose the Navy is hard to understand as these bases were only at the most a day's steaming from our main operations. Maybe the Italian Admirals did not relish the thoughts of a show down, but, whatever the reasons, the Axis naval forces refused to show up apart from E-Boats and Submarines. Our submarines were also kept busy for they are known to have sunk about twenty transports and supply vessels while our own light forces, cruisers and destroyers sank at least eighteen E-boats either by gunfire or driving them ashore. Thus, on the 10th July 1943 the Allies returned to the continent and enemy territory, determined to avenge the retreats from Dunkirk and Crete. By the end of July, Sicily was under Allied control and formed a stepping stone for the main conquest of Italy which obviously would be the next operation. Not only that, but it meant that the island of Malta could be supplied with all its needs and that the whole of the Mediterranean was no longer contested as Mare Nostrum. Again it meant that no longer would the Navy not have air protection while on passage from east to west or vice versa, Allied shipping could now pass freely, although there was still some slight danger from various small units of the Italian Navy. Their ships did not however show themselves until a much later date and under different circumstances.

After Sicily, *Euryalus* was detached from the squadron for special duties at various ports along the African Coast from Algiers to Bone, Malta and many other smaller ports, mainly to assist and strengthen the shore defences, against air attacks. This relaxed period did not last over long, for within the month, we were again operating at full pressure.

BOMBING OF THE HOSPITAL SHIP TALAMBA

With operation "HUSKY," the invasion of Sicily in hand, as many Naval ships as possible were withdrawn from the areas of the beaches. Some ships were obviously kept patrolling the areas in case of counter measures by the Axis forces.

The hospital ship *Talamba* was engaged in taking off the wounded from the beaches when she was bombed and sunk in the early hours of 10th July just before dawn. The following account was given by one of Reuters correspondents, an eye witness, he being on board a destroyer near the scene:-

The hospital ship *Talamba* was deliberately bombed in her death throes. It is a heart rending spectacle. Twenty minutes ago she was standing out some six miles off the southeast coast of Sicily, fully illuminated and away from other vessels. Axis aircraft swooped down and secured direct hits on her stern. Now it is 2230 and we have come alongside to rescue the survivors. By the light of the pale moon, I can see little groups of medical staff, the wounded and most piteous of all, English nurses clinging desperately to floating spars or bobbing in the water in their lifebelts. From them wink dozens of little red lights, (lifebelt indicators), for all the world like a cluster of fireflies. We circle closer and throw lifelines and rope ladders overboard. Cautiously we flash a spot light on the surrounding water to assess the position. The air is full of cries for help and I can hear the cries for help from the nurses struggling in the water. The great ship sinks lower. Even hard bitten sailors on board this hard fighting destroyer are mute with horror as they gaze down on the tragic scene.

Suddenly the white bows of the *Talamba* rear up out of the water, and with a loud hiss of escaping steam and air, she slides beneath the surface in a turmoil of confused water. It seems unbelievable that she could go so quickly. All that remains are a few floating spars and a big red cross on a wooden background which, with grim irony, wallows lifelessly in the waves, pointing its message skywards as if in mute reproach. Other ships have now approached but rescue work is difficult and dangerous as it is too risky to show lights with the bombers still about. Eventually we collect many survivors including nurses and the wounded who took part in the first invasion assault in the early hours of this morning. Down in the wardroom the survivors are made welcome and dry clothes and warming drinks are provided. Most of the survivors are too tired and shaken to talk. Only one small twist of humour relieved the grim tragedy. Our Number One, coming into the wardroom from watch found one of the nurses sporting his best and newest flannel trousers which a brother officer had supplied to her. This was too much for him. Politely but firmly, he led her to his cabin and gave her his second best pair to wear instead. His remarks were, "Chivalry can go too far." An hour later, the survivors were transferred to another ship and this destroyer was ready for action again, the crew in grim mood to avenge this further act of Axis brutality.

I make my apologies for repeating this story as I feel that this is one of the typical incidents that the men of the Navy have to face and still try to keep smiling. Or as the Navy says, "Keep a stiff upper lip." These types of incidents, although horrid and tear jerking at the time, served to give one that little bit of human will power to carry on with the job with added efficiency if possible. Although not involved in this incident, *Euryalus* was not so very far away as we were part of the bombarding force which was operating in that area near Syracuse. During this part of the operation we were part of the 12th Cruiser Squadron with our old friends *Cleopatra*, *Dido*, *Penelope* and *Aurora*.

By the middle of July 1943, Sicily had surrendered to the allies, so that there originated somewhere in the forces the saying, "Germany here we come." Whether it was from army ranks or from the navy I have little idea, except that suddenly it was on everybody's lips. This was however dampened down somewhat when the Prime Minister announced the success and added that this was not the beginning of the end but rather the end of the beginning. This island of Sicily formed an important stepping stone to the continent of Europe. Here we could establish airfields for further operations against the Axis Forces and build up valuable supply depots. No doubt, the complete capture of Sicily was a hard knock for the enemy, for now they were fully aware that with the forces at home and in the Mediterranean, they could expect little or no respite from constant attacks. For us in the ships of the Med Fleet, there was no let up to the hurrying and scurrying from place to place, always at high speed and with some important mission to perform. No, there was no time for leave in Sicily and in any case, it was presumed that the island would be that badly devastated by bombardments or enemy destruction, that it was considered to be not worth the while even thinking of shore leave. In truth, I am sure that not many of our ship's company were over bothered with shore leave; they were more concerned with getting the job done and going home. This was to be a while yet.

With the allies in possession of Sicily, and hammering at the door of Italy across the Straits of Messina, every effort was made to secure a footing in the mainland of Italy. Heavy bombardments by air and land soon rendered the adjacent towns across the straits, quite untenable. This was strongly supported by units of the Navy bombarding positions further up the east and west coasts of Italy making way for the troops which would soon obviously be landing in those places. Such a place was one of our assignments, called Vibo Valentia. This was a small port just up the west coast of Italy, and was being used as a base for E-boats and minesweepers as well as a stores depot for the Axis forces. Also it was part of the railway network up the west coast of Italy, hence its importance as a target.

This particular trip was typical of the many that we took part in, and was called the softening up process of the enemy's defences. Arriving off the port of Vibo Valentia about midnight, our two escorting destroyers were ordered to take station ready for the bombardment, which in reality meant, that they opened up their distances from us. Just before zero hour, *Euryalus* opened fire with flashless star shells to illuminate the target. Zero hour was when the star shells reached a certain height, so that all guns were ready loaded and trained on the necessary bearings. For the first few salvoes, flashless cordite charges would be used, so as to conceal our positions from the enemy batteries. At the appointed moment, a continuous ripple of gunfire from the three ships bombarding broke the stillness of the night. Perhaps it sounded more like a very heavy continuous drum roll, for there was little interval between the discharge of the guns from *Euryalus* and the destroyers. We were possibly endeavouring to beat each other in the number of rounds that were fired, for the navy is ever on the lookout for a chance of some competition between ships. Soon, fires and minor explosions were occurring at different places on shore and in the glare of the fires, one could plainly see the outlines of some ships in harbour. One of the destroyers seeing an opportunity to advance the allied cause, gradually entered the harbour entrance where she continued the bombardment of her own selected targets at close range. It is known that she scored several hits on several of the ships, and the shore defences became aware that this was not an air attack but a ship bombardment. As time for the bombardment was quickly running out, the destroyer turned about and rejoined us some four miles out to sea. At the approved time, the bombardment ceased as suddenly as it had started and while we made our way quickly seawards, we saw that many of the fires were obviously out of control. It was while we were watching through our binoculars that a sudden large explosion erupted from one of the fires. This was either a petrol dump or an ammunition dump going up. Possibly both, for scattered amidst the bright towering pillars of flame were many brighter flashes and flowering flames and sparks.

Speed was increased as the destroyers again took up their correct cruising stations as we headed for Bone and the restocking of expended stores. For some hours or so we remained at "Action Stations" until well clear of the coast of Sicily as although the island had been captured, there was ever the possibility of air or E-boat attack. Instead of going to Bone as we thought, we were suddenly diverted to Algiers a bit further west along the Algerian coast. Life was ever full of surprises.

On arrival at Algiers, we found that there were several ships of varying nationalities, mostly American. To our amazement, we were to berth near two American cruisers, named *Boise* and *Savanah*. Both of these ships, although cruisers, were much bigger and more heavily armed than we were. Little thought was given to these ships for we quite expected to be on our way for some operation before we could really introduce ourselves. How wrong again were our guesses? As the Captain came on board from an official visit, I as usual met him at the gangway with the current signals. Also at the gangway were the Commander, and of course, the gangway staff. As ever the Commander spoke to the Captain while I remained in waiting; just the usual practice when the Captain returned on board. To my surprise the Captain and the Commander both made for the Captain's quarters on the quarter-deck and at the same time signalling for me to follow. Nothing unusual in this for such things quite often happened, as this saved the Captain repeating certain things to the Commander and myself. Handing the Captain the current signals, I waited for any comments or further signals. There were no signals required, but a very searching question of, "How long will it take the signal staff to make a set of signal flags?" This was the same as asking, "How long is a piece of string?"

Although it was immediately in my thoughts, I did not make that suggestion, but mentioned that it depended on how many flags in a set, and how many of our own flags could usefully be adapted for use in the new set. It was then that I was informed that we should be given thirty-six hours to make a set of American signal flags, to be able to signal to the Americans as we were about to join forces with the two cruisers, and that an American Signals Chief would be coming on board to advise us as to what was needed. This did not mean that the American Signals Chief would be staying on board. Also, we should be receiving a copy of the U.S.A. standard signal book and that we should be expected to be able to comply with the U.S.A. signals. I was about to suggest that the time allowance was rather short, when the Captain cut me short by saying that I was to get moving and to report when ready to join the U.S. Navy as he also had the same time to get ready. Needless to remark, I waited no longer but beat a hurried passage to the bridge. Here, there was already an American Navy Chief talking to the signal staff, so that after introductions, we adjourned to the signal office to confer over the requirements.

The making of the flags presented little difficulty as we were able to re-adopt quite a few of our own flags and with a little ingenuity remake a number of others. In all I estimate that we had to make some dozen flags and remake about another dozen, which kept the whole signal staff well and truly busy for the working period. At the expiration of thirty-six hours the Captain was informed that we were ready to go. To prove our point we asked that we could carry out a simple signal exercise with the American ships. Not only were we surprised at the results but the Americans also were surprised just how quickly we could re-adjust ourselves to their methods. After a congratulatory signal from the *Boise*, (the senior officer), our Captain seemed in quite good humour, particularly as the next step was some gunnery practice. In this an aircraft towed what was called a sleeve target for us to shoot at. The Americans had first go and did some really good shooting which was quite impressive. Now for the "Limeys" to show their paces. Over came the aircraft with its towed target. Bang went *Euryalus'* guns and at the first shot, down came the sleeve target. A bullseye at first shot. A really impressive shoot from the Limeys and a very delighted gunnery officer, to say the least. All this was witnessed by all the ships in the harbour and loud were the cheers that resulted. I suspect that it was a fluke shot but the Yanks did not know that. The next few days we spent in signal exercises until we became really efficient and could hold our own with our new American friends. From there on we became good pals and exchanged pleasantries whenever possible. This included movies, ship visits to the ice cream parlours, mess visits and the exchange of coffee and tots. In all a really pleasant small episode, and one in which I found that the so called Yanks were very little different from ourselves except that what we called braces they called suspenders, and such like. I was, before not too long to meet some more "Yanks."

SALERNO

I wonder just how many folk had heard of a place called Salerno before the war made it an historical place, and a place to be indelibly inscribed on the minds of those that took part in those historic landings. However, from our berth in Algiers, I had not even given the place a thought, for at the time it was not even a town so to speak. An oversized village may have amply described it, positioned almost in the centre of a fairly large bay under the southern slopes of Mount Vesuvius just to the south of Naples. Although in peace time I had visited Naples and Vesuvius I was ignorant as to the exact position of Salerno. This was soon remedied by the arrival on board of the presence of Rear Admiral Vian with some of his staff, very early in September 1943. Sailing almost immediately, we headed a little bit north of east to rendezvous with a group of aircraft carriers. In this group of carriers, five were ex-large merchant ships remodelled as carriers, being the *Attacker*, *Battler*, *Hunter*, *Stalker* and *Unicorn*, with the addition of several destroyers forming a screen. Into the middle of this group sailed *Euryalus* to take command of the carrier group. This was about the 8th or 9th September. Meanwhile our friendly Yanks in the *Boise* and *Savanah* had sailed elsewhere for their required duties.

By midnight on the 8th/9th the whole group were steaming somewhere to the West of the Bay of Salerno when we were informed over the broadcast system that operation "Avalanche" was in force. This meant, as we were later informed in the early morning, that our force was to provide air cover for the Allied landings at Salerno. Never before had we been so fortunate to have five carriers for air support. At times in the past, we would have considered ourselves extremely lucky to have five aircraft for air cover, now we had five carriers all with fighter aircraft. This was defensive luxury in the extreme as far as we were concerned, and other carriers were elsewhere round the coast of Italy.

By dawn, the unaccustomed sound of many aircraft engines all revving at high speed assailed our ears. All five carriers of our group were steaming into the wind with full flights ready for take off. This was an extremely busy period for the signal department so that I ask for one's tolerance if this recollection of events is not quite in chronological sequence.

At a given signal, the first aircraft took off from each of the carriers, to form up in five groups overhead. Soon all the carriers' decks were emptied and course was reversed by signal, so that we should remain more or less in the same position for when the aircraft came back. Just as quickly as the aircraft had gone off, so more were ranged up on decks to take their places. The aircraft that had just taken off, had sheered away for the beaches over Salerno where they would patrol and give air cover for the landings, which had already started. After about three quarters of an hour, the next flights of aircraft were taking off ready to relieve those that were patrolling. All these aircraft were Seafires, (spitfires especially adapted for use on carriers), and were flown by Fleet Air Arm personnel. As the aircraft came back from the beaches, these were meticulously counted as a check for losses or the possibility of Axis intruders sneaking in. During the day, the same routine was followed, flying off and flying on, about every three quarters of an hour. Sometimes the numbers returning were not the same as those that took off, so that signals were quickly made for information. Sometimes we would be able to witness crashes on the decks, as an aircraft which had been in combat made a bad landing, either through their pilot's injuries or aircraft being damaged in combat. Throughout the day, the bridge extension speakers would give a running commentary from the aircraft flying so that one had a first hand report of the combats and casualties. Some of the aircraft would be more than busily engaged while others in a slightly different sector would not see any signs of the enemy. Each flight of aircraft would have a specified sector to be responsible for, and which were varied from time to time according to operational requirements. So the show went on without respite during the daylight hours. Each evening after dark, when the last flights were landed, the whole carrier force would steam out westwards just in case our position had been noted by the enemy ready for retaliation. Then at first light and even in the early dawn light, the aircraft would be taking off again. In this, I have forgotten to mention that we in *Euryalus*, plus the carriers already mentioned, would be designated "Force V." Whether this was a gimmick of the Prime Minister with his famous "V" sign, or just a lucky draw and omen from the coded signs allocated to various forces, is quite a good guess on anybody's part. We chose to think it as the choice of the Prime Minister. Probably wishful thinking or just plain boastful egocentricity.

It was while we were operating at Salerno that we received a high priority and secret signal during the night of the second day's operations, and into the third day. That morning, operations were carried on as usual, but, that night after dusk when the aircraft were returning to their carriers, *Euryalus* hurriedly left the carrier group and altering course to the south, we pushed on to our best speed. We were on our own, hence the value of very high speed. Course during the night was hardly altered, and then only by a few degrees one way or the other. Hour after hour the speed was maintained, and the almost constant conversation between Captain and Engineer Officer made one wonder just where we were off to. This was something really hush hush. Already the Army were pushing up from the toe and heel of Italy and the idea of the Salerno landing was hopefully to encircle the enemy. From the best of the matchbox navigators, it was estimated that we were heading for the area of Tripoli and this was confirmed when the Captain broadcast to the ship's company that we were heading for Tripoli. There we would pick up some troops and dash back to Salerno, where apparently the troops were needed as reinforcements.

Arriving off Tripoli somewhere in the very small hours of the morning of the third day, the soldiers were all ready and waiting to embark, which they did with great speed, or so it seemed to me. No sooner were the troops on board, than *Euryalus* turned about, and again at very high speed, retraced her path to Salerno. It was noted that some of the troops were looking quite sickly, so that the sailors in their usual chummy manner, were soon fortifying the troops with rum. I am unsure whether this was an official issue or whether the sailors forgot to drink their own ration. Whatever it was, it certainly was enjoyed by the army ranks of some five or six hundred persons. As was usual on these kind of trips, the whole ship's company would act as lookout while working about the ship. Many eyes make good lookouts. Fortunately the weather was kind so that progress was excellent and with the army fortified by "high spirits," there were few cases of seasickness amongst the troops. It was not until one started speaking to the troops that one discovered that there were many different regiments represented in our army passengers. Word had spread by the mess deck telegraph that these troops were going straight into action at the front. This news instantly endeared the troops to the navy so that quite a few more unofficial rum rations were distributed.

Arriving off Salerno, the troops were disembarked into landing craft and taken to the beaches. Here we were told, they would be forming a special battalion or whatever formation the Army calls such a body of troops. At least that was what we understood, which to us sailors seemed quite feasible. Off they went to much good humoured bantering from their new found navy pals. For us, it was to our stations for the aircraft of the carrier group "V", which went on for about another three days, after which the bridgehead had been established.

It was some time later that we heard that there was some talk of mutiny amongst the troops that we had ferried from Tripoli. This talk of mutiny, I very much doubted, at least from those that I spoke to I got a totally different impression, as they seemed a very level headed and sensible crowd. This talk I assumed to be some barrack room lawyer expressing his opinion, about someone in authority and their conflicting ideas of organisation, especially if the talk had been overheard by some unsympathetic ears. I only know that these particular troops had the respect and sympathy of all the navy in the ship.

After about six days of the carrier operations, the Carrier Group "V" was withdrawn and we returned to Malta for replenishing supplies of all kinds, and making ready for further supporting operations. The following signal was made by Admiral Vian;

"I share the disappointment of the pilots, that so few targets were offered; nevertheless you have ATTACKED the enemy, BATTLED with calm and HUNTED and STALKED with UNICORN success. You have ALL made operation AVALANCHE practicable and made history in the Fleet Air Arm." Originated 121150 September 1943.

Note: Many years later while on holiday, (October 1993 to be precise), I read some comments by some ex-Army people that were involved in the above transportation from Tripoli to Salerno. The following was printed in the Daily Mail of 4/10/93:

HORROR OF WAR. Your article on Britain's Secret Mutineers, took me back to one memorable night during World War II, when I was serving in the Royal Navy on the fast cruiser *H.M.S. Euryalus* in

September 1943, we were softening up beach defences, bombarding enemy shore batteries and troops in support of the Allied Landings at Salerno.

When our troops were bogged down on the beaches on the third day of the operations, *Euryalus* was detached from the rest of the invasion fleet and dashed at high speed without escort to Tripoli, North Africa to pick up British reinforcements for Salerno.

I vividly remember the sick faces of the British infantry as they stumbled on board and how amazed we were when they told us they had been pulled out of hospital, suffering from shell shock and other serious war injuries.

The following morning, as we put them, fortified with lashings of naval rum, in the landing barges, off the Italian Coast to sail straight into battle, the whole ship's company thought, "You poor beggars," and thanked God we were not in their shoes. We never saw them again.

Michael H Winter.

REPLY.... a couple of days later:

Your article on the so-called mutiny at Salerno, will hopefully clear our names.

We never refused to fight, or to engage in our duty but we refused to join other units. Eventually I was returned to my unit, the 5th East Yorks, and served with them for the whole of my Army career from 1942 to 1947.

After the war, I volunteered to fight terrorists in what was then Palestine.

I was no coward.

F. Jowett, Hull.

I attached the above comments from the papers of October 1993 since the ship was involved and it confirms my writing of the time or just after.

A FLEET SURRENDERS

Immediately after fuelling and storing, plus of course ammunitioning, on the evening of the 10th or 11th September, *Euryalus* found herself again unescorted and steaming at high speed to the northeast. Destination, question mark in large print. We had not overlong to wait, for the captain, as ever gave us the gist of his orders. He firmly believed that since the ship and her company were involved in any operation, we should all know something of what was expected of us. His exact words, I cannot remember, but they informed us that we were en route for Tarranto, the home of the Italian fleet, which had, for the most part, already agreed to surrender, and I believe were already on their way to Malta. Obviously, this was not part of the given information by the Captain, for nobody knew exactly what ships were surrendering. So we were in a very high state of preparedness as we arrived off Tarranto.

Here a rather large motor pinnace came alongside and several persons came on board. The names of those persons were probably known to the Captain, but for the rest of us, it was a question mark. It was mentioned unofficially later, that we had on board, Marshall Badoglio and Admiral Sara. The former I had heard of as a prominent figure in the pre-war conquest of Abysinia, by the Italians, but the latter figure was, as far as I was aware, just an Italian Admiral of lesser rank. Some of these persons that had come on board were soon landed again and we turned and headed for Malta.

Here we landed our mystery passengers and immediately put to sea again, where we joined forces with the cruisers *Scylla* and *Charybdis*, for what we reckoned was more bombardments. In the meanwhile the Enemy had made some counter attacks so that again we three cruisers were ordered to fetch reinforcements from Tripoli. This time it was not British, but American troops that came on board and were ferried as before at high speed to the beaches in Italy. During this operation, we heard that the old friend from the U.S. Navy, the *Savanah* had been hit by a radio controlled bomb and was in a very bad condition. Eventually she arrived at Malta for temporary repairs before leaving again for the States.

ORDERS FOR HOME

While on these smaller operations, we also learned that the Italian ships had surrendered to Admiral of the Fleet, A.B. Cunningham at Malta. Most of the units of the Italian Fleet were dispatched to Alexandria or further east so as to keep them out of the way of any possible retaliation by the enemy. Since the ship had been in the Mediterranean operations almost from the start, I had secretly wished to see the surrender of the Italian Navy, but that was a scene that only a few could witness for as I have remarked, we with Scylla and *Charybdis* were busy helping with the bombardment of the beaches, while a little further to the south two battleships were also adding their weight to the bombardment. By the end of the month, the Captain had informed us, one day while at sea, that we were to be relieved and go home and that he was leaving the ship at Algeria the next day. Within a few days of that event, *Euryalus* was on her way home via Gibraltar, completely unescorted, until the Clyde awaited us in the early days of October.

As was usual, a berth at the Tail of the Bank, (Greenock), was allocated to *Euryalus* and all hands in the ship turned to getting out the ammunition, as no leave was given until the magazines were empty. Never has a ship been stripped of ammunition so completely and quickly, for by the next day the first parties were going on leave. No, I was not included, but I did go ashore for a couple of hours in order to get off a telegram to the wife that I had not seen for nearly three years. One was not permitted to mention ship or movements so that I worded my telegram so that only the wife would understand. That was, "Many happy returns for Saturday on your Birthday." Neither my wife nor I had a birthday in October so I guessed she would follow my meaning. That's what happens in wartime, one gets as crafty as the enemy. I also learned that I would not be leaving the ship, but would remain on board for the refit that was to follow. So, *Euryalus* also "surrendered" to the Glasgow shipyards, to be virtually rebuilt after many thousands of miles of high speed steaming and having maintained the great name and traditions of her predecessors, and was indeed a worthy successor to the name.

During her short life of a few years some of her accomplishments were:

Two engagements with enemy battleships, the wearing out and replacement of some thirty gun barrels, the firing of thousands of rounds of 5.25 inch ammunition, the firing of many thousand rounds of oerlikon and pompom shells, the firing of six torpedoes at the enemy battleships, accredited with three enemy aircraft shot down plus a few more probables and part claims. Being war time, there was no home coming official celebrations, or the traditional paying off ceremonies. The time for celebrations would be when each member of the ship's company arrived home. It was certainly wonderful to enjoy the peace and quiet of the Scottish countryside and the bustle of Glasgow streets and tramcars, instead of the blast and roaring of the ten HA/LA guns and the blare of the "Actions Stations" alarms at the most inconvenient of times.

In the December, after returning from a most enjoyable leave I heard of my promotion to Chief Yeoman of Signals and Signals Instructor. This was now the peak of dreams. Each day was spent in bringing the signal department up to scratch with any new design arrangements and organisations. Many of the parts of the ship that had been known thoroughly by me were now ripped out and rebuilt to make room for the latest equipment available. This meant that daily tests were the normal events and little time was available for pleasure. In fact my only pleasures were the going to the local Dockyard Home Guard unit and using the rifle range facilities. This was usually in the evenings, when most of the Home Guard would attend to their drills and shooting. On these occasions I would attend, not in uniform but in overalls the same as the Home Guards.

Soon I became quite a good shot, and was extremely delighted when I was invited to form part of their team against rival Home Guard units. This of course meant a certain amount of free time being spent with them and a certain amount of entertainment. The real prize came when I was asked to shoot for them in the West of Scotland competitions, to eventually get the second best marks on the field.

However, by now the invasion of Europe was openly being spoken of and written about in the papers, so that daily we expected to be finishing the refit and to rejoin the fleet for the next big event of the war. Daily we heard of raids on enemy positions and installations, also of intensified bombings of enemy places. Time was really getting short, especially judging by the signals that we received.

EXTRACT FROM ADMIRALTY SPEECH

The following is an extract from a speech made by Mr. A.V. Alexander, the First Lord of the Admiralty on 23 September 1943.

The present day successes in the Mediterranean are in a large measure due to a very gallant band of officers and men of the Med Fleet and their sister service the Merchant Navy. Without their dogged persistence, courage and devotion to duty, our recent victories over the Axis Forces would not have been possible. For two weary, yet breathtaking years, when our fortunes have waxed and waned, I may now disclose that our entire fleet in that area consisted of THREE Light cruisers, *Cleopatra*, *Euryalus* and *Dido* and a mere handful of destroyers. By unexampled leadership, courage and devotion, together with masterful tactics and bluff, the men and ships of the FIGHTING FIFTEENTH, as they called themselves, harassed by bombardment, and hounded by the surface action of the enemy, from his own, INLAND SEA. This small but highly efficient force, held at bay and confined to their own harbours, the complete Axis battlefleet of seven battleships, sixty or so cruisers and destroyers and numerous other small craft. In truth, quite a proud achievement, for despite some regrettable losses, our shipping has always plied its lawful occasions in these dangerous waters.

To that very gallant force and the Merchant Service that sailed in their company, through BOMB ALLEY and STUKA LANE, I offer for myself, and I feel sure, on behalf of the whole nation, heartfelt gratitude and just pride of place.

THE SECOND FRONT

For months, every effort was strained to the limit to prepare for the assault on the mainland of Europe. Even in some of the remotest towns, and I suspect villages, weird, wise and wonderful objects were taking shape. All of the peculiars as I will call them, were most secret in the construction and use. Daily, one would see strange shapes covered with canvas either on the railways or on the huge transporter lorries trundling through the towns. The most secretive of ruses was adopted to secure the secrecy of the items. If one had any ideas of the eventual use, one just did not talk of such things. In any case the man working next to one, did not know or have any idea of what he was making. To him, it was just a component part of something. Many high ranking officers in the forces had little knowledge of what was being prepared, or for when. The only thing that everybody was certain of, was that the second front, as it was being called, would be sometime in the future. We in the navy, just knew that whenever the day came, we should be somewhere in the picture either as a bombarding force, a covering force for the vessels taking part, or just a part of a force to patrol the landing areas. Many of the old peace time exercises were reinstated as part of the daily routine, and where possible, wartime experiences were rehearsed to the full. Most important of all were the exercises of manning the gun turrets in double quick time, also the supplying of the necessary ammunition.

Until this time, 6th June 1944, one bombardment had been much the same as any other bombardment, with perhaps the slight difference of targets, or the numbers of ships forming the bombarding force. The landings in Sicily had been a taste of what to expect as regards bombardment and landings on enemy held beaches. Whatever had gone before faded into insignificance with these landings. Counting small craft, which landed the troops on various beaches, and all navy ships, there were over four thousand ships taking part in various places. A constant stream of traffic, (shipping), going to the beaches and returning to southcoast resorts and harbours was the normal sight. If one can envisage the traffic on one of today's busy motorways, then one will get a fair idea of the traffic, if converting the vehicles to shipping of all sorts. One can also imagine hundreds of aircraft passing and repassing overhead for this was the largest scale of operations ever undertaken, at anytime in history. At times, the sky overhead would be thick with aircraft of all sorts, either coming or going. Somebody somewhere was having one hell of a headache trying to keep trace of all aircraft and ships. It is amazing and surprising that collisions of either ships or aircraft did not occur. I was not aware of any such events happening, at least with the squadrons or flotillas. It all happened with much the same precision as bees when swarming, when collisions are unknown.

Apart from absolute secrecy, the main and decisive factors in establishing the Normandy beach heads, and the disposing of the German Armour and Artillery, was Naval gunfire. From the early hours of the landings, the devastating fire of the battleships, monitors, cruisers and destroyers and the many smaller rocket launching ships was of paramount importance. These ships accounted for and smashed up the enemy positions, of tanks, artillery and troop concentrations for anything up to eighteen or nineteen thousand yards from the beaches. Naval gunfire hastened the fall of Cherbourg, and the bombardment by battleships at a range of almost eighteen miles, was an important factor in the final capitulation of Caen.

I will try, however inadequately, to describe the bombardment of the port of Cherbourg. Two battleships, *Nelson* and *Rodney*, each carrying nine sixteen inch guns, each shell weighing well over one ton, hurled their shells into the town, much as we had done in the days of 1941 when we escorted the *Revenge* to the bombardment of the same place. This time, it was being hit by at least some sixty tons every minute of the assault. Great yellow brown sheets of flame and smoke could be seen through the artificial haze caused by the discharge of the guns and the resulting explosions. One of these huge shells, hitting a building would cause it to collapse and disintegrate in clouds of smoke and brick and concrete dust. It must be remembered that when these guns are fired, they are all targeted on the same spot, and although there will be a slight difference in the landing spot, the area is very closely marked in nearness to each other shell. Not a very pleasant experience to suffer when eighteen of these shells land almost together and at almost the same spot. Some time the salvoes of shell would be in unison and sometimes separately. As one closed nearer the shore as we sometimes did, to assist the military batteries somewhere further inshore, or one of the pockets of resistance to be neutralised, we could hear the rumble of the huge shells passing overhead. Again the runaway express noises, and some few seconds later one would hear the "Crrumpp, Thumpp" of the exploding shells miles inland as the shells landed. Perhaps if conditions were favourable, one would see the far off brown and ginger coloured smoke cloud rising on the still wind. This was bombardment on a super scale, for dozens of ships engaged targets on an unprecedented scale and certainly never before had such bombardment been known. It was a matter of Naval pride that no call for supporting fire from the army, was left unanswered, with the consequence that it became the most intense naval bombardment that presumably the navy and probably the world had experienced.

On the ships themselves, the crash and roar of the salvoes for such long and intense firing, would loosen the cork insulation on the deckheads and bulkheads. This resulted in one continually being showered by particles of cork and paint chips. Anything left in the shelves, such as cups or saucers, books or letters, would be blasted out of the shelves or corners by the constantly changing air pressures of the gun discharges. The eardrums would ring and vibrate to the constant drumming of explosive discharges so that unless one was fully protected, one's hearing was easily effected. Above and below decks, figures in white masks and gloves would move with apparent haste and disorder, but always with a determined effort to have the job completed. Those whose duty required them to be in the open, such as on the bridges, would suddenly go quiet as the firing gongs rang. This was to allow them to open their mouths slightly as a means of absorbing the shock of the discharge of the guns. One's mouth would become unaccountably dry and one would become distressingly thirsty. Not for a long drink, but just enough to wet the lips and cure the dry irritating taste of smoke and cordite. Then, when the shells had left the guns and the smoke had cleared a little, conversation, the passing of orders and commands would be resumed, until the ting ting of the firing gongs would interrupt again. Truly a case of pure undiluted bedlam and hell let loose, not for just a few minutes but for hours with only short intervals, during which one could relax for just a few moments. During these times, the whole of ship's company would be at "Action Stations" and only during the lulls in the bombardment could one find time or even the inclination to smoke. Meals as ever at "Action Stations," consisted of the old favourite, corned beef sandwiches, or perhaps a cup of soup, depending on the occupation of the galley staffs. Most of these worthies we did not always called them so politely, would have their "Action Stations" in the magazines so that they were not available for their normal duties in the galley. It was known that in some ships the galley staff would work overnight to produce meat or Cornish pasties, (tiddy oggies), ready for the next day at "Action Stations." During the lulls in the actions, an officer, (usually a Sub-lieutenant of the Paymaster Branch if carried), would broadcast on the ship's speaker system an update of the events since the last broadcast. Some of these broadcasts would give ample credits to the radio broadcaster of today. Whatever was broadcast was received with the greatest of interest by all the ship's company, for quite a few of them did not see daylight for several days, only coming to the open at night. That was just how intense the requirements of their duties were.

Unless one has seen the tremendously devastating effect of Naval shelling one can scarcely believe what is told. When one considers that a battleship on its own, can fire some three rounds per gun in each minute, and the usual shell weighs in region of a ton or more, it takes very little mathematical knowledge to assess the weight of destructive power that was being employed. A hit from these shells, just simply dissolves the target, and troops under such fire are very liable to become completely demoralised and consequently surrender. Gun emplacements, even if built in concrete, usually crack and crumble or dissolve at a direct hit. Accuracy is of prime importance and there were many instances of groups of tanks just disappearing in minutes when engaged by Naval guns. We heard how a cruiser was given a target of six tanks sheltering in some woods. All six tanks were completely destroyed within minutes. While HMS Nelson was on bombardment duty off the coast of Caen, she was asked by the army to fire on a target some sixteen miles inland. The target was not visible to the gunners on board Nelson, because of intervening hills. In just over one minute Nelson had obliterated the target leaving only an amount of debris and craters. It was also reported that the Nelson chased enemy armour from one hiding place to another near Caen, until the armour eventually dispersed or was eliminated as an armoured force, such was the intensity of the fire from the enormous number of guns employed by the navy – I have heard it reported as over five hundred guns of all sizes – that the enemy learned not to concentrate his forces within range of any Naval guns. Within the month, all bridgeheads were established. Harbours that had been subjected to intense bombardment had been repaired and were again working, while artificial harbours had been constructed. Liquid commodities, oil, petrol and water were pumped under the channel to the beaches to meet the ever growing demands of the Allied forces. This latter invention, (P.L.U.T.O.), was I understand the brainchild of a person that only suggested it as a kind of joke. This was found to be immensely useful and practical, like some of the other inventions that were used at the invasion of the continent.

By sheer good fortune, the enemy high command under Hitler had omitted to develop naval forces, so that we had little to oppose us at sea, during the landings. Our greatest threat would have been the enemy submarine force. Those U-boats that did attempt to interfere with the invasion, were quickly dealt with by the destroyers patrolling the channel to the north and south of the landing beaches. With the majority of the western seaboard of France under Allied control and with Allied forces moving almost daily, further into France, much of the Navy was withdrawn from the beaches. This left the Naval situation almost as it was before the invasion, except that the coastal areas of France, and the ports were under Allied jurisdiction.

After a few days' leave, *Euryalus* was allocated to the Home Fleet at Scapa Flow, where we performed almost weekly sweeps into the Arctic Circle and the northern waters of Norway. Our chief job here was to escort the aircraft carriers that accompanied the convoys to Russia.

ARCTIC CONVOYS

Since the weather at this time of the year, (August), is quite fair and the daylight hours are long, the constant threat of air attack was always with us. Fortunately for the convoy, the enemy had withdrawn some of his aircraft from the Arctic Circle routes to assist his forces in the battle for Europe. Leaving Scapa, our course would be to the north so as to meet the ships coming from Iceland, which had already been at sea for some days. On meeting them, course would be altered to the northeast so as to make for the Arctic Circle and beyond, hoping to make any rendezvous with other ships somewhere in the region of Nova Zembla.

From the time the convoys were sighted and course altered, it was general for the weather to change dramatically for the worse. The event was not by design or planning on behalf of the admiralty, it was just one of those phenomena that happen in the Arctic Circle. One could have a really clear day with bright sunshine at breakfast time, and then by noon, the weather would be, as the sailors termed it, an absolute pig, only in a slightly more forceful language. The weather then would remain atrocious for several days and then perhaps a couple of days more sunshine. Sometimes, against all ideas of weather conditions, one would have completely flat calm, perhaps a little fog, but mostly long rolling swells and huge waves of thirty to forty feet high, with strong gale force winds and driving rain and sleet or snow. Although these conditions made for intense discomfort for the crews of the ships, it meant that the threat of attack by U-boat was somewhat reduced. The reason for this was, that the U-boat had to come up to periscope depth to make an observed attack, and with the large swells he could, only with great difficulty make his observations with the periscope. During this short but precarious moment of observation he could be spotted, either by vigilant lookouts, or the patrolling aircraft. In either case, an attack would be the result, from which the U-boat would at least be forced to dive and take evasive action, thus depriving him of the opportunity to make a report of the convoy to his pals, who would be waiting for such an information. With this information, the enemy pals would concentrate some distance ahead of the convoy ready for a combined attack, (wolf pack), tactics. Such weather as I have just described would not interfere or stop air attacks which would come from the enemy airfields in northern Norway and along the Finnish coast. One may well ask, why in such weather was it necessary to have air patrols all the time? No doubt, the Fleet Air Arm pilots asked much the same question very many times. Hardly a day would pass but that some type of thick cloud would be visible on the horizon, mostly nimbus cloud which is thick and enveloping. In this cloud, one could generally expect a long range reconnaissance enemy aircraft who would tantalise the gunners for hours while he studied the convoy and its escorts in detail. By the time he had made his report on the convoy, he would have a far better picture than the folk in the convoy. With this information, the enemy would prepare his attacking programme, moving his aircraft from airfield to airfield as he deemed necessary to engage the convoy for the maximum period of time. In the meantime the wolf pack would be assembling and waiting for the information from the Air Attack Co-ordinator as to when and how the air attack would be made. Should the reconnaissance aircraft be shot down, then another would quickly be on the scene to replace him. There was very little let up in the attacking programme which would last for perhaps ten days or longer, depending on how far north the convoy had gone in its effort to evade detection. Sometimes it was necessary to go well inside the Arctic Circle before making one's way down to Nova Zembla. With the attack started, the aircraft would come almost continuously, in waves of a dozen or more and from different angles and forms of attack. Into the resulting turmoil, the enemy would suddenly attack by U-boat, adding further disarray to the sorely tried ships, as first they dodged the bombs and then the torpedoes.

Unfortunately sometimes, a ship would successfully dodge one mode of destruction to move straight into the path of the other. The merchant ships of the convoy being slow and cumbersome and fully laden, would lack the manoeuvrability to turn quickly in an effort to dodge. For those that were unlucky, or perhaps I should say unfortunate enough, to get out of the way in quick time, the result was a cold wet bath. Perhaps the rescue ships, usually tugs or small ships or trawlers, would be in time to rescue the crew, for it would be certain that if a ship was hit and damaged, she would become a marked target. This would inevitably mean, that the chances of being picked up would be very remote, for the rescue ship could not afford to stop for picking up, especially when targeted. This would mean that the bombed ship's crew would either have to remain on board until the last, or take their chances in the sea or boats if any. If it was the chance of the sea, survival was reckoned as two or three minutes at the most. There certainly were cases of people surviving longer, but very few and not for much longer. In any case, with the temperatures as low as they were, the crews would be clothed in all the thick warm clothing possible and once that became water-logged there was little point in trying to struggle on. Hard choices in very hard times, but that was the price to be paid, so that after each trip one became more philosophical than before.

Once the convoy was approximately north of the Kola inlet, and the entrance area for Murmansk, any carriers would reverse course and either proceed at best speed out of the area, or pick up a convoy of empty merchant ships ready for the home run. Until the invasion of Europe, the losses in merchant ships and Navy ships was very heavy, sometimes losing as many as perhaps twenty ships. Very seldom was there a case of all ships getting through without loss. However with the added requirement of the enemy for more aircraft at the home fronts, the situation eased somewhat. Even so, the trip to Murmansk was no picnic, and was certainly no trip that one might volunteer for. On most occasions the weather was that cold, that the guns had to be continually worked at intervals, to prevent them icing up solid. Also, to touch any metal part with the bare hands, was to leave the skin attached to the metal, leaving one with a piece of bloodied meat for a hand. When one removed one's clothes for any reason, one would usually find that the moisture from the body had already frozen and the clothing was solid. Until one became experienced in the Arctic trips, it would be quite common to find that one could not go to the toilet as the trousers were rigid with frost. This happened on the *Kelvin* in the very early days of the war, so that the information, although seemingly very trivial, was of prime importance in one's hand over notes after the convoy trip. The decks of the ship and the moving fittings were constantly being chipped and cleared of ice, so as to remove another hazard from the sailor's life, or at least attempt to remove it. Below decks, one would always find icicles on the ship's sides, where the condensation had frozen. One soon learned the tricks of the Arctic Convoys and it was at one's own peril, that any precautions were ignored. No matter what type of ship one happened to be serving in, there were peculiar difficulties that only that ship or the type would experience. Much of this may have been due to the construction, as little study of Arctic conditions was made before the war, as very few people realised that a war could be fought in those conditions. Frost bite and snow blindness became quite a common complaint with lots of the seamen and such things took time to combat in any large scale treatment methods. This could be likened to the rationing systems, as until they were required, little thought had been given to the problem. The question of survivors in open boats raised many problems as much of one's survival was dependent on keeping warm under the intense cold conditions. For example, the term "wind factor" was unheard of until well into the war, when scientists realised that for every unit of wind strength, the temperature would be affected by a corresponding drop of the thermometer readings in the body.

In addition to the ever unpredictable weather conditions, there was ever the threat of attack by German heavy ships of which Germany had two in particular, the *Bismark* and *Tirpitz*. Both of these ships were larger and more heavily armed and armoured than any ship of our own. These two ships kept most of the navy in Northern waters for the greater part of the war, and to a certain extent restricted the offensive operations of the Navy in other areas. The *Scharnhorst*, another of the enemy heavy ships was indeed sunk in Arctic waters by Naval units, but it was not until the final destruction of the two former ships that the Arctic Convoys could move with at least some degree of certainty and without constant threat of destruction.

I was only to do two more such trips in to the Arctic before I was returned to barracks for other duties. A few days' leave and then again, drafting orders back to the Clyde, to join the naval contingents en route for the Pacific where the war was still in full swing. At that time neither destination or ship was known, although one could make some intelligent guesses if one tried.

PACIFIC BOUND

While in barracks for the few days respite, and having been the Duty Chief Petty Officer for the night, and during the process of my rounds, about 0730 one morning, I saw the P.O. from the Drafting office posting his daily DREAD SHEET. This was the preliminary notice of any drafting. Out of idle curiosity, I walked over to the notice board to find that my name was on one of the sheets, together with several other Chief Yeomen. This information alone, told me that it was to be a large drafting requirement. Now, the brain started to race and intelligent guesses came to the fore. In all, there must have been some dozen Chief Yeomen detailed, with about one hundred to one hundred and fifty other signal ratings being listed. The ship was so far unnamed but just a designated Party number, which I now forget. Not that it mattered overmuch for we should not know the final details of this party until it would be posted in perhaps twenty-four hours or perhaps a week or more. That evening, being off duty, I again cycled home to Bexleyheath, to return the next morning by 0800 after having informed my wife of the "dread news" of imminent drafting. It was while cycling back, somewhere about Stone at the top of the hill, I noticed a strange light coming up from the distant horizon. Thinking that perhaps it was some new aircraft, from one of the Essex or North Kent airfields, I pulled in to the side of the road to watch the progress of the lighted object. The object seemed to travel at phenomenal speed, leaving what appeared to be a trail of smoke behind it. The first jet propelled aircraft were just coming into service with the R.A.F. so that I was rather intrigued, not having seen one before. Soon the object was almost passing over the top of me and moving at tremendous speed and at a goodly height. If this was an aircraft, then the Allies had certainly produced a winner. With the objects passing, I resumed my pedalling for Chatham and then, there were two loud bangs, more like cracks of thunder than explosions. Endeavouring to puzzle this object out as I pedalled along, I was before long entering Rochester, where the Navy would possibly have patrols about. Without incident I reached the barracks at Chatham where I reported in, as was the custom. While at breakfast with the other Chief P.O.s, somebody happened to mention the strange object they had seen. At this I immediately pricked up my ears like the proverbial nosy donkey, and mentioned that I also had seen the strange object. This was a general signal for a get together to compare sighting reports. We found that we had seen much the same thing at about the same times. After breakfast I decided to consult one of the officers that I had previously known, from a previous ship. He told me that although he had not seen the object he had unofficially heard about these things. The sightings would be of great interest to his pals in the intelligence section and he would quote me. The next morning it was rather dull and cloudy so that I saw nothing of importance on my way to barracks. I did however hear the almost simultaneous thunder claps at about the same time. This I also reported to the officer that I had spoken to. It was not until several days later that there were reports of several mystery explosions in various parts of the London area. When it was later reported that the enemy had launched long range rockets, (V.2s, as they became known); I realised that I had seen some of the first rockets to be fired against this country. The V.1s, had been called Doodle Bugs and had been in use some time. These sounded more like the engine of a two stroke motor cycle but louder. If these were sighted, they looked like small aircraft. If they were heard, then one paid one's undivided attention to them, for if the engine stopped the Flying Bomb, (doodle bug), was about to descend. On hearing the engine cut out, one promptly made for some kind of shelter in case it landed anywhere near. Since these bombs depended on the amount of fuel supplied to the engine performance, they could land anywhere and not as targeted. If no shelter or cover were available, one simply laid oneself in the gutter and put one's arms about one's head and ears as some slight form of protection. Immediately the explosion had occurred, one looked about for signs of the devastation, so that one could assist some unfortunate person, assuming that they were in a state to require help. No one wore anything special, just plain ordinary clothes, and definitely nothing that might be considered smart. A bomb exploding, made little difference between peer or commoner, rich or poor, smart or ragged, consequently one wore the most appropriate clothing that one had available. Since all items of toiletry were on rationing, one was not over particular in shaving habits, for razor blades were a very scarce commodity as was soap.

The V.1s and V.2s were to cause great havoc and loss of life before they finally ceased with the over running of the firing sites, well into the next year.

By the early Spring of 1945, the finalisation of the drafting orders were made. With somewhere in the region of six hundred naval ratings, we boarded the train just outside the dockyard gate of the barracks, and having loaded our baggage and hammocks, we were soon on our way. Guesses and more guesses, all the way to London, until we eventually passed through stations that were recognised as being to the north of London. This could only mean that we were en route for Liverpool, or further north, as we had all decided that we were going somewhere where convoys congregated. Lots of the so-called matchbox navigators made their predictions and put out good reasons for their decisions. On the train rumbled, never stopping at or in a station but always well outside. When we reached and passed Carlisle, everybody decided and agreed that our destination was Glasgow or Greenock. Yes, we were getting back to the early days of the war when we knew the Clyde area better than our own towns. After about twenty hours' journeying, we duly arrived at Greenock, there to unload all kit to a waiting lighter. The powers that be were certainly not going to send us on holiday to the States or Canada. By late evening, our fate was partly known when we were ferried out to a large transport decked out in the colours of the previous "ORIENT" line. It did not take us long to find out the name of our home to be, for the next few weeks. It was the Orient liner *Orontes*. What a difference it was to travelling on the French liner *Champollion* in pre-war days, when I travelled home for Mother's illness and funeral! Here, every inch of space was taken by soldiers, sailors and airmen and, of course, not forgetting the Women's Services, for some of these had arrived on board later that evening. No time was lost once the service passengers were on board and without ceremony or fuss the *ORONTES* sailed from Greenock. All the old familiar places returned to mind; Tail of the Bank, the Cumbraes, Ailsa Craig and out to sea heading west, to skirt the coast of Northern Ireland. Supper that night was a simple meal without frills, to be followed by boat drill and boat stations just in case it would be needed. This lasted quite a while as the *ORONTES'* First Officer and the Senior Naval Officer (a Lieut. Commander) did the inspection of the various stations, while the women officers of the service women checked their contingents. I would have imagined that all told, there were some fifteen hundred or more bodies on board. All was well, and the ship soon settled down for the night.

Next morning, with breakfast finished, all service personnel were informed by broadcast that they would be required to assemble as per their own service custom at 0915. Since there was a little bit of sea running, nothing really as far as the Navy was concerned, but it was noticed that some of the other services were looking a little off colour. However, with the other services the Navy went to what we termed divisions. There was much mustering and remustering, checking and rechecking also delays while the Army and R.A.F. checked their members more thoroughly. Some were obviously suffering from slight or worse, attacks of sea sickness. It was while all ranks were waiting for the dismissal orders that the broadcasting system called for the senior signal rating to report to the bridge. As is usual, and sensing a job of work to be done, ALL the C.P.O.s got in the rear rank. Whatever the job was, nobody wanted it, until the appearance of Signal Bos'n, (Commissioned Officer), whom several of us recognised, and knew. Commenting on the smart appearance of the rear rank, he quickly looked around and asked if there were any VSls, (Signal Instructors), on board. Since we were all wearing our badges of rank there was little point in denying the presence, which happened to be myself. With a laugh, the Signal Bos'n remarked that it seemed that I had won the lottery for the job, so that as is customary, the remainder of the Chiefs heaved an audible sigh of relief. With those closing remarks, yours truly made his way to the signal bridge of the *ORONTES*, where there were several Naval Officers and WRNS Officers in conference. On spotting me on the wings of the bridge the Senior Naval Officer called me over and informed me that as of then, I would be known as the WRNS Sea Daddy. This involved seeing that the WRNS Ratings were employed correctly on signal duties during the daylight hours, and that NO naval rating was to be allowed to mix with the WRNS except during recreational periods and in the Recreational area, that was allocated. This space was, as I later found out, in full view of the signal bridge. Since most of the WRNS were Communications Ratings; about forty of them; it seemed that I was about to take on one hell of a job. I was only thankful that the conduct of the WRNS was not my concern except during the day when on the bridge. The WRNS communication ratings would be assisting the *ORONTES* signalmen if required, so that I decided that they should start their instructions right away. This was to be my first acquaintance with any of the female services, and it seemed that from the WRNS officer spectators that were standing near by, I made a favourable impression. To start with, they were taught how to use the Aldis signal lamp and the procedures to use, so that they might be helpful when the time came. By the fourth day out, they were becoming quite expert at reading Morse and helping the ship's staff in the signals.

Having access to the bridge proved to my advantage, for the Captain's sea cabin and associated domestic offices were also on the bridge. Obviously, everybody on the ship soon became accustomed to my coming and going to the bridge, and very few people questioned me at any time. I soon found that the captain's bathroom had a small laundry room attached so that if I required, while on the bridge, I would use the bathroom facilities. In this, I had to make friends with the Captain's Valet, which I did. This privilege was jealously guarded by me, especially as we were heading south, I anticipated going into white uniform before very long. Having washing, drying and ironing facilities proved a great boon, for I was able at times to complete my laundry needs without much inconvenience to myself.

It was just prior to our sailing, that we heard the great news that Germany had accepted the surrender terms and that Hitler had killed himself with several of his immediate staff, in the Berlin bunker. This at least took much of the worries of the welfare of the folk at home from one's shoulders, as now they would at least be able to sleep peacefully. We also heard how the German U-boat Fleet had agreed to surrender in accordance with the peace terms. The only thing that bothered us was, whether or not there were any renegade U-boat captains that would continue the war. Fortunately there were none that the allies were aware of, so that our journey was redirected through the Mediterranean. With the alteration of course to the east, watch was kept for Gibraltar as we passed. This we passed during the night so that I delegated myself to be on watch until we had passed the rock, for we were not stopping. No signals were exchanged, so that as far as anybody was concerned, *ORONTES* had not passed. The reason for this, I presume, was that the previous Axis partners could still be helping the Japanese with certain informed intelligence, with ship movements being of prime importance. Straight through the Med, no stopping at Malta as we expected, but on to Port Said.

At Port Said, we stopped sufficiently long enough to top up fuel and stores and to wait our turn for a pilot and passage through the canal. If I recall correctly, passage through the canal was started about 1000 or shortly after, so that we should leave the canal about 1800. All went well, and with very little signs of the war that had recently been waged from this area, or perhaps there was, but one did not look hard enough. By the time we reached Port Suez, the weather had taken on the usual glorious blue skies and little breeze, to help cool one down, so it was with some pleasure that we pushed on with our speed to make an artificial breeze.

Eventually passing out of the Red Sea and into the Indian Ocean course was altered slightly to the south east. Again the match box navigators predicted Colombo as the next port of call, and again they were to be proved wrong, for course was again altered further to the south. To me, the whole trip seemed unreal, not being in the ship's official organisation, I was not in a position to glean information from the signal traffic that may have been passing. Day after day steaming at about twenty knots into the flat calm of the Indian Ocean, and to further the unreal atmosphere, there were the females on board which dispelled much of the idea of wartime navy. Soon, it was only too evident that Australia was our destination. Then, it was not long before the rumour of our final place of arrival leaked out, or was deliberately made known. This was to be Sydney, New South Wales. Soon we should be altering course to the East so as to pass through the Tasman Straits before turning up for Sydney, another couple of days' run. Passing through the Tasman Straits, a large bottle nosed dolphin attached himself to the ship and would, hour after hour remain calmly swimming some fifteen yards in front of the bows. It was regarded as a good omen for this dolphin to accompany us, and it seemed that he lived up to his reputation, for the weather was good all the way to Sydney. Arriving at the approaches to Sydney, called on the charts, The Heads, this was two very large promontories, almost twins to look at, except that one was on the right hand and the other on the left. Passing between these headlands, the ship altered course almost 90 degrees to port before making the long run up to Sydney harbour. Once there, we were soon berthed alongside at a place called Woollomolloo. Hope I have spelled it correctly, or I shall incur the wrath of all genuine Diggers, so coming from a mere Pommy, I hope they will find it in their great hearts to forgive me. If memory serves correctly, we berthed at about 1700, and by supper time the ladies of the womens' forces had all disembarked, leaving the fellows in charge, but not for long. Orders for all the passengers were issued by their respective Commanding Officers, (C.O.'s.), to be ready to disembark first thing in the morning, with the Naval Contingent going to a place called Golden Hind. This was the depot for all Naval Passengers, and was some forty miles outside Sydney, and getting well into the beginning of the bush country.

TO C IN CBPF

At Golden Hind as I looked around me, I was amazed to find that there were already many naval personnel installed, and from various conversations, it appeared that the British Pacific Fleet was about to be built up to maximum strength. After a few days' finding my way about the huge camp, I found myself outside the Drafting Office, where they required to know all the particulars regarding myself and family. This resulted in a few days, with the issue of a new set of identity discs. The information given, was also required for other purposes such as next of kin and illnesses that one may have had, plus of course the usual medical examination. While in the drafting office, I met again an old friend from pre-war days on the *Valiant*. Naturally, we passed over old times and yarns. About a week later, I was sent for by the camp Signal Officer, who was a cadet on the *Vindictive* and was now a Lieut. Commander. Again passing the news of the day with him, he told me that there was a requirement for a C.Y.S as Staff to C. IN C., (Commander in Chief), British Pacific Fleet, which was now rapidly forming and taking shape. If I wanted the job, he would recommend me, but the final selection would be by the Fleet Signal Officer, in a few days' time. This was too good an opportunity to miss, so that I gave him my immediate affirmative answer. Some weeks later, I was again sent for by the Signal Officer, who without much pause introduced me to the Fleet Signal Officer. From the start it was obvious that he had been studying my service documents, and from that he asked many various questions, jumping from subject to subject, almost a cross examination. He also seemed to know about my being the WRNS Sea Daddy, judging by some of the questions. The main concern was, if I was prepared to move about instead of being on just one ship, and could I drive a car. In replying to both as yes, I qualified the latter in that I did not have a licence with me.

"That's O.K.," he could soon arrange for me to get a licence, and about four days later I was told to report to C. in C.'s Office in Sydney where I should report to him. Needless to say, I started to wag my tails, for it seemed that I had at least a dozen of them. As I arrived at Sydney station, I was met by a Leading Seaman who informed me that he also was working at C. in C.'s office and that he had been detailed to collect me. For this, transport was provided in the shape of a jeep appropriately marked C. in C.B.P.F. At the time I had little idea where we were or where we went to, except that we finished up at a large block of offices, where he drove round to the back entrance. Dropping my kit in the lobby, I immediately went in search of the Fleet Signal Officer, where I was introduced to two other Officers of Lieut. Comdr's rank and whom I recognised as signal officers that I had seen before, while serving in the Med Fleet. I was then told that I was given a few days in which to find my feet and get to know the city, as I should be required from time to time, to drive to various places. The other requirement was, to hold myself in readiness to join a ship at a couple of hours' notice. Next I was told to get myself some digs for I should be living ashore. For this, I contacted the entrance office where I obtained a couple of addresses from the list of names that they held for such purposes, so that I chose a place not too far from the office. Quickly I settled in to the new job, making myself known to the various staff officers, and always informing the Fleet Signal Officer when I anticipated going off duty, or for any special instructions. In this duty, it was the custom to put in at least twelve to fifteen hours duty a day. This I did not mind, for it made the time pass most quickly.

Day by day progress was made with the formation and organisation of the Pacific Fleet, as so far all British Navy ships had been under the over-all command of the U.S. Navy. Admiral Sir Bruce Frazer had been appointed to Command the B.P.F. Admiral Frazer, (later Lord Frazer of North Cape), commanded the Home Fleet at the Battle of North Cape when the German battle cruiser *Scharnhorst* was sunk. On several occasions during the days at Sydney I met Admiral Frazer in the course of my work, also on a couple of occasions when later he attended the C.P.O.'s Mess Functions as a guest; of that, later. To the sailors of the fleet, he was known as Bruce, but that title was strictly reserved for use when referring to the Admiral, and definitely out of his hearing. Always, he was quite cheerful and smiling and was ever willing to listen to one's information when on official duty. One hardly needs to comment, that he always seemed more than busy.

Before many days the staff were busily engaged with their American counterparts, in preparing for the attacks on various islands in the Pacific. This was mostly of the Philippines group, although there were other places such as Mindanoa, the Marianas, the Marshall Islands and many other strange sounding and previously little known places. The Admiral with the members of his staff would think nothing of flying off from Randwick airport, (the services flying base at Sydney, later on returned to a race track), and fly some thousand miles plus to the bases in the war zone. The most warning that one got of these moves would be perhaps five or six hours, usually one or two, before take off, usually at night, and would be away for perhaps five or six weeks. Sometimes, when my presence had not been required, it would mean that I had many spare duties to perform such as going to the airfield for some reason or other. During the spells in Sydney, I made many friends, especially in the grocery and dry goods lines, and also the canteen supplies stores.

From these good people, I was able to obtain supplies for my own use and the use of the Staff Officers (Signals) for they also lived onshore and fed themselves. Very soon, I was able to send home from these supplies, one parcel each two or three weeks, as all supplies at home (food) were rationed very strictly, and anything that I was able to do to ease the home situation, was more than welcomed by the folk at home. Thanks to the efforts of the merchant navy, only one parcel ever went astray. That parcel contained not food, but a cuddly toy koala bear that I had paid quite a price for. Whether it was lost in a ship by sinking, or whether it was stolen I still do not know. Since it was almost life size and was for my son, who was quickly growing up, the loss was all the more acute. I was able to send the parcels because the forces were maintaining excellent canteens run by volunteers from the ladies of Sydney. These were opened from about 0800 daily and would not close until about 2000, so that food did not become a problem for myself .

The jeep that we had been allocated was quickly wearing out so that arrangements were made for me to go to the store yards (military) and collect a new one. Arriving at the store yards, I found rows upon rows of vehicles so I just helped myself to an almost new one by signing a document to say that it was required for the Admiral's Staff, which in truth it was. This jeep became my pride and joy, and soon we had it repainted and embellished with the letters C. in C. B.P.F. emblazoned on the sides and the signal staff emblem in blue and white. Great care was always taken of the vehicle for it was used almost daily by the Signal Staff Officers and by myself. This was especially so if Ships' Officers were calling on the Staff, the signals jeep would be used at full pressure, transporting them from and to the various quays and jetties. Quite often, I would be required to collect these Officers and it saved many formalities when entering or leaving the Offices of the C. in C. In this way, I became a fairly well known figure in Sydney and in the headquarters, and most probably amongst the Signal Officers of the Pacific Fleet. In fact, I had the honour, (maybe dubious), and the pleasure of being referred to as "FIX IT," for it seemed that I was able to arrange many things unofficially, but I must add, "always honestly." Just a little persuasive talk and the imposing looking jeep with the magic wording on the sides, did wonders, Probably most unfair to the Admiral, but as they always say, "All's fair in Love and War," and after all, we were at war, although not with the Admiral.

ATOM BOMB DROPPED

Eventually, the good days at Sydney came to an end when the Admiral and his staff would transfer to the battleship *King George V.* or *Duke of York* but not before having experienced some attacks by "Kamikaze" aircraft. These aircraft were usually flown off from one of the Japanese owned islands, by pilots who were quite willing to commit themselves to suicide attacks on the fleet, using the aircraft as a missile. This meant that although the plane may have been severely damaged in the run in for the attack, the pilot would steer the plane to hit the ship. The plane being loaded with explosives, if it hit the target, was the ultimate dream of these pilots. Life was indeed cheap in Japan. From what I witnessed, not many of the planes got through as they were usually shot down well before hitting their targets. In my opinion, if the attacks had been more intense and numerous, many would have achieved their purpose of hitting the ship. Obviously not all were destroyed in the attacks which resulted in the ship being a casualty and possibly sinking. However, the stranglehold on Japan continued and soon the combined fleets were operating on Japan's own doorstep, just off Tokyo Bay. This we were able to do by the steady whittling down of the Japanese navy. Then, one morning on the ship's radio the news came that a new invention had been exploded over Nagasaki on 8th August causing enormous damage and numerous casualties. Still the ships patrolled the area of Tokyo Bay with little or no opposition. Then again, some few days later, the radio news informed us that a second explosive device had been exploded over Hiroshima on the main Japanese island, with more than the same deadly effect than at Nagasaki. These bombs were what we now call atomic bombs and the destruction which they cause is horrific. At the time, it was no more than was deserved by the enemy for they had attacked the U.S. Navy at Pearl Harbour without warning. Retribution and revenge had indeed ensnared the Japanese, as whole rows of buildings had been converted and vaporised into so much dust. Some days later, the Japanese nation on the orders of their Emperor, (THE SUN OF HEAVEN), and a supposed divinity, surrendered to the Allies, under threat of further destruction. All

Japanese forces consequently surrendered but there were many acts of ritual suicide by many senior Japanese Officers, when this order was received by the Japanese forces. Admiral Halsey of the U.S. Navy, who was the overall Admiral of the Pacific Fleets, and was flying his flag in the U.S. Battleship Missouri, accepted the surrender terms on board that ship in Tokyo Bay. This was the official ending of the Second World War, much to the relief of all people.

Meanwhile, I had been loaded, with the remainder of the Staff, plus my staff jeep, on to one of the carrier store ships for passage, as far as we were concerned to the Philippines, to await further instructions. Of course, we heard the news of the atom bombs being dropped on Japan so that we all became a little dubious as to where we should finish up. No need to have worried, as we were speedily diverted to Hong Kong where we should meet up with the rest of the Staff. The passage to Hong Kong was uneventful except that many preparations were made for the eventual landing, because at the time the island of Hong Kong was still occupied by the Japanese and there was little way of knowing just what the reception would be in spite of the surrender orders.

Hong Kong is situated some two hundred miles north of the Equator in the China Sea so that temperatures at that time of the year justified the wearing of Naval tropical rig. Arriving at Hong Kong, we were met by a supposed pilot boat who showed us the way into harbour, for there were many wrecked vessels littering the harbour. With one of the signal officers and myself, the jeep was landed and we drove to a very large building on the hillside overlooking the harbour about a mile from where we landed. We were to take over the building for use as a future headquarters for the Navy and the Army. One never gave thought now that the surrender had been signed, to any further hostilities. Entering one of the first floor rooms I was amazed to find a Japanese soldier who immediately sprang to attention and saluted. I immediately turned round, quite expecting to see an officer or some one behind me but there was nobody there so the salute must have been for me. Of course it was a mistake on the man's part, for seeing me in white uniform with a peaked cap he jumped to the conclusion that I must be an officer. At least that's what I thought. However, when I spoke, the man bowed and made obeisance as though I were the Admiral himself. Handing the man over to a Royal Marine who was not far away, as he was better able to deal with him, I sorted myself out and sized up the office. Then moving on, I came to a large room containing several desks. This was promptly earmarked as the Signal Office. We had already been warned to watch for booby traps, so that every mechanical item was left severely alone, as now that war was over, I was not very keen to finish up as a number on the casualty lists. The building that we were looking over, was about two hundred yards long by some fifty feet wide and consisted of three storeys above the ground floor. This was an ideal place for an H.Q. Outside the building was a concrete pathway leading to some underground workings, enclosed by a big steel door. Opening the door, I saw that there were steps leading down. In the half light, I counted some sixty steps before losing track in the bad light. This needed investigation as who knows what may have been hidden in the tunnel. Obtaining a torch from one of the seamen's working party, I then went to investigate the steps and anything else that may have been there. Again I opened the steel door and turning on the torch, I saw that there was an electric light switch on the wall. At least that is what it appeared to be. Gingerly I operated the switch and immediately went down flat, just as a precaution. There was no need to worry for the tunnel immediately was flooded with light. Moving down the steps without haste, I noted that there was a passageway leading off to the left. Ignoring this passage, I continued on to the bottom of the steps where a cross passage was situated. Moving to the right hand passage, it came to an ending at a room fairly heavily secured by another steel door, with peculiar Japanese markings. Retracing my steps, to the left passageway, I encountered several rooms leading off and all to the left, none being on the right. All the rooms were quite large which could have indicated store rooms so that I assumed the set up was that of an underground refuge. Moving on, I again met a steel door which was locked and with the key still in the lock. This I opened to be met with brilliant sunshine, and some steps leading down. Following these steps, I soon found myself about six feet above the main road from Victoria to Wanchai. Some hundred yards away to the right, were the buildings of the old barracks, H.M.S. Tamar. Retracing my way to the tunnel entrance, I reported my findings to the officer for his record and reports.

During the next couple of weeks or so, we were so busy getting everything in working order that there was really no time to look around for anything else. Also, there was the question of getting the colony back to its normal life. Fortunately, most of the local business people had been imprisoned in Stanley gaol or had been made to work for the Japanese. This meant that their expertise could be used to help get the island working again. Such people as City administration staff, electricians, water works officials, the tramway workers, in fact anybody that could help were put to organise their respective trades and organisations. In this, it fell to my lot to try to organise local working parties from the released Chinese workers, most of whom had already been working for the Japanese. It also fell to me to assist the local, Police Inspector, not to do his job, but to help where possible in that I had access to the staff jeep. What with the famous lettering on the jeep, and a Police Inspector for company, there were very few places that were not accessible. Needless to say, the Police Inspector and myself soon became friends, especially as he spoke quite a bit of Chinese, or perhaps I should say Cantonese. This latter is because there are two main Chinese languages, Cantonese and Mandarin, and of course several others but these were mainly based on one or the other with certain dialects, for the want of a better description. Although in the early stages of our re-occupation of Hong Kong, such things as bottled beer were sheer luxuries, and rationed, so I always invited the Inspector to share my humble rations, whenever he visited me, mostly in the evenings. In his company I soon learned to speak a little of the language and was able at least, to get the Chinese workers to understand what was needed. Soon the police and the other utilities of the island were working quite well so in many ways the island became self supporting, and I was able to devote more time to my own duties, especially now that the Admiral and his staff were installed at the headquarters. Also at the headquarters were the Army under the command of General Festing, at least I believe that was his rank or it could have been Lieut. General. In any case, he was always referred to as General. Also, about the same time the first of the WRNS arrived to assist the Navy, mostly in the telecommunication and general office workings, for communications were now most important. This also meant that there were a certain number of WRNS Officers who were accommodated with the WRNS in a house some way up the Peak (hill) where they lived in some seclusion. The place was manned by Chinese staff for domestic duties, as were all the messes so that there was some considerable numbers of Chinese employed by the forces.

The Chinese domestic staff of the C.P.O.'s mess consisted of some half dozen persons which included three amahs, (Chinese laundry girls), who would do all one's laundry for a few dollars a month. In addition to the laundry work they did, they also performed what would be the duties of a chambermaid. Since they were always in the mess from before daylight until well after dark, these girls fed in a room just off the mess room. Although the pay was not so much, the job of amah in the C.P.O.'s mess was much prized and I don't recall having a change of girls for any reason. One of the reasons for this loyalty to the mess was that they lived well, far better than in other messes about the Island. Probably because most of the Chiefs had experienced rather tough and rough times in their own younger days. Apart from that, at one time I was instrumental in obtaining extra rice rations for the mess employees, for which I received the thanks of the mess staff. This was their life sustenance, and they appreciated a little help. About this time also, I was elected as mess caterer so that I had quite a lot of dealing with the mess staff. This job meant that I was responsible for the food purchases, the menus for the mess, the cleanliness of the mess and for the well being of the mess staff. To do this, each member of the mess was allowed so much cash each day and with the totals paid each month, I would purchase the food required for the mess. In doing this, I had the services of an excellent number 1 Chinese boy, who would attend the early markets to obtain our requirements. If by any chance, the mess debts for food came to more that the amount allowed, then each C.P.O. would be required to contribute an equal share of the deficient amount. This seldom amounted to more than a few cents, thanks to the number 1 boy. No doubt he bargained and bartered with keen business acumen, to his own advantage, as he was in charge of the mess staff and the cooking. Number 1 boy, was worth his weight in dollars and he was highly delighted to receive a pay rise after only a few months. After some months, the mess staff was increased to seven, and we had also acquired a permanent Chinese work force of eight boys. The signals' requirements for Chinese office workers gradually grew as replacements for Naval staff increased for demobilisation reasons, until we eventually had some one hundred and fifty boys and girls employed. When I talk of Chinese boys and girls,

I would ask you to remember that although we thought of them as boys and girls, many of them had families and were much older than our ideas of boys and girls. In the event of the staff requiring additional workers for the heavy work, we would inform the dockyard and the next morning we should receive the numbers of casual labourers, (men and women), that we required. These would usually be left to my care.

The heavy work that I mentioned just previously would be the rigging or unrigging of the radio aerials and masts in the event of typhoon warning or for the intake of signal stores which became more or less a regular requirement every few months. I must add here, that in the course of a few months during the typhoon season, I learned to swear most proficiently in Chinese. Not that it was my custom to use bad language at the labourers, but when they took it into their minds, a mule had nothing on the Chinese labourer for stubbornness. I soon learned from my friend, that the usual labourer had suffered considerably at the hands of the Japanese, so that to ease their burden of work, the Chinese would either develop a stubborn attitude or a non-understanding one. Very few Chinese were completely ignorant of the English language, especially those from the city or towns for they were in daily contact with British folk. Apart from that, if one offered the labourers a cigarette as some reward, they usually thanked one most profusely, or if one called for a stand-easy period during some rather hard work they would readily understand. If any doubt, one had only to mention the works office at the dockyard for dismissal and they were changed people. In all, I think that I got on very well with the Chinese for I was given the name of Mr Seemut. Probably not very complimentary as Seemut when converted to Chinese or the nearest wording, means "Sox," so it was Mr Sox, from then on. They must have regarded me quite favourably for when my time came to leave, the Chinese labourers gave me a pair of ivory chop-sticks suitably inscribed, but more of that later.

Another job that became my lot was that of Sea Daddy to the WRNS again, as apparently my record of previous employment as such, had caught up with me. Not that I was privileged in any way except that if the WRNS encountered any bother with the Chinese staff then MR SEEMUT was sent for. As I have already explained, the Chinese staff could be stubborn if they took it into their heads.

Most of the problems at the WRENERY were domestic matters, so that they were soon settled.

With the city of Hong Kong getting back to normal, the next big problem was that of entertainment for the population. Since many of the Staff Officers of both Navy and Army were keen riders, and as some horses were available, it was decided that the racecourse at Happy Valley should be put into working order, and that races would be held as soon as sufficient horses and riders became available. The horses were obtained from various sources, most coming from Australia. Although I say horses, the correct term is ponies, at least that is what I understood, although just what the difference is, I am unsure. However it fell to the lot of the Navy to get the track at Happy Valley in working order and where possible to rig fences for the jumps. In case the reader is wondering just what this is all about, yours truly, (Fred), was delegated as Honorary Clerk of the Course. This made me responsible for the supply of the fences and the positioning of them according to the plans as supplied by the Fleet Signal Officer, a Commander and a member of a well known Brewing family. This person was also to be one of the jockeys, so that when I was asked if I could ride, the answer was, "Yes, a rocking horse, Sir." Signals were made round the fleet calling for volunteer riders for the races. Eventually the big day arrived, a Saturday afternoon meeting, and it seemed as though the whole population of China had arrived, plus a fair sprinkling of British folk. The guests who included the Commander in Chief and the Governor were there to open the event which went remarkably well considering that all of the riders were strictly amateurs and had probably not seen their mounts before that day. Even a tote was organised by the fleet paymaster staff, so that the event at least raised some badly needed money for the purchase of the equipment and the feed for the ponies. I think that after that event, a race meeting was organised for each month. From then on, the races were advertised in the local papers which were then coming into being again. I mentioned that the Commander in Chief attended the race meeting, and this brought to my mind the little episode when the Admiral stood on the bridge just off Tokyo Bay when one of the escorting destroyers appeared to be badly out of station. Turning to various members of the staff on the bridge, he asked them all, one by one, just how far they thought the errant destroyer was away. It should have been two-and-a-half cables distant, (approx. 500 yards). The first answer came from the Gunnery Officer, this was, "600 yards, Sir." Next the Torpedo Officer, who replied, "Nearly half a mile, Sir." Then came the turn of the signal staff, whose answer caused a slight uproar on the bridge, "Three furlongs and no fences, Sir." A deadly silence reigned for a moment, then uproarious laughter, led by the Admiral who was after all, a keen race goer. "Quite appropriate," replied Sir Bruce Frazer, observing that there was quite a sea running and considerable movement on the destroyer. So the Admiral was keenly interested in the racecourse project.

At one of the meetings, it was usual for the Chief P.O.'s to gather at the finishing line, which normally was not too far from the paddocks. On this particular day, the Signal Commander was to ride a horse named Charlie Chase, a well known contrary horse, and just like the Chinese labourers, a stubborn starter. As is usual at any race meeting, the horses were paraded in the paddock for the public to admire or to select their fancy. All went well, until the Signal Commander mounted Charlie Chase, who incidentally all the signal chiefs had backed for something like two hundred dollars, (about three pounds ten shillings), a tidy sum in that day. As the Signal Commander mounted, Charlie decided that he would go back to his lady friend in the stables. No matter how his jockey tried, he would not give in so that, still struggling to get Charlie facing the right way, the race started, leaving Charlie still short of the starting line. By dogged persistence Charlie's jockey coaxed him round, and to the amazement of all the. public, he was off like a rocket to eventually win the race by a small margin, and to run straight to the stable for his lady friend. True love never did run smoothly, at least on that occasion. By Charlie's win, the signals staff reaped a rich prize of many hundreds of dollars, somewhere about eighty odd pounds, English money. Charlie became the favourite of the signal staff after that, but never again to win at such great odds. By the time I left China and Hong Kong, the racing was beginning to be taken over by civilian authorities and was flourishing well, to the great enjoyment of the population.

TYPHOON SEASON

At different times I would be required to go over to the mainland, Kowloon, by car and then on to visit some sites in the new territories. These sites were possibly radar sites for use with the Kia Tak airport. I enjoyed these trips very much, for it gave me a chance to see something of the inhabitants and customs of the folk outside the city. Also, while the signal traffic was getting well under control, and things in general settled down to something like normal, the senior ratings of the staff were given leave in rotation to go to Macao. This was a Portuguese island at the mouth of the Canton River. Although Portuguese, most of the trade was done by the Chinese and the place differed very little from Hong Kong except that it was under Portuguese rule and used that country's methods of trade and the language was basically Portuguese. One character on this island, who was referred to as "Champagne Charlie," and was considered by the service personnel as a millionaire. Whether that was true is unknown, but judging from the manner in which he entertained service people he must have been in that bracket. I heard of him while on that short break of leave, but was not entertained by him. In any case I had only about 48 hours on the island before I was due to return to Hong Kong. It seems that this character was so thankful to the British troops and the Navy for liberating him, that this was his method of thanks. Returning to Hong Kong I had barely settled down to my routine than the typhoon season was about to begin. This meant that the radio masts and aerials had to be prepared for instant collapsing, so that I and the Chinese work force were kept busy for quite a while. Later in the month we received our first typhoon warning. At full speed the masts were dismantled and all cracks and crevices, anywhere, were sealed off. Doors and windows were shuttered. In fact it looked to the uninitiated as if the island was again preparing for a siege. This was virtually true, for if the winds of the typhoon found a crack, it would be the end of that building. Something like the story of the little Dutch boy that placed his fingers in the hole in the dyke when he saw the water trickling through. Fortunately on this occasion the typhoon passed us by so that we had a brief respite. The trouble with a typhoon is, although the direction of the centre of the typhoon can be predicted with a certain amount of accuracy, there is no certainty that what is predicted will occur, as typhoons like many other occurrences have a nasty habit of changing direction at the last minute. One learns to disregard a typhoon warning at one's peril and cost. All typhoons are given names, usually in alphabetical sequence so that they can be tracked and warnings issued as required. If one should be in the direct path of the typhoon, one battens down everything possible, as quickly as possible. The reason for this is that the winds are so strong that cars have been lifted and flung about like cardboard boxes, and when the centre passes over there is no wind at all. Just nature luring one into a sense of false security. After a short period of no wind, the whole affair starts again but with the wind in the entire opposite direction. So, should one have been caught napping in the lull, and perhaps opened windows to air the place, the next few minutes would be entirely disastrous, with the wind filling the opened space and then literally exploding any walls with the force of the wind. In addition to all this, it usually rains, not in torrents but in bucketfuls and it normally is recorded as somewhere about five or six inches in perhaps half an hour. Normally everything stops as soon as the warning announces that the typhoon is in the immediate vicinity. This is the general signal for all persons to take shelter in the strongest building available. This is as much to protect oneself from flying debris as for any other reason. It is strange to be in the street one moment with crowds moving about, and then suddenly, whoosh! the street is empty, the rain starts and heavy manhole covers are tossed high in the air like so many plastics balls in a fairground shooting gallery. The whole chaotic bedlam denies description which will do justice to the damage caused. Typhoons as such, are peculiar to the China Seas and although some other areas have their equivalent winds, they are referred to under a different name, such as hurricane. If one is near the coast or even in harbour, one will find boats and some ships up to hundreds of tons in displacement flung up on the adjacent roads as though they had fallen off a transporting vehicle. The worst of the typhoons generally occur about October or November but one must not take that as a directive because of the contrariness of the weather clerk who usually gets everybody confused as to his intentions.

HONG KONG DAYS

Not being able to celebrate the ending of the World War II, as did the folk at home, and being near Christmas, the C.P.O.'s Mess of H.M.S. TAMAR, (our depot or barracks), decided that the Christmas celebrations should be something to remember, with D-25 being the first of December, so as to allow us ample time to organise events in the mess. Being the Mess Caterer the menu automatically became my responsibility, and I was authorised to spend extra money on the event. As was the case with all senior ratings messes on shore, the mess had its own bar, chiefly beer in normal times, but for this event special approval had been given for spirits and wines to be available. Next the guest list was debated. Many were the suggestions made until one of the C.Y.S. suggested that he would like to invite the Signal Commander. Somebody else suggested the Commodore and so on. Eventually the debate became so intense that it was agreed that each mess member should be allowed to invite two guests, and with general invites to the whole of the Admiral's staff and of course to the Admiral himself. The Staff invitation would naturally include the Officer's Wives and daughters if they wished. Consequently, with the reputation for entertaining being very high in the C.P.O.'s mess, we could not let such an occasion tarnish our record. Everybody put themselves out to do their utmost, so that by the big day, the mess was the envy of the island. My Chinese work force set to in their spare moments to make confetti which went into two large waste paper baskets made up as bells. These bells were hung at each end of the mess, high in the ceiling, about thirty feet up, amongst the rafters. Outside the mess doors, obtained by means undisclosed, was the largest fish tank seen outside an aquarium, and containing numerous tropical fish of various kinds. Water proof lighting had been made by the electrical chiefs and the tank was illuminated giving a wonderful effect to one's entry.

Daily the question arose as to who of the guests had accepted our invitation to the cocktail party at 1130, on Christmas Day. One by one the replies came in, bar one, and that was the reply that we were waiting for. Yes, especially the signal staff as we had far more to do with the Admiral Sir Bruce Frazer than any of the other C.P.O.s. No, I do not think that he was keeping us on tenterhooks, but rather that he was waiting to see just what his own requirements for the day would be. Some ten days before the big day, the Admiral informed us through his Flag Lieutenant that he would be delighted to attend. This brought renewed energy to the mess members for never before had they experienced having invited the Admiral to a mess party.

The big day arrived at last. Never before had I seen a C.P.O.'s mess so full of C.P.O.'s in overalls making the place look as though the usual mess inspections were just of no account. Some time before 1130, all mess members cleaned themselves into their best suits, and paraded outside the mess as a sort of dummy run, and in true Naval style we all mustered for our rum ration as for a normal day. I somehow suspect that many of the mess members did not drink their tots but probably saved it, so that their particular guest might share the honour. From there on, proceedings were a bit confused for as I went to meet the Admiral as our guest, he arrived at the bottom of the stairs leading to the mess. As is customary with a flag officer, he had been met at entrance to the depot by a bewildered young officer who had not been forewarned of the Admiral's arrival. He need not have worried as far as the admiral was concerned, for I heard that he had arrived without his cap, let alone wearing it. This at least signified that he expected no ceremony, so that as I met him, I saluted in the normal service manner and escorted him to the mess assembled outside. Some thirty or more C.P.O.s sprang to attention, far smarter than any guard of honour was capable of. Introduction to all mess members followed as the Admiral and Flag Lieutenant passed by. This duty was performed by the President of the mess. As though by the magic wave of the conjuror's wand, the remaining guests arrived at the mess stairs to be escorted to the mess by their sponsors. For this day and occasion only, we had obtained four additional mess waiters, (at mess expense), who immediately took the various orders for drinks. For those who were abstainers, there was ample coffee, for our mess was renowned for its ever ready cup of coffee at any time of the day. What a wonderful Chinese chef, especially with the menu of canapés that he provided! Precisely at mid-day, (by the mess clock), all celebrations were suspended for a few moments while the Admiral spoke a few words of thanks to the mess. During this period, all guests and mess members had been politely shepherded from under the bells. As the Admiral finished and wished everybody a Merry Christmas, so the bells overhead were actuated by pull strings, and about thirty pounds of confetti was released, to be blown by the fans all over the mess and the guests, much to the delight of the lady guests. The party continued until about, 1400 when all guests left the mess but, not until the President had extended an invitation to all to attend the impromptu dance and concert that evening, to be held in the mess. The Admiral offered his apologies, but most of the other guests readily accepted the invite. This also went with great enjoyment and hilarity for the guests were invited to become honorary mess members by sliding down the stair banisters. For this feat the stair extended over two floors in a spiral fashion, so that considerable speed was built up at the dismount stage. In all, a very good time was enjoyed by all, and when the guests received their honorary membership cards a few days later the praises for the party were quite overwhelming.

Many British people that have served in the Far East, know of and can play the game Mar Jhong, but very few can play the game as the Chinese play it. Once the cards, (blocks actually), have been shuffled and the walls prepared, and the cards dealt, no word is spoken until the winner declares his hand. When that happens, all the pent up feelings and frustrations of the game are released and Babel is recreated. Stakes are agreed beforehand, which are usually in dollars, and are immediately taken by the winner. All that one hears during the game is the click of the pieces. It is a most fascinating game when played the Chinese way, so that when the number 1 boy offered to teach me the game I was more than pleased, and even more so when I was invited to play the game with him and some members of his family. On this occasion, it was followed by a typical Chinese meal prepared by his elderly mother. Needless to remark, I was somewhat dubious about accepting, but I did so as I felt that it would help me to know and understand the Chinese ways of life a bit better. I am really glad that I did accept, for it was something that one would never forget.

The house was situated in the middle class district, and on entering the house which was spotlessly clean, I was introduced to those members of the family that were at present available. The family were introduced to me by the elderly mother, and what I presumed, was in order of seniority in the family. There were in all some ten members of the Yan Luk family, and I was then informed that the meal would be served before the game of Mah Jhong so as to allow us lots of time for the game. They were seated round a large round table, covered by a spotless white lace table cloth, with the feeding bowls and chop sticks all set out. Sitting next to me was the number 1 boy, quite smartly dressed in blue denim blouse and trousers. This was the usual dress; more of a national dress for the workers. Number 1 boy interpreted the various questions from his mother and for my replies. He also guided me through the various dishes explaining what each dish was made with. It seems that one eats whatever one takes, a help yourself idea, and that one leaves a little of the present course in one's feeding bowl which gets mixed and eaten with the next course. I was informed that a full Chinese meal would consist of some two dozen servings, so that by leaving a little in the bowl at each serving one made up the final course. I shuddered at the thought, but then, I was thinking along the lines of English menus. Real Chinese food is prepared and served so that the next course compliments the previous one. In one of the dishes I found that there was a small piece that I could not chew, and then noticed that the others that had had a similar problem, just spat the offending item on to the lace cloth beside their feeding bowl. This did not seem or appear offensive in any way. In fact when I spoke to the number 1 about it, he confirmed my thoughts that this was the custom of the old Chinese. Today, I would guess that the modern Chinese person acts in very similar ways to ourselves when eating out, at least. At the end of the meal, one was given a glass of some kind of white wine, or at least I presumed that is what it was, which was inclined to be a little on the dry side and seemed to me to taste more like rice wine. With the meal over, I thanked the mother in my best Chinese that I could muster. She was highly delighted, and on accepting my cigarette, seemed to consider the praises for the meal very ample indeed. The game of Mah Jhong that followed was carried out as the Chinese would play it but in a more refined and dignified atmosphere, for there was none of the usual bedlam and retrial of the game afterwards. However, it did teach me quite a lot about the way that the Chinese played their national game. This method was taught to my sons at a later date.

With the passing of Christmas, work steadily increased so that before we were really aware of the fact, Easter came and went with very little thought. By the time we were really on top of the work it was almost Whitsun holidays. At about that time, it was suggested that the communications staff should try to organise a sweepstake draw for the English derby. This really started as an office draw, but by the time various officers who were visiting the H.Q.s had been enticed into parting with at least ten dollars for a ticket, the affair snowballed until we decided to try to make it a draw for the whole fleet. Various senior officers were approached for their approval so that in the end it was as official as one could make it, with officially printed tickets and naming the various draw officials, which included several of the senior officers. This draw exceeded the expectations of any of the original organisers so that in the finish, it was being run on similar lines to the sweepstakes organised by the newspapers. If I remember rightly, when all tickets were counted and the calculations made, every horse drawn would be worth at least one hundred dollars, with prizes for the first three horses home, amounting to ten thousand dollars, (about £120), for the first horse and proportionate amounts for the next four horses. Results would be as received by the radio from the B.B.C. and the pay out would start where possible the next morning when the banks were available for business. Ships from the whole Pacific Fleet took part and I felt sure that the first prize was won by one of the destroyers away on anti-piracy patrol. Lists of winners were signalled round the fleet, and the C. in C. was enticed to perform the draw, which was made in front of the H.Q.s with as many staff witnessing as could be spared from duty. Although this had been organised by the signal staff, who had purchased numerous tickets at roughly half a crown each, only one prize came our way, and that was for drawing a horse. Really not enough to have a good drink with, so that a whip round was made for a general party which took place on the Saturday evening in the mess, to celebrate the success of the Fleet Derby Draw, for the 1947 derby.

Time was passing very quickly, and before I realised it I was informed that it was time for me to get ready for home. Letters were written and posted in double quick time, and farewells to various officials and other people were started. One thing that I had promised myself before leaving China was, that I would take home a carved camphor wood chest made by the Chinese. For this I consulted with the number 1 boy, who came with me to the maker of these items. This item, really an object of art, for it depicts the story of the Great Wall of China and the warriors that fought over it and for it. Number

1 boy, as I understood part of his speech to the tradesman, explained that he and his family wanted to buy it for me when I left the island. This was to get the best possible price for making it. Almost daily I would visit the tiny workshop and see the chest being made and carved. The tools that were used being most primitive, such as old car tools being ground down and sharpened to make the carving tools, or plane irons, or screw drivers and chisels. The craftsman's young son of about six or seven doing much of the carving work. The chest I brought home with me as part of my baggage, for I remembered only too well the fate of the koala bear that had never arrived. When the chest was finished, I went with number 1 to collect it, so that it was with some surprise that I was told that he and the other boys in my special working party were buying it for me as a present in appreciation for the good things that I had done for them. Due to later constant movements, the chest became too large for the premises that we lived in, so that when Keith, my eldest son, asked if he could buy it, I readily gave it to him on condition that it should never leave the family.

The chop sticks, I have already mentioned and these I still have. These are suitably inscribed, "To MR SEEMUT from thankful workmen," or words to that effect since it is in Chinese. One other important gift that came to me quite unexpectedly, was a pewter tankard from the WRNS thanking me for my services, and this was presented by the Chief Officer WRNS with the Fleet Signal Officers standing by. The only thing to be done now, was to wait for the ship to take me home. This was the transport *ALCANTARA*, which sailed from Hong Kong in the October, with yours truly on board.

Under my care, also went some half dozen or more large boxes filled with various items for the families of the various senior officers of the staff. The contents of these boxes were, as in my own case, gifts for the family such as silk or china tea sets and such items as had been collected since the end of the war. In my own case there were presents for the kiddies, leather shoes, nylon stockings and of course tinned food items, that we could obtain from Australia. The cost of the transport was paid for by the officers and my boxes were included in the freightage. All that I was apparently responsible for was the handing over of the cases to the various authorities when I arrived home, all the cases being consigned to the addresses on the cases. Obviously I was not the only Naval person travelling to the U.K. and since I was an ex-member of the Admiral's staff I was left severely alone by the Naval Officer in charge on the transport. For me, it was almost like being a passenger on the ship in a peacetime cruise. Bearing in mind my role on the transport when I took passage to Sydney, I more or less adopted the same role on the way home, so that I was considered as part of the crew. This of course was unofficial, and when one remembers that perhaps some several hundred service men and women were taking passage and returning home, I opted for a little bit of comfort where possible, for the six week journey home. Apart from a few flying visits home before we sailed for the Pacific, I had not had a real leave for over four years, so that the eventual sight of Southampton was really a treat for sore eyes. Here the cases spoken of earlier, were cleared through the Customs with my own baggage included and sent off to their various destinations. My own baggage arrived home within two days and by what is now known as British Rail. Really an excellent service even though under almost wartime conditions. For myself, having very little luggage other than service kit, I was passed quickly through the routine of rejoining barracks and was sent on leave for six weeks. More of that, later.

A-BOMB REMARKS

During the years 1960 until the disbanding of the Civil Defence Corps, I became a member of that organisation, as did my wife. Because of my service training and ability to lecture to a degree, I was soon promoted to the rank of Sector Warden, so that it became more or less a duty to attend various courses and lectures. The subject of one of the lectures was the bombing of Hiroshima and Nagasaki. This and the technical details revealed, was the subject of much subsequent discussion in the training of the Defence Corps. When I revealed that I had seen the destruction caused, although not having witnessed the actual event, I was able to give the Harmondsworth Unit the benefit of a talk about the devastation that was seen from a casual observer's view. The following are some of the notes that I made after the lecture that started the discussions, as we were prohibited at the time from taking notes. These notes were the basis of a talk that I gave the Unit, and which I now refer to.

On Monday the 6th August 1945, the most devastating and consequently the most controversial event of the war, and possibly the one that the world has ever known, occurred over and to the Japanese city of Hiroshima. An American Flying Fortress, (B29), dropped a single bomb from about 32,000 feet, which devastated the whole city and the surrounding areas. As the bomb was dropped at roughly the time that folk were going to work, (probably in the region of 0745-0815), not much notice was taken of the single aircraft flying almost out of sight. I would suppose that those that did see the machine, did not recognise it as an American aircraft, but most probably thought that it was one of their own. The bomb itself was set to burst some five hundred feet above the ground, (an air burst). Within a matter of moments of the bomb bursting above the ground, some two hundred thousand people had been either obliterated completely, killed by the explosion, or permanently disabled. Exact numbers will never be known as whole families were wiped out completely, so that the figure given is an approximation and the most moderate of estimates.

News reporters that later landed, were unable to get true estimates, as no person was able to supply accurate details of the event, which was so colossal as to be incomprehensible to the ordinary individual. One reporter described the city that he saw as the likeness of a huge waste dumping ground covering some three-quarter mile square, that had been repeatedly overrun by bulldozers. One young lad that had been found wandering destitute, told the reporter that, on the morning of the bomb, he had walked from what had been his home, towards the city centre. On the way, he had seen some of the people that he knew or recognised, lying in the dust and rubble, their faces bloated and covered with very large blisters, and with yellowish oily liquid coming from their eyes. He told the reporter that everywhere there was just so much rubbish and smoke blackened walls where once there had been a great city.

This catastrophe had happened on what would have been a Bank Holiday Monday at home, when the celebrating folk at home would be enjoying their first Bank Holiday, since the commencement of the war in 1939. Nobody blames them for their right to enjoy themselves after the deprivations and years of greatly subdued anxieties of the war. They had not been the war makers.

On the Thursday, three days later, 9th August 1945, a second such bomb was dropped, this time on the Japanese city of Nagasaki, a naval port and dockyard. On this occasion, the bomb burst, either accidentally or by design, on the ground, (ground burst). The bomb itself was approximately the same size as the Hiroshima Bomb, but the effects were different. Some sixty-five thousand people were killed or permanently maimed. Again these figures are not definite, as the atomising or vaporising effect of the explosion again erased whole families, so that records are not complete. A total of one-and-a-half square miles of the city were totally destroyed. Clouds of smoke and dust, all radioactive, were visible two hundred miles away and significantly identified by the peculiar mushroom shaped cloud that we now associate with atomic or nuclear explosions. The huge Mitsubishi foundry and factory resembled a child's meccano model which had been stamped on by an angry child who could not get the model quite correct. Before the war, there had been a large hospital on the outskirts of the city, that had completely disappeared as had the staff and patients. People that happened to be within a radius of over half a mile were simply incinerated or "cinderised" by the blast.

From these brief notes, there arose many questions that required answers. The most important being, "Would the atom bomb be the end of all wars or would it be the end of humanity?" It was not only the effects of the explosion and the vast numbers of people that could be killed in one explosion, but the effects of the radiation were enormous.

In 1946/7, several more tests were carried out on an uninhabited island in the Pacific, a coral atoll named Bikini Atoll. This test consisted of several old warships, mostly from the defeated enemies, anchored in the bay. On the vessels were some 5,000 animals of all kinds, ranging from pigs, goats and rats to other creatures that were available. Some of the animals were even wrapped in protective clothing for a particular test. The bomb, being monitored all the while from drop to explosion, which occurred at about 500 feet, (Air burst). In all, some fifteen ships were sunk or so severely damaged as to be beyond repair. Millions of gallons of water were flung into the air and everywhere suffered from gamma radiation. It was also estimated that on the ships would have been some 35,000 crewmen, all of which would have been killed or so severely injured as to make them permanently disabled.

Three weeks later another A-Bomb, this time suspended in a water tight tank, some twenty to thirty feet below the surface, the whole contraption then, was exploded by radio control. This time, two battleships and one aircraft carrier were sunk completely and several vessels damaged beyond repair. All effects of the explosion were recorded in detail.

In 1949, Russia exploded an atomic device and so the atomic nuclear race started.

In 1952, the USA exploded a device at Einiwetok placing the USA in the lead of the race again.

In 1954, the first H-Bomb was tested, the bomb having approximately twenty times the power of the first atom bomb. This bomb apparently almost got out of control so that the effects were felt at least 1000 miles away. This involved the Japanese fishing fleet, as fish is the staple diet of the Japanese, and their fishing boats wander at great distances from the homeland. In the case of the Japanese trawler *Lucky Dragon*, which was fishing some 1500 miles from Japan, the crew suddenly broke out in large blisters after hauling in a good catch. As the days passed, all the crew became affected so that the captain decided to return home for medical treatment. Returning to their home port, medical experts immediately placed the ship in strict quarantine where it was established that the whole catch was contaminated, the ship was contaminated and the whole crew were suffering from radiation sickness and the associated ailments. Already many of the Japanese people in the areas of Hiroshima and Nagasaki were suffering from diseases similar to haemophilia and blindness which was later established as due to the effects of the radiation.

Without going into the details and scientific data, which in any case I cannot remember, for there are such things as "half life" or "roentgens," "strontium 90," and many others that I did not take note of, for security reasons. According to the Commission for Atomic Energy, a dose of 600 R is sufficient to kill any person, so that it is estimated that the human being can tolerate a dosage of 0.3 R per week. According to the experts, the fall out that happened on the *Lucky Dragon* was 01 R in each hour of her journey back to Japan, making a total intake of radiation at about 500 R. One of the unfortunate crew died some eight months later. Just how the experts arrive at their figures I am at loss to understand as one needs more than an elementary education to grapple with such problems.

These notes that I have embodied in this. chapter, are NOT in any way to be taken as a cry of support for "BAN THE BOMB," which is now becoming a craze. Rather I give the notes in that one may give due consideration to the pros and cons of the acts of war.

For myself at the time that the bombs were dropped, it was a just retribution for having involved me in the war, also since it brought a speedy end to the war, I was more than thankful that the whole shooting works were over, for I had heard it remarked that the powers that be had expected some several millions of casualties, and I was not anxious to test their theories in the smallest way. Amen to that.

A WELCOME HOME

Obviously I had already, informed my wife that I was on my way and I gave my estimated time of arrival at Bexleyheath Station. Unbeknown to me, my wife had prepared my son Keith so that he and his friend Tony from next door could come to the station to meet me. As with many other things, one's ideas do not always go according to plan and I arrived at the station some hour earlier than expected. This meant that with few buses, I was obliged to walk from the station to home, about three-quarters of a mile.

Arriving at the back gate, a small head appeared round the kitchen door, took one look, immediately disappeared inside and yelled, "Mum, here's that man." Just what his thoughts may have been, I cannot really tell, except that here was somebody that was about to usurp his assumed authority as the eldest male in the house. Oh yes, this was quite a normal thing as one found out, the kiddies being left so long without an adult male member of the family to guide them, just assumed that responsibility themselves, and no stranger was going to usurp that responsibility. I suppose that in reality, I was a stranger, for apart from snaps, I had very little idea of Keith's behaviour or he of my responsibilities. Obviously, he was not going to accept the situation without some objections.

These objections came later in the day or evening, when he was told by the wife, to get ready for bed, which he delayed as long as possible. At that, I also told him to get ready for bed, as his brothers had already gone upstairs. Promptly the reply came, "You go back to China, we don't want you here." The fact that this was coming from a seven year old was just not right to me, but to him, he had every right in his own mind. However, matters moved on and after a few words from Mum, who, as far as he was concerned, was the boss, things started to get back to what was normal. The next day, after a frosty start between myself and the children, matters improved and before long we settled down to a normal family life. As was natural, the younger children, Kelvin and Malcolm, took their examples from Keith because he had been the male boss of the family, being only second to Mum. By the end of the leave, after being told that I would now be home, we soon became pals with constantly improving relations between all of us.

Life was not to be all roses, for in the midst of all the joys of being on leave the telegraph boy arrived with a telegram for myself. Yes, it was a recall from leave and to report to barracks. Never in my wildest dreams did I think that perhaps I was indispensable, but this was too much, as I still had about two weeks' leave to finish off. Arriving at the barracks about mid-day, I was informed that I should report to the Drafting Office where I should receive my instructions. This I did, to be informed that on the next day, I should be drafted to *H.M.S. Ganges*, for instructional duties. The vicious wheel had turned full circle and I was to be back where I had started.

Without wasting any time, I informed my wife of the fate that had befallen me, and with many mixed feelings, I prepared myself for the morrow and my journey to Shotley.

The next morning, I caught the early train to Waterloo Station, thence to Liverpool Street Station and to Harwich, where I arrived in the late afternoon. This arrival was to be somewhat different from my previous arrival, for reporting to the Transport Officer, I was given an escort of a young seaman to help with my baggage. This lad would be going over to the training establishment, so would accompany me all the way, by picket boat and assist with the transporting of my gear to the C.P.O.s mess. I was still somewhat dazed and annoyed with the suddenness of the move which I could see no reason for, as there seemed to be plenty of C.Y.S. in the depot. There was a reason, and that was, that most of those that I thought were available were going out on demobilisation, whereas I still had quite a few years to serve. Apart from that, I was considered the most likely candidate for the instructional job, which would start on the following Monday. There was only one little item that added some sunshine to the very dark clouds that seemed to cover me. That was, that the job meant an extra shilling a day on my pay, (5 pence at today's rates). Riches untold.

The next day if I remember correctly was Thursday, and as I was not required for duty until the Monday, I requested permission to have a long weekend to make up for some of the leave that had been curtailed. It appeared that it was the custom of the *Ganges*, that all new Instructors should meet the Captain on the first Friday after joining the establishment.

HMS GANGES AGAIN

Promptly at 0900 the next morning, I presented myself outside the Captain's office in my best suit ready for the meeting. It seems that there were two C.P.O.s to meet the Captain, the other fellow being of a preceding letter in the alphabet, so that I would be the last one to see the Captain. In went the first fellow, to spend some ten minutes being questioned. As he came out, he smiled and said "Your turn now." Meeting a Captain did not unduly perturb me, for in the last job, while on the staff, Commanders and Captains had been quite an everyday occurrence, so that this to me was just another Captain. Tapping gently on the door of the office, I waited for the usual call of "Come in." Stepping smartly in the door, I faced the Captain and saluted in the usual manner. As the Captain looked up from his papers, I was amazed and delighted to find that I was facing Captain Bush, the old friend of *Euryalus* days, in the Mediterranean. Without more ado, he extended his hand exclaiming, "Well, if it is not the boy himself." Yes, we spent a very pleasant forty minutes passing over old times and my bringing Captain Bush up to date with my history. Not that I suppose he needed a lot of telling, as I noted that he already had my service documents in front of him. During the course of the conversation, I mentioned that I had had my leave curtailed to come to Shotley, and that I had asked for a long weekend to adjust matters that I had left undone, as I had returned in some hurry in response to the telegram. Captain Bush immediately informed the Duty Officer that I was to be granted a long weekend, returning for duty on the Monday morning. I needed no further telling but was packed and ready for the next bus that was leaving for Ipswich so that I caught the earlier train for London and Bexleyheath, than would have been the case if I had caught the normal weekend trains. A great weekend until the Sunday evening was enjoyed, then I caught the train to get me back to Shotley late on the Sunday evening, ready for the Monday start.

The Monday starting was a bit of a myth, as I was required to take charge of a new intake of boys for training into signal boys. Eventually some forty boys formed the class which was to be shared between myself and a Petty Officer Telegraphist, that being the usual as instructors. The lads were from all walks, some from good schools, most from elementary schools, some from Scotland, some from all parts of the British Isles, and one from the Falkland Islands, also the usual sprinkling of ex-Greenwich School boys. All much as it had been in the days of the distant past, when I had joined. In fact there was very little difference in the main joining routine. One good thing about taking on a new signals class was, the boys had all been instructed and passed their preliminary squad drills and marching, so that one did not have to bother with that. With the class present, I gave them all a short lecture as to what were my expectations of them and that nothing but the best would be good enough for our mess, which was no. 39 on the Parade Ground and consequently under the eyes of everybody that mattered. Not only that, but the class number was to be 240, that of the class that I had been trained in. With all the coincidences building up, I also informed the boys that I should expect the same excellent results from the mess and the class as had been obtained when I was a member of that class. All the omens seemed good and in my favour. My only feeling of uncertainty was, whether or not I would be able to live up to the example that I was quoting, for not only did it involve signals, but many other subjects as well. Although one had various assistance in these matters, the ultimate results would be my responsibility. Not only that, but I informed the class that the Captain was an old friend and that no doubt he would be watching the progress of number 39 Mess in the Hawk Division, with more than the usual interest. In more than a few instances this proved to be correct in more ways than one, and quite a good guess on my part. I was quite unaware that standing just inside the mess as I spoke to the boys, was the Divisional Officer and the Second Divisional Officer. When I had finished my pep talk, they both entered the mess and introduced themselves to the boys and more or less repeated my pep talk with certain various additions, regarding the division and the duties of the divisional staff.

BOYS TRAINING AGAIN

For the remainder of the week, the boys were employed on learning all the Morse code, the semaphore signals and the Naval flag signals. The latter varied slightly from when I had learned them, there now being several American signal flags embodied in our own code, each with a special meaning. This made it all a little more complicated for the lads, but they would learn, and do it fast or else. The Navy had been caught out in 1939 by not having enough trained ratings in the various branches, and I, for my part, was trying to ensure that it did not happen again if I had anything to do with it. During my pep talk to the lads, I had informed them, the reading of comics and associated papers were now taboo and the only reading material that would be allowed, would be signal books and letters. As ever, there was a witty fellow in the class who remarked that, "all his letters were French," and from his dialect, I guessed that he came from one of the famous dock areas. I let it pass, telling him that I only spoke English or Chinese. From that moment on, I never saw anything but signal books when I did the rounds at night. Oh yes, it was part of the duty of the instructor on duty to go round and ensure that all boys were in their beds for "Rounds" at 2100 or just after. The rounds as previously described in the early chapters, was still the same as it had been, even in Nelson's days, and would probably be the same in another fifty years' time, if there were to be such a thing as a Royal Navy. There was one slight difference that I soon found out, and that was, that the boys were allowed to smoke if over the age of sixteen. Then it would be in a separate area of the mess and at certain times during the evening. Here, I will give a little story of smoking and its consequences. One of the smoking periods was that time after the supper meal until the order "OUT PIPES" and prepare for rounds. The "Out Pipes" had been sounded and the boys turned in, ready for the Officer of the rounds. I being the Duty Instructor that night, was waiting outside the mess for the rounds to visit the mess. Suddenly, looking up the rows of beds, I saw what I thought was smoke. By this time I had got to know most of the lads, so noting the bed from where the smoke issued, I went to the bed and asked for the cigarette. "What cigarette Sir?" replied the suspected offender. Feeling absolutely sure that I had not been mistaken, I ordered the offender to get out of bed. I searched through the bed and under the bed. There was no sign of the cigarette, but there was the smell of puffed tobacco. As the "Rounds" were approaching, I gave the boy the benefit of the doubt. One must have proof, not just suspicions.

The next morning at 0900 divisions, the boy was absent from parade so that I enquired if anybody had seen or heard of where he might be. "Yes Sir," replied his crony, "he has reported sick." Naturally it was my duty to know what the sickness was about, as this had to be reported to the Divisional Officer, who in turn would have to report to the Parade Commander, in case it was a serious complaint. The only thing that I could do was to inform the Divisional Officer, that I did not know and that I would find out and let him know in due course after divisions. With divisions over, I told the class leader to take charge and march the class to the signal school, while I went to the Sick Bay to make enquiries of the absentee. Finding the Sick Berth P.O. about to start on the patients, I asked if the absentee; I gave his name; had reported sick, and what was his complaint. When I was told that he had burned himself, I knew just what had happened. However, I got the story from the lad himself. When I had asked for the cigarette, he had jammed it between the cheeks of his buttocks, feeling sure that he would be quite safe. It was, but he did not reckon on the burns that would follow. Also, he had taken the pain of the burning cigarette without even fluttering his eyelids. The only thing was, that he could not march about all day with a blister each side of his buttocks. The Sick Berth P.O. gave a knowing wink to me, and told me that he would soon have him right again, which he did. No, I did not report the offender, but gave him a good talking to, informing him, that to wilfully injure one's self so that duty could not be performed, was a most serious offence for which detention in cells could be awarded, especially if the crime went to the Captain. Needless to say, when I reported to the Div. Officer, he had a good laugh and acting on my request for NO action, we let the matter drop, but, like all these events the news leaked out, probably by his chums, so that he became one of the establishment heroes. Incidentally, that boy became one of the class leaders some while later when selections for that post came up. This was done after about four weeks when the Instructors would select the most suitable lads for the job. Myself and the other Instructor decided that we would select the Petty Officer Boys, (two of them), and that the other members of the mess would select with our approval, the two Leading Boys, as after all they would have to take orders from those selected. This was probably against the selection rules, but it gave the other lads the knowledge that they had selected the leaders by common consent. Whenever possible, we allowed the lads to decide for themselves just what they wanted to do, and as far as we were concerned, it proved to be a winning decision.

Every evening when I was on duty, that was every other day, I would do as my old Instructor had done, and walk up and down the mess, from after supper to the time for "Rounds." In this time, it was a matter of shooting questions about signals, at the boy whose bed I stopped at. It was surprising just how quickly some of the lads picked up the signal knowledge, especially when one remembers that most of the lads had spent the best part of their school time in the air raid shelters. That also applied to the time in the evenings when their homework was being done, or should have been done. An air raid shelter and its environment, is not the best of places in which to indulge in swotting up. I will admit that some of the lads had very little idea of spelling, but as ever, the Navy Schoolmasters would sort that problem out, and to my idea, they were some of the best in the world.

On duty one evening, after supper, walking up and down the mess as usual, I noted that one youngster was sitting on his bed, not swotting but just looking blankly about the mess. The name I know well even to this day, but will not embarrass the fellow in any way. I say fellow, he is more than likely a Petty Officer by now. However, asking him what his trouble was, he openly admitted that he wanted to go home. Not an uncommon thing with new lads, especially if they were an only child, and had been cosseted to a degree. This lad had little or no interest that he could tell me of except to get home. Yes, I talked to him and suggested that he gave the Navy another chance by staying for another month, during which time he should endeavour to take up some sport to get his mind off being away from home. There was not much sport that he would be good at, or so he told me. At the time, the mess cross country running was just coming on to the calendar, so I suggested that he had a go at that. This he agreed to do, so that I advised him to put his name down for it as it would not matter if he could not run so long as he completed the course. At the training runs that followed, he came in well to the front, usually one of the first three lads home so that I decided to leave him in the mess team. I say that I decided, because I had always been interested in running, having made the team for whatever ship I had been in. This meant that I was selected to take the running teams for Hawk Division. Daily I would have the lads out on the playing fields in their working clothes so that they would appreciate the change to running gear when the time came. Anyone watching us would have come to the conclusion that I was a disgruntled Chief giving the lads a shake up, so I dissuaded the lads from giving any other impression. Not only did the cross country team practice on the playing fields, but they also practiced on the famous steps of Faith, Hope and Charity that led down to the pier. By the time those lads were ready for the race, those steps meant nothing to them. It was just an obstacle of the course and they could all take the numerous steps at a fair pace without tiring, and with our young friend usually in the lead. The proper course for the run started on the football fields just away from the mess, down to the foreshore of the Orwell past the running track and Shotley Pier, along the foreshore of the River Stour for about a mile, then turn across the fields to the Ipswich Road and back to the playing field gate, with the finishing tunnel at the north end of the parade ground. The course would be about five and a half miles over all types of ground. A really tough course, as the course from the Stour to the Ipswich Road was an uphill run all the way, part of it passing through the muck and slush of a farmyard. On the actual race, our young friend went into the lead by the time the course opened on to the Ipswich Road, about one-and-a-half miles from the finish. From there he practically sprinted the last mile or so. Needless to say he led the field by a good margin to be followed later by the others. If I remember correctly, his timing was something of a record, so that for a time he became the champion of the mess, to his delight. There was no more talk of his wanting to return home, so I left it at that. By now, we and the boys in the mess had really settled down and we were all trying to prepare for what was termed the twelfth week signal exams. From the previous exams at Shotley, it was known that to fail this exam could mean "Back Classing" and this they all dreaded doing, as it was considered as a slur on the boys themselves. The exams and the marking, were all done by the Signals

Officers and the results would be communicated to the Instructors who would, in the case of any boy's failure, either recommend that the lad failed or passed depending on his character and progress during the previous three months. Fortunately there were no failures in 239 or 240 classes. We did anticipate a couple of failures but those that we expected to fail managed to get their passing marks without a lot of trouble. The next hurdle for the lads would be the sixth month exam which would take them to the end of June. During this three months, the lads would intensify their knowledge of signals so that they would be performing at quite a bit of pressure. In these months they would also learn the elementary manoeuvres and intricacies of fleet signals, as signalled by flags or Morse. All this would be as well as attending school daily and for doing a certain amount of seamanship, for as ever, the signalmen of the fleet had to know how to handle and behave in a boat as well as the various knots and splices. In addition, they were all expected to take part in the various sporting activities of the class, mess, division or the establishment. No spare time here.

As remarked, the cross country running had been completed, with Hawk winning the trophy against five other divisions. Soon it would be time for the establishment athletics where division competed against division for the main Athletic Cup and the Victor Ludaurum Trophy. The latter would be awarded to the individual that accumulated the most individual points during the two day meeting, and involved all sports in the athletic menu. The biggest event of this meeting would be, the twenty-five mile relay race. Here, each lad competing would run a quarter mile before handing over the baton. This meant, one hundred runners from each division, of which there were six. Quite a bit of organisation needed for this, for until the second mile, each division had to move one place outwards from the inner lanes before it became a free lane. For this, I had selected nine good fast runners to start and then moving to the more average runners in sequence of timings, then finishing off with about a dozen of the fastest runners in the division, to finish off with our young friend that wanted to go home. He was without a doubt, the fastest fellow in the establishment. By the time that Hawk had completed the half-way stage, the division was going wild with excitement, for we were already over a complete lap, (a quarter of a mile), in the lead and the best runners were to come. The result was that Hawk completed the race long before the others, and when our last runner handed in his baton he was cheered to the limit. Even my wife and sons who were at the meeting as guests, cheered until quite hoarse for the success of Hawk. In addition to the above, one of our P.O. Boys had taken part in almost every event, and establishing a new establishment record for the pole vault. By a clear lead he had won the coveted Victor Ludaurum Prize. I was delighted, particularly when my wife entered in the three-legged race which she also won. No, this was not the end of the affair, for when I went to congratulate the lads on their grand effort, they, without further ado, picked me up and chaired me round the whole establishment. As we passed the Officers' mess, Captain Bush wanted to know what the commotion was, so that his remarks of, "I might have guessed who was the Instructor," so that I was later sent for to be complimented by an old friend. The next day it was to be back to work as usual with the lads sticking out their chests like the proverbial prize bantams, for they were indeed the cocks of the establishment.

In the meantime through all this excitement, signals and yet more signals were consumed by the lads so that when the annual fete at Ipswich took place, the lads were selected to perform with the signal display, which vied with the field gun display. This was the highlight of the year, at least for the lads, as here, after they had completed their display, they would be permitted to mingle and mix with the crowds. This always did mean that the public would hand the lads cigarettes or sweets and pop, while the local girls found obvious pleasure at captivating a young sailor, if only for the afternoon. No doubt, the Instructors and the Naval Police had an attack of blindness after the displays, for some of the lads had managed somehow, to visit the beer tent against strict orders. There was no need for me to worry, as my class of lads all verbally reassured me that they were all teetotal. Of course, I laughed and told them that I was also teetotal. I suppose that they believed me. Whatever the case of the lads, none of them let me down by going astray.

Each day, their signals knowledge improved, so that soon I was able to exercise them as though they really were on ships at sea. Another favourite trick of mine, was to let them use the telescope for part of their exercises, and then at some predetermined point, they would have to reverse the telescope so that the imposed image given, appeared to be miles away. Also, I would engage one of the lads in conversation about something entirely different from the signals that they were reading, and then deliberately shout something unintelligible so that they got used to reading signals under all sorts of conditions and with strange interruptions. These little tricks were not employed during their examinations, but I reasoned that if they could get reasonable marks with the interruptions, they would get far better marks under ideal conditions. Their examination results proved my point, so that I would have been happy to have any of them at sea with me as signal boys or junior signal ratings.

After the Christmas leave period all the class went into the phase of what was called doubling up. This meant that they had completed their school exams, which all passed well, and that all training sessions were now devoted to signals.. This affected the instructors in that they had to prepare their lectures the evening before, for the whole of the next day. For the lads, it was a super effort requirement as no sooner had they finished one session, than it was double away, sometimes to the other end of the establishment to be ready for the next session of instruction by their own instructor. I think that all the instructors that ever went to Shotley must have been in the acme of fitness. Even after a few weeks of being an instructor, for one always had to keep with one's class, even at the double. Beside this sort of gymnastics, the instructors were expected to be correctly dressed when they called the lads at 0600 daily.

The only day that any let up was permitted was on Sundays, when all work was reduced to a minimum. Even so the mess had to be cleaned to brand new condition, by 0900. At that time, all lads with their instructor would be required to parade for Sunday divisions, (inspection and march past with the band of the Royal Marines), to be followed by church parade. For this, the messes were arranged in sequence of seniority from the right, and would move towards the front of the parade each Monday morning. Something like a huge game of draughts until one became accustomed to the routine.

On one particular occasion, Hawk division were about in the middle of the parade muster. All lads were correctly dressed and very smartly turned out. As was usual, a P.O. Boy would be in front to march the mess past the saluting base where the Captain was standing, to take the salute. Soon, it was our turn to advance in line. Smartly our P.O. Boy gave his orders, and very smartly the lads advanced with yours truly the regulation six paces in the rear of the last rank. At the order "Eyes right" by the P.O. Boy, one could almost hear the click as the eyes went to the right, and the salute given. Just after the order "Eyes Front" was given, the Captain's voice rang out over the parade ground, "Chief Yeoman Smith, you are too close to your party, the regulation distance is six paces." This was soon adjusted by me and checked for distance. I had been the regulation distance. All that was happening was, that Captain Bush had seen and recognised me and was impressing on the parade that he knew everybody by their names. This was of course entirely incorrect as there must have been some two thousand ranks on parade. Knowing Captain Bush as I did, I guessed it was one of his methods of impressing his powers of memory on the lads. As a matter of fact during the next week he sent for me and explained the matter in just the way that I had guessed. It certainly impressed the lads of my mess and many other messes that knew me.

Another part of the various gymnastics that took place was that of weekly mast drill. Here, the lads were lined up under the mast just clear of the quarter-deck in ranks of six, just as we always had done. The drill was exactly the same as when I had been a boy. The first six would man the futtocks, (rigging), and would start to climb at the order "Way aloft." After the first six had cleared the half moon, (about one third of the way up), the next rank of six boys would be started on the climb. This would go on until the class had completed their climbing up and down the mast in the required time of three minutes. One could not afford to linger for the mast was 180 feet high, and to climb up and down in the three minutes was no mean achievement. As far as I was concerned, so long as the lads climbed the mast and came down in near enough the time required, I was quite happy, so that I would accept four minutes as the required goal, and this I feel sure almost all the Instructors accepted.

On the morning in question, I announced at breakfast time, that mast drill was on the agenda for that morning. This meant a reduction in the lad's breakfast time as mast drill usually started about 0820, so as to be clear for daily parade at 0900. Having announced this drill, I was approached by two of the lads as they wanted to know if they could be in the first detail of six. Thinking nothing of the request, I readily agreed, as from my own experience of mast drill, it is most frustrating to be climbing the mast to find one's way blocked by some slow climber, or perhaps somebody that was not quite sure of themselves on the mast. Promptly on time, the P.O. Boy reported to me at the foot of the mast, that the mess was correct and ready for mast drill. Thanking him, I ordered the first six boys to man the futtocks. Smartly the first six took up their positions with one foot ready on the rigging, ready to race away at the words, "Way aloft." I noticed that the two requestmen were in this detail with one at each side of the futtocks. At the word, the two raced away leaving the others almost standing. Almost neck and neck they climbed until the rigging closed in for the climb over the half moon. Whoever was leading at this point, was obviously going to be the leader over the next part, for this would only take two abreast for a short distance. I will call them, lads "A" and "B" although their names are still remembered by me. Lad "A" being in the lead, was really tearing away from his chum, who was endeavouring to catch lad "A" but without much hope. At the top, Lad "A" had quite a lead so that his way down was now clear. At the half moon on the return downward climb, Lad "B" seeing that he could not overtake lad "A," swung himself outwards away from the mast and let go. Sensing at least a crippled lad on my hands, I shouted the words that stop everything, "STILL." Even the remainder of the boys on the parade ground stopped what they were doing, that's Navy training, as "STILL" means just that. With a "ploomp" lad "B" landed in the safety net that surrounds the mast. Not knowing the exact state of the lad's injuries, I started to cut him free from the entangling ropes of the net, and telling one of the other lads to phone for an ambulance. With the aid of some of the lads who had come forward to help, we lowered the lad "B" to the ground. Also I sent a messenger to inform the Officer of the Watch of this incident. He was quickly on the scene. Asking the lad "B" just what had happened, I received the astonishing reply, "I beat him down, didn't I Sir?" Not fully understanding just what he meant I told him that he had certainly beaten him down. By then, the ambulance had arrived on the scene so that I requested permission from the O.O.W. to carry on with the Mast Drill. Again the lads manned the rigging and away they went, probably not as though nothing had gone wrong or as it should be. At the return of the last lad down, I left the P.O. Boy in charge to get ready for divisions and reported to the O.O.W. that mast drill was completed and that one lad was in the sick bay. I regretted that I was unable to answer his question as to what had happened, for I really did not know. However I meant to find out quickly, as I could not imagine the

Commander or the Captain accepting my ignorance of what had happened.

The Commander was already on the trail, for he had seen me report to the O.O.W. and was waiting for me as I finished reporting. There was little that I could inform him about the incident, so I told him I was on my way to the sick bay to interview the lad if possible. With that the Commander accompanied me to the Sick Bay so that there was no problem of seeing the lad. Taking us into the emergency operating room, there was the lad as large as life and with a grin like a Cheshire cat at the sight of me. Although he had some bandages to prove some injury, he said that he was O.K. At this the Commander asked him what had happened. "Nothing really," replied the lad, "except that I jumped the last bit." The Commander was taken aback somewhat. "But why jump when you could have come down in the normal way?" The astonishing answer was, "I would have lost the bet for being the last one down, instead I beat boy "A" and won the bet." . The bet was for SIX penny bars of Sharpe's Toffee. The Commander immediately called for the Medical Officer who reassured the Commander that the lad was quite well and that his rope burns would soon heal, and also that X-rays had been taken. A report would be made when the results were known. There was little need to worry about the lad, as by dinner time he was back in the mess ready and waiting for his dinner and only the rope burns to show for his exploit. Naturally, the affair went round the establishment like wildfire, as many of the lads had been on the parade ground ready for the morning divisions when the event happened. The lad was eventually given a real telling off by the Divisional Officer as one could not have the boys jumping off the mast for a silly bet. Oh yes, the lad that did not jump paid up his six bars of toffee, and the rest of the mess also contributed one bar of toffee each to the lad that had jumped. They looked on him as a bit of a hero. To be quite candid, I and many of the other Instructors also admired his pluck, as I feel sure the Officers did. The boys were the sort of lads that I had under my care. Just tell them that they could not or should not do something and they would do their best to prove you wrong. When I say this, I do not mean that it was a case of open breach of the rules of discipline, but rather with a sense of pure excitement. Eventually the time came for them to take their final exams. This they did with more credit to themselves and to me. Some of them eventually made officer rank and one even reached the rank of Rear Admiral, but that was several years later.

With their results made known, I was called in to the Signal Officer's office and congratulated on the good results; also, I was asked, since I had passed educationally, if I wished to consider going through for Officer rank. It seemed that every person that mattered had recommended me as Officer material. This step I talked over with my wife, who after all would have to share the results of that decision. It meant that I would be liable to several more years of foreign service and absence from the family, if I accepted. Foreign service was then reckoned as at least two years and service was world wide. For a long while we debated this matter, and the decision was made that as I was now within a short while of normal retirement from the Navy, I would forego the Officer selection opportunity. Going back to Shotley, I informed those concerned of my decision and requested that I be returned to my parent depot at Chatham. After a short while in which I was granted any leave that was outstanding to me I reported to the signal school at Cookham Camp just outside Rochester in Kent.

After my previous rather full life, the life here proved rather dull, but that was only to be expected until the next call to "ACTION STATIONS," or until I became a fully-fledged civilian with the title of "Mr."

As the Navy says on the successful completion of a job, "EVOLUTIONS COMPLETED".

Although I have recorded some of the highlights and incidents of that rather full and successful career, there are still many events that I can recall that would require many more pages. Space and time (age) are rapidly advancing and it is my sincere desire that this volume of memoirs should be available, at least to my grandchildren. May they never have to partake of the experiences that befell me between the years of 1939 and 1946.

EPILOGUE

It seems very strange that the sacrifices made by the Royal and Merchant Navies are more often than not completely overlooked.

Much more strange is that fact than when we remember that not only Great Britain but the entire Allied cause depended on the ministration and steadfast devotion of those Navies.

The oceans of the world are largely responsible for this sad lapse of memory, oceans which no matter the weather, calm or storm, snow or blow, shine or rain, bear no trace of the conflicts that raged over their waters, or of the sacrifices. To the traveller on land, they may spot or mark their memorial bronze or the broken column or even the preserved shell torn sites which indicate that sometime in the past, a nation battled against nation for supremacy.

At sea, there is no such pilgrimage except to where "X" marks the spot on some chart or map, for the white, blue, grey and green waters will hold forever their closely guarded secrets. Even the summer sunlight can hardly filter down to the depths where the multi-coloured seaweed sways to and fro with the waves, hiding the twisted limbs of ships, and the corals will camouflage the whitening bones of men.

The following is an extract from the Naval Prayer Book:-

"It is largely upon the Navy, and by the Grace of God, that the safety and welfare of the country doth depend."

If one remembers, that according to the history books the war officially ceased in 1945, but to many, myself included, the war still continued in distant places and did not finish until the men came home. For some, unfortunately, they never came home and their war only ceased when their names were added to the War Memorials. It should also be remembered that the war literally turned the world upside down, not only for the service man, but for civilians as well. Never again would life be as it had been known before 1939, due in most cases to wartime inventions that were later redeveloped and adapted to suit peacetime purposes.

Amen, so let it be.